P. Roberts 7-91

AFTER THE CONQUEST

BY THE SAME AUTHOR

Blackbird

AFTER THE CONQUEST

Tony Cartano

Translated from the French by
Steve Cox

SECKER & WARBURG
LONDON

First published in England 1988 by
Martin Secker & Warburg Limited
Michelin House
81 Fulham Road
London SW3 6RB

British Library Cataloguing in Publication Data

Cartano, Tony
After the conquest.
I. Title II. Bocanegra. *English*
843'.914[F]

ISBN 0 436 08811 8

The author and publishers are grateful to the following for permission to reproduce copyright material: Simon & Schuster Ltd, *Popol-Vuh*, tr. Dennis Tedlock (p. 254); Peter Owen Ltd, *Journals of Anais Nin*, vol. 6 (p. 271) and Weidenfeld & Nicolson Ltd, *Armies of the Night* by Norman Mailer (pp. 370–1). The passage from Cervantes' *Don Quixote* (p. 225) is from the Tobias Smollett translation, reissued by André Deutsch in 1986

Typeset by Deltatype Ltd, Ellesmere Port
Printed in Great Britain
by Billing & Sons Ltd, Worcester

Author's Note

THE CHARACTERS AND events presented in this novel have only one relationship to reality: they are the product of the same imagination. Any similarity, no matter how suggestive, should therefore be credited to the natural functions of fiction.

Clearly the narrative owes a debt to B. Traven, whose cryptic life lies somewhere in the background of this fictional venture. Here Will Wyatt's book, *The Man Who Was B. Traven* (London, Cape, 1980; published in New York by Doubleday under the title *The Secret of the Sierra Madre*), provided the catalyst for a series of departures into the imaginary. For – having recorded the distant source where the venture begins – I must add how thoroughly its matter, shape and expression then diverge. To press Traven, the author of *The Death Ship*, into an expedition not his own is an act, not of borrowing, but of literature: it is only the myths that change and evolve.

T.C.

'The creative person should therefore have no other biography than his works.'

B. Traven

'Tell me how you die and I will tell you who you are.'

Octavio Paz

'The world is so taken up of late with novels and romances, that it will be hard for a private history to be taken for genuine, where the names and other circumstances of the person are concealed, and on this account we must be content to leave the reader to pass his own opinion upon the ensuing sheets, and take it just as he pleases.'

Daniel Defoe

Contents

Prologue

NOWADAYS, EACH TOUCH of diplomacy seems more and more afflicted with unreason, as if pain had taken over as a principle of government. That, rather than the discretion required by my position, is what leads me to withhold my name. There is already enough *trompe-l'oeil* in the story I am about to present, without including the details of my personal involvements. In any case the authenticity of the following documents and papers cannot be invalidated by my anonymity: what counts is the conviction, not the trademark.

So I take it that the reader will believe me when I come straight to the point and assert that I knew Michael Mateos, the hero of this book – knew him well.

We met at Oxford over twenty years ago, when we were students at Magdalen College. A taste for literature as well as for English beer brought us together, and the friendship was cemented by the ordinary quiet course of student life. Then, after my return to Paris, when I wrote him two letters which went unanswered, I took it that Mateos and I had lost touch, until a trick of fate caused our paths to cross in Acapulco. In that haven for rich tourists, where the natives starve, as Orson Welles remarked, I was making my début in the very honorific and anything but onerous post of French vice-consul, while Michael was embarking on the hunt for ghosts and shadows which, fifteen years on, would ultimately cost him his life.

He only just escaped from the hole I pulled him out of in Guatemala, a few months after we met in Acapulco. I had arranged to dispatch him back to France, and when I myself returned there was a new surprise in store: I found him engaged to Beatrice François, a cousin of mine by marriage. They had seemed briefly attracted to each other at a party I had given in my Oxford days, but I had no idea that they had been in touch since then. My fellow student was certainly destined to make a much greater impact on my life than I could have imagined, and I must admit that in spite of our old friendship there were many facets of his personality that still eluded me when he and Beatrice fell head over heels in love and he lured her away from the straight and narrow path which her background ordained. I was a witness to the quick civil ceremony, performed in the town hall of the 7th arrondissement, which Mateos attended alone as if he had no family to support him. Although this last point did not unduly surprise me, I was then far from suspecting that his character itself stemmed from a deeper puzzle . . .

Our paths diverged again. When next I saw him in London he had left Beatrice and his job in television and become involved in various business ventures which had brought him to the top of a small press empire. It was he who telephoned me at the embassy to invite me for lunch. I found him unchanged. Slightly plumper, perhaps: for years he had benefited from the slim build and statuesque posture common among the high plains Indians on his mother's side; now that he was past thirty he was showing the signs of his father's Germanic inheritance. His father! That was the great secret, of course. But that day he talked only about his quarrels with Beatrice, their child, and the divorce, as well as about the rich pickings which had come his way from the counter-culture that sprang up and went to seed during the decade then coming to an end . . . Manifestly, the more the physique had softened the more the man had hardened and solidified, to the point of looking cramped in his new role of dynamic young press baron. When I expressed my surprise at his altered situation and comportment, he changed the subject. 'I have something to tell you in confidence,' he said, and started to talk about a strange kind of expedition he was determined to undertake, and for which he needed my advice and help. 'You don't mean you're back on the same old track?' I said. He smiled, and suggested that if I had no objections he would prefer to continue our conversation in my office at the embassy. He never turned up, of course. When I telephoned him at home three days later, a voice with a strong cockney accent informed me that 'Mr Mateos 'as set sail for Mexico City.' I was going to ask for details, but the man had already hung up. His choice of language felt to me like a sign of some hostile irony, although in fact it concealed – but how was I to know it? – one of the major themes of the symphony to come.

I always found Michael Mateos an elusive character. His temperament, culture and frames of reference were foreign to me, and awkward to approach. And to compound the difficulty, this puzzle was nothing compared to the convoluted splendours of his father's life, as if the son had worn himself out on the trail of that famous and forever mysterious man . . .

The final contact with Mateos took place in his absence, when some months ago the tragedy of circumstance caused me for once to mix official with family business. At the Quai d'Orsay we were the first to receive the news, and it was I who had the painful duty of breaking it to Beatrice on the telephone. In ten years, my cousin had only seen her husband on two or three occasions, but I knew that she still had some affection for him. So I was not surprised to hear her say that she would deal with the formalities herself.

There was talk of a mistake, an accident. How else to explain Michael's having gone to his death in Poznan? Although he was American by nationality – and God knows whether that factor alone may have muddied the story that follows – the task of taking delivery of the body and of the dead man's meagre effects fell to me, a French diplomat. In Warsaw, the embarrassed authorities deployed a wealth of linguistic ingenuity. Given the situation, Poland did not need yet another martyr, especially one who hailed from a country for which such an incident might count as provocation. Yet the death of Mateos did not merit a single line in the Western press, because somewhere in high places it had been decided to gloss over the death of this particular individual. To put it bluntly, both sides washed their hands of the awkward remains of a difficult man whom no one was anxious to claim. Hence my own good offices . . .

The deputy minister of foreign affairs gave me a friendly reception in his office. It had been agreed in advance that not a word of our conversation was to touch upon Poland's domestic affairs. In return, every formality had been waived to enable me to fly out from a military airfield with Mateos' coffin, destination Paris via Berlin. It was at that meeting that I was given the steel attaché case that contained the manuscript which Michael had sometimes titled *After the Conquest* and sometimes *Bocanegra*. As I was leafing through a thick folder – one of the several that held pages typed on various different machines, as well as some in Michael's own handwriting – the interpreter explained that these papers had been found in a hotel room after the 'accident' which the authorities had been so keen to hush up.

In order not to weary the reader with a welter of cautionary remarks and preambles, I shall disregard the questions that the manuscript raised for me, except to promise that all the answers are in the story. Even at Oxford, when we were twenty years old and experimenting with the muse, Mateos and I knew that there was no easy guide for beginners – a literary judgement I have had no reason to change.

A few brief comments though, in conclusion.

Few people were aware that Michael's father was none other than W. H. Raven. He confided that much at the time of our encounter in Acapulco in October 1965, along with his crazy determination to leave for Chiapas in search of the great man's traces. At that time I had not read any of his father's books, though I knew of Raven's world-wide reputation, and the unsolved riddle surrounding his identity. Naturally I hurried to catch up, and as years went by, little by little, I learned more about the man whom my friend has placed at the centre of his book. During his lifetime nobody was in a position to identify Mateos' father as the author of the novels published under the name of W. H. Raven. The wildest rumours circulated: that he was an American millionaire suffering pangs of conscience, an Austrian archduke on the run in Mexico, a leper in Chiapas with a bandaged face; and even Jack London who, contrary to general belief, had not after all committed suicide in 1916!

Mateos himself believed that anything was possible . . .

Xavier M.-P.
Paris, September 1984.

BOOK ONE

1

ALL AT ONCE the stillness of the sky seemed to break. The great blue vault bulged as if heaved by a swirling, unexpected, cosmic breath. Until that moment there had been nothing whatever to suggest the possibility of such a brutal transformation of the natural balance. For months, the gulf and the interior beyond it had stewed in the torpor of a perpetual tropical autumn. Along the coasts a flat sea lapped against burning sand, unmoved by the tired wing-beats of a hungry gull. From time to time the Atlantic wall of *ceibas* and palm-trees trembled to the shriek of a parrot, or swayed slightly to the rhythm of a croaking giant frog. Further away, on the hills surrounding the lake of the Original Legend, only the creeping insects found their way through the thick tangle of languid vegetation, while unknown species of huge gaudy butterflies fluttered high in the canopy of trees which disgorged an occasional shower of screeching firebirds. Their piercing calls flared up on contact with a naked sun and their scorched little bodies would then plummet in free fall, out of blue valleys into yellow plains, to glide along banks of vanilla plants and finally lose themselves in an ocean of contrasts. Rivers and marshes threaded through the undergrowth and, lapping and murmuring, ran gradually dry, merging into the sombre depths of the tropical jungle. There in the heart of a self-created, perfectly inhuman greenhouse ruled ebony, sapodilla and caobab trees.

Nothing had moved for what felt like an eternity, so the torn sky over to the east was all the more disconcerting. Starting as a tiny spiral stirred up by the gentle trade winds of the Azores, it had allowed itself to be enticed by the warm sea currents which had swept it, now full-grown and monstrous, out towards the Caribbean. There it swerved suddenly out of its track, shaking its wild mane in a killing frenzy. It slashed the sky open, plunged headlong into the gaping hole, and surged into the Gulf of Honduras.

The whole body of the mineral and vegetable universe, caught until now in the heat's solid grip, broke into a violent shudder whose spasms pulsed throughout the animal kingdom, where creatures cowered in the nearest ooze, lost in profound ancestral fears.

As for the humans, they ran for their temples . . . The wind howled high off the scale, it drowned their shouts of terror with their prayers. A chant went up, a flimsy shield against the hurricane's roar, recalling the prophecy of their ancestors. 'Listen! Listen! . . . White circles will appear in the sky. Words will be slaves, and men slaves also . . . That day will come, listen, it is coming!' But the announcement of a new god and a new world only increased the terror among the huddled crowds.

The surging black sea convulsed to its heart and reared suddenly upwards to attack beaches and estuaries. Squadrons of shredded clouds mingled with the columns of sea foam, and when their twin strength hit the warm land it doubled and redoubled until soon it was no longer possible in the pervading whirlwind to distinguish either the nature of the surrounding elements or the exact origin of the movement that drove them.

The wind howled up the river and smashed into the cordillera, where the backlash raised a tumult of waves on the surface of the lake and drove them up against the crumbling banks. The press of cloud rolled on, deeper inland, submerging everything in its path as the vapours of the humid continent rose to combine with the water sucked towards the eye of the cyclone on its crossing of the ocean. The men who sheltered in the sanctuary prayed to the god of rain.

The drops of frozen water did not bring the vegetation to life but fossilized it beneath a shower of stinging arrows. Now the squall blew harder and a first line of banana trees was uprooted. Minutes became hours, hours years. The spurting, the sap, the labour, slavery, seed and blossom, forests, cascades, erosion, rooting and slow ripening of things and creatures, the marvellous machinery of the living world, everything was jeopardized . . . The arm of death shot out, an elastic tentacle uncoiling at a speed much greater than the wind's, sweeping through space with one decisive gesture. Down a sixty-five-mile swathe it left only desolation. But no sooner had the giant whirlwind completed its murderous raid than it withdrew, as fast as it had come. Suddenly there was calm, an absolute, ominous moment of suspension as if the sky was ready to collapse on to the earth, this time to bury it altogether . . . The lethal crown of cloud remained, but at its centre a kind of clearing had emerged, lit by a blinding glare. The temple worshippers ventured hesitantly out and then they saw the eye that watched them. Prostrating themselves before this nameless god, they begged forgiveness. Since no clap of thunder responded, and no breath of wind rippled the leaves of the uprooted trees, they went back to work, meaning to repair whatever could be repaired before day gave way completely to night . . .

Driven by the storm a rowing boat had been wrecked and smashed to matchwood on the beach. The corpses of its nine crewmen were starting to rot in the reviving sun. Three years later, when a proud frigate dropped anchor in the bay, no trace of shipwreck would be visible along the shore; the white horses would prance across immaculate sand.

The eye measured twenty miles across. Around its central glassy stare, the spiral took its iridescence from the swirling bands that whipped at shorelines, streams and rivers. But the further from the periphery the more violent the giration. Unable to reach shelter in the heart of the mountains, many tribes tried in vain to escape the lightning that speared down from the sky. Those who were not killed submitted to the invader. Converging on the zone of calm, a swarm of boats had gathered at the estuary. They had crossed the bar without too much difficulty, glad to have escaped from the raging high seas and perhaps from the death which had not spared other crews.

The cyclone shifted slightly. The sky spun, and spun again. Flocks of fugitive birds, almost invisible to the naked eye, vanished into the breach, drawn in and swallowed by the monster's mouth. The eye had winked, rolled round upon its axis, turned bloodshot and contracted to an incandescent ball, discharging a warm sticky rain of the viscous matter in its orbit, as if it had finally discovered the means to renew its strength. The beast flexed its muscles, coiled and stretched; its flabby belly hardened to draw tight as a drum skin; when the tail of the white-hot spiral lashed at it, it clanged like a bell that all the region heard. Both the living and the inanimate shrank back in a sigh of utter dread. In such a turmoil it was no longer possible to tell the men with copper-coloured skins from those who wore white breastplates. Caught in the same frenzy of terror, some believed that they were witnessing the creation of a new kind of seed, others that it was the end of the world.

This time the winds did not subside.

And so savage was the havoc that its lethal echo was felt even in the bowels of the earth, rousing the Great Volcano which now decided to add its own voice to the concert. After clearing his throat a few times, the token of too long a silence, the bald-headed old gentleman bellowed out loud as if to display his strength to the rival on the surface. Shock waves coursed from the heights and depths of the continent and collided thunderously with the marine intruder's opaque screen. Everything merged into utter confusion . . . who now could distinguish between an uprooted bridge and a flooded road, a swamp swarming with caymans and a gold mine, a flattened port and a snow-capped peak?

The cyclone's eye is nothing more than a slavering black mouth. Pieces of railway track and lengths of telegraph wire are tossed between its fangs. A man slides up its rasping, pustular tongue, drawn inexorably towards the vortex of the throat. He tries to cling to bumps in the ground, slithers on all fours like a beast unable to walk, reduced to the condition of a primate barely able to crawl. Flat on his belly he claws at the earth with bleeding hands. For a moment he manages to gain a few yards of ground before he is torn away by the spinning top of a demented glottis whirling with such speed and violence that it emits a high-pitched whistling howl.

The whole world seems to have been turned inside out like a glove and is being ground against itself in a vast flexing of champing, oily mandibles. Crushed nuts and fruits gush their saps and juices in a multitude of syrupy torrents, still in spate as they pour in random dances through the jungle to mingle with the oil-bearing waters of the gulf. More ships, driven by powerful engines, seem to have succeeded in running the gauntlet of the unchained elements and bring, if not deliverance, then at least food and medical supplies, to bind some wounds and bring a little relief. People rise cautiously upright, but above their heads the living arms of sea have merged so fully with the lava flows that it is not possible at this hour to forecast the end of the storm. Some special machines have arrived from the north, juddering, stinking, belching smoke, and with them some other men with even whiter skin. In their mouths is nothing like the hoarse roaring of the Great Volcano, but sonorities that leave only the memory of the oceanic hail and wind. With their automatic weapons they have fired in the direction of the mourning stars and orphaned sun until the half-light has been succeeded by a night of full moon, rustling with the ghosts of the past.

With his glinting teeth the gringo has crushed and shredded the *chicle* from the Petén, chewing it over and over again before spitting out the tasteless wad at last and treading it into the dust under the heel of his hobnailed boots.

In a small country town in the Sierra de Guatemala, near the walls of the ruined church next to the government barracks, lying on the ground between two broken branches is an ancient stone gargoyle. Her disfigured nose juts upwards at a sky restored to a near-perfect azure, and it seems that her broad and gaping mouth gives out strange music which – if the legend is believed – may still evoke the true, authentic story of a murdered memory.

2

ON 18 FEBRUARY 1640, about five o'clock in the evening, the crew and passengers of the *Santo Domingo* believed they heard the trumpets of the angel host sounding in ears deafened by the howling wind. The calm of a morning during which the lookouts had reported the first signs of land had been succeeded by a driving hailstorm. Then all at once the sky cleared, and the ship was caught in shafts of light that gleamed and pierced like metal. Young Alfonso de Seguida leant on a bulwark and scanned the horizon, hoping to glimpse the marvellous shores of his dreams, which were to rescue him from the decay of his lineage, the crumbling manor of his native Novayas and the boredom of the lecture halls of Valladolid. Until now, he thought, the crossing had been a good one, hardly even disturbed on the twelfth day by the death of a seaman committed to the sea after Fray Xavier de Leon had held the mass for the dead on deck. A friendly east wind had blown nearly all the way, and they had suffered no sickness: even scurvy had been contained, although some of the crew had developed sores as a result of eating the salt meat unavoidable on shipboard. Contrary to the fate of many of their predecessors on the ocean voyage, thanks be to God their souls had been spared. The captain had told Seguida how, on a previous crossing, several of his men had been struck down by an unknown affliction which had turned their minds. But his passenger hardly had time to conclude the optimistic train of thought that a young man of twenty-two is entitled to entertain, in the teeth of all the evidence. Already his eye was drawn and held fast by the host of black clouds scudding upward from the south. From his place in the forecastle the almoner proclaimed that there in the shadows Gabriel and his angels were at war with the hosts of Beelzebub. And he ordered all the men to say what prayers they knew, even if only in the common tongue. His harangue was drowned by the whirlwind that caused the entire ship to shake and groan. Some swore by all the saints, some fainted, some knelt in humility, but the massive figure of the boatswain, Mattin the Basque, stood firm in the thunder and lightning as he bellowed to the crew: 'Hold on! To your posts! Lower the top-mast! Strike the mainsail! Stand out to sea!' The captain leant over the table nailed to the floor of his cabin and laboriously wrote in his log: 'Struck mainsail to avoid being driven on shore. So great a gathering hurricane I have never seen. God have mercy upon us, the maelstrom's prey . . .' Wedged beneath the lashings of one of the ship's longboats, and battered by the huge waves that surged across the deck, Alfonso de Seguida closed his eyes and saw the death-mask of his late father, and the tear-stained face of the mother he had left in Novayas; and as the images were jolted by the fearful rolling of the ship they in their turn gave way in an infernal round to visions of a paradise on earth teeming with lush fruits and magical birds . . .

Driven out to sea, the galleon fought the storm for two days and nights.

By the time the giant hands reaching out of the night decided that they had been adequately entertained by the plight of a fragile cockleshell attacked by raging elements, the *Santo Domingo* was a shambles. It drifted on the face of the now quiet ocean like a ghost ship, a messenger from Hell, and manned by shadows. But the dwarfish figures who began gradually to stir on the shattered deck were still alive. They had lost only two, but among them Mattin the Basque, found crushed beneath a spar beside the helm he had refused to leave.

Injuries were dressed, and some of the damage repaired.

Alfonso de Seguida they found unconscious and half dead. When he came to, raving with thirst and fever, the pain threw him into convulsions that left him so exhausted that the ship's doctor – powerless to help and too busy spreading ointment on minor wounds or mixing draughts for ladies swooning with nervous shock – would give little for his chances. In this he was at variance with Baruch Cordavoro, a Jewish astrologer from Gerona, and a fugitive from the local and ancestral persecutions which his family had long suffered. He and the high-spirited young cavalier had made friends on the voyage. The eminent scholar had left behind him disciples who had travelled from all over Europe to follow his teaching. He recalled with bitterness how his great grandfather had moved to Genoa at the time of the expulsion of the Jews from Spain. A generation had elapsed before he had been able to return to Catalonia . . . Seguida, who was weary of university sophistry and rhetoric, tasted the secret charms of the cabbala, learning the rudiments from Baruch during long nocturnal conversations enhanced by observation of the stars or commentaries on the *Zohar*.

Cordavoro diagnosed a fractured tibia and various minor sprains. He himself tended to the rest of his friend's needs; he drew upon his own ration of drinking water, and fed him broths and tonics. The fair weather had returned, and the gentle Caribbean trade winds now swelling the sails of the *Santo Domingo* revived the sick man's taste for life. The nearer the end of the voyage, the stronger he felt, and soon he no longer needed the splint that Baruch had fashioned and was able to move about on deck, limping slightly, leaning over the ship's side to watch for the first signs of land in the waves below. The galleon had been blown off course by the storm, but the captain had taken new bearings and they were sailing west-north-west.

Just over three weeks had gone by when one morning Seguida rushed into the cabin where the astrologer was annotating a grimoire and dragged him up on deck to show him the giant seaweed clinging to the ship's sides. They hardly had time to erupt with delight because already the lookout was calling 'Land! Land!'

Passengers and crew embraced. Drums beat, trumpets sounded, flute and viol struck up a dance. Fray Xavier de Leon ordered the *Te Deum* to be sung. The captain, a taciturn realist from Majorca, did not attempt to curb the general enthusiasm but let masses, rosaries and pagan celebrations proceed without pointing out that the ordeal was not yet over. The *Santo Domingo* had just passed through the Yucatán Channel and the land far over to port was Cape Catoche. That night, when thirst and feelings had been satisfied, the captain informed those whose minds were clear enough to listen that they still faced several days' sailing along the coast before starting to reach across Campeche Bay for a landfall at the port of Tampico. And once in the bay, watch out for French and English pirates! They all told each other, starting with Alfonso de Seguida, that they had come through the valley of the shadow of death and that having survived it, they were no longer afraid of a mere game of hide-and-seek with fate.

Next day a great bird of unknown species flew above the galleon for several hours: it was as if it meant to lead them in the right direction. The seamen interpreted its presence as a favourable omen, and Cordavoro's secret studies led him to equally encouraging conclusions. The sceptical captain reinforced the watch and ordered the gunners to overhaul the *Santo Domingo*'s complement of sixteen iron cannon, eight on either side.

The scholar and the cavalier were able to resume their conversations, except that this time they took a no less serious but more intimate turn. Baruch revealed his intention to place his talents at the disposal of the Marquis del Valle, descendant of Hernán Cortés and provost of Cuernavaca, who had summoned him to New Spain; and Alfonso was overjoyed to recognize his friend's sincerity in thus expressing scorn for what some men considered to be his art. Now the student in search of adventure and fame knew that he had encountered a philosopher, surely one of the best minds of his time. That such a man should have chosen to go and subjugate his learning to the court of a vulgar aristocrat with a thirst for pomp and clowning seemed inconceivable to him. Cordavoro retorted laconically that anything was possible in this New World they were about to enter, and begged his companion to tell him instead what reasons had driven him to make the long crossing. Seguida talked about the end of a lineage, and about the last chance he represented to sire an illustrious new line under a different sky and different auspices. The Jew replied that the Presence, the feminine element in the world, must be united with the Husband. On that condition alone was universal harmony maintained. Alfonso pondered Baruch's words, but did not fathom all their meaning . . .

Three days after this discussion the *Santo Domingo* stood in unscathed to Tampico harbour, to be met by a cutter of the royal navy. The galleon gave the Citadel an eight-gun salute from her port side, and was greeted by three in return. All the passengers and crew gathered on deck and heartily cheered the appearance of the Viceroy's standard floating above the tower that overlooked the rampart.

The royal coastguard ship cleared a way for the conqueror of the ocean through a flock of shallow longboats swarming with the semi-naked bodies of dark-skinned men and women.

When the ship had berthed, Cordavoro and Seguida found themselves standing at the foot of the gangplank. The two of them embraced, and the older man said: 'What lands are these that I have come to? Are the people violent, wild and lawless or do they welcome strangers and respect the gods? Where am I to carry all this wealth? And I, where am I to go?' And the other smiled, because he recognized the words of Ulysses on his return to Ithaca.

Yet the journey which was to take them from Tampico to the capital, and which lasted twenty-six days, combined the charms of the Odyssey with the discomforts of a merely human ordeal in which heroes were out of place. They met more midges and other winged and stinging insects than German alchemists or beautiful Sevillanas. On the first night, at the Dos Caminos tavern, the maize tortillas and the pulque made from fermented agave sap seemed welcome to the two friends after the limited diet of the crossing; but over-indulgence in both these native products was repaid next day, and the day after, by upset stomachs that kept forcing the travellers to dismount in haste and relieve themselves behind unknown shrubs which their Indian guides called by unpronounceable names. To make things worse, their little company was robbed five days later by a band of brigands who spared their lives only in return for all the provisions they were carrying by muleback. It was worse than death. There was much wailing, and many entreaties to God, and Seguida had to exert all his authority to start the group moving again. After nightfall, near the camp he had pitched on the banks of a stagnant lake, the Castilian shot a plump drake by the light of a full moon, and in the morning the Indians were cheered to discover three hares caught in the snares placed round about on the previous day. The convoy's spirits revived, and they set off southward with the certainty of covering the twenty-five leagues that separated them from the silver mines. Cordavoro had located their position on the map obtained in Tampico, and the natives confirmed it with a profusion of gestures at the stars. They reached their destination, but the joy of survival was destroyed by the unspeakable state of health and abominable working conditions suffered by the Indians who worked the mines. Cordavoro knew something about the writings of Bartolomé de Las Casas and the part played by the Spanish Jesuit nearly a century before in defence of this exploited labour force. He had never imagined that the situation would have remained so unaltered, and in fact so much more tragic than anything suggested by the tales told in Spain by those returning from the West Indies. To his great surprise, the Jew realized that for the new masters of this land the Indian still incarnated the devil. A good Indian was a dead Indian, dead if possible in the bowels of an underground gallery out of sight of the Whites who guarded the entrance to the treasure grotto with the zeal of Cerberus and the faith of a money changer in the Temple. Yet when Seguida disclosed some of his own feelings, the astrologer hid behind a wall of silence: the Inquisition kept watch, and it showed no mercy to heretics like himself.

A few hours after the travellers' arrival a minor earthquake put the camp in uproar. Part of the mine collapsed, burying several dozen of the supposedly soulless human beings who laboured inside it. The guards had to use their blunderbusses to restore order among the survivors, and the commandant announced his intention of sending a punitive expedition next day to raid the hill tribes for replacements. He even invited the new settlers to join it: then they would have a strong escort out of Chichimec territory, which was swarming with renegades. Alfonso de Seguida refused point-blank, saying that he and his men wanted to leave at once. The commandant greeted this unexpected snub with a bellow of laughter. 'Just as you like, caballero!' As for Baruch, he did not argue with his hot-headed friend's decision, but made sure that they were well armed and well supplied.

For four days and three nights nothing disturbed their slow

advance through narrow passes and high plains. They saw smoke rising from occasional distant camp fires, killed two or three snakes, and kept a sharp watch around the big bonfires they lit at night to ward off the cold and any prowling animals. At noon on the fourth day they were rounding a rocky pleak when their eyes were drawn to a wheeling silent ballet of birds silhouetted black against the sky. Zopilotes. The Indian guides, who were converts, crossed themselves. Vultures signalled the presence of death. Alfonso and Baruch spurred their mounts and galloped towards the sinister carrion birds. At the edge of a narrow ravine they found the bodies of a dozen men scattered across the dusty, stony ground, wherever battle or flight had caught them. One of them, obviously the leader, had been crucified on the shaft of a shattered cart now reduced to smoking ashes. A dying horse lay at his feet, panting very feebly. Seguida looked away, 'I thought the savages worshipped them like gods,' he growled. 'Their ancestors perhaps,' Cordavoro replied. 'But nowadays . . .'

Instead of eyes, the crucified man had empty raw sockets, and his broken lance was buried in his heart. Not far away, perched on the horn of an ox butchered to leave nothing but the head and stripped carcass, a motionless vulture defied the interlopers. They had no time to take offence or drive off the surly scavenger, for a faint human whimper reached them from below. Alfonso de Seguida dismounted, drew his sword and clambered down to the wagon lying overturned below. When the soft muffled sobbing broke out again, he was in no doubt about its source. 'A woman!' he shouted to Cordavoro, who had been joined by the guides.

She must have been about fifty years old. Her face was screened by dishevelled grey hair, her rich clothes tattered and torn. She was still breathing, and with wrinkled hands one of which still wore a gold ring set with a precious stone, she was trying to cover her half-bared breasts. The blood that trickled from her parted thighs was almost dry. Alfonso covered them with the satin sheet she lay on.

Cordavoro and the Indians built a stretcher out of the materials strewn around the site, and Seguida fetched drinking water and did what he could to comfort the lady whose present state contrasted so sharply with her obvious pedigree. When she revived a little, or at any rate enough to see that she was safe from further harm, she whispered to her rescuer that she was the wife of the corregidor of Pachuca. The Chichimecs had spared her life, but they had raped her.

Throughout the rest of their journey, Seguida rode alongside the stretcher, which was strapped to a mule. He would have stopped at nothing to prevent the death of the exhausted woman who see-sawed between delirium and utter misery. He prayed. She was nothing to him, but when he looked at her he saw the face of his mother, lying paralysed on her sickbed in Castile . . .

For the first time since leaving his ancestral home, he began to regret having left her. When he confided these feelings to his philosopher companion, Baruch told him: 'One day, which given the infinity of space and time is not so far removed, men will not care about this world below. All these lands, even the furthest and wildest among them, will be furrowed with highways as broad as the valley you see over there. And out of it, out of the bowels of the earth which will have been bled to the last drop, a vast city will rise, peopled by strange machines. Then, weary of too great a power, mankind will long for other worlds which it will build in its own image, the better to throw them down. Desperate for new ideas, and in order to prolong the apocalypse, humanity will bring war to invisible planets, products of its own imagination, simple reflections shining out of lifeless screens, travelling through the seas of heaven, paintings without souls. And when these senseless worlds have been created and thoroughly destroyed, no one will give further thought to the folly of departures or the joy of arrivals. Self will merge into fixity and movement combined. Men will be nothing but desire – mere, absolute, insatiable desire. Perhaps on that day it will be time to conceive of dying. Meanwhile . . .'

Those were the words of Cordavoro as the company came in sight of Pachuca, but Seguida said nothing, and there was no knowing whether he felt some relief, or on the contrary the most terrible dismay.

The corregidor had felt sure that he would never see his wife alive again, and he gave the two travellers a royal welcome. They were careful not to say all they knew about the rescued woman, and in view of her condition there were no special celebrations, but Baruch and Alfonso were treated like lords for a few days before they could resume their journey to Mexico City, when the viscountess was out of danger. They were given fresh horses, an escort of six armed men, and supplies of exotic fruits, distilled spirits from the Old World, and tobacco. Best of all they took with them a letter of recommendation to the Viceroy . . .

Except for a day and a half of wind and rain, they reached the capital with no misadventures. The only surprises left in store were the customs officials and the military inspection which they had to undergo a few leagues away from their destination, but the corregidor's carte blanche took care of that.

Once they had crossed a wide river, the hitherto steep and narrow road suddenly emerged into a huge basin out of which grew turrets and campaniles, domes and towers, churches and monasteries, an architectural symphony so miraculous in these latitudes and at this height that the riders reined in their horses to admire the splendour of the spectacle. Cordavoro chose this moment to inform his companion that their paths must separate. Alfonso protested in vain. The astrologer reminded him that a man of his race was certain to find trouble ready and waiting in a place like Mexico City, and it was better for him to pass by unobserved. On his own, he could ride past without being noticed and continue his journey to Cuernavaca. Friendship compelled the younger man not to insist, and they said their farewells, promising each other that they would soon meet again.

That at any rate is the impression a reader may derive if he consults the *Travel Diary of a Spanish Gentleman.* Recovered by some miracle in a village in Chiapas, in the possession of a Lacandon chief who exchanged it for a few cheap glass trinkets, this brief record was published in Mexico City twenty years later by the agency of Baruch Cordavoro. History does not relate whether the scholar had set out in person to look for his lost friend, but in the absence of concrete evidence it is a tempting supposition. In any case, a copy of the book is in the keeping of the British Museum in London. This is how Alfonso de Seguida describes his arrival in the capital of New Spain and the events that followed:

'Hardly had I recovered from my surprise at the spectacle of a teeming common populace in which Portuguese merchant rubbed shoulders with Creole adventurer, plumed savages with mestizo slaves, than I had to contend with a further revelation. Truly the strangest marvel of all was the one that awaited me at Court. There I was received with far more than the customary considerations of honour. No matter what the relative insignificance of my rank, it appeared that my letter from the corregidor of Pachuca had the power to sweep away every hindrance and open every door. For the first time since my arrival in the New World, I felt that the aim for which I had sacrificed those ties which bound me to my origins was becoming accessible. Everything seemed to lie within my grasp. Here, a bold, ambitious man enjoyed privileges as great as the highest born. After the months of privation I had endured, how should I not have been seduced by the marks of friendship and gratitude that were showered upon me? The ardour and inexperience of youth caused me, utterly forewarned though I was against their fatal effects, to confuse appearance with reality.

'And what a performance it was, in fact, worthy of the finest theatres, the most hilarious harlequins! Never had I seen such a saraband of plumed and feathered heads. The sartorial display which was in vogue among the Spanish nobility reached here the very summit of grandiose extravagance. Gigantic lace ruffs, outmoded on the old continent, doublets of sumptuously ornamented brocade, many-stringed necklaces, enormous rings, every kind of romantic cape and hat imaginable . . . And all this amid a still greater concourse of men of God belonging to every order, clad in every variety of robe, some with angelic or haggard faces, others with smooth or sinister expressions. This contrast between worldly frivolities and the ubiquitous Church was exacerbated by the rather malodorous blend of strong exotic perfumes and vapours of holy water and incense. Through all the pores of amply uncovered flesh, the warm and humid atmosphere of the Palace exuded a heavy sensuality. Never had I seen anatomies so shamelessly displayed. This world that men called new was strange to say the least, and I wondered how much the strangeness might not stem from some secret influence, some vengeance of the savage races. The men wore cod-pieces which left no doubt as to the state and configuration of their intimate selves, and during the ensuing fiestas I surprised more than one of them publicly and most aesthetically expressing the deeper virtues of his identity. The dress – if I may call it that – of the ladies was even more captivating: a tight bodice clasped their busts and emphasized the roundness and fullness of their breasts. These were always uncovered, and among the youngest and prettiest women it was customary to reveal the nipples too, using cosmetics to enhance their colour and mass. By night, it is true, they covered their heads and shoulders with black or white mantillas, but the reality of a figure thus concealed is divined with increase of pleasure through the folds of sheer openwork veiling. And the more the upper parts of their bodies seemed intended to draw glances and longings, the denser the mystery of the lower parts. To say that their skirts – *vertugadins* they call them here – were ample would be an utter euphemism. Nothing so voluminous, and necessitating such a deal of layered hoops and furbelows, had ever been ventured anywhere in Spain.

'With a lump in my throat, I called to mind the full-length portrait of my blessed mother which adorned the great hall in Novayas. She was young. A modest vertugadin of harmonious proportions gave her the look of a princess. When I was old enough to understand, she had told me that she disliked that painting, and that if it had not been for my father she would have disposed of it. In Castile, whatever the marquises and courtesans might say, the once fashionable costume had become indecent. So the Inquisition had decided. From the day when the Holy Office had threatened with excommunication any woman who should dare to wear them, my mother and her own mother had burned these objects of Evil. Later on I learned that the metal framework could impair procreation and prevent the natural course of childbirth. In Mexico City, I do not know whether such an exorbitance of skirts served to conceal the pregnancies due to fornication and adultery, but what I am sure of is that beneath their inordinate swaying they hinted at so great a wealth of unknown worlds that the most untried of explorers must long for the delights of their discovery . . .

'Our voyage by sea and then on land had not afforded my passionate instincts either the time or the leisure to awaken in the simple fight for life against the rigours of Nature. Yet it will be understood that such a company of charming forms did not take long to stir the springs of my virility, and stir them rather too strongly, to judge by the train of events they set in motion . . .

'In spite of the decorum which governed the customs of the court of New Spain, I was quickly overwhelmed with opportunities to practise the various talents natural to my age and condition. The Viceroy gave a great fiesta for Easter, and I was invited.

'Fanfares and native dancing preceded the tournament, which was celebrated in the old-fashioned style. Negro lackeys served exotic refreshments, while jousting with bamboo lances competed for the guests' attention with falconry displays. But all this commotion was nothing compared to the challenge issued by the Viceroy that afternoon to the numerous lords of the capital and to those who were visiting from their respective provinces: three fighting bulls were to be killed in the royal arena, and His Excellency invited brave young cavaliers to enter in the lists. In reward for his bravery, the foremost was to receive a casket full of gold and precious stones. It was certainly not the lure of gain or even pride that impelled me to take up the challenge. Rather, I believe that in that moment I had but one aim in mind: to regain my sense of what I was there for after braving so many troubles and misfortunes, as if the corrida in which my father had instructed me since childhood now brought me the means to revert to the essentials – to the truth of my own life, which amid this clamour of buffoonery seemed compromised. And yet, was this not also pandering to the arrogant lust for attention that spurred the crowd? Perhaps; but no matter.

'Caught up in the tide of my emotions I ran to the stables where I kept the splendid mount presented to me by the corregidor of Pachuca. In the region of Novayas, and throughout the length of Old Castile, there had never been anyone to rival Alfonso de Seguida in the grim duel between the great wild beast and the single rider armed with sword and lance! . . . Driven by the mountain wind blowing into the basin of Mexico City, I became reconciled with myself, with those forces buried deep within myself which my labours in the libraries and lecture halls of Valladolid had seemed to have exhausted.

'So I fought, and emerged victorious from the ordeal. I was carried in triumph. The ladies threw flowers and applauded. I knelt at the Viceroy's feet.

'Thenceforth it was one long whirlwind. The pendant I clasped around the neck of a beautiful courtesan whose favours were to be mine next day . . . And then the banquet, with its wines and fine dishes, the masked ball where I was showered with compliments, the whispers, the sway and rustle of fine fabrics . . . Behind the black velvet masks, such smiles and tender eyes . . . And at night, until the small hours of the morning, the dalliance with two ladies who did not tell me their names! . . .

'As may be imagined, so much success could not fail to kindle the envy of those whom fortune did not favour. In the days that followed, the hostility towards my person became a topic of conversation, and nobody spared me the knowledge. It did not please the gentlemen of New Spain that *gachupines* – Europeans – should come and pluck the fruits of their own coarse attitude towards their wives. To tell the truth, this resentment was no more than a point of pride, for these creoles readily acknowledged their preference for mulatto women, enlisted either as conjugal outlets, by means of concubinage that no one sought to condemn, or else as spices sprinkled over the insipid dish of marriage, or with a view to both these appetites. By tacit agreement between the contracting parties – revealing the inferior status of these women of colour – those who indulged such tropical affections were granted the special excuse that "Once one has suckled at the breasts of these daughters of slaves, the appetite persists" – as the local wisdom had it. As if the sweet beverage which good fortune bestowed upon me, during one night of fever, contained some drug or powerful philtre . . .

'Thus my first response, which had been to consider this new land as devoid of the prejudices common to our European countries, quickly dissolved into a general disaffection. The appearance of freedom coincided with a spirit of caste more rigid by far than that of the old continent. Truly a strange mosaic! And it took me two weeks to disengage the dream from the reality.

'One day as I was leaving the Palace in response to a noble lady's invitation, I suffered the jeering of the creole gentlemen all along my way. Their favourite gibe, and by now I had become familiar with its meaning, took the form of two words rapped out to the beat of the whips they were fond of carrying. "*El es!*" they hissed, meaning "Another one", and implying: "There's that poor fortune-hunting *gachupine* who gives himself airs the better to jump our women." On that day, then, as I was walking past the church of Our Lady of Balvanera, the insult was accompanied by a surreptitious trip.

'I fell flat on my face, to a chorus of jeers. My assailant – possibly the husband of one of my conquests – took the opportunity to help me to my feet by plying his whip, striking left and right "to teach you a lesson". Reeling, I strove to evade the lash that curled towards my face. Seized by an ungovernable rage, I drew my pistol and fired at my enemy – fired at his stomach, aiming to kill. Cries went up. He collapsed. I went over to him and observed that he was dead. His companions kept their distance, but I heard one of them speak the name of the Count of Arfilaz. The commander of the royal guard! A protégé of His Excellency! My hopes were dashed for ever. I knew that the life I had saved in the person of the corregidor's wife would count for nothing against the life I had just taken. All that remained was instant flight, thereby also avoiding the dishonour of a death inflicted in a dubious combat, outside the rules of the caste to which I belonged. I ran to the church and hid there, awaiting my pursuers, but none appeared. At nightfall I would be able to leave this blessed sanctuary . . . and fall into the hands of providence! The lands I had entered were vast, and still mostly unexplored. I would go away, far away . . . After all, was that not the goal of which Baruch and I had dreamed on the deck of the *Santo Domingo*?

'But providence did not lead me directly on to unmapped paths, for it chose a more roundabout course as the surer means of plunging me completely into the fate it had in store, whose claws still grasp me as I pen these lines . . .

'Curiously, it was the divinities of rain and rivers who heard my call. That night a cloudburst swept down on Mexico City. The gutters became torrents, the marshes heaved like a rough sea, and the Rio Cuantilán, swollen by the breach of dykes protecting several canals, burst its banks and in a matter of hours had inundated the city of twenty-two convents. The frightful panic brought about by the sudden flood exceeded my every hope in taking me beyond the reach of my pursuers. But although saved by the waters, I was soon forced to flee them myself, as if my good fortune had suddenly been reversed. From apse to sacristy, cloister to presbytery, I therefore retreated towards higher ground, driven by the whims of the flood. While the elements raged, thunder and lightning marking my path through the depths of darkness, my frantic footsteps guided me through anterooms and chapter-houses. Suddenly, muffled by the roar of the waters that surged through the streets, I heard the sweet sound of singing. I stumbled towards the chorus of female voices growing more and more distinct. *Veni . . . Creator . . . spiritu* . . . Nuns. I was in the precincts of a convent.

'In different circumstances, without that atmosphere of catastrophe which seemed to have been created by my crime, the situation would have seemed comic, and even favourable. In that night of deluge, however, it only crowned my confusion. Not knowing where to go or what to do, I rushed into the first doorway I found to my right, with no prospect but surrender to the hazards of an unknown fate. I blundered up against the cold dampness of a wall, then my shins hit a wooden plinth, and I toppled forward on to what I recognized as a bed. Now I set out on a groping inspection of the place, and my hands quickly identified the presence of a candle-holder and a pewter basin. Then something extraordinary occurred. Some will see it as a sign of divine intervention, others as the appearance of a natural phenomenon common in these latitudes. For my part, I must confess that I remained utterly mystified. My knowledge of the physical world, augmented by lessons from Baruch during the long crossing, had not prepared me to face such an intrusion of the supernatural, or at least of the inexplicable. Yet later I learned that these freaks of nature are not unusual in the New World. Believe me, then, when I say that all at once the room where I stood was aflare with celestial electricity. There was a loud report, and fire blazed through the narrow open loophole in the wall. Sparks crackled all about me, with such power that I shut my eyes, cowered down and thought that my last moments had come. I would be burnt to ashes, expiating the crime I had committed but thereby escaping from those in store. Would to God it had been so! . . .

'Well, then, following I know not what mysterious process, not only did I not succumb to the thunderbolt, but when I dared to open my eyes I saw – only imagine my terror and bewilderment! – that the candle was lit and was casting its tranquil light upon the cell (for such it was, of course). No cataclysm. Everything appeared calm and serene. A familiar, orderly universe in which objects had resumed their time-honoured place and function. In my relief I lay down on the wooden platform without giving any further thought to the incongruity of my presence, too preoccupied by the wonder of what I had just witnessed. Had I lost my reason, I asked myself, or had I been so unhinged by the dramatic sequence of events that they had blunted my perceptions?

'A feeling of great fatigue had overcome me, and before my eyes glazed and my head began to throb, it was not difficult to lay everything at the door of a most natural bout of exhaustion, which was more convenient and less painful to my baffled mind than having to re-examine the foundations of my own thinking or the principles of life that I had come to hold.

'Gradually and not unwillingly allowing my consciousness to ebb, in the end I slept. How much time elapsed I do not know, but aroused from sleep by footsteps and whispers I came thoroughly awake when I heard the bang of a door, the clank and thud of a drawn bolt, and most of all the shrill cry, rapidly stifled, of a woman close beside me, almost in my ear . . . Leaning against the wall with one hand over her eyes and the other clutching the crucifix that hung from her neck, I saw a nun, clad in the black habit of her kind. Thinking it was a bad dream, some apparition as frightful as the hallucination I had previously suffered, I myself uttered a long wail of fear and bafflement – but against expectation, it was the dark-robed vision which voiced a spate of calming words. "No, please, whoever you are, man or demon, do not cry out!" And the face emerged in all its youth and beauty in the candle's half-light . . .

'The idea of a nightmare dissolved at once. Appearance and reality combined in a touching image – mystic Venus or Madonna incarnate, as you will, and in fact I hovered for some time between the two versions, according to whether the voices of decency, legality and my own heart inclined me to honour the sanctity or else the femininity of the person I confronted. "Madame . . . sister," I finally stammered, "you will forgive this late intrusion into your . . . privacy . . . but I have been driven by an unkind fate, and by the rising flood, to seek refuge in your house . . ." She smiled. "Do not apologize, sir. And be so kind as not to take to your heels now. Our Mother Superior would be angry indeed if she were to meet you straying in the corridors of this convent . . . Our prayers have been answered: already the rain has stopped, and in a few hours' time, before the dawn, the waters will have begun to subside. Then I shall be able to lead you outside these walls by a secret passage . . ." The little nun was bold! I scarcely had time to feel surprised before she was sitting next to me on the wooden sleeping platform. "You have not told me your name." I made my excuses and introduced myself. Quite perceptibly, she meant after her initial alarm to make the best of my presence in a cell which was locked, you will recall, from the inside. In a quiet, unhurried voice, Sister Maria-Angelina told me how ever since her childhood she had been isolated from the world and immured in convent after convent until she was old enough to take her vows here, at the convent of the Immaculate Conception. In this way a shameful father (it pleased me to imagine that it might have been the Count of Arfilaz, the man I had killed), a Spanish grandee whose name she left unspoken, had washed his hands of the bastard daughter presented him by one of his Olmec servants. Moved to tears by this story, and captivated by the sweet innocence that filled her words, inwardly I raged against the dismal fate which she had undergone and which I longed momentarily to put right. In order to excuse what followed, shall I invoke the irresponsibility consequent upon such high-flown feelings? To tell the truth, who can say what godsend drew both of us from confession to caresses, and from a stir of feeling to a surge of heart and body? For my part, I would like to believe that it was a matter of erecting an impenetrable barrier, a wall of total incomprehension between myself and the remote or recent past. A means of making a radical break with Law. A simony, an absolute pledge of my own heresy, given for all time and for love of life . . . Releasing a loving being from a premature death . . . I know – and my judges were bound to invoke this argument after my arrest – I know that some people will see this act of charity and of genuine human affection as the sign of my profound malignancy and sheer hypocrisy. What does it matter now? Why should I lie, when I have so little left to win or to lose? Except a little breath of life. Destroyed by the unknown sickness that consumes me, I wander – in guise of conquest – from province to province through an ever more dense and hostile jungle which I know too well I shall never escape . . . So I can only repeat what I declared in the court room at the time: that during those few hours of a happy night, Maria-Angelina and I shared the comfort of our secrets and the pleasure of our bodies, and it never once entered our heads that our words and actions might have been dictated by some dark or malevolent power.

'In our satiety, we forgot the time, and so it was naked and entwined that daytime found us when a shaft of morning sunlight slanted through the loophole to die upon our outstretched bodies. A bell tolled and was answered by several more, and the ominous clangour started us awake. Our silence, our haste to rectify our folly, the prayers of Maria-Angelina – nothing availed, of course. When my blessed companion drew open the door of her cell we found ourselves standing face to face with the Mother Superior and five or six sturdy nuns. I attempted to force my way through their screams and furiously milling arms, but in vain . . . As for unsheathing my sword, I was not coward enough to use it so, and in any case the idea never occurred to me. Instead I flew into the arms of punishment with the same artless energy which had propelled me till now through the twists and turns of my young destiny.

'How I escaped the lethal thunderbolts of the tribunal of the Inquisition is another mystery that lies at the root of the slow death I am suffering today. Sometimes I ask myself why I have not succumbed to the blasts of the hurricane, the arrows of the Indians, the lances of brigands, the poisons of witch doctors, the lash or blade of Arfilaz, the quicksands of Cuantilán, the torturer's blows, the enemy's musket balls, the pitfalls of a hostile nature, the puma's claws, the serpent's sting or the cayman's jaws, rather than suffer the thousand deaths of a body which is falling to pieces little by little, shred after shred.

'I was arraigned, of course, before the Holy Office. Through some chance effect of the flood, I suppose, that jurisdiction called me to account only for my act of foul seduction. Arfilaz vanished from my life and memory into the rising waters, as if in their sympathy the elements had seen fit to wash out that stain for ever.

'The Viceroy heard the news of my crime and my imprisonment, which naturally caused a great commotion in Mexico City, and he intervened on my behalf. How could I have been so naïve at that moment as to imagine that my rescue of the corregidor's wife could still be keeping me in credit? Yet that is what I was asked to believe one morning when, instead of taking me for yet another session of questioning, I was bundled into a coach that set off, under escort of course, for the royal palace. In reality I now have good reason to think that His Excellency knew from the start who had been responsible for the death of his captain of the Guard. Let the reader judge . . .

'For what other motive than my coercion into their own godly scheme would my judges have agreed to shut their eyes to the corruption of a soul that belonged to God alone?

'They spared my liberty and life in exchange for liberty

and life themselves! In the service of King and Church, for the immortal greatness of Spain and the Christian faith!

'The needs of the Conquest had reasons unknown to the very Commandments. The secular power dictated to the spiritual in this New World even more than in the Old.

'So they ordered me to take command of the latest of many expeditions which had attempted to pacify the last rebel tribes in the far south of the country, with fire, sword and crucifix. How utterly astonished Cordavoro would have been to find me transformed overnight and against my will – had I the choice? – into a soldier of fortune leading a band of lawless mercenaries against the very sanctuaries that might still harbour a little of the wisdom we had come to this land to seek. One treacherous irony of fate that I did not discover till much later was that, for a reason still unknown to me, the Viceroy had signed the warrant disgracing the Count of Arfilaz on the very day he died, and it was he whom I replaced as the head of this small but formidable army.

'In the fortnight it took to complete the preparations, I was considered to be under arrest. It was impossible for me to leave the confines of the barracks and I had to undergo rigorous military training which I escaped only to give ear to the vengeful sermons of the half-dozen priests who were to accompany – or rather were to guide – the expedition. They spared me no detail concerning the cruelty and vile morals of the Indians whom it would be my duty to conquer in order that they might accept the authority of the Crown and more particularly of the Church. Out of the company dispatched to the Petén four years previously, only two men had survived to report the massacre of their companions and how the savages had sacrificed the Franciscans who had come to bring them faith and holy scripture on the altar stone . . .

'One day I was summoned to the Palace. I was expecting a royal audience, but instead they took me to one of the towers in the north wing. After a maze of stairways and anterooms I was ushered beneath the low ceiling of a cabinet room at the foot of a short flight of steps. There, seated behind a severe desk strewn with books and papers, I found an impressive-looking man who rose to his feet as I entered, emerging from the semi-darkness as a fair-haired giant with an open gaze. He motioned me to sit down in the chair facing him, measured me from his commanding height, and without further ado informed me in a frank, open tone:

'"My name is Boot, Pieter Boot. No doubt you have heard of my father, Adrian Boot?" (I was about to answer no, but he forestalled me, not pausing for breath and speaking with the same conviction.) "In 1614 Philip III decided that of all the brilliant engineers that Holland could offer, none was more fit than Adrian Boot to complete the task of draining Mexico City which a host of predecessors had left in a pitiable state, under the constant threat of a sudden rise in the water level. Nor could any other man provide Acapulco with the fortifications necessary to protect New Spain from possible attack from the east. As you know, my father completed his two tasks, but what you probably do not know is that at the same time he embarked upon an unrivalled study of the savages whose souls are in our charge – always supposing that they have any, and black souls they are, if heed is paid to my learned father's discoveries. Whatever reproaches may be levelled against you in certain quarters, sir, I would have been glad to accompany you on your expedition and to find the answer to the questions raised by Adrian Boot's treatise. I tell you this because a few days ago, on my way back from Acapulco to the capital, I met another very learned man who spoke very favourably about you although the news of your vile crime had spread as far as Cuernavaca province. So, since the King's service detains me here in this office, I would like to share my family's secret with you. Come over here, if you will, and look at this manuscript . . ."

'After the misadventures I had survived and the ill treatment they had caused, the man at once inspired me with undivided trust. I plunged with genuine interest into his father's text, which he told me was a copy of the original, and what a surprise it held! I moved from close attention to what I must describe as genuine fascination. Boot showed, with an appearance of scientific rigour which I could not gainsay, that the ten Indian kings of the original Mexico City were nothing more nor less than the incarnation of the Beast of the Apocalypse. Today I would no longer have the energy to reconstitute the intricacies of his reasoning with the necessary precision, but the following were its principal elements. There were fifteen letters in the Indian alphabet. If the letters composing the names of these monarchs were given a numerical value from 1 to 15, according to their order in this alphabet, it would be seen that the sum of all these numbers amounted to 666. The number of the Beast!

'When I exclaimed out loud, Pieter Boot stood up and roared:

'"And the beast which I saw was like unto a leopard, and his feet were as the feet of a bear, and his mouth as the mouth of a lion . . . Who is like unto the beast? Who is able to make war with him? . . . And it was given unto him to make war with the saints, and to overcome them: and power was given him over all kindreds, and tongues, and nations. And all that dwell upon the earth shall worship him."

'We dwelled at length on the abysses that gaped out from this manuscript, all the more so because the Dutchman had a hearty supper served, with plenty of wine and strong drink. When, late into the night, he had me driven back to the garrison, I fell, replete and content, into a sleep of the just which I had not enjoyed for weeks.

'At the five o'clock reveille for the changing of the guard my mind was still drowsy, but I could feel a revived enthusiasm at long last superseding the sad resignation with which I had hitherto accepted my fate. Baruch had not deceived me. The mirror of the possible was refracted here in an infinity of promising reflections. To be sure, it remained to be seen how much light was shed by hope, and how much by delusion. But the venture was worth the living. As long as men like Boot still existed . . .

'That was the happy state of mind in which I spent my final days in Mexico City, never to return . . .

'The company I led consisted of a hundred Spanish soldiers or mercenaries, together with a further hundred Indians who were responsible for the sizable supply train which must provide all the needs of the expedition for the eighteen months' travel through more than four hundred leagues of plains, mountains, forests and inhospitable jungles . . . The fighting men would bring about fifty war-horses, the Indian auxiliaries upwards of eighty pack horses and mules, to carry artillery pieces, munitions, clothing, and food and water. The Indians also had to drive an immense herd of several hundred head of assorted livestock in which oxen, donkeys, pigs and a squawking horde of poultry combined to produce an indescribable uproar of clucks, squeals and bellows.

'And when this cohort set out along the southward road among the fireworks and popular celebrations, it was with some pride and satisfaction that I sat on horseback atop a nearby hill, and looked down over the motley army which it was my mission to lead into the land of the Lacandons and the Itzas. In its wake rose a cloud of dust which now obscured the ramparts and bell towers of the capital.

'But once past the cheerful bustle that greeted us from village to village, it was time to organize my party, and take the men in hand. While I took charge of pitching camp, Fray Sebastián, the senior of the Franciscans, took much of the latter task upon himself by directing evening prayers.

'A fortnight later, not having met with a single problem other than the desertion of two Zapotecs who slipped away in the direction of the volcano Popocatepetl with a mule and two casks of rum, our vanguard entered Puebla, where we were greeted by Bishop Manuel Fernández de la Paz. Forewarned of our arrival, he had stayed the execution of three pagans accused of stealing the consecrated wafers from a church, together with the monstrance which they mistook for an image of their holy sun. Don Manuel was most anxious to afford us the privilege of seeing them scourged and hanged in the main square, thus allying the edification of the faithful with the necessary emulation of the valiant warriors who would soon be fighting the wild men of the South.

'Thereafter we traversed plains, mountains and upland passes without meeting a living soul. The solitude caused grumbling and unrest in the increasingly straggling, disorderly ranks of that army of the Petén, which by now had left all its swagger and good humour far behind. In the gloomy succession of dawns and sunsets with no other prospect or purpose than to rest from the day's forced march, weeks and then months elapsed with such monotony that nobody even noticed the place and time that marked the dreaded onset of the rainy season.

'Once we had finally emerged onto the vast marshy plains that lie before the isthmus of Tehuantepec, we had to endure day after day of torrential rain. Our progress was slowed, and several dozen men, mostly Indians, perished during the crossing of swollen rivers. Not to mention the toll of our livestock, which was decimated: allowing for what the detachment had already consumed, the figures now gave cause for alarm. We had spent two months trudging through the mud and rain, and before long we were going to run out of fresh meat . . . As for the men, in addition to natural calamities they also fell prey to contagions. Before we reached the shores of the Gulf of Tehuantepec our Indian auxiliaries had dwindled to about fifty at most, and we had lost almost a quarter of our fighting strength.

'By now those damnable carrion birds, the zopilotes, never left the sky above us. Death was our permanent companion.

'So we entered that increasingly hostile and alien world, and marvelled at the snares and prodigies of nature. Thus far, only our intelligence, courage and physical endurance had been put to the test; henceforth we must immerse ourself body and soul in this sulphurous morass of vapours alternately foul and enchanting. I knew nothing any more.

'During the first stage of our venture I had let myself be borne along on the flood tide of my feelings, following the pace set by my horse and the company. But as we made our way into the dense forests of the South, suddenly I found myself longing to turn tail; or, failing that impossible retreat, to look back, with a sense of both regret and nostalgia. My destiny had seemed to match my wishes, yet now a gaping breach had opened between myself and those living springs of history where I had sought to quench my thirst for something new. I had begun to take the measure of this gulf as we were leaving La Venta, that last gasp of civilization, where we gathered a little strength before plunging into the endless tunnel of Chiapas. Now the weight of separation dragged me faster down a steep descent where I felt sure that the stake was life itself. Deadly as they were, Neptune's tempests had contributed to our rites of passage in the crossing. In a sense they were what had cast me up on the shores of Mexico, their sound and fury completing the inner upheaval I had longed to undergo. The whole sequence of these events, including Arfilaz and Maria-Angelina (how I dreamed of my little nun as I swayed to the rhythm of my horse's steps), belonged to the same pattern. Even the expedition, and the transformation of my hopes into a headlong race for death . . . even that did not betray the visionary plans that Cordavoro and I had made on the deck of the *Santo Domingo* while we stared up at the constellations and the stars . . .

'One cannon was swallowed by the marsh, dragging with it a mule and the Indian who was leading it. The majority of our company we had to leave behind us at the mission of San Cristobal, the last outpost of Christendom in this enigmatic land. Together with myself and the unquenchable Franciscans, only the soldiers, the seventy-two who remained, were to persevere, mostly on foot and leading their mules or horses by their halters, through the impenetrable screen of trees and lianas, a labyrinth rendered all the more hellish by the universal humidity; it drew a veil across our senses so thick and so disorienting that they could not tell a fallen branch from a snake, a monkey from a demon of the night, mosquitoes from the fulgurations of our own baffled minds . . . What shall I describe? A world of pumas and caymans, iguanas and sapajous, magnificent stands of ceibas and matapolos, colonies of parasites and insects, birds of paradise or nightmare, fugitive visions of sleeping glades where eagles hovered overhead, proud shapes which proved to us that in spite of everything, we still belonged to the same world . . . The further we advanced, the more we merged into this vibrant, pulsing bestiary in the heart of shadows.

'Curiously enough – and this was something that only increased my own uneasiness and my men's irritation – the villages where we had the good fortune to be welcomed after days and days of dreadful solitude showed us savages who were capable of remarkable kindness and wisdom. We were a long way away from those bloodthirsty creatures who peopled the imagination of the capital. Yet some veterans of previous expeditions – the flower of my army, if it still deserved the name – insisted that appearances were not to be trusted: within their small frail bodies, these fishermen and hunters contained horned devils which, under the effect of magical substances, were violently transformed into fearsome warriors. I remembered Boot's manuscript. Everything I could see – the peaceful scene of celestial lakes where flower-decked pirogues cruised, the quiet labour on fields of maize that belonged to the entire community, the women and children smiling and at play, the skilled musicians, impish bowmen, potters whose speed and expertise rivalled the finest craftsmen of Castile – everything told me that the Beast could not dwell in this vicinity. During the several nights that we spent resting and feasting here, and under the influence of the tobacco leaves rolled for us by the Indians' nimble hands, I was assailed by sensual dreams more intense than I had ever experienced. Virgins of Castile, the wife of the corregidor, courtesans of Mexico City, Maria-Angelina and Lacandon wives and daughters entwined in an endless round of cries and caresses. I was burning alive. Racked by privations and sleeplessness, my body was no longer my own. My liberated spirit went prancing into the days to come, reckless, and determined to risk everything . . .

'The little dark-haired men taught us how to build and handle pirogues, and we paddled down ever more sombre rivers. We were able to load a dozen horses into the larger boats, and they followed us along that final stage of a journey whose end we now knew was in sight. Driven by a strange and savage longing to make an end, we forged on without pause, readying our weapons, steeling our hatreds, swearing and blaspheming against Heaven, utterly in thrall to the mire, and to the vermin that devoured us.

'This was our state and our condition when we reached the shore off which lay the isle of Tayascal, sanctuary of the rebellious Itzas, for whose sake we had come here after so much suffering, remorse and illusion.

'We had hardly had time to draw the perimeter of our camp, when we heard the muted pulse of drums echoing far behind the curtain of mist that hung above the waters of the lake. This throbbing echo accompanied our toils until nightfall. Then, after sentries had been posted along the shore and around the single remaining cannon, and while the exhausted men were saying their prayers around the great bonfire which blazed in the midst of our makeshift fortress, the sound abruptly ceased. Silence took hold of our distress, which was surely the keenest of all the fears we had been forced to withstand for upwards of a year . . .

'Three days and three nights passed in this way, in a terrible alternation of threatening din and utter calm. At dawn on the fourth day, one of my foot soldiers ran screaming towards the lake, where he threshed for a few clumsy strokes, then drowned before we could go to his rescue. Driven beyond endurance, the poor wretch had forgotten that he could not swim: we soon perceived that his headlong flight had begun with discovering the body of one of his companions who had stood guard that night on the eastern flank of the camp. It was riddled with arrows, mutilated, torn unrecognizably by the fangs of the wild beasts we sometimes heard howling around us, and mangled – what remained of it – by the jaws of the aquatic monsters that inhabited Lake Tayascal.

'Fray Sebastián told me that we must wait no longer, but attack at once. I proffered cautious advice, but did not insist too strenuously on the need to reconnoitre the terrain and devise a proper strategy, for I knew that the monk had given me an order. "Here ends your mission. It is God who takes command of His Majesty's troops." I had forgotten the Viceroy's words, but Fray Sebastián took care to remind me. It was part of the bargain: I was to be made use of, that was all, until the time came for the final assault under the sole banner of Our Lord Jesus Christ. One privilege alone was to be granted me: that of fighting, either to conquer or to die. In exchange for a brief lease of life, I had accepted a destiny. More than my freedom, I had signed away my free will. A base suppression.

'Bullets winged blindly towards the island. With a chorus of war-cries, to vengeful hallelujahs, our boats set out across the misty waters. On the other side all was silence. It plucked at our nerves. Our paddlers redoubled their efforts, and ten minutes later the first pirogues grounded in the full light of day. The fog had lifted with the speed of a curtain torn away. Blinded by the risen sun, the men did not see the hail of arrows. They had no time even to fire a few musket shots or to arm their half a dozen arquebuses . . . The shrill whistling was already upon us. Swish! And then the shouts, the groans . . .

'Standing in the bow of his boat, Fray Sebastián defied the storm of arrows with his upheld crucifix until one of them pierced his left shoulder. I was immediately behind him when he fell, and I took command of the retreat. As we withdrew, still under a shower of missiles, desperate to reach the shelter of the mist before we were all massacred, I observed that the whole length of the shore was barricaded with logs and bristling with Itza lances as far as the eye could see. Tayascal was impregnable.

'A direct assault across the water, feebly supported by sporadic cannon fire often falling too short to be effective, was doomed to fail. Fray Sebastián, with his shoulder bandaged and out of the fight, eventually had to agree that this was so, on the day after that ill-fated attack in which we lost three men, one of the unfortunate horses pressed into the crusade and, above all, the hope of ever succeeding in our venture. Back in our camp, as well as those killed we counted a good dozen more or less severely wounded.

'Yet – and this I knew well – there was no alternative but to confront the Itzas, although none of us could foretell the outcome. In any case, while we salved our wounds not one of us gave a thought to resuming the northward journey and plunging back into the inferno of the wild selva.

'So, a travesty of a siege began. How on earth was a mere battalion of exhausted soldiers and priests to encircle several leagues of unknown, hostile shore? In obedience to the idea that great deeds require submission to the spirit of legend, so that – come what may – those deeds should be carved on the monument of exploits achieved by the grace of the Christian faith, Fray Sebastián decided that we had been chosen to wage "the siege of Tayascal", and the expression stamped itself into the memory and imagination even of those who gave no credence to it. It sufficed, for the moment, that the words existed. Amen!

'And so we lived on, miserably, among these dreams of a victorious Iliad for several more weeks. Until one morning when, instead of laying siege, we were astounded to discover, on waking, that our camp was itself surrounded by a host of Indians armed with spears and bows and arrows. Ten against one, mustered in stealth during the night from the isle and the mountains round about. We never would have dreamed that those virgin lands could be so crammed with savages. They teemed along the lakeside, in the trees, in pirogues, or hanging from lianas, their heads crested with many-coloured feathers, their faces painted in three colours, red, gold and black, lurking behind the rocks we had chosen as the natural boundary of our garrison. They never stirred, but watched in silence. A multitude of piercing eyes.

'"Do not move!" I shouted. "Do not fire!"

'Having consulted Fray Sebastián, we agreed after half an hour of that intolerable confrontation to send an embassy. What alternative was there, if we were to avoid our certain murder?

'Fray Sebastián, two of my lieutenants, three mercenaries and myself were led towards a pirogue which took us to Tayascal. Our discussions were fruitless, as if the Indians had known from the beginning how matters would stand. One of my soldiers, a veteran of the Petén who had a smattering of our enemies' tongue, assured us that we ran no risk. The Itzas were past masters of this kind of diplomatic compromise. It was afterwards that we would have to redouble our vigilance. If the embassy failed – which meant, for our part, if these rebels were to refuse their allegiance to our God and to His representatives – then either flight or combat was inevitable.

'On the island we were greeted by a chorus of trumpets, flutes and tambourines. In different circumstances, the event would have seemed pleasant, as if we had been arriving at the climax of popular festivities where we were the invited guests. The friendly tenor of the reception seemed to be further confirmed when, during the procession which took us from the shore to the summit of the hill overlooking the rest of the island, armed warriors soon made way for groups of half-naked women who, amid lilting laughter, flung handfuls of flower petals over us. And so it was that we reached the cabin of Canek, their chief.

'From that point onward, I remember all that followed only with appalling imprecision, as if every sublime emotion oscillated between doubt and delirious joy. Did it matter what was said or done, since after more than a day and night of ritual celebration, the pleasures of feasting to our hearts' content on fish and succulent game so overmastered all our conquering plans? What matter if the sacred grasses had warped our understanding, since on that night my fortune led me to Sanikté? Her name, she gave me to understand as we lay side by side in the undergrowth on the warm and aromatic earth, was the name of a white flower which she would show me when daybreak came. In the fever of love which dazed my senses in the hours that followed, I called her Maya. She laughed, and let me know with her body, all her body, that Maya pleased her well. O mysteries of a destiny only to be conceived by a mind long past the reach of reasons, and caught in the grasp of sovereign passions! I was there, in Tayascal, in the depths of that incorruptible jungle, and these infinitely good wiser beings responded to fire and sword with weapons far more divine! And I loved you, Maya, priestess and ambassadress of the race which invented the language of the stars. I worshipped the magical powers within you, I bowed before the offering of your breasts, I revered the sacred light in your eyes, and communed with all my soul in the holy sacrament of your belly. Ecstasy! There would be no truce . . . Maya, Maya, my love!'

So ends the *Traveller's Journal of a Spanish Gentleman*, handed down to us by the man called Alfonso de Seguida, my ancestor. Its resurrection now allows me to speak up on my own account, as if consulting a memory that I had given up for dead gave me the necessary impetus . . . For the present, are we to conclude that, like so many Conquistadors, his reason eventually gave way, caught in the web woven by abstinence and illness? History does not say, but legend preserves at least two versions of the tragedy's conclusion.

One of them, the Spanish source, claims that, contrary to Seguida's story, it was the Itzas who sent an embassy of Indian women to the camp of the Christians, in order to seduce them and get them drunk, before the tribe's attack . . . According to this same tradition, Seguida was bewitched by Princess Sanikté in person, who was the daughter of Canek, the chief. At dawn, the pagan warriors merely had to slaughter the sleeping men. Fortunately a divine revenge ensued, for Sanikté found herself pregnant by Alfonso and gave birth to a son who, when he grew up, made a treaty of peace with Spain and converted to Catholicism.

The other version, from an Indian source, says that the union between Sanikté and Alfonso de Seguida saved the Itzas and the Conquistadors from killing one another. Canek was wise enough to ask for the marriage to be observed according to both their rites, the Christian and the Mayan. Fray Sebastián was angry at first, but in the end he accepted the compromise as an unhoped-for method of introducing the worm into the bud, which is how the story turned out. He set only one condition, that while he and half their band would remain to pacify and convert the people of Tayascal, Seguida must travel to the frontiers of Yucatán to join up with the expeditionary force which had been based there for several years. Just as the priest had intended, the Castilian did not complete his ordeal and would never achieve his redemption. Imagine the heartbreak the lovers must have suffered at the moment of separation. In that tropical sanctuary, one of them had found meaning for the turbulence which had ruled his life until then; and the other had probably read in what happened the immeasurable human anguish contained in the ancient legends.

Seguida soon succumbed to the terrible sickness of the black fly which consumes flesh and sinew and leaves the face a mass of open wounds. It was probably during those weeks of affliction that he wrote the bulk of the *Journal* quoted above.

The despairing Maya Sanikté threw herself into the waters of the lake. The son she had borne a few days earlier was called Chama.

Three years later, a new army arrived from Yucatán, which Alfonso de Seguida had never reached. Chama was baptised by Fray Sebastián's successor, on the day they consecrated the little church built on the ruins of the Itza temple. It had been destroyed after Canek's death, which followed soon after his daughter's. Jutting from the façade of that new sanctuary was an impressive gargoyle which the Indians named Bocanegra, marking the blend of awe and terror aroused by the carved stone figure. One day, they were sure, after years, or even centuries, they would see its grotesque black mouth disgorge some token of truth that would recall the sweet song of Maya Sanikté.

BOOK TWO

I
THE STAKES

1

Paradise? You're kidding. A shit-heap, an ulcer on the world. You've got fevers, mosquitoes, gunmen popping up all over like plague-ridden rats and shooting at anything that moves, especially if it has copper-coloured skin, those Indian crazies asking for their rights, just asking for genocide and helicopter gunships and napalm . . . The Jesuits in the old days used to say that the only good Indian was a dead Indian. Nowadays, if you persist, and if you've first managed to prove that in spite of your American nationality you're not working for the CIA or United Fruit or some well-heeled landowner, maybe someone will whisper in your ear. 'No political detainees in this country,' they'll say. 'Don't bother looking, you won't find them . . . They're all in the graveyard, or some bulldozed pit . . . Here there are nothing but political killings . . .'

Michael Mateos knew what he was talking about. He had seen all the guerrilla warfare and all the massacres a man could stomach. The first time, when he was twenty-five years old, not only had he had nothing to lose, but whatever he might have said or thought, he had some compulsion to go where the blood of his ancestors dictated. At forty, when he had finally discovered what he had come to find, Michael no longer had visions of some hypothetical last hope.

Right now he was satisfied by a soupy warm beer in the Los Faroles cantina, by the harbour. Once the gooseflesh had subsided, getting out of the Guatemala trap had given him a glow of satisfaction that he was unable to explain. After all, there was nothing so humdrum about sitting in an empty bar while outside a sickly sun shone down on deserted streets – curfew time, under the state of emergency – and listening to a reedy voice from a crackling radio issue resounding but contradictory victory communiqués. But Michael was in a hurry for permission to ship out to Le Havre on board the *Bahia*: he was missing his son Pablo (and not before time!), and he had to make that detour to Paris before heading for Poland and the final secret of W. H. Raven, the writer who was his father. Twice he had been compelled to make his way to Central America in order to 'merit' – the word produced a sardonic grin, and he signalled to the barman half-hidden behind the counter to fetch him another *cerveza* – to merit, okay, not *the* truth, which he didn't give a damn for, but *his* truth, small, selfish, radical, lethal or pleasant as it might be.

First there had been the hurricane. Not a chance of outrunning that tropical spectacular. Caught between the two arms of the river, thirty-five miles from the estuary, after a journey through mountains and jungles, he had been forced to go to earth yet again in order to save his skin. There, deep in that den of misfortune, the will to write, to write the whole thing through, had given him the patience to wait. Until then, all of his various attempts had ended in failure.

The messages from the weather station in Puerto Lapiz had been crystal-clear: 'Hurricane originating in the South Atlantic has turned west past Barbados and the Lesser Antilles. Wind speed at the eye-wall upward of 160 miles per hour. Low pressure 950 millibars. Hurricane warnings posted for Kingston, Jamaica. Tidal wave forecast. Probability of massive natural disaster in Yucatán, Chiapas, Honduras and eastern Guatemala.'

This son of a bitch was called Bocanegra IV. Michael knew all about its notorious ancestors, the cyclones of 1640, 1926 and 1966 (that one had nearly cost him the use of his leg, and sometimes the limp still recurred) . . . The tempest's ancestors (it might have been a good title for Raven) instead of his own! 'Yeah, it's the way my luck runs,' he grumbled to the barman, who was a circus of twitches and scuttled away without a word after leaving the beer on the table. On the wall a calendar advertising Anis del Mono told him that the date was *Viernes, 2 de octubre, 1980*.

Now that the hurricane had subsided, faster and with less damage than the forecasts had suggested, this bitch of a war had broken out, a sticky, murderous war.

The barman switched off the radio and Michael called to him to put it back on. The heavy beat of one of last year's American hit songs blended with the buzz of the flies.

In a few days' time, Michael felt certain, the boat would finally leave port for its next Atlantic crossing, and his last, he hoped. Safe. No wind or squalls. In the end, he was feeling like a tourist – disenchanted, of course, but all the same with a natural tendency towards escapism. If there was no pitching and rolling he could resume his story where he had left it, on the day when Bocanegra IV had hit the region.

Alfonso de Seguida would soon be dying his fine death.

And what about me? thought Michael, just as a submachine gun chattered in the alley outside.

2

I WAS BORN on 6 August 1940 in Oaxaca, Mexico. So my passport claims. Such statements have always felt to me like some sort of feeble joke, yet I have to recognize that the sentence rolled off my pen with all the force and impact of the obvious. And the phenomenon is doubly inexplicable and perverse considering that I myself have often had my doubts, though without quite knowing why, about the accuracy of these biographical assertions – for example imagining a birth date two years earlier, as if for some reason my mother, my father or some other party had wished to conceal the true circumstances of my arrival in the world. And furthermore there are these notes, this story, this work I have set myself to carry out after years of repression and months of reflection and hesitation, and which in theory cover the life, the work and the personality of W. H. Raven. Even though – but need I spell it out? – the uncertainties attached to my own origins are very much involved with the mysteries of Raven's identity.

All this must appear ridiculously confused, I know, but it is also something like the form of words I used when I tried to describe the situation to Virginia over fifteen years ago. It must have been in February or March of 1965.

Alec Simpson, the deputy director of the channel, was throwing a reception to celebrate his retirement. Having no liking for the man, and no taste for that kind of event, I had decided not to go. But the people from the studio had finally dragged me along. And they were right, after all: idealist or not, I had responsibilities towards my team and it was up to me to carry them out. This was no time for performing some sea-green incorruptible routine, not while the question of the finances for the Mexico shoot remained to be settled, and by a committee on which Simpson would continue to be an honorary member. 'Michael has a teensy tendency to mistake himself for Antonioni.' (We had just had an argument about *The Red Desert*, which I had seen at the Fulham Road Classic the night before.) Okay, one day you'll make your big film, but for now we're in real time, got it? The rat race. All the top brass are going to be showing their faces at the Hampstead bash. Don't be so fussy. Anyway, who are you, what are you, hm? Producer-director on TV at twenty-five, that's not so bad. Always looking for more, all of it, all at once! (At least that was one thing I knew I'd inherited from my father: the Señora and Charlie had told me so often enough.) After less than a year's work, I had three films to my credit – a pseudo-symbolist trial-run with a flavour of half-baked Cocteau, a short piece televised as part one of 'Saturday Night and Sunday Morning'; a goodish TV drama based on a Somerset Maugham short story; and a straight documentary on Cardiff and the Welsh Black Hills. Nothing to complain about there. So if I really wanted to make that trip, I first had to make the reception.

We went to Simpson's place, and I played the game. I disliked the glad-handing, back-slapping side of show business, but I was determined to get that budget approved. Not that I had fallen suddenly in love with Mayan temples or the mural painters of Mexico City. I had put my name forward as soon as I heard about the plan to make a series about Mexico past and present, presented by the art historian Paul Arthur Smith, but my reasons were nothing like what my friends and colleagues might have supposed at the time. Not many people knew that I was born in Oaxaca, and if I was the subject of any gossip or tall stories it was in connection with my American nationality rather than my place of birth. In any case, all through a disrupted childhood and adolescence I had learned to forget my origins, leaving them buried among the debris of an orphan's memory. Who could have suspected that there was Indian blood in my veins? Perhaps the tint of copper in my skin and something aquiline in my profile might hint at an unusual background, but they were generally interpreted as signs of the same kind of immigrant history which had produced so many millions of American citizens. I could just as easily have passed for Spanish or Greek, and my surname didn't contradict the notion. Mexico was a country I had left for good at the age of five: it was distant memories, a haze on my mental horizon. There was no obvious reason why the prospect of shooting a series there should capture my imagination so strongly that it made me ready to discard my principles. Yet I felt as if my life was only just beginning, and as if all the years before had been a means to place me on my marks with my feet secure in the starting blocks, mind and muscles straining, and eyes fixed on a horizon, knowing that it was not the finishing line. Even if it didn't last, I would rather chance a royal sprint and a killing pace than plod through the mud across country. Nothing was prohibited as yet – not even a journey back . . .

As it happens, I was not to regret that duty trip to Alec's. An evening which had seemed likely to be particularly depressing, an arena for market forces, favours on sale to the highest bidder, suddenly transformed itself into a decisive turning point in my life. Whether by chance or by predestination, Paul Arthur Smith arrived, late as usual, but bringing a couple of American friends. I was standing by the buffet in the music room, listening with half an ear to my cameraman, Ron, through the general roar of conversation, when Paul came up with a glass of champagne in his hand.

'Michael, I want to introduce you to Professor George Lippman. He teaches literature at UCLA and he knows a great deal about Mexico, as you can imagine. I thought you'd like to meet him . . . Oh, sorry, and this is Mrs Lippman, Virginia Lippman, his wife.'

I finished off my bourbon and turned round to put the glass on the table, or rather to cover my confusion. When I faced them again I had no idea whose eyes I should avoid, those of a man who five years ago had published a thesis on Raven, or those of his beautiful and considerably younger companion. I stuck out my hand towards Lippman and stammered:

'Mateos, Michael Mateos . . .'

The beginnings of a cordial smile froze on the other man's face, and his hand went limp and slipped out of my grasp as if it had burned him. Then he screwed up his eyes and I saw his astonishment turn into a gleam of manic interest. But the professor didn't dare come out and ask the question that I feel sure he had in mind; and the suspicion tinged with curiosity that seemed to invade us was heightened by Virginia's playful, sensual grace as she clasped my free and ridiculously suspended hand before saying in a warm voice which struck me as quite assertive for someone so young:

'I'm delighted to meet you.'

She looked stunning in a close-fitting black sheath dress, her bare shoulders set off by a gold Colombian necklace which further accentuated her youth and the perfection of her body and face . . . Ron, hovering beside me, was visually undressing her. I knew from the knowing look he darted at me that we had both been struck by the same idea – another of those professors who marry the girl who needed special tuition . . . There are situations, aren't there, where sheer triviality offers the most convenient, if not the most reliable, way out of a sense of mounting insecurity. With her short blonde hair, she reminded me of the Jean Seberg of *Breathless*. After all, she must be closer to my own age than to Lippman's forty-odd. (Later on I found out that she was just turned twenty-two.)

Visibly taken aback by this awkward outcome of his introduction, Paul Arthur Smith put all his natural tact into picking up the burden of conversation.

'Lippman is in London for a few days. He'll be taking part in Hunter's programme, this Friday, on great literary riddles . . . We met in San Diego . . . At the moment he's spending a year as a visiting professor at Trinity College, Oxford. When do you go back to Los Angeles, George?'

It was Virginia who answered.

'Early this summer, probably . . .'

A press of people drew Paul and Lippman into the next room, and I was left face to face with the young woman. Ron had already made tracks towards the plump brunette from the *Daily Mirror* he'd spotted as soon as we arrived.

In general. I tended not to fall for instant feminine appeal. After a few brief liaisons I had swapped young love for the masculine arrogance that young men are liable to confuse with emotional independence. I had reckoned without the arsenal of armour-piercing weapons which has been described by so many analysts of the patterns of love, and which found a sitting target that day. Though I must also admit that the unwelcome connection between Lippman and my father played its part, first in my stunned response, and then in my readiness to pay court to his wife . . .

I had read his academic study over and over. It was called *The Unknown of Oaxaca: Fake or Riddle*, and argued from the fact that in his lifetime my father had systematically covered up his own tracks, to claim that the masterpieces published as *The Tale of the Chimera* and *The Cyclone's Eye*, together with all the succeeding novels, had in fact come from the pen of a man called Joe Cartridge.

According to Lippman my father was a mere imposter. He claimed that my father had met Cartridge on an expedition he made to Chiapas; that some time later this Midwestern anarchist on the run from the Federales had given him his manuscripts for safe keeping; and that when Joe was locked up in an Arizona penitentiary after fatally wounding one of the agents on his trail, there was nothing left to stand between the so-called author, W. H. Raven, and his chance of glory. Of course, while I refused to believe a word of Lippman's thesis, I could not fail to be disturbed when I read his book. For the first time in years I began to think again about the father I never knew, to the point of being obsessed by the blurred images and the flurry of facts that the Lippman version canvassed. At the age of twenty I would rather have had things cut and dried, the file closed, the case explained; at least it would have been some sort of guarantee for my own future. I wrote a long letter to the Señora, and she ignored my questions, as if she had forgotten that I even existed. Two further appeals went unanswered, and her silence underlined the intensity and frequency of my uncertainties. Yet I knew that she was alive and kicking, and had her eyes peeled for trouble, to judge by her vigorous statements to the international press. It needed the end of my studies and the beginning of my career in television, the passage into adulthood together with entering the world of work, for these distractions gradually to tail off. That is, until the day in the autumn of 1964, some months before this meeting with Virginia Lippman, when a blaze of publicity announced the appearance of a new book by W. H. Raven.

Controversy broke out at once. How was it that twenty years

after his death, when his widow had already scraped the bottom of the barrel, a brand-new novel could suddenly turn up? Naturally I hurried to buy a copy of *Tarantulas at Nightfall*, and was not at all surprised to find no trace of my father's hand and genius. The novel might be published under Raven's name, but it could only be a forgery – laboured, unbalanced in composition and sloppy in style. What squalid motivation had caused the Señora to allow such damage to the memory of the man who, after all, had been her husband? Was she implicitly admitting the correctness of the theories put forward in Lippman's book? Lippman himself seized his chance to proclaim from the columns of the *Los Angeles Times* that his candidate Cartridge was restored to life: he had been released for good conduct and was living peacefully in Santa Monica. Not far from the Señora's house . . . Quite a coincidence. I was in the middle of shooting my Welsh documentary, and that is what prevented me from following my immediate impulse and flying straight over to have it out with my stepmother once and for all. When I got back to London the Mexico project came up and I focused on that. If I could go back there and have things clear in my mind . . .

'Where are you staying?' I blurted to Virginia, who was telling me about her honeymoon in Mexico.

'The Strand Palace Hotel . . . It's shabby but it's central . . .'

At this point, Lippman reappeared and broke in. He came straight to the point and told me in a cool tone, but with what sounded like a tremor of underlying feeling:

'Mr Mateos, I believe we have quite a lot to say to each other.'

'I imagine so.'

'This isn't the place for conversation. Would you come to dinner . . . say tomorrow? I already have a lunch appointment. I'm seeing Hunter to talk about the broadcast . . . Call me at the hotel, it's the Strand . . .'

'Yes, I know.'

His eyes narrowed, but his tone stayed casual:

'. . . around ten o'clock, all right? We'll arrange the time and place.'

Virginia broke in:

'Michael' – she called me Michael, and I don't know if it was

Lippman or I who was more taken aback by her use of my first name – 'Michael has been telling me about a nice place, an old pub in Greenwich, where Dickens is supposed to have gone to eat fried fish, fresh out of the Thames.'

'The Trafalgar Inn.'

'It isn't exactly the swinging London you enjoy,' Lippman complained, 'but whatever you say . . .'

'Oh, there's more than just the Beatles in this country, right?' Virginia was smiling as she spoke.

The following day I did not phone at ten o'clock – I had an appointment – but just before midday. I had no reason to do so unless I was hoping to find Virginia on her own and talk to her. Not that I would have articulated the idea as clearly as that, although that hadn't prevented me from thinking about it all morning. Ron had come in to see me at half past nine: we had to sort out what equipment we would need when we arrived. I made coffee and we worked for a couple of hours. But in spite of the importance of what we had to discuss, I had trouble concentrating on the lists my colleague had drawn up. I surprised myself by quibbling – unusually for me – about details such as the number of cameras, the quality of the lenses and film stock, the means of transport, cost estimates and so on.

'Mrs Lippman's room doesn't answer,' the switchboard operator told me. 'Shall I take a message?'

'No thanks, don't bother . . .'

Disappointed, I decided to go straight to my office, even though that day I had nothing to do there. With some grinding of gears I threaded my Triumph through the traffic at South Kensington, which was heavy at that time of day, and headed for the Television building. Just opposite Harrods my bad temper suddenly switched to a fit of juvenile excitement which I made no effort to control as I stuck my head out of the open window and shouted her name. Halted by a traffic light I had caught sight of Virginia on the pavement, coming out of a record shop. A coincidence like that, which I would usually dismiss as a fictional liberty, now seemed completely in the nature of the equivocal situation which had brought us together. The idea of a miracle or stroke of good luck did not enter my mind for a moment. There was no doubt about it: that meeting expressed the logic of events.

I tooted the horn several times and leaned out of the door. 'Virginia! Virginia!' She saw me, waved one arm in recognition (the other was holding a plastic bag containing the records she had just bought), and ran towards me.

She had swapped her party dress for jeans and an Afghan jacket, with high-heeled Texan boots that made her look taller than the day before. But in fact the only difference I noticed straight away was the absence of make-up on her face, and that natural look, together with the more casual clothes, only added to her attraction. She crossed over in front of the Triumph, I opened the nearside door to the inevitable outburst of hooting from behind us, and she was sitting beside me. 'Incredible,' she panted, slightly out of breath. I said nothing, happy to watch her smile, before I let in the clutch and drove off.

She took a pack of untipped Pall Mall out of her jacket pocket and offered me a cigarette. I refused, without explaining that I did not smoke. I pushed in the button of the car's cigar-lighter, and the cigarette quivered between the fore and middle fingers of her right hand as she waited for the click. When it came, and she had touched the glowing end against the tip, she seemed finally to relax, taking two or three quick puffs as she leaned back. And I too was able to stop pretending to have my whole attention focused on the surrounding traffic.

'Usually it's always the people you're trying to avoid that you bump into,' she said. 'Have you noticed?'

'Yes, I'm always on the look-out against this kind of meeting . . .'

My clumsiness, or possibly her own good mood, made her laugh. It was a gentle, unaffected sound, but with a sparkle that conveyed the fresh and genuine quality of her manner. Aware of my confusion, I suppose, she went on:

'In other cases, with other people, it's no use trying to force the pace, lay plans, count your chickens . . . you know, Michael, those games you play when you're a kid – if my tenth footstep touches the crack between the last two paving stones, then my wish will come true . . . No good thinking the stars are on your side: those are the people you just don't see . . . How are you?'

'Fine. You?'

'Better than yesterday and not as good as tomorrow!'

'I meant to say . . . I put it badly . . . With me, every important happening in my life has always involved some coincidence.'

'And that scares you.' (Maybe her answer should have a question mark, I don't know now.)

'I'm not superstitious . . .'

Then came a brief analysis of my metaphysical options, which made no allowance for the supernatural. We were driving up the east side of Hyde Park in the direction of Marble Arch. The weather was fine, and people were strolling along the pathways and over the grass. These signs of the end of winter and of life returning brought me back to the present too, and to the moment's reality.

'Where shall we go, Virginia?'

She could not fail to notice the 'we', the fact that I was not excluded from the question.

She stubbed out her cigarette in the ashtray and declared her intention:

'I'm hungry.'

First things first. I kept driving northward, to Camden Town, where I knew a restaurant that served traditional English food. It was close to the second-hand market, on a barge moored in a picturesque position on the Grand Union Canal. Virginia was delighted by the idea. Whenever she and George had come to London they had visited museums, university libraries and foreign restaurants in Soho. It pleased her to discover a more unexpected city.

'You'd think we were on vacation,' she said as we sat down at a table overlooking what might have seemed a rather sinister stretch of water if it hadn't been for the primitive patchwork of brightly painted wooden shacks and buildings along the bank, painters' studios or craftsmen's workshops.

Thinking I was being smarter than the situation required, in keeping with the way I saw myself in those days, I looked straight into her eyes and told her:

'It's as if you were being unfaithful to Lippman.'

She smiled, but a gleam of resentment crossed her face, like the reflection of a deep disappointment or a stinging wound, and certainly sharper than the simple, natural pleasure of knowing that she was attractive and desired.

In a way (and this is what finally parted us, a few months later) I was succumbing to the same mistaken impression her husband had when he married her – that of dealing with a sex-object – simply because she had the wit to conceal her own sensitivity and culture beneath a veneer of disconcerting pliancy and an immediate grasp of things and people.

In reply, and indicating the split, the tremendous divergence between our points of view, she confined herself to giving me a few details of her life. She made no excuses and offered no justifications. Only someone like Lippman or me would think of such a calculating move . . .

'I fell in love with him straight away,' she said, then raised her glass to her lips, tasted it and gave a nod of approval.

Guessing, I told myself she must be the daughter of some Californian wine grower. But she continued:

'A scandal in the family!'

'Were you a student of his?'

'Hell, no! What gave you that idea! I met George in New York, visiting some friends of my mother, Sylvia Morrison . . .'

'The actress? She's your mother?'

'Yes. Does that surprise you?'

At that moment I did notice that she had the eyes of the famous tragic actress who had made her name on Broadway and all over the world just after the war, before becoming one of the Hollywood stars of the Fifties. The eyes were soft and yet devastating at the same time, as if they might melt or strike you, as she chose . . . But otherwise Virginia was nothing like her mother. Anticipating my question, she told me it was her father she resembled, and quoted the name of a big impresario. She saw very little of him since her parents' divorce over fifteen years ago.

'When he found out I was marrying George Lippman he jumped on to the next plane. For once he was trying to pull the same way as Sylvia . . . You see the picture: a college professor pushing forty, the son of a Central European immigrant who hadn't a cent; and the girl who had everything – youth, looks, a movie career for the taking! After drama school I'd played a few bit parts . . . not too convincingly.'

'That was your way to start a fight?'

'If you like . . . I wanted to study. When my best friends went off to Radcliffe I thought I'd die of jealousy. As soon as I could do it I used to be out of the dressing room and into the public libraries. Does that sound crazy to you, anachronistic?'

'In any case I understand why Lippman didn't pass up the opportunity!'

'He took my side . . . I'm doing a course in general linguistics at Oxford, and I help him with his research as much as I can.'

Behind these words I thought I detected a hint of uncertainty that invited me to go ahead, and to set my own pace. I wanted her, but more than that, and for reasons not clear to me then, I wanted to cut her loose from Lippman's influence – as if the counterfeit freedom I would soon be offering did not derive from the very same reflex of domination. We were living in a decade (the Sixties) when sexual licence still had some credit left: Virginia was only too ready to test the strength and reality of the semi-filial bond that tied her to her husband, and on my side I was all set to leap into the opening breach and trade on the subtle dialectic of master and slave. With hindsight such a bundle of bogus feelings may seem outrageous, but it certainly enabled our meeting to move fast towards firmer ground, as if it gave us a pretext and an agency for the expression of alerted sensualities. The conversation slid, drifted and floundered without ever moving off the ground where our own wants met and clashed.

The coup de grâce came, need I say, when I blurted out: 'I'm Raven's son.'

Virginia, who had been relaxed and laughing till then, stared back at me with a blend of pity and disbelief. An angry frown broke the perfect balance of her face. I reached out with my right hand and held her left wrist tight.

'Do you understand?' I said.

That evening I was the first to arrive at the Trafalgar Inn. In spite of the backdrop of factories and warehouses that lined the horizon, the muddy shores of the Thames sparkled in the glow of the setting sun. A gull soared through the golden splendour, untroubled by the wail of a distant siren somewhere downstream, towards the sea, and by the water lapping against boats moored at the restaurant's landing stage.

I sat at the bar with a glass of Bell's and thought back to the afternoon's events.

Virginia had not wanted to stay for dessert. I insisted that she must hear me out, but she was wary. I was no longer the young man of her own age whose company she could enjoy while she forgot about the husband she loved and the influence that stifled her just a little. All at once I had swung across to the opposite camp: Virginia had been trying more or less deliberately to distance herself from Lippman, and now, through me, she found herself back in his presence in an unacceptable, even shameful way. She did not protest, nor did she question my sincerity, but simply greeted my news as an omen, fatalistically. I too belonged to Lippman's sphere, a datum of his, an object to be studied. That was why he had taken such an aggressive interest in me the previous day, and why my own effect on Virginia had been to give her the impression that she could confide in me. We were pieces on the same chess board, and our desire was nothing but the spontaneous expression of that mutual involvement. From that moment on, I am certain that neither one of us envisaged anything but the liaison that would quench our energies. We were victims of a reciprocal fascination that we turned into a shield against George Lippman . . . Each in our own way.

In the meanwhile we dawdled over a Cona coffee, and that gave me the chance to mount a counter-attack. Backed up against a wall of suspicion, I fought to regain ground which had been sown with mines. I played on Virginia's surprise and dismay, and reinforced my own position by starting to reminisce about the muddied waters of my childhood. Strangely, that period of my life I knew least about became the one creed I could cling to if I wanted Virginia's good opinion.

'Doña Marina did the best she could to look after the Hotel Universal, the last trace of the wealth and glorious past of the Chama family. Her grandfather's ideals had swallowed what little remained of the Chama fortune when he went off to perform and die by the side of Emiliano Zapata. Her father had been a throwback to the line of degenerate drunks who had cluttered up the family tree all through the centuries in nearly every other generation . . .'

Actually I had no justification for turning to such distant memories, rooted in the half-breed depths of my own ancestry. My childhood memory's brief but vivid image of my mother, Doña Marina, offered my fumbling imagination nothing but shreds and patches which I somehow overlaid with the successive masks of my own longing . . . My mother's tales and legends were engraved in my mind more sharply than the real facts about the people who brought me into the world. And later on, when it was a matter of understanding and of methodically examining sources and archives, the investigation did not unearth anything so important or so necessary. At any rate that is what I believed before the journey, and that is what I told Virginia, sitting in my car that day.

'The Universal dated back to the French occupation. It was a weird architectural mishmash combining mid-century Napoleon III elements, particularly on the façade, with arcades opening on to an Andalusian patio with a decorative fountain. The muddle of styles made the whole place look like a cheap B movie set, except that instead of cardboard there was genuine stucco and marble, colonnades and terraces, wooden panelling and frescoes on the walls, though admittedly with fewer and fewer guests, flitting about the place like ghosts. A few rich Indians of mixed blood, down from the north – that sounds like an invention too, but they did exist – a minor employee of the railway company, *Ferrocarriles Nacionales*, some sort of European diplomat in between trains and beers, or maybe a young Yankee couple passing through, ready to embark on a tour of archaeological sites, and not sorry to leave the place – not that there was anything sinister about it, just that it was an obsolete anachronism without any compensating appeal . . . You didn't stay long at the Hotel Universal, let alone live there. Who would dream of taking that warren of corridors and those rooms with their damp and crumbling walls for anything but historical window-dressing? You moved on fast, or else risked losing all sense of rhyme and reason.

'Only Raven had found his niche there, when he came to the hotel during the Thirties, on his way back from Chiapas.

'He seemed to have the Devil on his heels, at the very least.

And that is where the theories diverge: some people, like Lippman, talk about an imposture and argue the case for my father having been in some sort of serious trouble which caused him to go to ground there, away from prying eyes; others – I'm thinking of Charlie's version, and even the Señora's – interpret his flight and his subsequent concealment as the stubborn determination to protect the integrity of his work, to put it out of reach of the vultures who were starting to find attractions in it that had nothing to do with literature. In any case Raven did make the Universal into the sanctuary he needed. And Doña Marina, who was an only child and practically an orphan – her mother had died in childbirth and her father, *capitán* Chama, lay bound to a hospital bed and dying – Doña Marina welcomed him with a concern not unlike La Malinche's when she succumbed to the tainted charm of the conquistador Cortés. This last point delighted the gossips in the *calle* Humboldt and round about, and I must admit that Marina did have it in her blood, the kind of heredity that doesn't just fade out in a few decades. A very distant ancestor on her father's side, the daughter of an Itza chief, was seduced by a Spaniard called Alfonso de Seguida, who had been put in command of an expedition sent to pacify the South-west in 1643.'

Virginia sat up and protested at that: she claimed that I was making fun of her, spinning tall stories to put her off-balance and make her lose sight of what she called my 'little game' and my 'sweet talking'. Not that she doubted the truth of what I told her, but given the situation between us it was understandable that she should suspect my good faith when I was spreading the historical detail so thick.

'Michael, you're even more paranoid than Lippman,' she exclaimed.

'And that's saying something, isn't it? But you have to believe me all the same . . .'

'I want you to take me back to the hotel.'

'There's something else I want to show you.'

'Okay, on one condition. I have to be back by five o'clock.'

'A chapel. A little cemetery in Swiss Cottage. And the grave of Charlie O'Sullivan – my real father.'

'You're putting me on! Just now you were telling me that Raven lived with Marina Chama for over four years and . . .'

'Yes, but it was O'Sullivan who made me what I am. *In loco parentis*. Of course the Señora used to send me the money from Los Angeles to London, every term, to pay for my school fees and living expenses.'

'Stop it, Michael. That's enough.'

'You think so?' I jammed on the brakes to park by the pavement opposite the cemetery where Charlie lies.

It was over a year since my last visit. I detested those places where death dresses up in monumental platitudes, as if it were trying to make itself invisible under a layer of make-up and social conventions. Even if the ritual did once have an essentially religious function, that aspect itself appeared to me improper in every sense of the word.

We walked in silence up the rise that leads to the chapel, and it was then I realized that Virginia had followed me to this incongruous spot without a murmur: what clearer sign could we have had of the unlikely attachment which had drawn us together since the night before? The same thought must have occurred to her, because it was she who opened fire.

'Whoever this Charlie O'Sullivan may be, you really are called Michael Mateos,' she said, as she pushed open the door of the little Catholic church. 'And don't talk to me about any Lippman conspiracy. Our friend Paul Arthur Smith called you by that name,' she added at once, turning suddenly towards me, so that I almost had to put my arms around her so as not to knock her over. She looked at me out of her grey-green eyes, smiled and slipped out of my embrace. Then she entered the sanctuary and continued under her breath: 'Unless he's another member of this circle of myth-mongers that you and George seem to get such a kick out of belonging to.'

She dipped her right fingertips into the water of the font, and crossed herself slowly and not at all mechanically.

'My mother,' she whispered by way of explanation. 'You didn't know about Sylvia being a Catholic. Not very regular nowadays, but still . . . She had me baptized.'

She genuflected in the middle of the nave, opposite a rather plain altar, and went to sit on a chair in the back row. As quietly as I could, I slid into the chair beside her and used my respect for the holy place as the pretext for leaning close and whispering in her ear:

'Mateos is my stepmother's name, the one the pair of them assumed in Los Angeles. In his Oaxaca days my father called himself by the name of Waldo Joven – it means "young" in Spanish. When I was born, Raven had already been parted from Doña Marina for six months.'

'And Michael, why Michael?'

'Charlie always claimed that it was in memory of Bakunin. I suppose Raven must have told my mother that if she ever had a child by him, then his first name was to be Michael. After he married the Señora and took off to Los Angeles with her, somehow – I don't know how – he must have learned of my existence. Apparently he never tried to see me, but by then he'd become rich and famous, and he did all he could to secure my future. I've always wondered whether he had some premonition of a tragic death not far away . . .'

'Maybe he was afraid of dying?'

'That's part of the inheritance too.'

As if from nowhere a sacristan in a grey smock appeared in the transept. He knelt in front of the altar then came in our direction, limping slightly. As he went past he darted a disapproving look, then melted into the darkness of the chapel as mysteriously as he had appeared.

'Raven had allowed for every contingency but one: that Doña Marina too might die . . .'

Virginia seemed to shudder. She moved closer to me, and our thighs and elbows touched. I took her hand and she did not withdraw it.

'As long as he stayed at the Hotel Universal, his anonymity brought him the most creative years of his life. He wrote *The Cyclone's Eye* there, for instance. On the other hand fame took him into the spotlight, and that unquestionably brought on his decline and destruction.'

'Of course it made it easy for his enemies, whoever they may have been, to pick up his trail again and then–'

'You really know your Lippman!'

No answer from Virginia.

'He just joined the hunt a bit late, that's all!'

'You know very well that it's not the same thing,' she protested quitely as she stood up. Her frozen hand had remained in mine, but as I rose to my feet she disengaged it and walked towards the door. I followed, and at the edge of the graveyard, just as I caught up with her and took her arm, we passed an old woman with her face hidden behind a veil, accompanied by a child who carried bunches of flowers. He was probably less than six years old and had trouble holding them all. We both fell silent as we turned down a side path.

Eventually I told her:

'Mateos is the name I took when the Señora adopted me, if that's the word for it. She was acting in accordance with Raven's will. Did he leave her any choice?'

'People often don't realize how a name can matter. I do, a little. My maiden name was my father's, who I'd hardly lived with at all. Whereas Morrison meant Sylvia Morrison. From that angle it did feel pretty weird to be his daughter.'

'In any case,' I went on, as if to avoid starting that sort of discussion, 'by doing that the Señora gained a useful lever for controlling my behaviour, if not my thinking. She was making sure I wouldn't get in the way of her schemes.'

'By claiming any financial or moral rights over your father's works, for instance?'

Usually the 'practical' American side of Virginia's character would have grated on my nerves. That day I felt it was part of her appeal.

'You're wondering if I still inherit?' I laughed, with real amusement.

On the path running parallel to ours, the old woman and the child had been tending a grave. Now they stopped and looked in our direction.

'One thing's certain,' I said, lowering my voice. 'I was an orphan, and illegitimate too. After two painful years of a kind of waiting game, the Señora sent me to England in the care of my Uncle Charlie.'

'You were almost seven years old . . . And you've never been back there?'

'Never. Do you see? Imagining that part of the scenario, Raven had wanted me to be educated in the best English schools, and he appointed Charlie as my legal guardian. His great friend and comrade in arms. The character of Harley in *Journey Without End* is him, of course.'

'I haven't read it.'

'Your husband rates it a minor novel, but I think he's wrong. Do you know the plot – a stateless seaman, forced back on board his ship in every port because his papers have been stolen? I don't believe Raven ever wrote a better account of just how wild and ludicrous that classic question of identity can become. Harley goes half out of his mind while he keeps insisting "I don't need papers to know who I am" and a string of officials play him the same old tune – "No birth certificate, no certified official status, then you can't prove a thing!"'

'A typical theme of his.'

'Round about 1920 my father wrote some articles for various anarchist papers in London under the name of Never. Another anagram . . . One more element in the puzzle, a facet of the magic mirror, a reference to Edgar Allan Poe, "The Raven". Do you know it?'

And she at once recited: '"And his eyes have all the seeming of a demon's that is dreaming . . ."'

'They shared their banners and their dreams, did Charlie and Never, the man who would be Raven. They were . . . what? . . . twenty-one or twenty-two.'

'My age,' said Virginia automatically.

It was a pretty commonplace response, and it caught me like a slap in the face. I came back to earth and saw myself telling things I had never said to anybody to a total stranger who happened to be married to a man whose work essentially amounted to undermining the fragile foundations on which, stone by stone, I had built my life. And here we were, Virginia and I, with all our youth, our strength and our desire to love, raking over the ashes of macabre stories, which was both dangerous and ridiculous. She was alive, and beautiful, and ready to love.

'Let's get moving,' I snapped in exasperation.

But Virginia had stopped dead. I took a single step, and heard it crunch on the gravel of the path, but she tightened her grip and I felt her long nails digging into my arm through the leather of my jacket. She nodded towards a gravestone whose inscription read:

CHARLES PATRICK O'SULLIVAN
1899–1962

And there, in front of a handful of faded flowers, their stalks rotting in a vase with no water, I talked about Uncle Charlie and his veteran fighter's memories which had become part of my own, because of Raven. All through the childhood years which I spent between school rooms and sports fields and the little house in the suburbs that Charlie paid for every month out of his wages as a lithographic worker, I had gathered the components of a legend, and I ended by making it altogether my own. The tension of living on the run, impromptu journeys, teamwork, comradeship, the joy of a libertarian life – in other words all the imagery that a proud and solitary adolescent will readily cement into a shell to protect him from his own worst dreams . . . Raven and O'Sullivan had been through the mill together, which is what made me take it all so seriously for so long.

When Charlie died of lung cancer I naturally arranged a decent funeral. He had always lived alone, but while he was around I occasionally managed to forget that I was an orphan. Now, as I told Virginia, I was left with a blank; not even a feeling of devastation, a glimmer of biblical undertones or whatever. No, the simple presence of death. And as if to drive off the shadow that hovered above our heads, I added:

'In Raven's case they scattered his ashes over the jungle. Did you know that?'

Virginia was too busy tidying the grave to answer.

'That's what the Señora has always claimed, at any rate,' I continued. 'But who knows if she really did obey my father's last wishes? I'd like to be sure . . .'

'What difference does it make?' Virginia sighed, before she withdrew into what seemed to me like a deep meditation, or maybe even a prayer.

On the way back to the Strand it was she who steered the conversation back towards Doña Marina. In the end, she must have imagined (and with some reason) that in order to understand me, to discern some of the light and shade of my character, it would surely be better to try to detach me from Raven for a while and turn to what might be even more secret aspects of my background. None of the writer's biographers had been able to delve so deep.

Besides, it didn't take much insistence for me to yield to a type of questioning so much in tune with the see-saw movement of my own emotional priorities. At that time I was a long way from resolving the problems set by such a division of affections. On one side, the huge figure of an overpowering father. On the other, the ambiguous memory of a mother too quickly lost, even though the impact of her heritage and the whole sense of history that attended it had powerfully influenced the brittle make-up of my character . . .

So I told Virginia about what happened on the day of the festival of the Shout.

(In retrospect, and also because I no longer have the slightest reason to sing in praise of the instinct of love, I realize as I sit in this shabby room in a Polish hotel that this part of my story is certainly where I took the fewest liberties with the truth. The events of 15 September 1944, when I was just over four years old, make up the solid core of the memories attached to my Mexican childhood. The rest is open to question . . . even my orphan years, or my stay with the Señora in Los Angeles. Parental recollections and photographic albums do not fuel my memory. Not that I would claim to belong to a rare species: there are plenty of people whose infancy lies beyond a door they cannot open. There is an age after which remembering becomes viable. Usually it is the time when the big decisions are determined, so in my case it was at six or seven. The amniotic fluid of the nutritive years no longer immerses us and we are free – in a manner of speaking! – to evolve on the arid surface of the social sphere. I remember the ship, and that first Atlantic voyage from west to east, the opposite direction from Raven, the conquerors and the immigrants. I remember docking at Southampton on a foggy night, the sinister echo of the foghorn, London streets flashing and crackling with fireworks on Guy Fawkes night, postwar rationing, my public school and its savage discipline which completed the petrifaction of my already numbed and traumatized mind and body. Luckily there was Uncle Charlie! The counterweight of his counter-education . . . the cult of my father's personality and work . . . the weekends . . . holidays of freedom and subversion in search of an ideal . . . I am the impure product of all these. Talk about the harmony of opposites!)

* * *

'Since morning, groups of people had been walking the streets to commemorate the anniversary of Independence, wearing masks over their faces and shouting out from *zocalo* to *barranca*: "Viva Mexico, children of La Chingada!"'

'George told me about that one day when we were sitting outside a café in Cuernavaca . . . La Chingada is the raped and abandoned mother, right?'

'The Mexican woman par excellence. The mother of us all, torn and humiliated, raped and then rejected by the conqueror . . . the father. Out of this combination of paternal deceit and violence come tearful solitary children born into a world they see as hostile and dangerous . . .

'On that day, clock time stopped from the moment the express train came into the railway station carrying the terrible news. You would have thought that everybody had passed the word to join the chorus. The pedlars hawked their goods in the square while children seemed to flock in from all directions calling: "*Muerte de Raven . . . Famoso escritor matado en Estados Unidos* . . ." Then came the lottery ticket sellers: "Special draw today! Big prizes, big prizes . . ." Then the murmuring chant of the blind beggars who prayed to "the Virgin for those who have nothing" at the entrances to bars already crammed with American tourists. Wrinkled old women with braided hair, pleading with the tourists to buy big coloured scarfs of their own design. Soon the mescal and tequila would be flowing like water . . . and even the Devil himself would not recognize his children.

'The Mexican people who are usually so cautious and silent were proclaiming their everlasting sorrow. The chanting rose skyward all day long until dusk began to fall, to the whistle of rockets and fusillades of firecrackers, in prelude to the great final shout. During that time Doña Marina was hard at work in the Hotel Universal. Of all the days of fiesta, and God knows the Mexican calendar is full enough of those, Independence day is one of the busiest. A horde of ramshackle buses came surging in from all the surrounding hills and villages and flooded the main square with a sea of sombreros and a roar of celebration, backed by little orchestras of violins, guitars and trumpets . . . For that occasion the Universal used to fill up with kindly middle-class women and good Christians along with a few foreign couples on the lookout for folklore and strong emotions.

'How I detested those fits of frantic cheerfulness when people would drink themselves sick on their own distress! In that respect my character ignored the calls of my blood, or at any rate of one of its components: and from there to thinking it was the other part that drew me to anticipate even more devastating follies, according to the gospel preached by Raven in his life and death and in his works – from there it was only one step that there was nothing to prevent me from taking . . . I shut myself in my room, looking for the comfort of my old familiar toys and especially for the protection of the cult objects hoarded there by my mother: an old bellows camera, a soft felt hat with a hole in it ("a bullet from a renegade's Colt," she used to say), some poisoned arrows in a carved and painted quiver, a thin handkerchief with embroidered initials too convoluted to read (was it WHR or UJB or MUR?) and no smell or perfume . . . a shelf of books that mostly seemed to be printed in old characters (my mother told me they were written in German, which I could not read, but she would show them to me and often made comments about them). One name still sticks in my memory, Stirner, Max Stirner, and I can still see the coloured illustrations in another book, with Indians and white horsemen unlike the Mexican kind, a novel by Karl May, perhaps, or quite simply a copy of the first novel published under the name of Raven by the Gutenberg Club in 1927. Later on, when I investigated the book, in the wake of all the experts, I found out that it had been published as a serial the previous year in *Vorwärts*, the Berlin socialist newspaper.

'Night had just fallen. My indifferent ears identified jaunty *mariachi* rhythms from somewhere outside the window – *Valentina, yo te quisiera decir* – and some facetious remarks made by onlookers flocking towards the square where the fireworks display would soon begin. Suddenly Doña Marina came into my room. I still have a clear mental image of her fine Maya face covered in tears. She never wept in my presence again, and I believed at the time that her eyes had grown as hard as her heart, steeled by the feeling of belonging to nothing but eternity. A sculpture in bas-relief . . .

'Without a word she took me by the hand, and I followed her, terrorized, through the impressive maze of the hotel and down to the garage. There we climbed into the old Hispano left behind by the man they told me was my father, when he walked out one day without a word of warning. In fact, as my mother knew perfectly well, Raven's own demons of perpetual flight had caught up with him again, and he had become infatuated with an American woman who was only passing through – infatuated enough to suddenly forget the four years of real happiness he had enjoyed with his lover in the Hotel Universal.

'The car wove in and out through the crowd of pilgrims strolling in *calle* Humboldt and their grinning masks clustered reproachfully against the glass. Toothless smiles and threatening hands intensified the terror that glued me to my seat. The torture went on until we crossed the bridge over the *barranca*. In front of the ice factory we passed a few more groups of latecomers, but jolting up the stony road that led to the church, cutting through the starlit night, the Hispano finally left the revellers behind. Doña Marina had stopped her sobbing, and the lump that swelled my throat had not yet turned to tears.

'At the top of the hill Marina Chama switched off the ignition and coasted to a halt a few yards away from the parapet that separates the chapel and cemetery of Los Milagros from the mines of Teopancingo, where it clings to the hillside overlooking the rest of the town. Through the thick darkness I thought I could make out the pale outlines of two figures slipping across the graves – the fireworks men.

'There, just as rockets began to burst red, green and blue around the Hispano as if they had made it a target, my mother spoke with a broken voice to say that she wanted to tell me a story. I was very fond of the bedtime stories she used to tell me while she held me in her arms, but this time it was a different kind of legend, the tale of La Llorona . . .

'After betraying her own people, an Indian woman, the daughter of a chief, left her tribe to follow a Spanish caballero called Matamoros. This aristocrat and red-handed killer maltreated her, but that did not prevent La Chingada, as they called her, from submitting to her fate without flinching. She loved Matamoros. And loved him so, in this blind, absolute way, for several years. One day the betrothed of this so-called gentleman arrived from Castile: she was a girl of fourteen and her haughty manner witnessed to her high birth. Till then, La Chingada had taken little notice of her people's lamentations or the sarcastic observations of good Creole society; and she might have greeted this new rival with the same indifference, as just another test of her love. Only she knew at once, without question, that now she would never belong to her lord, and in fact it wasn't long before Matamoros was riding off with a retinue of coarse drunken cavaliers on his way to Veracruz, where his lady's ship was waiting – his true lady, not a *chingada* and the mother of two young children. Early next morning, after strangling with her bare hands the children she loved best in all the world, but for the Master, La Chingada stabbed herself to the heart with a silver Toledo dagger left behind by her noble gallant.

'Ever since then, they say that every night the ghost of the Indian woman roams the streets of Mexico City, praying for the salvation of her injured children's souls and continually bowing before the Virgin of Guadalupe and all the saints. In adoration . . . Baroque paintings and sculptures reflect an almost untarnished image of her lover. She cries herself breathless, so much so that the common people finally heard her sobs and laments: they love and fear their weeping woman. Children are kept quiet with the threat of calling on La Llorona.

'The bursting rockets of the final display showered coloured rain around us. My mother clasped me tighter than ever before. I thought I was choking, and released the dark floods dammed inside me.

'The scream came loud and shrill, through rounded lips, so harsh that it hurt my throat. A single scream, on a note held for what seemed an infinite time, until my lungs were bursting and my head spun. For the first time in my life the shiver of death passed over and through me, and the presentiment of the tragedy that lay in wait, sooner or later, for my mother and myself. Today I say to myself that you have to invoke this kind of knowledge before the fact in order to explain the mute passivity that took hold of Doña Marina without a struggle on the day that Raven left her. She never asked him for anything, but confined herself – I suppose – to letting him know that he was the father of a son . . .'

* * *

It would be pointless to maintain the pretence that between leaving Charlie's graveside and reaching central London I had time to tell so long a story, and that Virginia would have listened without interrupting. I have telescoped the narrative using one of the most basic devices of fictional licence, for who nowadays would object to the compression of a string of separate real events into a single synthesis? Don't you agree, Raven and the rest? And then again, does it matter. . . ! I also remember Virginia making an allusion – which I felt was rather too academic in the circumstances – to Jason and Medea. In her version, Jason did not regain the throne of Iolcos after the witch Medea had caused the death of their two children. She preferred to accept the other tradition, the one in which Jason wanders wretched until he dies. That was closer to what she knew or imagined about W. H. Raven. I insisted: I didn't want the confession I had made to be picked up and fitted in to some sort of sweeping explanation, even if it meant that Virginia had begun to take me seriously.

'How could I forget the original moment when I lost a father and a mother at a stroke?'

As I spoke those words I leaned across Virginia to reach the handle of the nearside door. We had arrived at the hotel and I had parked my car in the taxi rank. My sideways movement brought me close to scent, hair, cheek, neck, and curve of breasts, their rise and fall . . . Before I straightened up again, I could not prevent myself from touching Virginia's lips with my own.

'Michael,' she breathed, and drew her mouth away. It was not a reproach but rather a sort of call for help, a drowning person's strangled cry. I chose to see it as encouragement. Why should I deny the obvious? I was mad about this girl who had burst into my ordinary life with all the melodramatic force of a thunderclap. Lippman or not, Raven or not, I wanted nothing but to love her. After all, the coincidence of such a meeting was in tune with the order of things, the script which had occupied my mind for months already. Now it was a matter of arranging the production. At last it might be my turn to share in the performance of an organized dream, a destiny made to measure. Quiet everybody, action! I had a part to play, I was an actor – after Raven and the rest – in the great universal comedy. No more kicking my heels in the waiting room of life, appearing in a walk-on role hardly worth a credit in the cast list. Even if a colossal distance still stetched between myself and the assertion of my destiny, with Virginia's sweeping entrance it was no longer a question of sheltering behind suppositions and allegories. The liaison which was soon to exist between us might have delayed my preparations and interfered with the departure for America; paradoxically, I believe it had the opposite effect.

On the spur of the moment, sitting beside her in the Triumph, I suggested seeing her to her room. She told me that Lippman must be back by now, and that in any case we were to meet again for dinner, the three of us. Had I forgotten our date on the bank of the Thames? I should never have accepted that damned invitation, I swore, and it was a cold reply she made. 'No, you shouldn't. I wonder which of you two will get to interrogate the other!' She stepped onto the pavement, but before shutting the car door she smiled and added: 'Please, you can grill George all you want, but leave me out of that.'

Virginia was not ready to be bait in a trap or the prize in a contest, and even if I had thought of her in those terms the intriguing ambiguity of her last words would have stopped me short. That is what lay on my mind at the moment when Lippman walked into the restaurant, which brought me back to a closer consideration of the immediate facts. The situation contained a political angle which I had been trying to minimize. To meet one of the most eminent and articulate members of the anti-Raven clan was no small matter in itself. But to face a man who had for years been doing his utmost to demolish the statue which posterity had erected to a writer who also happened to be my father acquired an extra, surreal dimension when it took place in the presence of Virginia, his wife and my mistress-to-be!

Professor Lippman came in with a purposeful air and waved when he caught my eye. At first his bulk concealed Virginia, who was walking behind him, and I thought momentarily that she had not come along or that he had prevented her because of the events of that afternoon. Until then I had not noticed how tall and powerfully built he was. At least six foot two, and though he was thick-set he had the springy step of a former athlete. The type who sweats the pounds away in endless Sunday morning runs, only to collapse with a coronary one day at the end of the tenth mile. I could imagine him younger, entering the Greco-Roman wrestling championships for his college colours. Only his balding head and little round glasses gave him any kind of typically academic look, though in fact his general manner conveyed a rather spurious impression of phoney nonchalance, because underneath, and particularly in the shrewd stare of his cold blue eyes, you could sense the man of principle, a rigid quality. That was all I needed in order to feel justified in my prior hostility.

Lippman stood over me and looked me up and down.

'Say, this place of yours takes some finding!'

'. . .'

'Here you are, young, cool, contemporary, and you do your eating antiquarian style. You British will never stop surprising me!'

'I'm not British. Hello Virginia.'

'Oh yes, that's right.'

One up to me!

'I chose the Trafalgar Inn because I knew Virginia would like it.' As a matter of fact, a setting so far removed from academic or fashionable circles could not help disconcerting my opponent. I liked this London plainness with its provincial Victorian flavour, and I was hoping that it would exasperate Lippman. 'Something to drink, Virginia? And you, Professor?'

In order to accentuate the distance between us I had made up my mind to keep plugging the 'Professor' routine all the way through the evening, to confine him to his academic quarters.

'A Seven-Up. No alcohol for me.'

The last straw – a lemonade drinker!

Still, Virginia ordered a Bloody Mary, and we went into the dining room next door.

It took some time to study and interpret the menu, while tacitly steering the conversation on to safer subjects in the intervals, although Lippman turned out to be more clumsy than I had wished or imagined. Virginia unhesitatingly chose a salad and the fried fish I had mentioned the day before. I ordered an oyster soufflé, which seemed a novel enough dish to intrigue the professor. Not to be outdone, he eventually decided to follow my example, after first wavering between the lamb chops and the T-bone steak. But he couldn't help asking for an extra portion of French fries. And when the maître d'hôtel offered him the wine list, he pointed in my direction:

'It's this gentleman who's the expert on intoxication and artificial paradises.'

The challenge was certainly deliberate, but I didn't take it up and merely ordered a Muscadet. Lippman announced that he would stick with lemonade. Virginia, who was sitting opposite me, said how much she liked Muscadet too.

While we were waiting we got on to the subject of psychoanalysis, and strangely enough, that is how the conversation really kicked off. It must have been Lippman who raised the topic, which seemed to offend him so much that he just had to take a swipe at it. That early in the Sixties it was not such a hackneyed issue as it is today, at least in Europe. At Oxford I had written a brief paper on the literary Freudianism of the 1920s, but my interest in the subject did not extend beyond that one academic excursion. The transition to the life of action, and a passion for journalism and the techniques of the image, had diverted me from a field of inquiry which in my personal case seemed not only pointless but even dangerous. The contradictory attitude of a writer like Joyce – quite as much fascinated with the theory as he was determined to reject the practice – seemed to me reason enough to suspect the reliability of such an existential crutch.

To tell the truth, the news that Virginia had been seeing a psychoanalyst for the past year only came as half a surprise. It even crossed my mind that Lippman rather enjoyed telling me about it, as if it gave him a morbid kick to hint at marital problems, and at the same time to assert by doing so that they remained within his scope and under his control. The real shock – and naturally I took care not to let it show – came when Lippman informed me that her latest appointment had been for that same afternoon. Virginia blushed, and that amused her husband, who did not know the true reason.

'I usually come to London once a week,' she said without losing any more composure.

As if to allay suspicion I inquired prosaically:

'By train or car?'

'That depends. In any case it's only an hour's travelling.'

So Virginia had sacrificed an appointment which must have meant a lot to her, to judge by the professor's belligerence. And to think that I had been parading my own 'case' all that afternoon, without suspecting the grave resonance and deep impact this reversal of roles must have produced. A man would have to be really naïve, or else thoroughly selfish, to underestimate the implications of that change of programme.

The professor suddenly broke the spell his revelation had cast.

'Bullshit! It's all . . .'

'George, please let's drop it for once,' Virginia protested, visibly exasperated.

'Some people have unfinished business with their father, isn't that right, Mateos? With Virginia, it's her mother . . .'

'Ah?'

The arrival of the wine rescued us, and when the food followed it prevented the atmosphere from becoming any more strained, though Lippman could not resist adding a little fuel to the flames by comparing the couch to a confessional and ending his tirade with the sweeping judgement that it was 'just another bunch of priests'. Virginia shrugged and concentrated on her wine glass. I laughed with the professor. After all, it was an honourable way out, and he was not completely wrong.

'Are you by any chance an atheist, Professor?' I asked him for good measure.

'Just an agnostic, my dear Mateos. I go along with the argument that the absolute is outside human understanding.'

Disregarding a remark that in other circumstances I might have taken for a personal attack, I inwardly congratulated myself that the conversation remained confined to the level of urbane commonplace. I even allowed myself the luxury of a joke:

'A bit of a communist, then?'

Then, from McCarthyism to the Rosenberg affair, the discussion edged towards more delicate ground. Quite obviously, and even though we were there to feel each other out, neither Lippman nor I was ready for a direct confrontation. Yet when I referred to the Vietnam situation he must have thought that I had stopped sparring and gone over to the offensive, not only against the American guilty conscience in general, but against himself. So he justified his own position: as a liberal, he had taken the risk of signing petitions against the war. What had I done myself, when the first bombs had fallen on the North a month ago? Yes, he was against it, but all the same it was the NLF that started it . . . The temperature rose. Things came to the boil when I asked him if he would have been ready to join the troops who had just landed at Da Nang, three days before. What about you? he exploded. It was a good question, and it might have to be asked quite soon if the scale of operations increased. I got very excited and declared my intention to desert. Claptrap he said. You think so? I retorted. It's what Raven would have done, isn't it? Sparks were flying. Virginia thought she could apply the brakes, but her sudden change of subject only set us off again.

'I've just been reading a fantastic book. *The Real Life of Sebastian Knight* by Vladimir Nabokov.'

Silence from us both.

'Do you know it, Michael?'

I pulled my wits together, and was about to say that I had been fascinated by the narrator's exercise in reconstructing the life of his novelist elder brother who had died two years before, when Lippman piped up:

'Sure, sure! Proteus and all that! The impossibility of writing a biography . . . especially when it's somebody close. The writer as con man, the prancing dandy of literature . . . The man's a monomaniac.'

'He's my favourite author,' Virginia said.

'Professor,' I intervened, 'need I remind you of what Raven wrote to Ganz, his German publisher, when he asked for a biographical note?'

So there we were, smack in the middle.

I plunged onward, quoting from memory:

'*Let it be quite clear that the biography of an artist has no importance whatsoever. If the man can't be recognized in his works, then either the man is worthless, or the works themselves.*'

Lippman almost choked with laughter. With tears in his eyes, he managed to splutter:

'And you . . . you . . . can say that?'

His glasses had slipped down to the end of his nose. He

pushed them back with his forefinger and thundered into battle with all guns blazing – categorical doubt, scrutiny of the facts, internal analysis of the works, and even psychological criticism.

'You're young,' he eventually asserted, 'but in time you'll see.'

'When he wrote that letter, Raven was as old as I am now.'

'Well, there you are.'

After an awkward silence which felt all the more uncomfortable because the restaurant was almost empty, Lippman resumed in a more affable, oddly friendly voice:

'Virginia thinks that being the son of a great writer – supposedly, I would say, but we won't go into that – is a terrible thing in any case. Is that your view?'

Still taking a conciliatory line, and also because it was a coded way to speak to Virginia under Lippman's nose, I explained that there is no necessary connection between the state of filial dependence and the privilege that is commonly assumed. Of course there is prestige, and a certain aura, but that imposes duties too. The irony is that you can find it a millstone round your own neck.

'The main thing is not to forget that the existence of your father and the genius of Raven are lost in a maze of receding questions . . .'

'I've read your book.'

'And?'

'Look, you either have what the Señora told you or else you have nothing, and it makes no difference which. I won't go on, but in spite of your deductions she knows a lot more than she pretends. Why would she confirm your Cartridge theory without a murmur? She's not the kind of woman who lets go of anything, once it's hers.'

'Now there I quite agree with you, my friend! Widows are possessive by definition, but she's a Tartar!'

'Never mind my stepmother's reputation. What bothers me is this posthumous novel, *Tarantulas at Nightfall*, such a bad book . . . Frankly, Professor, what's your opinion?'

'My main line of argument derives from a comparative linguistic study which supports the idea that your father (and there's no question that Raven alias Joven alias who knows how many more really was your father) was not the author but only the translator of the books published under his name.'

I listened. Lippman kept talking.

'The original texts lifted from Cartridge were in English, and I believe that Raven put them into his mother tongue before sending them on to a publisher in Berlin. Hence the clumsy turns of phrase, the faulty usage and awkward syntax that several other critics have also pointed out . . . Cartridge was a self-educated man, and his American vernacular was a double handicap for his translator. In fact – and I don't think you'll deny this – Raven came from a middle-class background. A German anarchist he may have been, but a bourgeois intellectual he certainly was.'

I smiled. The professor must have guessed how much I enjoyed his hesitations, and he tried to retrieve his position.

'I've been trying to locate you for some time, Mateos.'

'You mean the Señora didn't tell you where I was?'

'She hardly mentioned you. And then it was in such vague terms . . .'

'She acts as if I didn't exist.'

Lippman looked depressed. He went through the motions of queasy absorption in masticating his hot oysters. Virginia offered to share her fresh fish, but he waved her away. The danger was past. Lippman would rather have seen me respond to his provocation by coming into the open. His mistake was to have under-estimated my defensive capabilities, because I had a clear advantage on that particular ground. Certainly he was unusually knowledgeable about Raven's life after his landing in Tampico in 1925. On the other hand, like all the others who had tackled the problem, he had found the period before Tampico a blank wall, with a few chinks of light shining through here and there from Twenties Germany. They knew, for example, but not with absolute certainty, that in those days Raven had used the name Ulrich Jasper Bremen (hence the possible initials UJB on the handkerchief kept by Doña Marina). But was that even his true surname? Lippman thought so and I did not contradict him, any more than when he referred to the part played by this man Bremen during the Munich Revolution of 1919.

But I had Charlie! And nobody would be coming to interview him, in his graveyard in Swiss Cottage.

It was clear from the way she was looking at me that Virginia had gauged the importance of the secret she and I had shared for the last few hours, although we had stuck to generalities, for lack of time. She would say nothing. We were accomplices.

The professor was welcome to his monologue, what did Virginia and I care? Over the table, with our glasses of Muscadet raised in honour of our collusion, our eyes spoke a language that Lippman was unable to decipher.

'As I see it,' he said, '*Tarantulas* is a genuine production of Raven's own . . . a text he must have written in Los Angeles around 1942 or 1943, at the Señora's request. She doesn't deny it. In any case, with respect, my dear fellow, one question still remains: whether or not Raven is the true author of the Raven novels, is he really the great writer they say he is? I don't know, I don't know any more . . . In the long run my kind of proceedings only enlarge his reputation. Out of proportion. More than his novels, what matters is the mystery of his life . . . just the reverse of what you said before.'

'You surely weren't expecting us to agree?'

'Besides,' he went on without listening, high on his own words, 'everybody copies everybody.'

That literary cynicism was the inevitable counterpart of the sourness engrained in his character. How could Virginia have. . . ?

'You sicken me, Lippman. It's not just Raven you resent, it's writers and creators in general.'

'Easy now, fellow!'

If it hadn't been for Virginia, I suppose I would have left him sitting there. But now I wanted every detail, down to the last gasp, of what could possibly justify the attachment between two people who made such opposite impressions on me. I was not far off imagining that Virginia had suffered some total blackout of her own personality, as if Lippman were totally responsible for what choices she had made in her life.

Luckily we had reached the end of the meal. The coffee had been served, and Lippman added milk to his, complaining as he did so:

'Since the British have gone over to this espresso garbage you can't find a good demi-tasse any more. Of course in your case, Mateos, the only thing American about you is your passport. You've put a continent between us . . .'

'Throw in an ocean too, and you're nearer the mark.'

'I was joking . . . Why don't you visit us in Oxford before you leave for Mexico?'

'So you know about that too?'

'Paul Arthur Smith,' said Virginia.

'And most of all, don't miss my broadcast tomorrow, you should find it interesting.'

'I only ask one thing, Professor: don't mention me.'

He laughed.

'And why the hell should I do that? There's no hurry, you know. We'll see how it goes. Did you think we'd exhausted the Raven question this evening?'

'. . .'

'And now, if you'll excuse us: it's going to be a heavy day tomorrow.'

He seemed to put some extra stress on that 'heavy' day, and I wondered whether he had guessed my intentions. Then he asked for the bill and I let him settle it, taking advantage of the interruption to ask Virginia:

'Will you be there too?'

'I don't think so. George knows how allergic I am to studios and cameras, ever since my shotgun début with Sylvia.'

'Oh, then you already know the reluctant actress story?' said Lippman, with genuine surprise.

The ambush came from an unexpected quarter. He had thought he could just reach out and swat me with one hairy paw, and here I was, facing the giant with the only weapon that could penetrate his armour – Virginia.

Lippman's astonishment gave way at once to a smothered rage that flickered in his eyes, and then finally to suspicion.

'Rather than get stuck in the hotel, why not have Michael ask you over to his place, Virginia? You could watch the programme together.'

Stung by the dual rivalry that now divided us and which he had only just recognized, Lippman was playing with his own personal demons by adopting the role of the complaisant, liberated husband. Virginia told me next day how much he enjoyed this laying his head in the lion's mouth. 'The more George feels he owns me, the more he knows we're strangers to each other.' To have a rival, and not just a rival but W. H. Raven's own son, became the crowning glory, perhaps even the major success of his whole professional life. There are minds for which intelligence is synonymous with self-destruction. There is no limit to their cerebralism; the engine races on and on around the axis of its own isolation, left in cold storage, crazed and suicidal.

I ought to have given this Lippman a smack in the teeth. No doubt he was right: I must have been too young a puppy, for I did nothing of the kind.

Virginia sat in their Ford Anglia, outside the Trafalgar Inn. In order to have the last word, and to assure himself that he was still in control, before he bent down to sit next to her Lippman said:

'Delighted we've met, Mateos. Really. And this is just a beginning, don't you think? Don't forget that I still have a lot to tell you about your father, if you want to hear. Isn't that a funny situation?'

Looking back, it seems to me that the evening was shorter than my account may suggest. As if all the protagonists had done their best to short-circuit any possible arguments. Unless it was simply that the three of us had approached the meal like athletes going into a warm-up, as a quick preliminary exercise. We had to go through with it, whether we liked it or not. Our course was set, and there would be further encounters. Whatever we might have said or done that evening, nothing could have altered the sequence of the events required by our triangular commitment, even if our motives differed according to our various aims and experience.

The following morning, and early enough to spare my impatience, Virginia called me at the television office. I knew from her tone of voice that a decision had been reached and that the next step would follow. It would be pointless to try to fathom the nature of the quarrel which must have developed overnight. Certainly life had taught me to distrust a natural tendency to prejudge other people in accordance with my own objectives, whose definition and achievement too often were sheerly egocentric; but that day caught me unawares, and I must have surrendered to the autonomy of the process which I might have set in motion but in which Virginia had purposes of her own to pursue.

It all went very fast. The rest of the day was reduced to a mere interval, fixed, laborious, and exacerbated by the certainty of the waiting. I focused on my paperwork, and ruthlessly ignored the clamour of my feelings.

At eight o'clock, as arranged, I collected Virginia from the hotel.

My memories of what followed take the form of something like a cinematic montage, quick and sharp. But contrary to what might be supposed, the images have not subsided into the soft-focus haze which – either because of idleness or else for sheer convenience – is the standard artistic language for visual memories. Each one remains sharp and corrosively immediate. The silence, Virginia's soft mouth and her moist tongue, words . . . the clink of ice in glasses, the whistle of an artillery bombardment and mud-caked GI faces on the screen, the doorbell, a break for the caterer and the smoked salmon . . . Virginia's laughter when I snap the cork and leave half of it stuck inside the bottle of Chablis . . . her legs sheathed in seamless stockings, revealed when she folds them beneath her on the couch . . . I join her there . . . we embrace and kiss. The wanting. We are roused by the theme music and opening titles of 'Enigmas'. We eat fast and ravenously, and empty glass after glass of wine until the bottle is dry. The camera zooms in on the face of George Lippman; it wears a cheerful smile. Our eyes are held by the screen, glued to the image, while my right hand travels up her thigh until it finds the tender warmth of flesh. Virginia sighs, her head lolls back, I kiss her neck, she quivers. We fall upon each other. Lippman talks on: '. . . There are some men whose lives afford a puzzle so great that it obscures the very meaning of their work . . . Who can claim ever to have laid eyes on the living person whose novels are signed with the name of W. H. Raven? Without pre-empting the facts which I shall be presenting tonight, and most of which I cover in my book, I want to begin – in order to put things in perspective, and to eliminate one false trail – I want to begin by saying that the Raven who died in Los Angeles in 1944 was not the true

Raven. That man was only a figurehead, perhaps even a swindler, and in any case merely a forwarding agency who for over twenty years acted as the pipeline between Raven the writer – whoever he was – and his publishers in Germany, England and the United States. What I intend to do tonight is to trace just a few of the strands in this Raven network . . .' Virginia unglues her mouth from mine and says: 'Lippman the magnificent.' 'Easy to be smart at Raven's expense,' I complain. Virginia's mouth invades mine again. We roll to the floor, onto the carpet. Without letting go of Virginia's body, I rest my weight on one elbow, lean over to where the TV set stands on a low table, and turn off the sound. Slowly, and with great concentration, we remove our clothes in the silent white flicker of the screen, somewhere beyond our half-closed eyelids, until suddenly a brighter light is shining on Virginia's face – a voltage surge – a sun-drenched landscape, bleached, somewhere in the Mexican high plateau, light playing over neck and shoulders, summer lightning flaring on the tips of her breasts and picking out the bones and lacy fabric of her brassière. Raising my head as if that were gesture enough to deflect the intruding glare, my eyes are met by a flashlight close-up of my father's face, lying on a trolley in the Hollywood morgue. The caption reads: 'The pseudo-Raven, 16.9.1944.' Now cut to Lippman standing by a map of Central America. Forcing the pace of the amorous ritual whose tempo had carried us together until now, I unilaterally break the balance of touch and desire. Without waiting for both our bodies to be as perfectly naked as we had meant them to be, I hold and part her legs, pull her splayed body towards me and roughly enter her. The thrust elicits a harsh cry.

II

DEPARTURES

1

At precisely a quarter to ten on the morning of 14 September 1944 Waldo Mateos pulled the starter of his limousine. If the downtown traffic was not too heavy he would reach the studios in time. His appointment with the director David Robbins was for ten fifteen, and Waldo preferred to observe his habitual punctuality no matter what the circumstances. His tyres crunched on the gravel drive and he made an effort to choke back the sour taste brought up into his mouth by the jolt of starting. The party had ended very late – he might even recall the first light of dawn, although if you had asked him which drink had finished him off where he sprawled in the arms of a woman he did not know, he could not have answered. As he turned into the street he rejected the possibility of such a question, for his attention had been captured by the blurred image in the rear-view mirror of Ruth, leaning over the balcony, undressed and dishevelled, and aiming unreadable signals towards him. Scarecrow semaphore for a morning in distress. While he had gulped two mugs of coffee in quick succession, Maria-Concha, their Mexican maid, had told him just now that the Señora was going to see her lawyer in the afternoon. In fact just as the extra help were leaving, Ruth had come into the kitchen to ask her maid to call counsellor Bernstein on the stroke of nine o'clock that morning. The Señora's face was ashen, her voice shook with suppressed rage, and the makeup was smeared around her eyes as if she had been crying. It must have been about one o'clock, the maid reported . . . Mateos forced a smile, in spite of a headache already worsened by the prospects of the day, combined right now with the jumble of last night's drunken recollections. Maria-Concha bent her head and made a show of busily sorting out the piles of dirty plates, uneaten food and half-full glasses, in a kitchen ravaged by vandals or a storm.

Yet the party had looked promising at first: Ruth had set her heart on arranging a special celebration for the fifth anniversary of their moving in to Beverly Hills. While he appreciated her thoughtfulness, Waldo had nevertheless pointed out that they were hardly in a position for extravagance. Gone were the days of those luxurious receptions where Mrs Ruth Powell, the widow of the late movie mogul, could spend the Powell dollars without counting the cost. After Oaxaca the new couple had lived another few months in relative luxury, but eventually they had had to face the facts: the account at the Chase Manhattan had practically run dry. Creditors were standing in line, friends were sidling away, and the war effort meant higher taxation. True, they were getting a grip on their affairs, but the pressure was still on, as Mateos had good reason to know with the Internal Revenue always on his back. Very soon he had had to start providing for the Señora's needs. The house was eating up the Raven royalties. Officially, Mateos was just Raven's literary agent, and everybody both in and out of Los Angeles seemed to have swallowed this fable that Waldo Mateos looked after the interests of the famous novelist who was supposed to be living a hermit's life in some forgotten corner of Mexico. And then again, the man in the middle recalled, before the war most of that 'Raven' income had been paid directly into a Swiss account by his German publisher. For nearly four years, there had been no news from that direction.

So Ruth had promised to make it a modest party, and in fact apart from a dozen close friends there had been only a handful of other guests – fifteen or twenty at most – out of the thirty or more that the hostess was expecting. Nothing like the old extravaganzas.

In any case, these were the days when Hollywood was only just recovering from its wartime mobilization, and the big studios had hardly begun to set the dream factory back in motion. There were still plenty of absentees. Chaplin and

Paulette Goddard had been invited but had not replied. Anita Loos had sent flowers with a short note of apology. Gertrude Stein had cabled from New York. Apart from their neighbours the arms merchants, who turned up with their brood of spotty children spoiling for bop and Coca-Cola, the bulk of the other guests were scriptwriters and bit players. The press was certainly represented, but in the shape of some sort of public relations executive from *Variety* magazine.

At first, Mateos had been flattered by the presence of Dashiell Hammett. He came without his friend Lillian Hellman, whom Ruth had known since her late husband's days: Hammett told them that she was in New York, packing her bags for Europe and Russia . . . Ruth and Waldo were twice as delighted to see the temporary soldier, who was back on leave from his barracks in the Aleutian Islands after making the punishing flight to Los Angeles by way of Vancouver, Seattle and San Francisco. The creator of Sam Spade didn't look too bad in his corporal's uniform – dead beat, but not bad. Double scotches on the rocks, then, for the gallant defender of Uncle Sam, who needed no second invitation.

When another of their guests arrived an hour later from his nearby house on Ledoux Boulevard, Dash's spirits seemed to have revived; he stood on the veranda nursing his drink and telling the knot of people around him about the newspaper he edited on Adak Island for the benefit of the forces in the region. The newcomer attracted no attention as he slipped in among the guests in the drawing room. They nibbled their slices of brownie, washed down with Sonoma County champagne, and shimmied to the rhythm of 'Stompin' at the Savoy', played by the guitar of Charlie Christian, the young jazz genius who had died two years before at the age of twenty-six, in a Staten Island sanatorium. Listeners around the record player snapped their fingers and tapped their feet.

The new arrival was William Faulkner, who had greater debts and a more powerful thirst all on his own than Hammett and Mateos put together. They said he was finished, and his New York publishers kept him on a drip-feed of royalties and were reluctant to continue publishing him, yet he had just co-written the script for *To Have and Have Not*, which Howard Hawks had shot with Bogart and Bacall. Waldo had crossed his tracks once or twice and, having read and enormously admired *The Sound and the Fury* and *Sanctuary*, he hoped that some time he would meet a writer who to his mind overshadowed W. H. Raven. So he had invited him just in case, not really expecting him to come.

Mateos watched him for a while as he lounged in an armchair, resting his head on its back, his eyes hidden behind dark glasses. Clouds of smoke from the pipe clenched between his teeth screened him still further. Waldo was about to walk over and say hello, but was stopped short by the arm of John Davenport, an English novelist based in Hollywood whom he had met in Mexico City in 1940, after meeting Ruth. John had been one of the first guests to arrive, bringing with him a writer who lived, so he said, in a fisherman's cabin in British Columbia. Mateos did not recognize this man's name, which was Lowry, Malcolm Lowry. He was an odd-looking man, husky and thickset, more like a boxer or a stevedore, yet he leant on his wife's arm, almost swaying on his feet. Waldo had soon forgotten about him in the evening's uproar. Lowry had found his way to a bar stool in the corner, and there he stayed, unmoving, although his eyes looked far away, as if lost in stormy seas. Waldo noticed that, but he also noticed that he too was starting to get smashed. And that was when the resemblance struck him. Dash, Faulkner and the perpetually seasick sailor shared a curious generic look: the same thin elegant moustache, the same sharp, aquiline, thoroughbred profile, and the same contrast between the radiant energy locked inside them and the painful uncertainties betrayed by their public selves. Buttoned up in uniform, Hammett had style enough, and yet somehow Mateos did not see him very differently from the other two, one of them quite rumpled in his striped double-breasted suit, the other with his threadbare yachting blazer worn over an open-necked shirt.

The man who called himself Raven's agent caught sight of his own face reflected in one of the mirrors decorating the walls, and endlessly duplicated by mirrors in the drawing room and hallway. And he saw how much he differed from the three men he had just been considering: heavy jowls, shadows under the eyes, soft fleshy lips, receding chins fortunately rescued by a trimmed goatee beard. If there was any nobility at all in those features it was unquestionably of the sort which is generally ascribed to the old Europe, the Europe of down-at-heel aristocrats. Mateos smiled sourly as he told himself that maybe one day he would turn out in a monocle. At forty-six he was beginning to have just the type of complacent plumpness that called for such equipment. To compound the irony of his thoughts, Waldo drained the glass of bourbon which Maria-Concha had served him only moments before. Ruth happened to be passing, and her frown was aimed at Waldo. She recognized the signal: her husband was back on the bottle. After Mexico he had dried out in a Los Angeles sanatorium. A year later, a relapse, and since then no further trouble, but they both knew that the demon was not dead, only sleeping. Waldo had been very much on edge for several days, and would flare up over nothing. The heat had been rising. The truth was that the two of them had never hit it off too well: after the early raptures they had started to fall out, and financial troubles, Waldo's moods and Ruth's expensive whims had made the rifts permanent. They were no longer meeting but cohabiting. They made love less and less, and beneath a pall of desperation. In secret, Mateos had begun to write to Marina Chama in Oaxaca. And Ruth, who quickly realized the strength of the Indian woman's hold over her husband, took a lover, a petty gigolo from Santa Monica. There was also that son in Mexico. Raven might have left him behind – for Raven it was – but the boy was always on his mind.

Not that the Señora feared her husband's going back. She knew that he had bolted in spite of his feelings for Doña Marina, to avoid being discovered when a shady journalist from Mexico City had traced him to the Hotel Universal through his Swiss bank account and some intercepted letters. Yet again he had had to run for cover and change both his name and his life, and Ruth had happened along at the right moment. She had never brought herself to accept the conclusion that although Raven might have followed at first in pursuit of a love affair, he had stayed on solely for the sake of preserving secrets which he kept buried so deep inside himself that she could only glimpse them. Waldo – that was the name he used with her – Waldo had only missed a single trick, among all his strategies for survival: what he did not know was that Ruth really did love him. One day during a quarrel she had tried to tell him so, in the midst of the misunderstandings and recriminations. His answer was venomous, and interrupted by hiccups. 'In Oaxaca, once I was over thirty-five, I couldn't stand going through the same damn routine every day, everything so familiar, the hotel getting to be a prison cell, solitary confinement, and the people . . . the people . . . the jailers! Marina was no bitch, nothing of the kind . . . And yet . . . But what would you know about that? Now I'm nearly forty-five. I'm washed up, and I'm living with a Yankee whore!'

For some time now, the insults had yielded to indifference, so it took Ruth aback when her husband grew suddenly worried and irritable again. Several times she caught him muttering to himself about danger, and deadly enemies. At first she believed that Waldo was rehearsing ideas for the film scenario he had been working on, but the symptoms grew worse. There was the delivery man who brought a case of his favourite bourbon. The sleeping pills. The letters she saw him writing more and more often, most of them addressed to Mexico, she felt sure. His nightmares, and the words he spoke: '*Die Ziegelbrenner* . . . Kurt, Ernst . . . Suicide . . . Essen theatre . . . Mosquitoes, lice . . . Palu . . . Rio Muerto . . . Little Sun, Little Sun (yes, twice, distinctly repeated) . . . If you touch her! Bastard!' Ruth would have liked to be able to blame all this on the recent outbreak of mass psychosis still raging in California, whose victims suffered under the delusional threat of an immediate Japanese landing, with an armada of guns and periscopes. This psychosis was coupled with an even more deep-seated obsession whose theme was that the United States, and particularly Hollywood of course, was threatened from within by a whole fifth column of assorted spies, some of them posing as actors or newsreel reporters . . . What struck her even harder was the fact that instead of taking her advice and consulting a doctor, Waldo had hired a detective. A few days earlier, Maria-Concha had told her: 'The shabby man who visits the Señor this morning? I do not know. No, wait, his card says "Duvall", private something . . . The Señor takes him to his study straight away, and tells me to say nothing . . . But if the Señora says that it is for the good of the Señor . . .' And Ruth had reassured the maid, and thanked her for her special contributions to her master's health. The Señora didn't see too much harm in Waldo finding a few cheap memories of another life in the arms of the little Mexican girl. The real enemy was the Indian woman, so the Señora turned a blind eye. She would rather have Waldo squalid over this one than impassioned and romantic about the other. No more flights of feeling. *Finita la commedia!* It's all over. For everybody . . . She would do her utmost, go to almost any length, to hold on to him. The anniversary party was only a symbol, a recall to order.

Just as Ruth was about to introduce one of Dave Robbins' assistants, Waldo had drained his glass, turned on his heel and left her standing there while he went off with Davenport.

John was saying:

'Waldo, you must meet Malc, lord of Cuernavaca and maestro of volcanoes!'

The words alerted Mateos, and he stiffened. The other went on:

'You ought to have things in common.'

The man in the blazer was struggling to control his shaking fingers and take hold of the cigarette his wife was holding out, already lit. That was Waldo's first image of him when he came over to the bar. The drunk caught the eye of his host and muttered:

'Fire, you see. The shaking inside . . . Not long ago – the seventh of June, wasn't it, Margerie? – with my damned stupidity . . . bloody gin . . . I let our shack burn down.' His wife guided the cigarette to his mouth and ran a hand through his hair. He took a greedy drag, and as he exhaled he signalled to the white-jacketed barman to fill his glass. 'With two thousand pages of manuscript inside, you know.'

Mateos thought that his luckless guest was going to cry. John came to the rescue.

'Here's to the real novel, the one you showed me some chapters of, the one that didn't burn.'

'*Under the Volcano* . . . Yes, rejected by thirteen publishers . . . My stars . . .'

'A new version is being read in New York and London.' This was Margerie speaking. 'We should hear something soon.'

Davenport ordered another round for the little group.

'Here's to great writers!'

Waldo made a face as the stinging alcohol caught his throat. John continued to sing the praises of this man Lowry, mentioning his travels, the call of the sea, his stay in Mexico and his trouble with the immigration authorities, and saying that his friend was certain to go down to posterity as a modern Elizabethan. It was difficult for Mateos to imagine that the wreck of a man whose head kept nodding forward as he stood listening to Davenport could have the slightest relation, even of a malicious, incestuous kind, to genius. But in any case if anybody had suggested to him that night that he was entertaining three of the century's literary heavyweights, Mateos would hardly have believed it.

'What are you drinking?' he asked, to change the subject.

'Tequila. Coming from Mexico, I'm sure you know how it improves a man's metaphysical awareness,' Lowry replied.

Davenport burst out laughing. Waldo was embarrassed, but he felt obliged to enquire:

'What are you working on at the moment?'

'A writer . . . is making his confession; he ends it by admitting to a murder, long ago. My character – his name is Wilderness, aren't we living in a savage world? – my hero, if you like, is an absolute liar. All novelists are crooks, more or less. Don't you think so?'

'Maybe . . .'

'Wilderness steals manuscripts that belong to Erikson, his mentor and counterpart. Wheels within wheels – which doesn't excuse him. You know, guilt and so on. The good Samaritan . . .'

And he babbled a disjointed sentence in which Mateos managed to detect the words salvation and redemption. Under his alcoholic façade, the man had some dangerous, compromising things to say. Who was he really? What was he driving at? Mateos scoured his memory, afraid that somewhere their paths had crossed. A bar in Acapulco, a cantina in Parian, who could say? Better be careful. This blend of booze and genius seemed too 'true' to be good. Ah, now it came back to him: Oaxaca, 1938. The Englishman who kept reeling up and down the *calle* Humboldt. His wife had left him – not this one, it must have been a first marriage. Always wound up in the local jail after his benders. Then one day he was gone, and no one had heard of him again. He might have been dead.

Waldo announced that he had to rejoin his wife, who was waiting for him with some other guests.

'See you later.'

But there was no later, because the couple from British Columbia would turn out to have vanished as quietly and mysteriously as they had come. Mateos said to himself that the alcoholic might have recognized him . . . Anyway he would not be there when the signal for retreat was sounded, after the battle, the clash of the titans, the forward fugue, the suffering, insult, crackup . . . As if their brief visit – a quick skirmish – had struck the first chords of a symphony of destruction.

Ruth was part of a group which had gathered around Hammett. Naturally the talk was about the links between cinema and literature. But Waldo was annoyed to hear his own name spoken in the same breath as Raven's. He tried harder than usual not to betray his uneasiness. Ruth was laying it on much too thick:

'. . . till now we've refused all offers from producers. Raven has never been fond of what he calls the Hollywood pimping system, and Waldo has stood by his intentions. An extraordinary man! I haven't had the good luck to meet him, but Waldo tells me he's nothing like you might imagine . . .'

'Times are hard, Ruth. You do what you have to. And it isn't over yet.'

'Oh Dash, come on, how do you turn down a sixty-thousand-dollar contract with Mankiewicz producing and Dave Robbins directing?'

'Your Mr Raven has struck it lucky,' said one of the guests, a veteran cameraman.

'Oh sure,' said Mateos. 'Why, only last year I didn't even ask him before I let Duffy Cigarettes sponsor a radio series based on *The Tale of the Chimera*.' The group could not help noticing the sharp edge behind the even tone.

'That's the one about tobacco plantations in Honduras, isn't it?' asked Hammett.

'Guatemala.'

'Hell of a book.'

'Yes. Seven hundred and fifty dollars an episode. And a

hundred on top, for repeats.' Mateos spoke drily, and plucked a full glass from a passing tray.

Faulkner was sitting in a different chair and smoking a different pipe. He had kept out of the conversation so far. Ruth was annoyed with herself for letting things turn this way, and she was about to start off on another tack when the writer broke in with his unexpectedly sonorous Southern drawl:

'The salt mines!'

Mateos caught his drift. 'How much?'

'Three hundred dollars a week.'

'No, how much writing? How many scripts a year?'

'Now there you have me.'

The cameraman had arrived at the party with a younger woman friend. Now she repaid her hostess by coming unwittingly to the rescue. Obviously left cold by the last exchange, she asked Dash:

'When this war is over, do you think it will still be possible to invent heroes?'

'If you mean to say that people will have lost faith in them, then I agree with you. We're just going to have to exaggerate. I intend to get around the problem by writing about a father and son.'

Mateos was certainly disturbed by Hammett's answer, and in a different time and place he would have enjoyed taking the argument further. But although he was caught in two minds, the man in uniform was the lighter opponent. It was the bigger fish he wanted to tackle, the kind of writer he had dreamt of being.

'The movies have killed the best of us . . . of you! Ask Bill.'

To his surprise, there was something detached and strangely calm about Faulkner's reply.

'Nothing can ruin a writer if he really is a writer.'

'Even when he peddles his hide and his talent to the spiritual slave trade?'

'Waldo, please,' Ruth begged him, 'don't start on that again.'

But the Southerner was unshaken:

'Somebody once suggested that I should keep a bordello, and I have always regretted turning the offer down. A perfect situation, cash, comfort, privacy and pleasure.'

'Sure,' jeered Mateos. 'To each his own economic independence.'

'As long as you have pen, paper, tobacco and scotch . . .'

'No Jack Daniels?'

'Good lord, given an ordinary scotch or an empty glass, I take the scotch. And in any case, a second-rate writer is fooling himself if he pretends that he has no time to write because he has a living to earn. It's a bogus excuse. Only death can destroy the novelist. Death calls the play.'

The more Faulkner talked, the less could Mateos control his growing rage. The man was laughing in his face, taking the words and the bread out of his mouth, deliberately mimicking what Raven himself had tried to say in his own books. He closed his eyes, gave way to the burn of the alcohol inside him, and roared:

'Hogwash! You talk like a drunk's book, Bill, and you're not the first to do it. We've heard it all before.'

'True, true,' said the other. 'If I had never lived, someone else would have written in my place. It's *Hamlet* that matters, not the fellow who wrote it.'

'High-faluting stuff. But preening in the mirror has never been a mark of creativity.'

'Maybe not, but it is a sign of health. The only way we living writers can rate ourselves is to be measured against our own dreams of perfection. The touchstone is the splendour of our failures, the grandeur of our defeats.'

'Who's going to understand any of that today, I ask you, when it's not your own ambitions that judge you, but other people's expectations?' The words hurt Waldo, but he was forcing the argument to a head. He accepted the unreasoningly self-inflicted pain, as if the force of his resentment had finally put paid to the vestige of dignity he had meant to preserve.

'What does it matter? Okay, so the amateurs stew over the critics, but the honest to goodness writers stick to writing.'

'I'll drink to that,' Hammett broke in with a smile. He had come here to relax, not to get squabbling with a bunch of hacks, and be out-talked as well as out-drunk. 'Anyway, why keep making comparisons with other people? You'll grant me this, Bill: you have to do better than your best. Every time. Right, Bill?'

'We go where the devil drives,' Faulkner proclaimed. 'A writer is an amoral creature: he'll steal, borrow, pirate, poach, disguise, make up, dress up and double-cross everything and everybody.'

'The end justifies the means, then?'

'Exactly.'

This was too much for Waldo. Yet another candidate to fleece and provoke and torment him. What if this novelist turned Hollywood ghost-writer had only moved in to Ledoux Boulevard as a better place to spy from? And who was he working for?

He had to hit back, and fast. Not be caught napping. Get it over with, and all fall down.

He still had obscenity in reserve, and if necessary violence – both of them weapons he had been able to use whenever things had looked like going seriously wrong. An impartial observer would have found nothing unusual in the situation that night, except for the presence of a few minor celebrities. Both in spirit and content it was barely distinguishable from any number of social occasions as they happened in the Beverly Hills of the 1940s and as they happen still, give or take the proper variations, among the intellectual circles of the West. Yet for Mateos it was coming to seem unbearably close to the sounding of the huntsman's horn. A premonitory ritual.

He pawed with his free hand at the bare shoulder of the cameraman's girl-friend, and stared down the front of her dress, startling her so much that the jerk as she tore herself loose made Mateos spill most of the contents of his glass over the suit of the man standing next to her. Hey, can't you mind what you're doing? Waldo said nothing, not even to apologize. His hands shook. The last of the whisky churned in his glass. And his eyes still goggled, frantic, into that generous cleavage.

Ruth called his name. He let go of the glass, and it rolled along the floor to shatter against the fireplace with a crack that broke the room's silence like a gunshot, further magnified by the timing of Waldo's original gaffe in the space at the end of the record playing in the background.

'It's another of Waldo's attacks!' the Señora exclaimed, in a bid to defuse the situation.

An attack, damn right, Mateos exulted. Eat shit, it's free!

'Go see if I'm in Santa Monica!' he flared at her, and threw himself, not at his wife, but at Faulkner. 'And you,' he roared, 'you can shove off!'

He took hold of the lapels of Faulkner's jacket, hauled him to his feet and pulled him at arm's length out into the hallway. Bill made not the slightest attempt to resist, and let his hands dangle by his side, with a faint smile on his lips. The crowd parted in front of them. Hammett wanted to intervene, but Ruth stopped him – 'You don't know how far he's liable to go!' And this time she howled in desperation. 'Waldo!' The guests stood still and stared. Conversations were suspended, gestures frozen, jaws left hanging.

But Mateos was already walking back. With Faulkner gone he seemed to have cheered up again. The shakes had stopped, and he strode over to the record player. 'Let's get this party going!' Nobody moved. The Duke Ellington band played the first bars of 'Caravan' and still the eyes were trained on Waldo. He was shuffling to the beat of the music and humming along with it.

When he found himself next to Maria-Concha he wrapped his arms around her and danced her along with him, holding her indecently close and slowing his pace in order to rub more deliberately against her. Then he stopped dead, clamped his right arm around her waist and crushed his lips against hers. The young housemaid attempted to free herself, but could not. He was smothering her. Her head fell back, and she yielded. His left hand reached down to fondle her thighs, her groin and belly, shifting and caressing with the tune. Gradually he backed her up against the wall, the centre of attention, and proceeded to pull up her skirt to the tops of her stockings, all the while grinding his pelvis unambiguously against her.

Ruth reached out for the nearest available partner. 'Come on, let's dance.'

The buzz of conversation rose again. Order was restored and the party sprang to life. If the play was off, then the dancing or the screwing must come next.

The signal had been given. On your marks! Get set for the main event, the fortune race. Same old stakes, and no holds barred. A few guests who probably felt too sensible or too optimistic to admit the necessity of licence said hurried goodbyes. Others hesitated before starting their pallid drift towards the door. As for Hammett, he slipped away as soon as the drinking stopped and the party switched to a sexual free-for-all. He was supposed to report to HQ at eight o'clock next morning.

As he was driving down Sunset Boulevard, Mateos stopped at Schwab's pharmacy to buy some Alka-Seltzer, and took a couple of tablets in a big glass of water. This was the wrong time to crack up, and he couldn't afford to have his hangover interfere in his business with Fox. He was feeling more intensely aware than ever of the imminence of danger, but it would be a shame to be wrong-footed on that account. Certainly *Malasierra* was not one of the best of the Raven novels, and commercial interest in the book would tend to perpetuate the uneasy relationship in people's minds between Raven's exotic backgrounds and his working-class themes. As well as that, Waldo would rather have had Hawks direct, or better still Fritz Lang, than Dave Robbins. But his remaining reservations had collapsed when he heard that Joseph Mankiewicz would not confine himself to producing the film, but intended to handle the adaptation and the script.

When Mateos parked his limousine on the vast parking lot at the entrance to the studios it was exactly sixteen minutes past ten, and he confirmed the time with a glance at his wristwatch. The guard on duty in the security cabin asked him his business, and when Waldo told him that he had an appointment with Robbins, he nodded and dialled a number on his handset. He was still chewing methodically at his gum as he announced the visitor, hung up the receiver, and gave Waldo his directions. 'Studio B, Door E, second floor, left at the end of the corridor, then take the elevator to the fourth, and it's office number 104.'

Strangely enough, there was no great flurry that morning along the pathways criss-crossing this cardboard world. Mateos recalled visiting once or twice with Ruth – as seldom as possible, because there was no point in attracting attention – and being impressed by the unbelievable hustle and bustle that prevailed there. Yet at that time they had only been shooting a few war series of the *Why We Are Fighting* kind. 'You should have seen it in the old days,' Ruth sighed.

There is nothing more sinister than a studio where a film has only just finished shooting, except for the still more sinister atmosphere of the shooting left unfinished. That is what Mateos might have told himself as he followed a dimly lit passageway through structures of half-dismantled scaffolding, flats piled one on top of another, redundant painted backdrops leaning against grey concrete walls; but in fact his mind was elsewhere – on the footsteps he had just noticed shuffling somewhere behind him. Had he been followed? He quickened his pace, anxiously darting his eye into the surrounding gloom, which was broken all at once by a gleam of light – a bare electric light bulb swinging at the end of a long flex that dangled from a high metal ceiling. It startled him. Then a face emerged from the darkness, the portrait of a very beautiful woman, incongruous in the desolation of the setting. Mateos was not to know that this was the famous picture which hung on the wall of Laura's apartment, in the film by Otto Preminger. Though just for a second he seemed to recognize the features of Gene Tierney . . . perhaps because she was the star, he wanted Mankiewicz and Robbins to cast as the leading woman in *Malasierra*, as the Mexican adventuress who betrays the hero before she redeems herself by the sacrifice of her life.

The slamming of a door raised echoes in his memory, and Mateos asked himself some questions. He was starting almost to regret having given way to Robbins's arguments and the Señora's pressure. It was as if the intrusion of the cinema into Raven's work and his own entrance into a world he had deliberately avoided, engrossed in his roles as literary agent and husband of the widow Powell, signified a point of no return in his life.

He plunged into the corridor that led to the elevator, or so he hoped, since he might have lost his way in the press of his thoughts. After a life spent wandering off the beaten track, shunted from exile to exile, this was no time to miss the exit! New and broader horizons. Free at last no longer to think of anything, not even of the past, the chain of events which had brought him to the heart of this factory for producing truer goods than nature, had delivered him to the empire of appearance where the Ten Commandments themselves were only another fable. 'Thou-shalt-not-steal,' went the hammer in his head. 'Thou-shalt-not-kill.'

He hesitated before he pressed the red call button for the elevator. What if the danger was not behind him but in front, up above or below? He was tensing to spin round when the shots rang out. Three in succession, then one more, detached. Pause.

Mateos fell forward against the metal grille, and it jangled – funeral bells. He slid to the ground, trying to turn his head for a sight of his attacker or attackers, but the movement was never completed. In the fraction of a second before he died, his reeling mind framed the question which had long obsessed him – 'Will they come from Germany, from Mexico, or will it be from here?' – as if that instant of utter solitude contained its own incidental version of the eternal question, 'Where do I come from? Who am I? Where am I going?' Had he known, before extinction, what hatred and revenge had brought him down, then perhaps he need not have feared to go too far wrong in making sense of his own fate. But that atom of felicity was denied in his last gasp to Waldo Mateos, alias W. H. Raven. The missing link.

Not that it prevented Señora Ruth from staging one final sensation in its place. It was a masterly publicity stunt. On the morning after her husband's death she summoned the press to her mansion in Beverly Hills and revealed that the identity of Waldo Mateos had in fact been a cover for the great writer W. H. Raven. She gladly replied to all the questions asked both by journalists and by the police, and produced proof – in particular the original manuscripts of some of Raven's novels, and an old Mexican passport – that there was no mysterious figure living somewhere in Mexico. Case closed. But not altogether, because the widow managed to grab a lot more column-inches and newsreel footage with the tremendous funeral she organized. Raven's ashes were conveyed to Mexico City, where the governor paid them his solemn homage. Then the Señora boarded a Cessna provided by the authorities and flew down to scatter the remains of the famous novelist over the region of Chiapas, while in the villages below, Indian flutes and drums accompanied the drone and occasional backfire of the little plane's engine.

All over the world, they began to rediscover a 'major but still little-known writer'.

Malasierra was one of the greatest Hollywood smashes of the postwar era.

So Raven entered the second phase of his legend. But the apparent resolution of the enigma exploded the mystery and ushered in the reign of the annotators and biographers.

2

I DO NOT recall who it was who said that a story is the autobiography of an imagination, but there are times when you have to discard your forefathers, let sleeping ancestors lie. That is also essential for anybody who intends to start writing, and in particular for those who intend to finish what they started.

The death of Alfonso de Seguida, and my father's death too, are speculations of my own, which have fed my imagination right from the start of this whole story, and certainly since the moment of first meeting Virginia Lippman . . . Even though in those days it was beyond my capability – meaning that I had neither the means nor the will – to bring them to life. It will have taken this Polish winter of my quest's conclusion to bring out the urgency of the task. And the relative ease of performing it, for when I did begin to write it was with a pleasure never within my reach till now.

For years, it was forbidden territory – taboo. And it would be difficult to pin down the exact moment when the wish to create took over from timid flirtations with fictional devices. Perhaps it was a few months ago at Puerto Lapiz . . . However that may be, today I am possessed by the feeling that writing offers the means – the most pretentious means, no doubt, but also the least illusory – of mesmerizing death. Trying to arrest the dance of time for a moment, and to compass the curves of infinite space in a clumsy and probably luckless grasp, does not signify that the writer thereby passively accepts the idea of sacralizing the impulse that causes him to write. The poison contains its own best antidote. How many times did Uncle Charlie remind me of the deep humility of the man who put his genius into the service of the poor and the oppressed? 'For Raven, a worker was the whole story,' he loved to declare. 'Why should we bow down to some figurehead of a supreme authority – king, general, or artist blessed by the gods? Sure, he'd become a novelist, but your father knew that didn't entitle him to anything extra, didn't raise him above the battle.' And O'Sullivan believed that this was the reason for Raven's retreat into absolute anonymity: he would not lay claim to any special importance. What mattered were the men and the ideals which found expression in his writing. So I spent the whole of my childhood and adolescence convinced that my father was not merely a novelist but a hero in his own right. It was a terrific theory, and corroborated by Charlie's tales about their escapades in the London docks, fantastic nights when in order to escape from the bobbies' whistles they would vanish into a London particular, the creeping Thames fog . . .

Later on, in Los Angeles, some reluctant admissions by the Señora put a new gloss on Charlie's words. According to her, Raven's long quest for asylum obeyed more cryptic rules and more secret influences. Without labouring the point, but persuasively enough to support Lippman's insinuations, Ruth steered me towards the theory of a guilty conscience. What did he have to hide behind all those disguises and that devious game of switched identities? The thought of throwing light on this question presupposed that I myself was beginning to doubt the certitudes by which I had been living until then. As long as the clarification was not my own, the perspective stayed blurred. That is quite obvious now, but in the days of my first departure for Los Angeles and Mexico I still needed time to see things clearly.

Till then I had not properly come to grips with a dilemma mostly of my own creation. On the one hand, Raven's character almost completely eluded me because I indulged myself in uncritical admiration of its various facets. God knows how numerous they were, and how blindingly they sparkled in the light of past memories. On the other hand everything in and around me would have fallen apart if Raven had turned out not to be the man I believed in. Taken overall, the mystery deepened. So I waited, although I could not have said exactly what I was waiting for. But it is undoubtedly this breach in my defences that partly explains how and why I came to throw myself at Virginia Lippman with a mindless greed that overrode every possible objection. For pleasure's sake.

Yes, it took me some time to learn how to confect the deaths of heroes, even if only in a novel. And at the moment when we decided, Virginia and I, that we were going to meet in London every week, behind Lippman's back, I still felt incapable of spelling out their connections with the past, in the pattern of a story which first had to be traced to its beginning. With hindsight, it seems to me that the order of events runs from the coalescence of my own desires to the establishment of the actual facts, and it is this curious combination that frames the picture. Now I have resumed the work on these notebooks which was brutally interrupted by my stay in Puerto Lapiz.

So I was in Paris to see my son Pablo, after an absence of several years.

I knew that Beatrice would raise no objections. The boy was thirteen now, and old enough to understand, she told me when I called her on the telephone. She didn't even bother to ask what I was doing, or what had become of me, as if my long disappearance had been perfectly natural. He's in his third year at Montaigne, she told me, and a good student. A gifted violinist too, you've no idea. He looks like you.

Pablo's greeting was affectionate but not effusive. 'Father.' I could tell that he hardly recognized me – I had grown a beard, and lost weight – and I felt that he was growing up a little too quickly, like so many of his generation. But he made the best of things, and came out for a walk, and a trip to the cinema, and a drugstore icecream, without giving much away about what he must have been feeling. His air of indifference was bound to be resentment – along comes this stranger, after dropping out of sight without a word for seven years, and starts playing the fond father. It was asking too much of the child, or so I told myself at the time, perhaps to excuse my own attitude and because I knew that it was just a temporary reunion. Anyway, when I told him that I was leaving next day for Poland, all he could say was 'Oh really, Poland!' I wonder now if it wasn't sheer lack of curiosity on Pablo's part. It would be futile to dwell on my personal feelings about that. It brought home to me the passion and the follies which had eaten up my life, and the terrible sacrifices I had imposed on my own family.

That is a galling impression, and I must not surrender to it altogether, or else I shall once more lose the thread that it has taken me so long to spin. It is too soon to take care of the ghosts of the present, when the ghosts of the past are wriggling between my fingers, ready to slip away at the slightest sign of hesitation. The main thing is not to rush. There is no hurry now that the countdown has begun. Because I have chased time in all directions, in the end it has caught and betrayed me. Today I have reached the end of the story. A few days from now, once I have sorted out the intervening chapters of my life, I can make the trip to Schwiebus, where the naked truth is waiting at last, the truth about Raven and therefore about myself. Patience!

All the same, it is hard to slow down, hard not to skip events like hurdles passed, once books and documents have been consulted, noted, digested, forgotten, lost or destroyed. Down the years I have had access to more than enough references to fill two or three lifetimes. All of them – including those of living memory – were left behind in Mexico and Guatemala. Peace to their ashes! Here in the country where my deep roots lie, the missing ones, I sense that momentous events are on the move. The paradox is that after my constant hoarding, I should wind up dispossessed, stripped bare of everything but the knowledge of the facts, conclusively established. These lines are written on Polish writing paper which needs no skill with archives. I am attracted and fascinated by these blank white pages: it doesn't matter if my blindness flutters like a moth against their brightness or if, like Icarus, I should melt away my wings, my freedom and purity once regained. Fortunately for me, Lippman and his kind went out of my life long ago.

First, you remember, came Virginia, that stillborn passion . . .

Henry James said that for an American – if you could call me an American – Oxford typified the union of science and sense. 'A German university gives a greater impression of science,' he continued, 'and an English country-house or an Italian villa a greater impression of idle enjoyment; but in these cases, on one side, knowledge is too rugged, and on the other, satisfaction is too trivial. Oxford lends sweetness to labour and dignity to leisure.'

In my own student days this definition still held good, obeying the changeless but freely accepted laws of a ritual as calm and slow as the current that carried our punts between the Cherwell's reeds and water lilies. We were outside the century, necessarily. Belonging to the experimental theatre group, terrorizing the university poetry circle, haunting pubs and brothels, even joining the ranks of the revolutionary socialists – all this gave us the probably false impression of riding the tide of events. We skimmed above the age, ready for any journey and every folly. The postwar disenchantments had been succeeded by the victory of the Cuban revolution, and without giving too much thought to the fundamental differences between my organization and the fond beliefs of Charlie O'Sullivan I bounced from meeting to meeting and sat up all night concocting motions, pamphlets and polemics. *Ay! Compañeros!* All this exertion no doubt enabled me not to ask myself too many questions about Raven: I felt that it would have pleased my father to see his son joining the ranks of the Cause. Sometimes, when I was working alone in my room, or had drunk a bit too much, I used to wonder whether Charlie might not have exaggerated or even fantasized his stories, projecting his old desires onto remembrance and reality. Charlie did a lot of that. Broad, gestures, grand admonitions, lamenting for the downtrodden, the widows and orphans (he might have picked his own words more carefully!), he would hammer on the table fit to break it, his eyes rolling hugely in their sockets . . . Charlie the Menace! Hurricane Charlie! Yet now and then the story did not take, and left me caught in a blank listlessness that surprised my good friend. And as time went by, the more I thought about it, the more my doubts intruded. However hard I fought them, trying to reject even the ghost of a suspicion, still they would spring up again, the hydra's jeering heads. By the time I was twenty the questions had made themselves heard; or – to put it more clearly – I had realized that between that anarchist in London and the Raven of Los Angeles as revealed by the books, the press and the Señora's letters, the contradictions were insoluble. The worm was in the bud: work and pleasure – a wildly romantic cocktail of ambition and hedonism, I have to admit – gave me the means to ignore it . . . But my Oxford refuge also meant the pleasant whirl of youthful love affairs, three or four of them. The most serious happened in my third year and ended when the term did, in a furtive abortion. Nancy – that was her name – belonged to the same political group as myself, although (in fact because) she was the daughter of a Harley Street specialist. It was probably not her looks, which were plain, but rather what struck me as this outlandish blend of elements in her character that impelled me into an insidious seduction campaign whose weapons were the poems of Blake in one hand and the collected works of Marx and Lenin in the other, followed by the twenty-fourth edition of Dr Eustace Chesser's manual, *Love Without Fear*, and by Dr Ogino Kyusaku's method of natural birth control . . .

At any rate that was the memory of Oxford whose spell was broken by the presence in the city of George and Virginia Lippman.

'We can't possibly see each other there,' I told Virginia after a fumbled meeting in a bed and breakfast place in the industrial belt. Yes, even if I tended to prefer the libraries and smoky bar rooms of my Magdalen days, there are also factories around Oxford!

'Would you rather I come to your place?'

'Take my spare key to Old Brompton Road.'

'Then we can only make Thursdays.'

'That's the way it is. With Lippman round the corner, Oxford is hell. I can't take it.'

Yet I did make two visits there, to meet Paul Arthur Smith about our plans for the journey. Paul had tutorials to give, and couldn't come to London so often. When he phoned to ask if I could go to him, how could I refuse? He knew I could manage a quick day's visit. Anyway, it was my job. Obviously there was just one thing I was afraid of, and that was running into George and Virginia – on their own ground, you might say. So I asked Paul if we could meet at his house and not on university premises, and urged the greatest possible discretion. We hadn't been friends for long, and since I was unable to tell him the real reason for all this covert action I cooked up a feeble story about our expedition to Mexico being some sort of scoop. He made no comment about my guerrilla warfare precautions and gave me the benefit of his habitual British sense of humour. From there it was only a single step to imagining that Lippman had been telling tales about my background all over Oxford, and I took that step like a charging bull.

In particular I was goaded into intensifying those weekly encounters with Virginia, and I would spend the entire week waiting for Thursday to come round again. She used to arrive at my flat at about four o'clock in the afternoon. I never even asked her if she'd been seeing her analyst. It was a matter of routine, and we had decided never to mention it. To tell the truth, I didn't give a damn. Anything she might have said about Sylvia Morrison or Lippman no longer mattered once I had my arms around her. I must have figured in her therapeutic confessions, or so I supposed, but I hardly bothered about what she might say and think in the ebb and flow of considering our liaison. What counted was the charge in her gestures. Her hand on my thigh, her hair brushing over my neck or my stomach, her tongue and lips around my cock. The first impact left no room for talking. We were too busy with our bodies. Later on, when I opened the curtains to let the rays of the setting sun slant in through the studio skykight, and while she smoked a last Pall Mall, put her clothes back on and got ready to leave, there wasn't much time left for talking about what we both felt.

Perhaps I was too afraid that whether she knew it or not, under the pretence of caring about the film-maker and journalist Virginia might really have Raven's son on her mind. And on her side she must have been constantly persuading herself that the growing passion I displayed from one week to the next was not just the measure of my hatred for her husband.

Imagine how easily that Thursday of hope and longing, rehearsed and inflamed by days of suspended fantasy, could be transformed into an ordeal almost to be feared. In any case the whole became a part, the absolute became a pivot of uncertainty and vacillation.

'Are you bored with Oxford?' I would say, as a sign of good will.

'Yes. George never lets up for a moment, he never stops

talking about you and your father. I don't even manage to work any more.'

She was throwing me a lifeline, not knowing which of us was going to save the other from drowning. All the same I took care not to catch it, and would steer the conversation to more frivolous subjects, till it was time for her to hurry to the station for the nine o'clock train.

At the beginning I had imagined Virginia as an eternity. But no matter how sublime our moment's satisfaction, the violence of our desires tore open that perfection. As if the climax of appetite was producing its own antidote . . . I felt as if I was only living for those hours of pleasure, so that I even lost sight of the urgency and importance of my departure for Mexico. Yet quite soon, not more than a month after the night of Lippman's television appearance, I became certain that it was the other way round – that the erotic energy of those weekly reunions took its high voltage from the prospect of the journey itself.

It was an untenable situation, and obviously it could not last. We both did our utmost to prove that fact, unknown to ourselves of course, and yet aware.

I delighted in the way she made love, brusque and lascivious at once. She gave and yet refused herself. She loved to be taken on the instant, without preliminaries. 'Let's do it, quick,' she would gasp. I tried out different strategies, but always she reverted to that. Yet the rending harshness of her cry of rage signalled an invincible frustration. It was as if a sense of want, a cliff-hanging suspension, was the condition of her happiness, the better to lure her into the act again, and always again . . .

'Did you come?' I continually asked her.

She did not answer, lying with her thighs still spread, waiting till I could enter her again.

On those first occasions both of us felt convinced that we were locked in a sexual involvement more intense than anything either of us had experienced before. For me, that was a fact, and I had no a priori reason to doubt Virginia's word when she told me that she felt much more with me than with Lippman.

We had reached this stage in our story when Lippman

counter-attacked with a virulence and shrewd timing which neither Virginia nor I was ready to oppose. And maybe I was less ready than she was.

Lippman knew. I was sure of that, although she kept denying it. Besides, it somehow suited me that he should know – it was more convenient, more proper too, and God knows what a relatively proper young man I was in those days in my insistence on keeping up a front of solid principle. The connection with Raven had a lot to do with that, so much so that my reasons for seeing myself as an outright rebel rebounded on themselves.

In order to keep Lippman thoroughly aware of my liaison with his wife I took special and shameful care to leave my mark on Virginia's body, by sucking the base of her neck, nipping at the small of her back, smacks and attempts at flagellation with a belt, though this she rejected and called me a 'freak'. In fact it amounted to marking out a territory, not like a dog when it pisses but like a child at play, drawing an imaginary boundary just by making a line in the dust. Heaven on this side, Hell on that . . .

George Lippman's retaliation came in the form of a devastating anonymous article published in the *Times Literary Supplement* of 30 May 1965 under the title: 'W. H. Raven: Death of a Myth', and taking up three quarters of a page. I took the absence of a signature as an intolerably ironic gesture, combining provocation with deceit, although actually it was standard practice with the paper in those days. It could not be intentional, yet I saw it as clear proof of its author's determination to wound. In my flustered state of mind the lack of a signature guaranteed the article's authorship. In any case, who else could possibly have written it?

The article came out on a Friday. I brooded over it all through the weekend, but I couldn't wait until the following Thursday to cross-examine Virginia and make sure. As soon as I sat down in my office on Monday morning I dialled the Lippmans' number in Oxford, in defiance of the risks.

It was Lippman who answered.

'Oh, is that you, Mateos?'

'Yes.'

'Glad to hear from you after all this time. What can I do for you?'

'I wanted to speak to Virginia.'

'Again? This is getting to be obsessive, old boy. She's out at the library. Maybe you didn't know, but she's really going hard at her research work. Mine too, if it comes to that.'

'Why did you do it, Lippman?'

'We-ell, you wouldn't come to me, so I just had to come to you. Get things moving a little, right?'

'But why do it that way?'

'Do I ask you how to screw my wife?'

'. . .'

'You hear me, Mateos?'

'I knew the world was full of bastards, Lippman, but I've never met a creep like you before.'

'Watch out, you're getting carried away just like Raven – at his worst.'

'Shove it!'

'Ooh!'

'You have a death smell on you. It's the only thing that turns you on – death and the dead . . . Odd how that's all you need for thrills. You're stuffed with death! Raven only impresses you dead. You've never given a damn for his life or his work.'

And I hung up, without knowing that Lippman at the other end was bawling: 'Hey, hold on, you damn fool. Virginia's here, she wants to talk to you . . .'

Waiting for Thursday gave me three days of drunken misery. Alcoholic drunk, but also drunk on the rotten atmosphere of the situation, or so it seemed to me. I want to say that underneath I was not too unhappy about the turn of events, as if they confirmed my own natural tendency to push things to a crisis. Without knowing it I was launched on a process of fulfilling my secret desires: settling a troublesome affair, upping the tempo . . .

On the first evening I left the office at four and roamed the streets of South Kensington chewing over the text of Lippman's article and its implications for my relationship with Virginia. At opening time I went into a pub I didn't know. No doubt I was avoiding meeting anybody – I didn't want to see or talk to people, just to drink . . . one beer and one whisky after another, to get drunker faster. And when I reached my limit, some hours later, then I would go home with a bottle of Bell's just started, and sink right to the bottom of an empty night. In between glasses in flashes of sharpened lucidity, perched on a bar-stool or slumped on a wall seat upholstered in grey velvet, I had re-read and re-dissected that murderous text. The crumpled paper was soiled and creased; it had lived in the pocket of my jacket since it first appeared.

On the second evening, instead of going straight home I picked up a Soho prostitute who drove me in her car to a seamy hotel in Bayswater, and I spent the night there.

On the other hand on the Wednesday I worked late. Ron had turned up with two men and a woman from the film crew. We worked hard, and I put so much effort into the planning that Ron must have suspected something. He suggested that we all go for an Indian meal at the Ganges, a favourite restaurant of his. We had a good time, and without realizing it I began to forget my hangovers and my weaknesses. When I got home I watched *Citizen Kane*, the late-night movie on BBC 2, for at least the fifth time. Rosebud . . . Before going to bed I cut out the article in the *TLS* and filed it away in the cardboard folder where I kept all the important Raven documents. I fell asleep over a page of *The Plumed Serpent*: Lawrence's loaded prose and totemic musings on the love between a man and a woman were as good as the strongest sleeping pill in my state of mind that night. In any case they were nothing like the reading I needed in order to apprehend Mexico.

Virginia did not come. The morning post brought a brief letter explaining that she had caught a cold and couldn't leave Oxford. 'Love' – and she signed herself 'V'. In my vexation, but in no great rage, because I had been ready for something of the kind, I tore letter and envelope to pieces. The scraps of paper I let flutter down into the first litter bin I passed along the pavement.

In the hours and days that followed, it never occurred to me to question the suspicious ease with which I wiped the incident out of my mind. A loophole had opened up, and I jumped at it with the speed that only narcissism gives. Didn't I have every reason to doubt Virginia and condemn her silence? It was she who had let me down, who was distancing herself. In the narrowness of my view, her responsibility soon extended to the Raven question too. I blamed her for her husband's ramblings. What if she was in collusion?

Virginia telephoned my office at the end of the week, and I had my secretary tell her I was out. So as not to be caught at home, I asked Ron if he and his wife would mind my spending the weekend with them in their house in the suburbs, so that we could get some work done. The departure date had been brought forward at my own request, and was set for three weeks' time. On the pretext of having some technical arrangements to take care of, I planned to leave London a few days in advance of the others and stop off in Los Angeles before flying straight to Mexico City to join the rest of the crew. I had settled all these details in a discussion with Alec Simpson's successor.

When I came back from Epping Forest around midnight on the Sunday, I had no idea that I would find Virginia waiting there, sitting on the stairs outside my flat. Her eyes were shining, but when she stood up I saw with a touch of disappointment or even apprehension that it was not tears but desire that glistened there. She wound her arms around my neck, dug her fingers into my hair and drew my mouth down onto hers. I let it happen.

It was the first and only night we spent together, and our coupling was only an imitation of passion. No matter how great the quantum of feeling or pleasure on either side, it seemed that for both of us the programmatic aspect of our encounters ruled out the achievement of any real understanding. We did and said everything to one another. The order and intensity of things does not matter. The outcome remains.

For example she said: 'I'm going to leave Lippman.' I ejaculated inside her before she could take hold of herself again.

Later, as she was about to light her fifth or sixth cigarette, I ordered her not to.

She spoke. 'I love Lippman, and I also love you. That's what you both hold against me. You don't understand a thing. One of you tries to send me back to high school, the other treats me like some character out of fiction, competing in his personal mythology, and both of you are glad to fob me off with my analyst.'

'I thought Lippman disapproved.'

'For himself he may, but in my case it suits him fine.'

'I've never asked you anything about that.'

'Exactly. And that proves I mean nothing to you. Or not enough.'

She turned over towards the bedside table, and this time lit her Pall Mall, without a word from me. I went to the bathroom to piss, and called through the open door: 'You'll be going back with him. Anyway I'll be in Los Angeles next month, and we'll meet then.' She made no answer. No doubt she knew a phoney promise when she heard one. When I was lying next to her again she stubbed out her cigarette in the ashtray, then nestled into the hollow of my shoulder. Her left hand reached downwards for my cock and stroked it erect once more, and all at once she was kneeling over me and planted astride me. This time I saw how her eyes were swollen with real tears, and when the first of them brimmed over onto her right cheek I wiped it away with the back of my hand. Then I took her by the shoulders and drew her too fast into a jolting rhythm.

So we made love, and made love again, until there was hardly anything left to say, as if all our words had been drained into less and less violent, more and more weary and apathetic movements.

At eight o'clock in the morning I got up without a sound so as not to wake her. I left a note on the bed: 'See you at Dino's, one o'clock.' An Italian restaurant. Did I really want her to show up? Maybe. Unless it was all part of my scramble for an exit to the future . . . In any case, still in order to postpone the confrontation, I crept out to have breakfast at the Lyon's by the underground station. I wanted to be on time for my meeting at the television centre.

When Virginia sat down next to me on the apple-green plastic-covered seat, it was after half past one. I had drunk two Martinis, consulted the menu, decided that she wasn't coming, and ordered lasagne which would soon be ready from the oven. She had had her hair dyed brown, wore different clothes from the day before, and hid the previous night's ravages beneath big dark glasses and thick make-up – a bit too thick for my taste, I thought, not having recovered from the first shock of her appearance.

'I went to the hairdresser's, and I had some shopping to do

around here. Sorry. How are you?' She spoke in a rush, slightly out of breath.

I watched her closely. It appeared to me as if the natural high spirits which usually gave her so much of her charm had been turned into a façade of affected simplicity. Suddenly she seemed less beautiful than I had previously imagined her. My own bad faith may have accentuated the plumpness of her cheeks and the lowness of her forehead, but obviously I hadn't noticed them before.

'I'm sorry,' she said again, as the waiter brought my food. 'You were right not to wait for me. Anyway I wasn't all that hungry. Bring me one of your "Four Seasons" pizzas please. And a big glass of water.'

'And a half-bottle of Valpolicella for me.'

The waiter went off. Virginia talked on about her shopping expedition. I wasn't really listening: the lasagne was too hot, and I had burnt my tongue.

She had bought herself a sleeveless T-shirt printed with the face of Che Guevara, the Cuban revolutionary leader who had just disappeared, mysteriously leaving his post as minister of the interior to join the guerrillas of the Third World and so give birth to a myth which was to catch the imagination of many young people in the West. I was myself an admirer of Che. It struck me as offensive to turn him into just another consumer product, especially when it was Virginia who took part in the exploitation, and I told her so.

'It's for California,' she said. 'Sunshine again. You've seen how white my arms are. Pretty soon I'll be tanned – all over. You wait and see.'

I won't see anything, I thought. As much as Virginia had dazzled me on the day of our first rendezvous in Camden Town, so she now exasperated me in the role of Little Miss Average American. Now she was talking about her gypsy skirt, her espadrilles, her new bracelets . . .

'It's June twenty-first you know, Michael. It's summer.'

Yes, she was right. It was summer, the weather was fine and she was beautiful. It all seemed simple, and I might have been persuaded to think so, but I was not. There was one thing about her that stuck in my throat and floored me completely, and that was the awful triteness of her character. Ordinary, and therefore vulgar, she was, and I despised myself for having been so naïve. Trinkets and beads for the busy tourist. It took a hell of a lot more than that to go to my head, something genuinely exotic. So let's get moving! The adventure was only just beginning. Forget about imitations.

I was approaching my twenty-fifth birthday, with the feeling of having lived a quarter of a century ('do you realize, Virginia?') for nothing, or next to nothing. Hardly even a footnote. Nothing much had happened yet. Only the future waited, limitless.

Not only were we caught up in a dialogue of the deaf, but Virginia was thoughtless or else determined enough to carry the whole thing through with disarming nonchalance. I was torn between an urge to smack her in the face and relief that she was giving up so easily. Perhaps I would rather have had her suffer more conspicuously: then I could have cast myself in a better role – tenor in the big leave-taking aria.

She did not give me that final pleasure. I pretended that I didn't have time to see her to the station. We kissed one another on the cheek, standing there in the restaurant, and she scribbled an address on a paper napkin. I stuck it in my jacket pocket and walked to the door to hail a taxi, without a backward glance at Virginia.

The surprise I had coming late that afternoon when I returned to Old Brompton Road was considerably more painful than all these secondary symptoms of a low-key ending. On the still unmade bed – she hadn't even opened the curtains or aired the room, and it stank of stale tobacco and dry sperm – on top of crumpled sheets woven into a kind of funeral garland, lay the article by Lippman which I had cut out and filed a few days earlier, and scattered all around it, strewn across the mattress and the floor, lay all the documents and papers collected in the file. She had ransacked the room and tipped out the contents of drawers. Looking for what? Well obviously for what she had found, and read, and – who knows – possibly memorized for Lippman's benefit. I imagined the worst. And my foreboding was confirmed by a discovery that was even more dismaying: next to the *TLS* article Virginia had found a prominent position for the sheet of paper torn from my notebook where I had left my message that morning. Underneath my invitation she had written, in her tiny, almost illegible writing:

> As Lippman says, sciatica may not be such a drag as teenage acne. Take care of your spots, then maybe . . . No, it's not me you need most now. Run, don't turn back: I failed to become your Eurydice, you won't lose on the deal. Lippman is right: I'm just a wrong turning in your maze, a cul-de-sac at best. We knew it from the start, he and I. But unlike you, Lippman knew what makes me tick, and that's why I married him, because he saved me from suffocation. Right from the start you were just a new buzz for him, a temporary thing. I know you always thought the opposite – he was an albatross around your neck, you couldn't stand it. That's going to turn out to be your main mistake. Strength and certainty, even with your burning cock and juice, you couldn't give me that. Anyway how could you, with nothing to offer but sap and a young body? Believe me, Michael, for the sake of what we had together: as long as you reject Lippman's case for the inconsistency of Raven, the implausibility, you'll never do much better. If ever I have a child, I want it to be Lippman's, the old man's. Good luck. Virginia.

I realized at that moment what a defeat I had suffered, and how serious and irreparable it was . . . as if my egoism had rebounded against me, as if I had fastened my own chains, then howled when I pulled against them. But these were solid shackles. No matter how I screamed and struggled the fact was clear and sharp. At first I responded like a madman, furiously determined to deny what I was reading; then as the two texts branded themselves on my memory I gradually became calmer and more clear-headed. Successively, alternately, mixed in endless permutations, I read and re-read the article by Lippman and that last message from Virginia. Concertinaed images, stray lines, unexpected visual flashes, associations crisscrossing in a network almost too dense to penetrate, a virgin forest of signs shooting up through the slightest gaps of thought while the rustle of crumpled paper distorted the acuteness of jangled senses, shadows looming over a horizon of light, black on white, blood on night, with a quiver of stardust in between the lines, and the outstretched body lascivious in its silence, pumping heart, stiff legs, trembling, clumsy hands, my whole body a shower of curses, waiting for pleasure to be granted or withheld, but either way waiting, desire or its frustration . . . I would have liked to eat those sheets of paper, chew over their bitter black juice, swallow them down with all my strength and still be biting on them in my stomach, digesting them for the nourishing contents which were my urgent need.

That night I burned the papers, all their joys and pains together – watched their reflection in the mirror above the wash basin, writhing in the flames' embrace – and once I had done that I might have understood (as I do now) that I was being shown the elementary secrets of literature. Yet the mere fact of letting the flames consume material which till then I had thought vital to my existence, both as a stronghold and as the basis of a destiny still to be constructed, ought to have enlightened me. I was ready at last. No matter what happened, Raven would be given to me – one way or another. But after all, perhaps I was lucky not to be too confident too soon. The destruction of those concrete proofs of my 'proto-life' was ultimately part of the pattern: it fitted the character and image of the man whom I was left to discover, not by proxy, but in the flesh, on his own ground.

The version of Raven's death advanced by Lippman in his article had nothing in common – in its form, I mean – with the death of the man called Waldo Mateos in Los Angeles in 1944, which for reasons which this narrative will make clear now seems to me to be the only version worthy of belief.

In particular, Lippman wrote:

> The publication of *Tarantulas at Nightfall* marked the downfall of a myth. Critics were unanimous in their judgement that this posthumous novel owed very little either to the pen or to the imagination of Raven, and I myself have shown that this clumsy parody could not possibly have been written by the author of *The Cyclone's Eye*. So it is fair to ask whether the man whose ashes were scattered in a blaze of publicity over southern Chiapas is to be identified with the famous writer known as W. H. Raven. In the light of modern scholarship there are strong indications of a possible solution to the Raven mystery. The man with twenty-seven pseudonyms has lost a great deal of his cover story: the Waldo Joven of Oaxaca and the Waldo Mateos of Los Angeles were aliases of the real Ulrich Jasper Bremen, but no matter what his

baptismal name may have been, he was nothing more than the plagiarist of another man's genius. That man's name was Joe Cartridge, and I picked up his trail in Los Angeles.

For nearly twenty years the world admired the series of novels published under the name of Raven, and yet no one came forward to claim the authorship of the Raven books. In the following twenty years readers lost count of the spate of articles with titles such as 'The Raven Mystery', 'Who Was W. H. Raven', etc, etc, which kept the pot boiling with their own so-called solutions. It was an open contest, and the most outlandish versions were proposed: the President of the Mexican Republic, Adolfo López Mateos, was himself suspected, to the point of having to issue a categorical official denial of this elaborate hoax. With Raven, anything was possible: he was Swedish or Norwegian one day, Lithuanian or Irish the next. The closer the scrutiny, the deeper the mystery, as if each new line only added to the confusion.

Yet a key event had occurred in December 1945: while the director Dave Robbins was filming *Malasierra* on location in San José de Purua, he was visited by a man who introduced himself as Joe Cartridge and claimed that he was W. H. Raven's agent, or at any rate that he represented the widow of the late Waldo Mateos. I interviewed Robbins eighteen months ago, at his house overlooking Malibu beach, and he confirmed the story. I found myself back on the trail of the same elusive American whom I had last encountered three years previously, when a search of the Federal archives in Washington yielded evidence that according to his own account he had served a prison sentence in Relámpagos, a village in Guatemala, alongside a number of Europeans. He mentioned some of their names: Donovan, Guardi, Bieliski, Echeverria . . . and Bremen.

Dave Robbins told me that Cartridge had given him invaluable advice both on physical locations and on characterization in the film. He was a discreet observer whose perceptive suggestions always displayed a close knowledge of the background and plot of the novel.

In the meantime Mrs Ruth Mateos had maintained her rather strident insistence that her husband had been murdered by his old enemies, Nazis who had never forgiven him for the immense influence he enjoyed among the German working class and intelligentsia in the early days of the Third Reich. According to his widow, he was also paying the price for his role as a leading figure in the Munich Revolution of 1919 – two sets of old scores to settle. The idea is attractive, and I have not the slightest intention of casting doubt on the word of Señora Mateos. Why would she want to provide a false account? When I met her in Paris three years ago, on the occasion of the French publication of *North and South*, she struck me as completely sincere. But perhaps she too had been misled by the ingenuity with which her husband succeeded in devising a persona protected by multiple layers of uncertainties masquerading as truths. When I asked her about Cartridge, Ruth Mateos began by denying that she knew the man at all. When I pressed her further, she eventually admitted that there had been someone with that name who had looked after Raven's interests for some years, but she added that it was a long time since she had made use of his services and that she had no idea what had become of him. I was unable to draw her any further that day, and subsequent investigation has yielded no further trace of the man whom I have good grounds for identifying as the true author of the Raven books.

As a matter of fact, the principal begetter of the Raven myth was a man called Kuhn, an Austrian anarchist who had emigrated to Mexico. I met him in a bar in Mexico City in 1953, the year of my doctorate – unfortunately too late to take account of his key information in my thesis. He had just published a book of memoirs, at his own expense. I heard about it quite by accident, through a journalist friend. Kuhn had a Raven version of his own. He told me that in 1926, when he was editing a newspaper called *Der Syndicalist* in Berlin, he received a letter written in German and posted from San Cristóbal, in Chiapas state. The signatory, W. H. Raven, wanted advice about publishing a novel and some short stories that he had written. The letter ended with the slogan 'No God, no master', and Kuhn expressed his solidarity by sending the addresses of several publishers and newspapers, in particular that of the Social Democrat daily *Vorwärts*, the first to publish our author's work.

Kuhn gave me the same account that he developed in his autobiography, namely that he and several anarchist friends who included the poet Eric Muhsam quickly became convinced that these early Raven texts came from the pen of their former comrade in arms, Ulrich Jasper Bremen. As a young man barely past nineteen, Raven alias Bremen had been one of the chief editors of *Der Ziegelbrenner*. His involvement lasted from 1917 to 1920. By Kuhn's account, Bremen's prose of that era resembled both in style and content (he cited a number of mannerisms) the prose of Raven in *The Tale of the Chimera* and *Journey Without End*.

When questioned as to whether Waldo Mateos, alias Raven, and this German anarchist Bremen were one and the same, his widow would never deny the possibility, although her explanations remained exasperatingly vague. On the other hand every inquiry that I and my fellow researchers have been able to make in order to verify the identity of the supposed Bremen-Raven figure has led to a dead end.

If Mateos really was Bremen, there is no doubt that he did his utmost to cover his tracks and leave no clues behind him. Again I have to ask, did he have something to hide? And confusion makes his masterpiece when an examination of the death certificate for the Mateos shot dead in Los Angeles in 1944 discloses that the place and date of birth that it records are 'San Francisco, 1898'. How is it possible to verify such a claim, when it is common knowledge that all the city records were destroyed in the great earthquake and fire of 1906? It was only a short step to the supposition that Mateos might have borrowed the name and identity of an American born in that time and place, and I did jump to that conclusion. Later research proved that the Cartridge I had been looking for was a native of Chicago. There was no mention of anyone called Cartridge in the San Francisco records after 1906. Yet Cartridge really was born in 1898: his birth certificate showed that he was the son of Ursula Walser, born in Düsseldorf, Germany, and Burton Cartridge, born in Cincinnati, steel worker with US Steel. Fifteen years later his name appears on the list of trade unionists jailed after the strikes in the steel industry. After that we find him travelling the highways of the United States as a migrant worker. He had joined the Wobblies, the Industrial Workers of the World, moving from Springfield to Saint Louis, Saint Louis to Kansas City, spreading the word, a priest of revolution. That brought him up against the reformist trade unionists of the American Federation of Labour, and on one occasion he was injured so badly in a brawl that he had to go into hospital in Oklahoma City. In 1917 America entered the war. Cartridge distributed pacifist pamphlets and organized meetings calling for mass desertions. He found himself on the run from both Pinkerton agents and the Bureau of Investigation. He surfaces in Amarillo, Texas, in February 1919: six months in prison. Next year his trail peters out this side of the Rio Grande, heading for Mexico. Not long after that, he chances across the path of Bremen-Mateos.

I am not the only critic to have called attention to the stylistic problems posed by the original Raven texts, and books have been devoted to this question. One of the theories most commonly advanced explains the very Germanic overtones of the American texts in terms of the dual background of their supposed author.

According to the passport in his widow's possession, Mateos was born in San Francisco, of a Mexican father and a German mother. That is a plausible version considering Cartridge's ancestry and lack of formal education: he sprang from a popular culture, and was self-taught. But all these facts become illuminating, given the possibility that the rather ungainly language of the Wobbly was more or less successfully 'translated' by Señor Herr Bremen-Mateos.

In novels and stories which are meant to depict a world alive with working people, the uprooted and oppressed, the use of slang often rings false, and I have in mind not only the subsequent English translations but also the German 'originals'. The style is synthetic in every sense of the word.

Considering such a farrago of mysteries, who can really espouse the claim of Señora Mateos, that the truth was made manifest in Los Angeles on 14 September 1944? Only Joe Cartridge, if he still lives, could tell us the facts of the matter. If he reads this article, perhaps he may respond to our appeal. Why stay in hiding any longer, as if no one suspected that Raven was not Mateos? We beg him to pay no further tribute to this absurd legend. There is a host of readers who will not hesitate to recognize him as one of the unsung geniuses of our time. Nothing will persuade me otherwise: as long as we remain uncertain of what happened in 1925 in the confines of a prison in the Guatemala jungle, I shall continue to believe that that lurking, silent figure is beyond question the author of the books signed W. H. Raven. For how else is it possible to explain the fact that the famous Herr Bremen who landed in Mexico off a ship from Hamburg (as confirmed by records in the German consulate in Tampico), and who therefore had no first-hand knowledge of the social realities of contemporary America, could display so much vigour and such a wealth of pictorial detail in describing the adventures of a rebel from Indianapolis in his novel *Mr Steele*, or the tribulations of a migrant worker in *North and South* – two minor works, I agree, but none the less characteristic of our author?

The answer must lie in Relámpagos, in the locality of Tayascal, in the region of the Petén, and the best way to find it is to go and look, if only some clue remains there, so long after the events. I intend to keep that rendezvous soon.

Call that an anonymous article! Unsigned, that's all. No, Lippman, you and your phoney scholarship don't fool me this time. I shall be there before you. And if there's anything to discover I intend to do it first, not leave it to someone else.

The challenge is on, the race has started, and it's between the two of us. You like to play games, and so do I. Your gas, my flare, let's see who shines.

You've been a few jumps ahead of me till now, but point one, you don't know much about Bremen, and with good reason, because you don't know about the Charlie O'Sullivan episode. You think Raven went straight to Mexico, and you're wrong: he stayed in London for several years. And point two, you've eaten my poisoned apple: no matter what she says, Virginia won't back you, that's one thing I'm sure about. And that's why I am taking the extra risk of writing her a letter there, in Los Angeles, where I will arrive before you do. I leave tomorrow, at long last.

Dear Virginia

It's obvious that we shall never see each other again. Even if I denied it you probably wouldn't believe me. Maybe it's better so.

My bags are packed. Ron and Paul will be hard at work in a few days. Imagine how I feel.

It would be better for all of us if you keep the Mad Professor off my back. I'd like you to tell him that. This isn't a threat, but after what he's done to me (to both of us) I think that if we meet again, especially down there, something is bound to give. This is to keep my place in the anti-hero team, where maybe you've dumped me too fast. I know: it's me who's the bastard, not him.

You're getting restless – I can feel it. This letter is so disjointed. Torn up is the way I feel. Please bear with me, this last time. I've never been any good at writing letters, I really hate doing it. If you were here you'd tell me I don't like fair exchanges. It's true. I can't stand this kind of rhetoric. If I could, I would telephone . . . With everybody talking communication, no one communicates with anyone, do they? Maybe one day I'll be able to write with enough control to make myself understood.

By the way, keeping to the point here, tell Lippman to reread Raven's letters to Ganz, his German publisher, I think it was in 1928. They've just been published here. A researcher from the University of Basle discovered them – someone less short-sighted than your husband. He should give some thought to this: '*This country is hell. Writing in the jungle is worse than the most painful tortures the human imagination can devise. Sweat, fever, itching, mosquitoes, vermin sucking blood and brains as well.*'

Are these the words of an impostor?

And to prove that I wasn't lying either (or at least not so much as you may have thought) I will make you a confession:

The man had a mother, a centre of gravity dragging downwards in his guts, pulling his feet to the ground, tying both legs to the path of the clouds and the stars. He was eagle and cayman at once. Time flew by on his wings, while his body decayed in the ooze of the swamps like a waterlogged tree. And those forces pulled and sometimes ripped at him, especially on the days of the April moon when the wind from the South blew out of the sands and rattled the windows of everyday life. Crack! And a thousand splinters. Then the undreaming child would remember that he had no father. His decapitated head rolled into the sea and drifted with the swell. The blind eyes stared into the distance. The plugged ears whistled, full of brine. The swollen lips foamed with rage, speechless, bubbling green and blue.

In the flurry of the elements the man was sure of one thing only, and that was the amount of Indian blood that flowed in his veins, a slow, deep, stubborn river. And that gave a sense of something like eternity, though constantly resisted by the rest of his blood, the fraction belonging to the intangible and the possible. The split is never more cruel and strong than in our fictions.

And that is why the man would listen to himself talk and watch himself live.

I miss your body, Virginia.

I want you.

Michael.

3

THE RAIN GOD sat up. From his favourite observation post, Chac Mool saw a long way, almost as far as the footprint of time past, faint up above the horizon, on the side where the gates of death stand open.

It did not gladden him that people should trespass on his solitude. Dozens of men in leather harness, pale-skinned and sea-green-eyed, had scaled the slope of the sacred mountain to hunt him down. Moons passed, and Chac Mool roamed the land, swelling the rivers and flooding the marshy plains until the day when exhaustion stopped him running and he glided – no larger than a heart full of tears – into the depths of a sombre valley. It was then that the riders spread their nets and harried him with shots from their flintlocks. The weary god wept and bled. He did not understand the rancour they expended in confining him to his most cramped expression, he who knew only one boundary, that of the Great Circle which stretched from unknown seas and would sometimes carry him whirling into headlong adventures whence he returned exhausted, yes, but with a surge of new strength, a quickened awareness of his own existence – a fever that gave rise to short-lived follies. Chac Mool, capricious child, loved play and liberty. Captured, he grew aggressive.

A different set of men – not those who had caused him to discard his taste for pranks – had taken it into their heads to build him a pedestal on a hillside facing the sea. They installed him on it with great pomp and circumstance, after various ceremonies that the god pretended to endure without flinching. In fact, though, his sole response to the litanies addressed to him was to be conspicuous by his absence. The more they invoked him, the more he kept aloof. Month after month of terrible drought now fell upon the region, and the rain hunters bewailed their helplessness, but all in vain: many succumbed to the catastrophe, most of them children and the old.

Chac Mool was no longer anything but a mask, an effigy, frozen in his stance of moulded clay, able to do nothing more than stare at the horizon, deaf to entreaties. How could it be otherwise?

Yet with the passage of time the statue seemed to melt into its natural surrounding of rocks and shrubs, and his guardian presence began to be forgotten. Offerings dwindled, processions tailed away. Restored to his solitude, Chac Mool felt that the earth of his body was breathing anew. He shifted one arm, then the other, and gradually he regained possession of his movements . . .

The clay was porous; it gave the winds a hold. The friable image eroded and began to crumble. One day a stray pilgrim happened to pass by, and he noticed that the head of the god was disfigured by a crack as broad as his thumb, running from the right ear to the base of the neck, then between the shoulder-blades and down the spine. Soon he would begin to overbalance.

No one knows whether it was the nameless traveller or Chac Mool himself who spread the news, but what happened next may be taken for certain. Before long every village and household in the country had produced its crop of statuettes of the rain god, and where they appeared, so showers and downpours followed. Now everybody was determined to make his own little Chac. They made him into pendants, bracelets, rings; they carved him in stone and captured him on paper. Potters drew him crudely on their vases, while women re-echoed the divine image in their woven shawls and hangings.

Restored to himself, Chac Mool was able to stand up again and look around him at the sea and sky, out to the boundaries of time and space. And that day he came to understand that his future was to be eternally reborn.

The flight was dreadful, from every angle. Although Michael had been longing to be gone for several days, it didn't make up for the hassles.

At the airport, the formalities took an exceptionally long time. The police were on edge. There were rumours about the arrest of a French Connection big shot. Going through customs Michael had to submit to a thorough search of his luggage and a barrage of questions about the purpose of his journey. His good humour did not survive the ordeal.

After that it turned out that the baggage handlers were on strike and he found himself staggering down endless corridors with a suitcase in each hand. Then there was more standing about, then threading along another set of gangways before catching the shuttle service to the plane.

On takeoff Michael tried in vain to engross himself in the *Daily Mail* so as to avoid looking out of the side window and thinking about the chances of a crash – the front page had a photo of the previous day's disaster in Honolulu – and after that came a series of irritating incidents that jarred on his nerves, although they had started before the aircraft left the ground, when he found his seat in the non-smoking section occupied by a disabled old lady, and failed to object when the stewardess steered him to a seat at the back. There he found himself stuck between a rich kid travelling on his own to join a divorced father, and a stern-faced nun. Discomfited by the acrid smell that hung around her – a blend of dust and incense – Michael preferred to put up with the fidgeting boy who spent much of the flight driving a team of imaginary racing cars with accompanying sound effects. The nun smiled sourly and dropped an acid remark about American upbringing, which Michael did not bother to take up.

The meal was foul. Michael made up for it in whisky, under his neighbour's disapproving eye. The film had no chance to be bad, because despite some frantic banging by the stewardess the projector refused to work. Michael attempted to sleep, and when he was unable to do so he ordered another whisky. When the first turbulence hit the aircraft, he had downed enough drinks not to notice. The sister reminded him that he was supposed to fasten his seatbelt.

The captain made an announcement: 'Ladies and gentlemen, we are about to pass through a patch of rough weather. You are requested to put out your cigarettes, stay in your seats and not move about the cabin, and to follow any instructions that the cabin crew may issue . . .' A murmur ran down the rows of passengers, a ripple of apprehension, and indeed the aircraft now began to pitch and roll quite sharply.

The mid-Atlantic storm raged on for nearly two hours, a lot more than it needed to make Michael imagine himself as a living torch, a fireball spiralling down to its death in the cold of towering seas. As he clenched his eyes shut in the unlikely hope of sleep, his head filled with dreams of self-destruction garish enough to blot out his various plans and resolutions in the swoop from one air pocket to the next. Let's get it over with . . . But a rising tide of memory flooded back to fill his cringing body, the image of a young and sovereign Raven who had also faced the rigours of a sudden violent squall during his crossing on board the SS *Craven*. According to the official version retailed by the biographers and hence by Lippman too, the writer had sailed to Tampico direct from London. Thanks to Uncle Charlie, Michael knew that the order of events had been much more complicated: from Hamburg to London, then – for reasons still fairly obscure – a return to Hamburg (to settle some unfinished business?) before shipping out on a freighter bound for Baltimore, USA. Uncle Charlie had received two more letters, one from Philadelphia and the other from New York, and nothing after that. Later, Raven had resurfaced in Mexico, where he did land in Tampico harbour.

How had Raven stood up to the storm? Or was it the idea of revenge that kept him going, knotting his stomach too tight to be sea-sick?

Michael tried to summon up a mental image of his father's face. He knew it only from a handful of photographs, and even then he was not altogether certain who they portrayed. Charlie had always been wary of these documents divulged by the press. A bearded explorer in Chiapas in 1927, an underexposed silhouette among other silhouettes in a crowd in the Mexico City bullring, a young man with a moustache, cap pulled down over his eyes, in a sepia print taken by a photographer from Berlin . . .

The aircraft still ploughed on through the sky, while the passengers pretended to sleep or carried on noisy conversations as if such tactics had power to exorcize fatality. Michael gave up the struggle to organize his thoughts; he opened the old leather briefcase which went back to his Oxford days, and took out a book. *Los pasos perdidos*, a novel by the Cuban Alejo Carpentier, the story of a New York musician who takes refuge from civilization in a region of virgin forest. It was the original Spanish version: Michael had not forgotten the language since the distant era of Doña Marina, and out of loyalty to his mother he had made it a special study at school (when he was sixteen his teacher had even arranged to send him to Barcelona for a Spanish course financed from Los Angeles). The book he held in a feverish clutch was a present from Virginia. One Thursday at the beginning of their affair she had turned up with two gift parcels, the other containing a record, *The Flying Dutchman*, by the London Symphony Orchestra conducted by Sir Thomas Beecham (and Michael had told his mistress about the maestro's remark to a TV interviewer: 'Imitators borrow, real artists simply steal'). 'Was it on Lippman's suggestion?' 'Well, thanks for your vote of confidence! As if I couldn't tell what you liked. The other day you told me how highly you rated South American novelists, right? So I wanted to give you a surprise, a kind of name-day celebration.' 'Is it St Michael's day then?' 'No, but what does that matter? I didn't see you caring too much about birthdays and anniversaries.' 'That's what I mean.'

This story of a musician and his mistress escaping to a tropical wilderness made Michael uncomfortable. With hindsight it looked as if Virginia had wanted to give his destiny a mischievous nudge. He shut the book at page 99, midway through an account of guerrilla revolution.

In fact, without knowing why, and with no direct connection between the two stories, his brief reading had been disturbed by the memory of another text read several years previously. His French friend Xavier, called 'Froggy', had unearthed it for him in a bookshop in High Street, Oxford. The exact title of the book escaped him, but it was an anthology of short stories from Latin America. A story by Carlos Fuentes had stuck in his mind. One day a Mexico City office worker finds a statuette in the flea market representing Chac Mool, the rain god of the Aztecs. The replica is of little artistic value, and the buyer stores it in the cellar of his house in the suburbs. Soon afterwards, the cellar is mysteriously flooded. Who would suspect the statuette? And yet the terra cotta has started to drip; soon the clay has turned malleable again and, imperceptibly, it stirs. It has come back to life . . . Chac Mool grows, and his reincarnation appears to the clerk in his bedroom one day. A strange relationship develops between the two, a bond of dominance, a dialectic of master and slave. The owner of the house falls further and further beneath the sway of his uninvited guest, to the point of becoming his vassal, making new concessions with every day that passes. In the end the poor man is driven out of his own house and goes to his death in Acapulco. When one of his friends brings back the body, he is surprised to find that a stranger has moved in and has made himself at home. Enthroned in the dead man's armchair is an Indian with an impassive face. His skin has a greenish tinge, and his eyes are stony. He wears the dead man's dressing gown, he stinks of perfume, his lips are painted bright red and he is smoking a fat cigar . . . No, there I'm embroidering, thought Michael, I've let myself be carried away. Through brooding on that story, it's almost as if I'd written it myself. 'Miss, can you bring me another whisky?' The air hostess was having the greatest difficulty in moving along the cabin, tottering from side to side; she had no time to answer before the pitching aircraft propelled her down the aisle.

Michael noticed that the boy sitting next to him had fallen asleep. The nun had her eyes tight shut and was praying, tense fingers plucking at her rosary, lips faintly twitching. The wings of her coif shook with the lurching of the plane, and she looked more like an airborne witch on a sabbath night than a merciful bride of Christ. No doubt because of the Fuentes short story, Michael recalled some stunning images from the film *The Mummy*, with Boris Karloff, which he and Froggy had seen at the university film club around that time. Xavier was a fan of the genre, whereas Michael was almost impervious to the supernatural, even when it was transformed by the skill of the production, and he had found it very funny. Now, as he looked at all these people unable to persuade themselves that they had an appointment with the sea, he felt like laughing again.

These thoughts had hardly crossed his mind when the battering miraculously stopped. The plane levelled out, and through the windows he saw the lightning succeeded by shafts of sunlight slanting through a carpet of fleecy clouds. The nun heaved a heavy sigh. It was over.

The flight captain announced that they were about to fly over Halifax, and the passengers cheered. Saved! An hour or two from now and they would be in New York. The stewardess arrived with Michael's whisky. She had straightened her uniform, tidied her hair. The boy was awake and demanded a Schweppes. The nun stood up and headed for the restroom.

Suddenly Michael flashed the vivid image of himself shaking hands with Charlie O'Sullivan on the deck of the *Queen Mary*. In answer to the Señora's request, and to the last wishes expressed in the will of Waldo Mateos, the London Irishman had come to collect the orphaned son of his old comrade.

After draining his glass with a single gulp, Michael asked the boy's name. 'J.F.,' he grumbled.

'Like the President?'

'Yeah, Jack. What's yours?'

And thanks to the ensuing conversation Michael managed half to forget the misadventures of the flight and the unwelcome ghosts which had prevented him from sorting out his thoughts, as he had planned to do.

Luckily the air connection between New York and Los Angeles was as calm as the first half of the journey had been rough. Michael slept soundly. He even woke up without a hangover.

III

RETURN TO THE SOURCES

1

The weather was hot, 92 degrees Fahrenheit according to the thermometer hanging by the door of the motel attendant's hut. Even on the twentieth of July that was high for Los Angeles. No chance of a dip in the pool, which was visibly too dirty. I was there at my own expense, and not yet on the production budget, so I had to settle for a down-at-heel motel off Hollywood Boulevard. All the same my room, number 7 (I was glad when the Chicano receptionist handed over that key, and not sorry to discover a touch of superstition in myself), came with both air conditioning and a shower. Three dollars extra. I was expecting to have to stamp on a cockroach in the bathroom. At least that was better than having to tout for hospitality from the Señora, who had not been informed of my arrival. I wanted to take her by surprise, confident that she would be delighted to see me.

'Hallo.'

The click that followed when I dropped my dime into the public telephone woke me from my torpor. A sound of thunder in my head. They have no call boxes in Los Angeles, only free-standing phones placed in the open air, and in this case in the blaze of the noon-day sun.

'Hallo, Señora Mateos?'

'Yes.'

'It's Michael.'

'Who?'

My throat was so dry and tight that I could hardly swallow.

A trickle of sweat rolled down my left cheek.

'. . .'

'Hallo, who is that, who do you want?'

'Mateos, Michael Mateos, Señora.'

There was a further silence, but this time at the other end of the line, before her deep contralto continued sedately:

'Oh, it's you. You're in L.A.? You've decided then . . . at last! I thought you'd never come. You know, it's not such an awful town as they say. All this talk about smog, pollution, earthquakes, I hope you don't believe a word. Just fairy tales to keep the tourists away.'

Talkative as ever, dear Ruth. Her cardinal quality, the laying of verbal smokescreens, seemed not to have deserted her. Having said that though, honesty compels me to admit with hindsight that she never reneged on her legal obligations towards me. Until I was twenty-one I received the allowance due to me, via Charlie, and afterwards – instead of replying to my letters and my questions – she was generous with her money on several occasions. Bear in mind that after my father's death the Raven industry staged quite a remarkable recovery.

She was still talking. It was time to interrupt.

'Just the way Raven tells it in his books, Mother – that Yankee guilty conscience.'

'What's the matter with you?' The tone was sharper now. 'You know I don't like that name . . . Anyway, what kind of silly talk is this? Where are you? Where are you calling from? You must come over right now. I shall be expecting you.'

I took evasive action, claiming a series of appointments in connection with the film I was preparing to make. Ruth seemed to appreciate the fact that I was not there solely in order to open old wounds, and she even ventured the kind of remarks that parents feel entitled to produce when they want to congratulate their offspring on getting off to a satisfactory start in life.

'I'd ask you over to dinner, but I have an invitation I just can't break.'

And she launched into some explanation that I hardly listened to. It was her turn to run for cover. Apparently she had had second thoughts about her original urgency. I didn't know what had caused her to change her mind, and as a matter of fact I paid no attention to the question, because it suited me not to. I told her that I had made arrangements too, and that I had to see some people who were working on the co-production. Actually it was next day that I was supposed to have lunch with the network correspondent and another man who was in charge of technical liaison with the film crew. If there was anything we needed, particularly film stock, Ron and I would need to deal with him.

I had no inclination to visit the house in Santa Monica, at least not straight away. I needed time to think: the ground had been too thick with mines, for too many years, for me to charge in with my eyes shut.

'Tell me where I can get in touch, anyway. I'll call you . . . You've kinda caught me on the hop!'

And she laughed.

I gave her the number and address of the motel.

'Fancy you staying in a hole like that! Really, you might have let me know . . . Oh, it's just the sort of madness your father was capable of.'

'Really?'

I was about to cash in on that advantage conceded in a careless moment, but I was interrupted by the tapping of a hand on my shoulder. When I turned round I saw a huge black man with an impatient expression.

'You 'bout done, Jack?'

'I've got to hang up, Ruth. I'll call you.'

'No, no, I'll call . . .' she was insisting as I put the phone back on the hook and made way for the basket-ball player.

I spent the rest of the day driving around town in the little Chevvy I had hired at the airport. The traditional tour around the film star mansions, for old times' sake. Not that I was much interested in which had belonged to James Stewart or to Marilyn Monroe, and the whole trip was really a pretext for driving along Ledoux Boulevard and locating Waldo Mateos' old house, where I had lived for a while before leaving for England. I spent some time sitting opposite William Faulkner's house, but did not go as far as the crossroads and the broad gateway of 'our' place. Parked in the car with the windows lowered and the sweat making my back cling on to the plastic of the seat, I sat stock-still, with my mind a total blank, as if I hadn't recognized the place at all.

In the end I reversed into a U-turn and it occurred to me to take a look at the studios. My professional status ought to be good for a pass, I thought. Of course it was Fox I had in mind, not Universal, whose studios were open to the public and whose legend did not concern me for the moment. It was a sudden sick attraction to the long-gone stage, or so I supposed, where the final scene of Raven's life had been played.

On the way, and though I can't explain the change of direction, a glance at the local map persuaded me to head for Westwood and the university.

I lunched on campus – Coke and a hamburger. It was annoying to find no beer or any kind of alcohol available, but two notices in the hall of the Student Union restored my good humour. One of them announced a showing of *Malasierra* at the film society the following night, the other a discussion, chaired by Prof. Lippman, on the theme of 'Utopia and social reality in the works of W. H. Raven'. It was scheduled for 27 July, by when I would have left town. In any case I knew perfectly well that Virginia was due back on the same day that I would be taking the plane to Mexico City. There was no risk even of an accidental meeting at the airport, because I would be leaving in the morning and the flight from London and New York did not arrive till evening.

Virginia would find my letter, and that was all.

That afternoon I went swimming in the Pacific. I had driven west on Sunset Boulevard to Santa Monica, making sure to steer clear of the Señora's house, which I had located on the map.

The Pacific was the forbidden fruit. The quiet waves carried me, the sun burned on the sand, and haunting echoes sounded, memories clustered under eyelids closed against the heat. I had come here, or maybe a few yards further on (not a grain left of my sandcastles now), with Maria-Concha, the Mexican maid whose bottom my father used to pinch – she told me so herself one day as she scolded me for one of my bouts of opportunist whining, when I would cling to her in search of lost caresses. The Señora disapproved of my going to the beach: with a pool of our own, we weren't so poor that we needed the ocean. I used to hear her grumbling about Maria-Concha, my accomplice.

A pelican skimmed across the waves. The sun dipped

towards the horizon. 'Michael, *nos vamos a casa . . .*' A bunch of children passed by. I dressed quickly and walked back to the car park. Just before I'd lapsed into daydreams an idea had crossed my mind: why not push on to Malibu and talk to Dave Robbins? It would give him a surprise to see the only son of Waldo Mateos, alias Raven, materializing like the Angel of Desolation! No, a waste of time. Everything the old film director might have to tell me, I had already examined in detail. I wasn't here for that.

Back at the motel I found a message from the Señora. 'Meet me tomorrow, 8 p.m., El Choclo. Ruth.' The Chicano in reception told me about it in his broken American. (Odd that I spoke both of his languages, and didn't know which to use with him. America, and California especially, had become foreign territory. I was a United States citizen but my reflexes came from the Old World.)

'*Es que* . . . El Choclo, restaurant *mejicano* . . . *Muy* easy, everybody knows . . . *Típico*.'

Ruth had some nerve.

I was being followed. The tail had been there all through the afternoon, or at least I had noticed a big orange Buick pull out behind me as I left the downtown Chinese restaurant where my colleagues had taken me. After joining the urban freeway I tried to accelerate, but I found myself caught in the stream of cars which pours onto those overpasses at a constant fifty-five miles per hour, no matter when, or how dense the traffic. Bumper to bumper, an unforgettable feeling. The Buick had left the restaurant's parking lot only a few seconds after me; now it sat right on the tail of my little Chevvy. In the rear-view mirror I had a clear sight of the driver's face – a big man with a huge moustache and sideburns, greying hair, and a flashy shirt unbuttoned over a hairy chest. A truck cutting in from my right forced me to swerve, and a horn blared on my left. My heart gave a jump. I had missed the Hollywood turn-off, there was nothing for it but to go with the tide. And the man was still following me, unless my imagination had begun to play tricks. After all, who was likely to be tailing me like this, so carelessly, to say the least? I decided to put it out of my mind and to keep right on driving. It was only four o'clock, and there was nothing to keep me in town until my appointment with the Señora. Just because I found myself in L.A. I needn't feel obliged to be cast in a Bogart film!

The suburbs of the metropolis, and I kept on driving, with nothing but the stream of vehicles behind. Situation normal. I passed several side roads without turning off, determined to enjoy a long ride. The weather was distinctly less hot than the day before, with an overcast sky and a northerly wind. The Chicano had grinned when I asked if there was any chance of rain. '*No señor!*' As if I didn't know!

After three-quarters of an hour's driving I took a random turning. The freeway had slanted inland and my idea was to rejoin the ocean by finding a shortcut through the hills that divided me from the coastal road.

The first bends took me by surprise. They were very sharp, and the roadway narrowed sharply too. I told myself that this might not be the right route, and my eyes went mechanically to the rear-view mirror. Far back on the curve I thought I glimpsed the orange nose of the Buick. I stepped on the gas, and the tyres squealed on the next bend. I was climbing steeply now, driving flat out, and I didn't dare to look back again.

Close to the summit a few scattered houses appeared among the rocks, fine buildings with swimming pools. The caustic response they evoked momentarily took my mind off the man with the moustache, the Señora, Raven, the reasons for my trip to Los Angeles, and deeper still, the importance assumed in this context by every detail of an adventure I had embarked on with delight, looking forward to the real shock, the impact of returning to my native country, Mexico.

'Raven couldn't have stood it, living in this republic of power, bankrolls and bullshit.' That was my father's son speaking, with my militant back to the wall, trying to recreate what he must have felt at the sight of so much wealth and corruption. 'After all he'd been through!'

'Christ!' The exclamation was torn from me by the breath-taking view at the top of the hill. I stopped on the far side and got out of the car to get a better look at the landscape spread below from west to east, from the Pacific to the first foothills of the desert. And perhaps, more unconsciously, I wanted to stick my neck out and see whether my shadow was still on my heels, or maybe waiting on the road. And in fact after walking along the verge by the wall of an estate, I stood still for a few seconds admiring the landscape to seaward, but then I could not prevent myself from looking back and catching sight of the Buick from the restaurant, parked about a hundred yards away. There was nobody inside it. The guy had disappeared. That gave me the courage of curiosity. After all, it had to be better to sort this whole thing out. I marched off in the direction of the abandoned car, and when I got there I called out: 'Hey, are you there? Show yourself!' Only the echo replied. 'There's no point playing hide-and-seek any more. If you have something to tell me, now's the time!' Nothing. I was starting to feel silly. What if I'd imagined this little drama, projected my own fantasies onto a mere coincidence? The other man must think I was either crazy or pretty dumb – although in that case there was nothing to prevent him from replying. He could not be far away, and he must have heard me. This last thought triggered a rapid retreat. I was really scared now. If my reasoning was correct, it meant that the character with the moustache and the Hawaiian shirt was only interested in me. And if so, why?

Before I fell back to the Chevvy, I had had time to peer into the other car and see that there was some photographic equipment lying on the front seat. As I scorched off, determined to lose this snooper, light dawned in a brilliant flash: the Señora was having me followed. Not knowing what to make of my schemes and intentions, she had hired a private investigator who, before our rendezvous at the Choclo, would turn in a detailed account of my day, complete with photographs. Bloody hell, Ruth, don't you think that's going a bit too far?

I raced down the winding road that fell towards the sea, driving with all the skill I had, meaning that I was also weighing up the risks – for wouldn't it be too ridiculous to skid on the thin layer of sand that covered the road in places, and go hurtling down among the cactuses at the bottom of some ravine? The fear was there, but deep inside I was also glad that a race was on. It put a tiny dash of justification into the cocktail of feelings I had shaken for myself before leaving London.

When I came to the junction with the coastal road, there was still no Buick in the mirror, so after halting at the lights I slid into the dense traffic on the coast and headed southward to

Malibu and Los Angeles. All the way back I kept checking to make sure that I had shaken off the tail. He did not appear again.

Back at the motel I only wanted one thing, and that was to shed my clothes and get under the shower. Tepid first, then ice cold.

Then I stretched out naked on the sheets (I had got rid of the squalid-looking bedspread the previous day) and tried to gather my thoughts again in preparation for dinner with Ruth, my stepmother.

She had taken the risk of launching the first attack, hadn't she? I had to allow her to make her move, not charge in head-first and shove her dirty tricks department in her teeth. She held most of the master cards, but if I played dummy I had some trumps as well. Knowing her, she was bound to show her hand eventually. And when she did . . . Well, she'd have to spill whatever she had told Lippman, and in particular – since there was no possibility of her deceiving me – she must say how far she'd gone in bamboozling the Professor and generally clouding the issue. And why had she done it?

It was getting on for twelve years since I had last set eyes on the Señora. I nearly said eighteen years, because the only images that had really stamped themselves on my memory belonged to that period in Beverly Hills after the death of my mother. Actually the Señora had come over to London two or three times; she had met Uncle Charlie, although he would never talk about her visits. He knew that my stepmother still intimidated me (even the mention of her name set off uncontrollable shaking fits). He knew how much I detested her. Unreasonably, of course, since rather than just sticking to the letter of my late father's requests, she had always treated me with evident affection. Later – much later – it had struck me that she must be really lonely, this ageing ex-actress who lacked the kind of personal memories that would amount to a solid past. She only kept going thanks to the myth, and the royalties, bequeathed by a husband whose literary fame had been a posthumous chapter. Things are never simple for the living. It would be an exaggeration to say that I felt sorry for the Señora. Anyway, at the time when I was about to meet her again, those kinds of consideration were not uppermost in my mind.

Once, when I was twelve or thirteen years old, she had paid me a visit at Farlow School, near Bournemouth, where I was a boarder. She made me a present of a watch ('it belonged to your father'), an assortment of little cans of fruit juice in a plastic net – guava, mango, custard-apple, orange, passion fruit ('they tell me there's still rationing in England') – and a tin of *frijoles* ('do you recall how much you used to love those damned black beans, back at Ledoux Boulevard?'). The headmaster let me off school in the afternoon: it's not often that you're visited by a stepmother from Los Angeles. The Señora took me to the beach, and I ran about on the sand, played pinball (the first machines were just coming over from the States), and ate icecream. The Señora – still as beautiful as ever – did a lot of laughing but not much talking.

That was my last memory of her. After that there had been letters, articles, newspaper photographs, the whole mental apparatus that still occupied my thoughts when, at exactly a quarter to eight, I put on my safari jacket and set off for the Choclo, which was a five-minute drive from the hotel.

I got there early, and had to fill in the time at the bar. 'Señora Mateos will be here any minute. I bring you the house special, a margarita, *no*?' Ruth seemed to be well known at this place, which was a typical Mexican restaurant, on the chic side. 'Single or double?' asked the waitress, a pretty girl in a low-cut dress. 'Make it a double.' It's unbelievable, I thought, how this city of *Nuestra Señora la Reina de Los Angeles* gives the impression of being an anteroom (only almost too bright and too beautiful, whatever people say) to the country where I was born among shadows, as if I had been deaf and blind . . .

Naturally tequila had been a familiar temptation in England, but with the magic of the salt and fresh lemon it had never tasted more appealing or more dangerous than it did that day. As Ruth was obviously not a jot more punctual than before, I ordered another double margarita. She arrived at eight forty-five.

'Oh Michael, I'm absolutely mortified. Say you forgive me, please!'

She had grown old. If anyone had asked me right then, I could not have said her exact age. Fifty-seven or fifty-eight, perhaps. I had been so involved in counting the years that I had forgotten to count hers. If she had not come straight over to me (having picked me out at first glance), I am not sure that I would have recognized her immediately. She had put on weight, especially around the face. Too much make-up emphasized rather than concealed the dark shadows beneath her eyes. Her lipstick traced baroque parabolas, and her mop of red hair, sparser now, was a cluster of waves and curls, when once she had worn it falling straight down to her shoulders, with a fringe of silk above her eyes. As soon as she sat down she lit her everlasting cigarette, probably so as to pre-empt the issue of a kiss of greeting. I had shot to my feet like a jack-in-the-box and made as if to stick out my hand – a clumsy gesture, because I was holding a glass at the time. She had laughed. Same old laugh.

With that half-smoked cigarette between her lips she presented the classic picture of the older American woman, smart and sophisticated but a slave to slimming regimes and techniques for self-improvement or relaxation. Close up, her skin seemed paper-dry and full of lines, and I could see on her hands and arms the liver spots which are the first signs of irreversible decline.

They showed us to our table. I had barely opened my mouth except to say hallo, watching her all the time. She had assumed her familiar jaunty manner, throwing back her head to blow a cloud of cigarette smoke, or to laugh – just as she used to in her starlet days, and in Raven's time – but you could feel how tense and nervous she was, ready to unsheathe her claws if she had to.

'Two margaritas,' she said to the waiter who had taken over from the pretty girl behind the bar. 'Seems it's your kind of drink,' she added, glancing down at the empty glass I was still holding.

Later on, after the Napa Valley wine – two bottles – and the coffee laced with raw tequila (which she turned down, pleading the start of a headache), she reproached me with drinking too much. 'You know where it got your father.'

And she launched into a grand tirade about self-destruction which utterly contradicted the pious idyll of the authorized version she had been preaching over dinner. All through my childhood I had been brought up on this myth of the upright revolutionary, till I was sick to death of the theme. Still, ducking my questions and interrupting what I said, Ruth went on rehearsing the virtues of the great writer.

'Before the war, *The Tale of the Chimera* sold more than one and a half million copies in Russia alone, and two hundred and fifty thousand in Germany . . .'

'Till it was banned by the Nazis, and burned. I know.'

'Michael, I'd rather you didn't make jokes about such things. Those are the people who killed him. It's the answer to all your questions – you, the reporters, and this Professor Lippman you seem to know better than I do.'

'I'd like to believe you, really, but I'm sick of this whole story of the unsung hero dying for nothing after who knows how many changes of identity. You know, Ruth, I've never really believed that version, not since the day you first produced it in reply to one of my letters.'

'You seemed so anxious, so desperate!'

'Guilty, that's right. Didn't you claim it was because of me and my mother that Raven was forced to run for cover?'

Apart from one detail, she then confirmed the story of that final day as I had imagined it and as I have already recreated it. Ruth didn't remember whether or not William Faulkner had been there at the anniversary party. To be totally accurate, nor did she give me any indication of the setting where Raven was killed. I thought the *Laura* set was a possibility because the dates fit and because in that film it happens that the plot revolves around a substitution of identity whose subject is a murder victim.

'Listen, Ruth, it will soon be twenty-one years since my father died. Don't you think it's about time for the truth? I'm begging you, please, if he was guilty of anything at all that you're still keeping back, I absolutely have to know. Don't let me leave for Mexico without giving me at least some clue to the guilt I feel . . .'

'I see this Lippman has done a good job. Michael, you'll learn one thing from life, I hope: don't believe everything they tell you, and stay in control.'

'Straight lines aren't always best.'

'Do I seem so dumb to you?'

'But what about Cartridge, does he or doesn't he exist?'

Well, the least I can say is that at this point the Señora launched herself into a lyrical tour de force, linking the Indians of the Petén to the voyages of the Conquistadors, by way of the revolutionary exploits of W. H. Raven . . . She only just failed to throw in the libertarian Spain of 1936, echoing the theory once put forward by a particularly shrewd commentator. When I asked her not to exaggerate, because we both knew that Raven had never been anywhere near the Aragón front or the Durruti column, she let slip one fact which was news to me. 'When I first met him, it was all your father talked about – going over there! *No pasarán*, he kept saying it over and over again while we were driving down the road between Oaxaca and Mexico City. The fact is – and I wonder if he truly didn't know – it was all over, or almost. The battle of the Ebro had been lost, and Moorish troops were marching through Madrid not long after. What he did know perfectly well – and how he found out is another story – is that his brother Otto had fallen over there, at Teruel.'

'You mean he had a brother?'

'Didn't I ever tell you? Never mind! Well, it was a *half*-brother.' (She put a heavy stress on the 'half'.) 'Didn't your mother ever tell you either?'

How was I supposed to answer that? She probably expected some retort, but seeing that it wasn't going to come, she kept on talking. I stiffened. What if she was deliberately putting me on to a false scent, to keep me guessing?

She threw out some tortuous allusions to a family secret which she claimed Raven had not disclosed till very late in the day, and which she'd never so much as mentioned to anyone but me, and so on.

'But look, what is it you mean to say here? Okay, you confirm that my father's name was really Ulrich Jasper Bremen, and that he came from Germany?'

'Yes, of course.'

'All right, let's have it!'

'I don't know if I can tell you. You have to promise me not to repeat it to anybody, anybody at all.'

I protested: I wasn't a kid any more, I hadn't crossed the Atlantic to be told what to do . . . Today I felt quite capable – 'more capable than you, Señora' – of tackling Raven in all his shapes and sizes, even the most shameful and degrading.

'Oh, that's not it. By no means. It's even possible – now this is my personal interpretation, but Waldo was afraid of it too – that this gives us the real explanation for his death. Okay, since you insist, I'll tell you the truth. Your father was a natural son of Kaiser Wilhelm the Second of Germany. There, are you satisfied?'

'You're kidding me!'

'No I'm not, you heard me. A one-night stand, when the Kaiser went on a hunting trip in the eastern provinces.'

'Who was the mother?'

'You've got me there. Waldo always refused to go into detail. His story went something like this: "She was an actress called Helen. She belonged to a touring company which put on a performance at the castle where the Kaiser was staying. Her imperial lover discarded her, and then she left me in the care of a local peasant woman who brought me up the best way she could. I was the sixth mouth to feed in the family and I was quick to pick up the trade of bricklayer from my adoptive father, Carl Bremen. When I was ten, I didn't know how at the time, but my parents found the money to send me to the town school as a boarder. After poverty and work and learning my place, which was low and almost hopeless, I found that I had intellectual gifts, and they told me I had a brilliant future ahead of me. But when I was sixteen, with nothing but a certificate in my pocket, I decided to go off and make a start in life. I felt it would be sheer selfishness to keep on living at my adoptive parents' expense. Also, I had always called Carl my father, but on the day I left for school he had decided to tell me how I had arrived in the Bremen family, or anyway half of the story, the half about my mother, the actress Helen somebody . . . So I set my mind on finding her, and to help me do that I joined the first touring company I met. Then came Berlin, and then Munich. I never found a trace of my real mother, but in the years I spent searching, I stumbled across the identity of my illustrious parent. Much to my horror. What else could I do except escape from such a past, such a bad joke?" '

The Señora stopped for breath, and to put away a plump spiced prawn.

I was at a loss for words.

Ruth went on munching as she spoke.

'That was all I could get out of him, and you'd better believe it. God knows I made him tell the story often enough. To make quite sure, you see . . .' She swallowed, and took a mouthful of Mondavi. 'So, Michael darling, I suppose your curiosity is finally satisfied.'

My head was in a tangle, and swimming with alcohol. The Señora had shuffled the deck, and I was playing a new hand that I didn't recognize. But one detail had caught my attention. (How often it happens: you make a staggering discovery, one to make your blood run cold – now I was the grandson of Kaiser Wilhelm, wasn't I? – and yet you home in on some minor detail, as if amongst this spate of crazy revelations there is only one point of reference worth clinging to before you go flying into space.) Raven's first trade, his childhood trade, had been bricklaying, and suddenly I had remembered that the paper he edited in Munich was called *Die Ziegelbrenner*, which literally means 'the brickmakers'.

The Señora concluded:

'Let's change the subject.'

She bombarded me with questions about my future plans, and the film I was making in Mexico. She refused to let me pay the check, and said she would get angry if I insisted. 'If you really want to do something nice for me, drive me back to Santa Monica. I came here by cab. And this damn' headache . . . they started to get worse as soon as your father died, and once they get going no amount of pills and tablets will help, they don't go away. Sometimes I have to lie in the dark for a day, or maybe two, not eating and not seeing anybody.'

On the way out of the restaurant I thought I saw the man with the gaudy shirt tucked away in a booth which had been out of my line of vision from where we sat. I was not able to make sure it was him because my stepmother was already shepherding me towards the door. 'I'm so glad you're here.' Was I having another hallucination? Maybe Ruth was right and I shouldn't have drunk so much. But if it really was the character I thought I'd seen following me in the Buick, then it was a whole new game again, and the clouds were already gathering on the horizons opened up by the Señora's fantastic story.

She chain-smoked all the way back, and when at one point

she apologized for doing it I told her that I didn't mind, although I thought it was surprising for a migraine sufferer to be a heavy smoker too. Ruth didn't bat an eyelid. 'My dear boy,' she drawled, 'it's the only drug that calms my nerves a little.' I kept quiet – I had other things to worry about, and no window to let them out through. In any case, I found that I rather enjoyed the smell, perhaps because it reminded me of Virginia. But Virginia meant Lippman, and with that I was back in the same vicious circle again.

When we turned into the drive, the crunch of gravel beneath the tyres reminded me of the sound made by Waldo Mateos' limousine, on the day when he drove to his final rendezvous. The night was warm, but I could not suppress a shudder. Fortunately this was a different house, with a different garden.

I parked the car by the front steps, and the Señora asked me in for a nightcap – not too enthusiastically, I thought, and told her no thanks. I had learned enough for one night: with this much new material I was going to have to go back to the beginning and rewrite the script. Ruth must have noticed the way I was looking around at the house, the grounds and the floodlit pool. The words came out in a rush: 'You're sure you don't need anything? It would be a pleasure . . .' And she fumbled in her crocodile handbag, looking for her chequebook. I cut her short. 'Ruth, you remember the character in *Mr Steele*, facing his judges? "Make no allowance for extenuating circumstances, because I'm innocent." Please don't do that.' She lowered her head in the darkness, and I felt that she was blushing. I got out of the car and walked round to open her door, and then she kissed me on both cheeks. Her lips even brushed my mouth on the left side, and I quelled an urge to wipe it dry. She stood at the top of the steps outside her door and bared her yellowed teeth in a broad smile. 'So it looks as if we won't be seeing each other again.' She laughed.

Poor woman, she didn't know how right she was.

As I drove off, the beam of my headlights swept across the bonnets of some vehicles standing in the garage at the other end of the garden. Next to an old Ford and a small English convertible stood an orange Buick. I don't know what prevented me from jamming on the brakes and going back to hammer on the door where the Señora was hiding along with all her fads and fancies, but instead of that I shot off down the drive in a panic, and drove away feeling still more shattered than I had just before.

It took me a good ten minutes to snap out of it, and when I did I found myself parked outside a neon-lit chain store. Even in 1965, Los Angeles already had the kind of big multiple stores which are now known universally as supermarkets, and they even stayed open past midnight. I decided to stop and buy a six-pack.

I had kept a close eye on the rear-view mirror, and I was confident that no one was following me. All the same, after collecting my supply of Budweiser I ran back to the car and beat another fast retreat, and even after that it still seemed a good idea to switch boulevards two or three times, as a precaution.

Back at the motel I double-locked the door of my bungalow. The air conditioning was in good working order, and I lay on the unmade bed fully dressed and holding a bottle of beer which I had opened by jamming the top between the bathroom door and the door-frame, cursing as I did it, because I had been in such a state of panic that I grabbed at the first brand I saw, when I should have looked for cans.

Obviously the Señora had arrived late at the Choclo because she had been conferring with her spy, and I jumped straight to the conclusion that the spy was Cartridge. Not only had Joe the Wobbly not departed his life, but maybe he hadn't even moved from that house in Santa Monica. I was sure of it now. Ruth was living with Cartridge. Not bad, I thought, two birds with one stone. Only one thing worried me: was this also the same man who had been her lover in 1944? If that was the case, then dear Ruth had been nothing like the naïve innocent she had pretended. In fact she became suspect number one: nobody would have more to gain from the death of Waldo Mateos. As Cartridge's accomplice she would stay in control of the situation. Calculated risks. I could just imagine her pleading in front of a jury softened up by her expert theatrical tears. 'I thought I'd married a genius, and suddenly my whole life fell apart: he was just a crook, a rat! I loved Waldo Mateos because I believed with all my heart and soul that he and a great writer called W. H. Raven were the same man. Could anyone dream of a more cruel disillusion? My love meant nothing, because I had built it on a lie. I know that I should never have listened to the man I'm accused with, but what was I supposed to do? You must understand how it feels to be hurt, and cheated. Cartridge offered justice. He was the author of the unforgettable masterpieces that all of you have read, the noble spirit behind them, and he too had been cheated and left for dead. His longing for revenge did seem horrible at first, but gradually it crept up and took hold of me. At first I paid. Cartridge was blackmailing both of us, Waldo and me together. Then I went right over to his side. Waldo dug his heels in and tried to resist. He hired shyster lawyers to scare Joe and me. He hated me ever since the day he heard from one of his cronies that I was sleeping with the man he'd broken – broken his work as well as his life. But what could he really do to us? He'd tied his own hands. He had very little room for manoeuvre, because his own anonymity put him at our mercy. If he made a fuss or came looking for trouble, it would rebound against him.'

So that was why the bitch was so determined to protect and perpetuate the hero image, the portrait of a Raven made for legends. Natural son of the Kaiser, no less!

But what am I saying? If all these fine theories stand up, they mean that Raven was not Raven, and my father was really a swindler and a shit. No, Lippman, you don't get me like that! After all, why does the man absolutely have to be Joe Cartridge? My first guess was a private detective. The second theory, a lover, was even more likely. I wasn't going to argue with my stepmother's right to companionship, twenty-one years after my father's death. But if I wanted to be sure, it would be better to go and find the man, and ask him the question myself.

Halfway through my third beer I fell into a heavy sleep. I came out of it around nine o'clock next morning, with a dry mouth and sore eyelids. Before dozing off I had seemed to hear some funny scraping sounds along my door. I paid them no attention and told myself it was the wind blowing in from the ocean. Tomorrow the mist would be gone and the day would be hot again.

Just before waking I must have had a terrible nightmare which left a few brief flashes in my mind, like a taste of fresh blood, an acrid taste. Talking to Cartridge. Pursuit through a maze of gloomy streets. And each time I tried to fly over the cliffs and away, to escape from the bullets, despite all my struggles I never succeeded in spreading my wings. I only stayed nailed to the ground, pathetic. And the other man was still catching up. I tried to fight, but the more I picked my punches and the harder I hit, the more I kept missing, or else landing so softly that my fists sank into the face or stomach of my pursuer with no apparent effect, except for the sardonic grin under the shade of the moustache. I huddled into my corner and tried to make myself invisible, but the rat that stuck out its snout behind a stone just in front of me always went for my throat in the end. I shook myself, and shuddered, till I did not feel the bite, then lashed out with an uppercut and two or three right hooks, but as soon as I backed away again and put my guard up, my opponent would close in once more with his piercing stare, tail and snout twitching, a thread of blood beading the corner of his mouth, ready to spring.

I woke up too with a sticky, damp sensation on my stomach. So much for my self-imposed abstinence since the break-up with Virginia. I shed my clothes and headed straight for the shower.

An hour later it was my turn to be skulking about a hundred yards down from the Señora's house, on sentry duty. With a little luck the man in the Buick would still be inside, and would come out before too long. This time the hunter would be me.

Sitting there with all my attention focused on the big double gates at the entrance to the grounds, I did not realize how amateurish I must look. Doubtless I might have regretted not having learned more from thrillers about how experts keep surveillance, but I must admit that in those days I was silly enough to dismiss that genre of literature as second-rate. Life took precedence over myth, and yet paradoxically I dreamt of nothing so much as constructing my own personal, made-to-measure myth! Need I point out that since then my opinion has considerably changed?

This is it: the gates open, the orange limo noses out, slows to a stop. My heart pumps – the man with the sideburns is driving, I'm sure it's him. (But is he Cartridge?) He turns left, past the spot where I am parked. Ignition. Let's go.

A short drive over to Venice, the canals, beach, then a sudden screeching U-turn. Could he have spotted me already? I don't think so, because now he drives on, quite slowly, forcing me to stay so far behind that I'm worried about losing sight of him. We come to the Fruit Market. I recognize the place – I went there often with Maria-Concha. This is the moment. He drives into the parking lot, I accelerate to join him, and park opposite him, nose to nose. He's seen me. He gets out as fast as his belly allows, and I'm on to him already and grabbing him by the neck of his shirt (a different one from yesterday, but equally loud). He protests: 'Mr Mateos, please . . .' It's an admission, and another good reason to tighten the lock on his left arm. 'Come over here!' He shouts, this time with pain. 'Are you crazy? What's the matter with you?' I frogmarch him behind the wine traders' building. There's no one else there, we can have this thing out. He's red in the face, gasping through his open mouth: you'd think he was choking. Physical violence usually sickens me, but on this particular day I feel an incredible urge to hurt, rip, crush, wrench, burn and torture; I would never have believed that I could suffer such a loss of control.

'You're making a mistake,' he wheezed. 'It's all a mis . . . misunderstanding. Careful . . . my heart . . . let go . . . doctor.'

'You're Cartridge, right?'

I have no idea what my reaction might have been had he said yes. Was I a killer? Was I capable of murder? The Raven fantasy, if it was a fantasy, made anything possible.

'No, no . . . I'll explain . . . name's Sam . . . Sam Nicholson.'

Even though he was in pain (I had him in a choke-hold, with my cheek rubbing against his) his wince became a grin. He was laughing at me. I tightened my grip, he jerked, struggled feebly, and then sagged up against me, and when I let go he fell to his hands and knees. His eyes pleaded. I realized now what I was doing. A man in his sixties was lying at my feet and begging for mercy, if not for pardon.

'Get up!'

He held out his wallet and mumbled: 'Look . . . papers . . . Sam Nicholson.'

That was his name all right, as his driving licence showed. I helped him to his feet. 'Okay?' He nodded, walked a few steps while his breath came back, and then beckoned me to follow him. We walked towards the colourful booths in the market, so typical of Los Angeles. 'Come on. I need a drink. We'll talk there.'

We sat at a table, him with a tonic, me with a papaya juice (oh, those little cans in their plastic net at Farlow School), and collected ourselves again.

'I'm sorry about . . .'

'You have a hell of a short fuse, young fellow.'

It was the first time anyone had ever said that kind of thing about me: at school, on the playing field, in bars or in my television job, the general impression was that I wouldn't hurt a fly. This was the first time I had ever flown so totally off the handle.

'Just like your father.'

'You knew him?'

'You're bigger and darker, but the same eyes. Ready to er . . .'

'Kill? Is that the word you're looking for?'

'Hey, now don't you start that again. My doctor would never forgive you. Once is enough for a cardiac case!'

I was beginning to take to Nicholson – which really was his name. I liked him as much now for his sense of humour as I had loathed him before his furtive behaviour.

'Let me give it to you straight, Michael. You don't mind if I call you Michael?'

'That last night in Beverly Hills, the party with Hammett and the others, the day before his death . . . you were there?'

'Yes, but that isn't the most important thing. You mistook me for Cartridge, but I was only his lawyer. Joe died about four years ago.'

'Then he's not the author of *Tarantulas at Nightfall*?'

'What gives you that idea? Oh, I get it, it's that blood-sucker Lippman.'

'Has he been around a lot?'

'You wouldn't believe how often. I had to take drastic steps to protect Ruth's privacy.'

'But . . .'

'Wait, I'm coming to it. Actually we've been living together, your stepmother and I, for about fifteen years. We met at the time of the Cartridge trial. Yes, I'd been looking for character witnesses. After a long investigation, with some clues from Joe, I had managed to trace your father. He was friendly enough but he insisted on the utmost secrecy. He agreed to give me invaluable information about his companion on the expedition to southern Mexico and Guatemala, but only on the express condition that I kept his name out of it. He explained who he really was. I could only tell him how much I admired his work, and that naturally I would only use the facts I needed for my client's defence, without stating my sources. We met again. On the second occasion, Ruth was there . . . Years passed, and you know what happened. All right, Michael, there's only one ambition that Ruth and I still have today, and that is for a quiet life. And I ask you frankly, why would you want to spoil our share of happiness?'

He smiled. His face had relaxed into the calm good nature of a man living in comfortable retirement. He seemed sincere. Yet I felt there was still a couple of things that needed explaining.

'What about Dave Robbins and his whole story?'

'Maybe the old master has a few gaps in his memory. Actually it was me who went down to San José Purua, to look after the Señora's interests . . . and Raven's too, of course. Lippman did the rest, I suppose. When he interviewed Robbins he must have kept plugging away at his Cartridge theory till he had Robbins confusing the two of us. What difference did it make to him?'

'Yes, but none of that explains why Ruth has never made any attempt to deny Lippman's allegations, and you aren't giving me the key to the Cartridge puzzle either. Mr Nicholson, I assume you must know about the letter my father wrote to that Swiss professor, a man called Derauss, I think it was in 1938, where he claimed to be an American citizen?'

'Okay, Michael. Point one: the Señora doesn't think much of Lippman's half-baked theories, and she doesn't understand why you are taking them so seriously. After all, it only contributes to the Raven myth . . .'

'That's what bothers me.'

'Hang on, now. Ruth and I have nothing to hide, except the fact that we love each other. Why should we want to stir up the past, when the embers have taken so long to die down? I told you, we want to be left in peace. If you think about it, nobody is better placed than me to puncture this Cartridge thing. Me, I knew Joe. He was a terrific guy, one of those second-generation Americans who made this a great country, although not the way a lot of people think. He was a genuine hero: all he cared about was peace and freedom, that's what counted. A man like that, and they break him, they treat him like a renegade, scum of the earth. They hounded him right out of the country, into exile, and that's how he came to meet your father, when they both signed on for an ethnological expedition. It was their sense of adventure, breaking new ground, that brought them together, but they also shared the need to escape from a world which had betrayed them both and where the values they stood up for weren't worth a nickel. Joe did help Raven, it's true. He passed on his experiences as a migrant worker and a fighting trade unionist, a unique legacy . . .'

While Nicholson paused for breath, I told myself that Cartridge had given the writer the essential continuation of what he had begun in Germany.

'Afterwards, there's no question that something strange happened. Cartridge would never say what was at the bottom of it, not even to me. Their friendship must have taken an awful hammering for Joe to claim the authorship of your father's books when he was bitter and up against it later on. Do you write, Michael?'

'No, I don't.'

'If you ever try it, you'll see what a distance there is between raw experience and putting it into words, even for a writer like Raven, who always took the opposite line, that there are no good novels without experience.'

'So you're saying that Raven stole nothing from Cartridge, except for his life . . .'

'If you want to put it that way . . . And that's why Raven must have written the letter to Derauss you mentioned. Some sort of self-justification, a sense of guilt, in spite of everything . . . A tribute to his old friend caught in that vicious circle of jails and courtrooms again. Naturally, when Raven was in hiding himself – but you know that, anyway – he couldn't possible tell the *whole* truth without giving himself away.'

Sam Nicholson asked me to keep him company while he

looked around the little market stalls. 'The Señora is expecting me back for lunch. I'm supposed to be out shopping, you know!'

In between stalls, we chatted some more.

'Tell me, Sam, why did you follow me yesterday?'

'Oh, sure, I understand your reaction. It was a dirty trick, I have to admit. But it's like I told you: Ruth wondered what was on your mind, and we wanted to do everything we could to prevent you from unintentionally stampeding around and forcing the issue so much that we'd have to come out of our cosy shell.'

'Is that true?'

'Let me tell you something, Michael, if you don't mind. You're a strange character. Ruth was telling me last night. Why are you so determined to complicate things? Do you hate yourself so much that you want to blacken your father's memory?'

'But it's just the opposite. I want to clear him of suspicion altogether.'

'With *Tarantulas* he's in the clear . . . By then – which was when I knew him – he was finished, or at least his genius was finished. As for clearing his reputation, do you think you're going the right way about it?'

'Does Ruth know what really happened in southern Chiapas, in the Petén?'

'Now there I promise you she doesn't. If there is a Raven mystery, that's where it lies. And your father never spoke a word about it, not to her. Your mother, though, she must have got wind of something.'

'What makes you think that?' I snapped.

'Don't get riled, it's just an idea.'

'Tomorrow I'm leaving for Mexico City. As soon as we've completed the first shooting schedule in the capital I shall be going on to Oaxaca. And who knows. . . ?'

'I say drop it. What's the good? Raven's work is a fact. Isn't that enough?'

'No, I don't think so.'

Nicholson invited me to lunch in Santa Monica. I gave a polite refusal, claiming a final appointment before leaving.

'The Señora would have been glad to see you.'

'Are you so sure?'

'Come on, Michael, you're incorrigible!'

And he insisted on my accepting a cheque for five thousand dollars before we separated.

'Do it for my sake, please.'

This time in the end he got his way.

2

No exit. *Salida prohibida.* Forbidden territory. Deserts of eternity . . . As night fell a cloud of dust blew up out of nowhere and settled over the smoking ruins of the town. Wind fanned the flames of devastation, quietly. The sky turned from pink to violet, washes of colour over giant arabesques, spongy lianas gradually absorbing the glow that rose up from the earth. The horizon's dark green turned almost black. Under the spell of heat that caused the air to shimmer, senses and instincts roamed freely like so many rare gases in suspension and doomed to destruction, too volatile to endure. The dome of sky had lost its stars, a choking void. A bird crashed into the seamless wall and plummeted down. Only the wings remained stuck to the dome for an instant before they too flared up and were gone in the twinkling of an eye.

The tears dried up before they ever surfaced.

In his dismay the man did not recognize the path he had just trodden. His footprints hardened to leave hardly any mark, blending indissolubly with the original mud. Had he turned round he would have glimpsed the rapid movement of the earth cracking, gaping open in a fissure that stretched out of sight towards the folds in the ground raised by the previous cataclysm. But his ears were deaf, and his mind too busy. The man walked on.

His long stride aimed towards the fixed point shining over there, behind the fiery mountains. The further he advanced, the more the gleam was refracted into a multitude of rays as intense as the source itself. Far away, he could feel it, ran a river of light. And on the other side, if ever he should reach it, lay the calm confluence of sea and sun.

He stumbled forward, counting down towards zero. Ground covered . . . hardly any. The mistake, he said to himself, wagging his head, was youth. He wanted to be old, very old, a Methuselah, wrinkled and creased as the ground he trod, his eyes so accustomed to the flashing in the darkness that they finally kept still in their sockets, set in their gaze.

An impact jarred his thoughts. The shudder went all the way through his body too, and his head slumped onto his chest. He woke up.

Or so he thought. But the roaring returned. And the pressure tightened once again, twanging his facial muscles taut. Caught in the shaking, he could not make a move of his own volition. He told himself he wanted to resist.

Yet when the order came, the sinister howl of a dog baying at the moon, only his reflexes had worked. Obediently he moved towards the door. As he was about to jump he realized that he was stark naked, yet curiously the sight of himself reduced to the state of nature boosted his confidence and he started to laugh out loud, impervious to the jeering behind him. From that altitude the land they were overflying in the B 52 reminded him of the padded patchwork quilt his mother had made for him when he was four years old. He would not be parted from it for anything, and would always fall asleep in his cot sucking at one of the stiff corners of the coverlet. When his mother had died and they came looking for him to remove him to a world he did not know, the only thing he wanted to take with him was this single treasured object. Later – he had forgotten when – they had taken it away, considering that he was too old for such childish fads; and by then after being so thoroughly sucked, chewed and nibbled at, the quilt had taken on the look of a piece of rotted meat, all frayed and dry. Below him a great sprawling body lazily offered him its belly, thighs and breasts. At this speed, curves and undulations seemed to transmit endless signals of distress. The naked man shivered in the grip of the icy slipstream. When he looked down between his own thighs he could see his limp cock jiggle in the wind. In his exhilaration, one thought surfaced: jump, out and away, into thin air . . . Nothing and nobody compelled the crazy gesture. Conscious of the silence now surrounding him, he was obeying an impulse from his guts, and nothing more.

The fall was practically instantaneous, and then the spouts of flame blossomed with a crackling thunder of serial detonations. The lethal bomb ripped space apart and buried itself deep between the soft round breasts cupped and dangled in the hands of a woman with a hidden face. Like an overripe mango the vulva dilated and voraciously absorbed the explosion . . . Overjoyed with this awakening, the volcanoes started to roar.

At that moment Michael Mateos opened his eyes, convinced that the aircraft was in distress with its engines spluttering and in flames. It took him two or three seconds to realize that in fact the DC 9 had just lowered its undercarriage and they were arriving in Mexico City.

Michael's drowsiness as the plane took off in Los Angeles had quickly turned to a deep sleep which he made no effort to resist. After the encounter with Sam Nicholson his stay in California had been tame. Perhaps his hopes had been dashed, but not his illusions. In his heart he felt certain of only one thing: here, in the kingdom of artifice and showmanship, every scrap of dialogue wore such a fancy dress of camouflage that it came to sound like instant parody. The Señora was not exempt from the rule: it made no difference whether she was sincere or not, she played too big a part in the show. It was no good blaming her for the excellence of her acting. Michael was out of his depth, so lost in the traffic of events that he lapsed into some of his most asinine routines, as if mixing his drinks and playing the stud might fabulate the answers that reality kept refusing. He drowned his dilemmas in a night of American cocktails and Hollywood Boulevard whores . . .

Early next morning a racking headache jerked him awake from the drunken coma of a bender which he was reluctant to recall. Around his aching body, drenched with sweat, only the squalid sheets still held some touch and smell of love. The girl, with her thick, coffee-coloured skin and dry cunt, had done her job and left. Michael looked at his watch: five twenty. The plane took off at nine. No point going back to sleep, so he might as well pack and head straight for the airport. There, after returning the hired Chevvy, he ate a heavy breakfast on a painfully empty stomach (he had skipped dinner the previous night, and cocktails were no substitute). For once he would put up with American coffee, which he loathed – a sudden urge to drink pints of it, cup after cup, had germinated under the reviving jet of the shower.

He craned his neck to peer out of the window for a glimpse of Popocatepetl, feeling certain that he was bound to recognize it, but although he looked hard he saw nothing but the blanket of cloud above the city. Too late. He cursed himself for that, and for having missed the flight along the Sierra Madre. While the plane had been climbing to its cruising height, he had been grounded in sleep. The sense of frustration suddenly gave way to a literary echo – he tended to pride himself on the frequency of their occurrence. The upward flight had reminded him of a passage from a writer he very much admired – more than he did Raven, although he had never dared to spell out the heresy in so many words. *Under the Volcano*, which had been his bedside reading for over three years, had taught him more about Mexico (or at least the Mexico he was pursuing through his own father's books) than a library of studies and documents. He could not fail to make the connection. On top of that, he was haunted by the idea that Lowry and Raven might very well have met in Cuernavaca or Oaxaca. There was nothing to prove it, but nothing to refute it either. Although in any case he had often told himself that if he ever wrote a life of Raven he would certainly hesitate to bring the two men face to face. Perhaps they had not run into each other till later . . . in Los Angeles, who knows, after their paths had crossed on other occasions without their knowledge.

So it did not worry Michael that his arrival in Mexico City should come under the twin signs of Raven and of Lowry, even if the premonition had yet to be corroborated by facts. And after all he was only here to shoot a documentary. The rest was in the nature of a contingency plan if time permitted. Of course he intended to slip away as soon as he could to Acapulco and Oaxaca, but to strike out from there down to southern Chiapas and beyond was a leap that only his imagination allowed him to make. Yet the identity checks Michael was obliged to endure at Mexico City airport seemed to him to be a good omen, a confirmation of his digression via Lowry. His American passport was scrutinized, and his bags turned inside out. Back to square one, he thought, containing his impatience. And he thought too about the problems which Lowry had faced with the immigration office, not to mention what Raven must have been through during his travels across the Atlantic and in North and Central America. It was a fine start . . . Far from being iron-clad safe-conducts, all his impeccable visas, credentials from the London embassy and letters from the Mexican minister of culture only seemed to impress the officials as so many more good reasons to suspect this American citizen born twenty-five years ago in Oaxaca, and domiciled in London, England.

When two hours later the taxi dropped him at last outside the Hotel Regis, Mateos was relieved, after such a welter of official harassment, to see the friendly, smiling face of Paul Arthur Smith, who sat waiting for him in an armchair in reception. The art historian came to meet him, and in honour of the occasion he shed his very British detachment, took his colleague by the elbow and led him over to the bar. '*Una cerveza, amigo!*'

Let it drop? Okay, I let it drop. The Señora and her good friend Nicholson should feel satisfied. I knew my limitations, but to go from there into playing the game of utter abdication was going beyond the role of the pretender, the anti-hero (or rather quite simply the character in search of his own existence), which circumstances had dealt me. I despised myself for being so frivolous, and as quick to lose my temper as I was to run away. But to take my mind off all this, there was the job, and I threw myself furiously into it. The series of films which I made with Paul certainly does not deserve to go down in media history, but they were as good as any of the work I produced during my time in television. When they were screened two years later the critics praised their lyrical power and the enthusiasm of the images. What they did not know was that in the interim – I mean between the shooting and the cutting, which I did only after my return from Central America – I had completed an essential chapter of my life, after which I was to abandon the camera in favour of the journalist's pen. It was the prelude to my writing, which did not come until much later on – not long ago, in fact.

What else could I do except my job, once I had arrived in

Mexico City? The Señora had literally stopped me in my tracks with her Kaiser story. Whereas it ought to have revived my interest and given greater point to my quest, what happened was that her thunderous revelation produced an utterly purgative effect. It wrung me out, and left me to start all over again. The Cartridge trail, defused by Nicholson, had also petered out in the desert of probability. The Raven biography had come uppermost again, set back on its foundations. It all seemed so distant now, so impalpable and bookish, that the very idea of looking back began to fade out of my mind, melting smaller and smaller each day under the leaden sun of our locations. I would see about it later. Now that I was back in the country of my birth I thought harder about the man I was over there, in England, who no longer had much in common with that past which did not belong to me. The few moments when I did allow myself to flirt with the reminiscences definitely connected with Raven referred me straight back to the old Europe, as if the story had no life, and no meaning, except in that perspective. Not in this one . . . After all, this fable of the Kaiser was situated over there and harked back to European events belonging to history books quite unrelated to the carved stones which portrayed the dramas of the Aztec race I had come to film. In addition, Uncle Charlie had never breathed a word of all this hokum. Taking one myth with another, I preferred the one about the anarchist hunted by the police and fascist gangsters of the world. To find myself the bastard grandson of Wilhelm II shattered the very reality of my childhood, or so I told myself in the days of that first visit to Mexico, not suspecting that as the years went by the theory would grow more and more enticing. But tortuous was the path that would lead me to Bocanegra . . .

The most successful episode in the television series is probably the one called 'The Falling Eagle'. The subject had not been included in the original synopsis, but I fought for it so passionately that Paul agreed to make room for it – and here it is revelant to explain that Smith was the real moving force behind the films: it was his idea, his scenario and his commentary. Working on behalf of a project not my own, and involving myself in a collective assignment, undoubtedly played a considerable part in my very temporary 'cure'.

Hardly had he risen to the summit of his glory than the young emperor Cuauhtémoc was pitched into a headlong fall. Abandoned on all sides, by the gods as well as his allies, the Aztec prince reigned only for the duration of the siege of Tenochtitlán. The warrior was only a child, and it was easy for Cortés to dispose of him. The legend tells that the hero's tomb could never be found, as if the murdering conquistador had intentionally robbed an entire grieving nation of his burial place. From then on this absence, this lack, was to symbolize the invisible birth of a country, the Mexico of all the solitudes, whose one hope would forever remain to discover that cradle-tomb again, and in doing so to discover its own origins. A vain hope, naturally . . . And for the purposes of the film we pretended to go in search of the tomb of Cuauhtémoc ourselves. It was the pretext for many other visits to existing sites, but also for a commentary which I wrote myself. Unknown to me, that digression into historical allegory, with its inexhaustible implications of heights and depths, rise and fall, preyed upon me from the inside, eroding whatever fragile defences and comfort my profession afforded. 'The Falling Eagle' was to keep me company for a good while yet, forever spiralling downward into oceanic depths . . .

But more than the proud Aztecs, perhaps it was the Otomi – said to be without shame – who most fascinated me. From Toluca to Jilotepec we inspected the folk remains of that lowly civilization. As I saw them, these eaters of rats and lizards, these inveterate pulque drinkers, painted women and erotic rituals – the outlets for a powerful sexuality now sadly out of favour – did not constitute an inferior category. The Otomi were crude, and yet I loved their way of life which mocked at Aztec puritanism. Fermented agave juice is sickly stuff – 'absolutely foul' was Ron's reaction – but pulque, what a paradigm of drunkenness!

Still, it goes without saying that the Aztec nation, with its legend of the suns and its taste for cataclysm, did more than retain my sympathies, but stood at the centre of our concerns. The four suns that preceded our own universe – Four-Jaguar, Four-Wind, Four-Rain, Four-Water – showed the omnipotence of the elements and the weakness of man, a being who had 'descended' to the earth, constantly in flux, unstable and perilous. The man was eaten by jaguars, then, when the storm had quenched the second sun, the jaguar-man was transformed into a monkey and consigned to a rain of fire in an apotheosis of thunder, lightning and volcanic eruptions. Finally, at the end of a deluge that lasted fifty-two years, a single couple survived. Punished by Tezcatlipoca, the rival of Quetzalcoatl, the man and woman were metamorphosed into dogs. The pariah dogs whose bodies are thrown into the *barranca* . . . And we owe our existence, we men of the fifth sun, to the Plumed Serpent who travelled to the underworld and spilled his blood on our bones to give us resurrection. It was not in Jerusalem that these things happened . . . In any event, at that stage, it was perhaps natural that all these mythological perspectives should wake grievously deep echoes inside me. Think of it as a slow maceration, with its highs and lows, to the beat of pulque, tequila and mescal . . .

At a more or less conscious level I knew that this professional assignment hardly began to explore my personal concerns: the heart of the matter lay hidden somewhere else, further off, and deeper still . . . After all, on my mother's side was I not descended from the Mayas, with their great philosophical tradition, a race more ancient and distinguished than the Aztecs themselves? Nowadays I have come to see those flights of historical fancy as mere arrogance, futile and pathetic.

In concrete terms this expressed itself by hastening the tempo of events. After three weeks' intensive filming we decided to give ourselves a few days' break. We had kept till last the traditional sequence on the shrine of Guadalupe, which was to conclude the series, since the celebrated Dark Virgin has succeeded the moulded clay idols in popular veneration. In any case, Ron had been having some problems with his cameras and with obtaining the proper film stock in Mexico, so we were waiting to hear from Los Angeles, where I had arranged to send a cable for any extra equipment we might need.

All this presented me with the opportunity which I had been expecting even as I dismissed its likelihood. When Ron suggested that we should go to Acapulco, 'tan ourselves brown and live like millionaires', I jumped at the chance. Acapulco would bring me closer to Oaxaca, but not all the way. A respectable distance from my native town . . . Raven had only passed through the place, a tourist like myself. The trip would not commit me to anything much. After parting with Nicholson in Los Angeles, I had cashed his cheque, and the money was safe in my wallet, in big bills. There was nothing to stop me packing my bags and taking to the road. Ron and I would spell each other at the wheel of the old crate we borrowed from the Mexican assistant. '*Con cuidado, niños!*'

It was a travelling fiesta everywhere – Mexico style, if you like, but mostly in our own way, with the hopes and intentions common among many men of our generation, brought up according to British laws and British ways, and with British prejudices too – a real holiday, in other words. And that is how we came to be prowling the beach at Caleta in pursuit of a couple of American girls we'd met in a club the night before. We never did find out if they had stood us up, because I was stopped in my tracks by a sudden shout. When a voice called out '*Vieille noix de Magdalen, par tous les saints de la révolution*', I recognized Froggy at once.

'What are you doing here?'

'What about you?'

Even in bathing trunks my old friend from Oxford was looking as distinguished as ever. A bit thinner, perhaps, and wearing horn-rimmed glasses. Although his hair was longer it barely covered his ears, whereas mine were completely buried.

Xavier had taken his degree in political sciences, before going on to follow his family footsteps into the salons of the Quai d'Orsay.

'Just a minor post here to start with, you know,' he told me later, when the three of us had sat down for the first glass in a long night's drinking.

This meeting was welcome, of course, because the Parisian had been a good friend, and excellent company. Still, I could not help seeing it as a bad omen too, a message from fate to steer me back onto a path which I had been ready to leave. It was like putting the clock back to the beginning, on the other side of the Atlantic . . . And yet we were at ease together as we roamed through the backstreets of the harbour, probably fascinated by the common memories still imprinted on us both in an invisible ink, even if we were still too short-sighted to make them out.

Xavier never knew it, but it was he who unwittingly struck

the spark that lit the powder, which by now was bone-dry and ready to burn. We were feasting on grilled *camarones* when he began to shake with laughter as he recalled our poetic and political pretensions at Oxford.

'The problem with our generation,' he said, 'comes from our inordinate love of ourselves, the amour-propre that we believe we exorcise by constantly projecting ourselves onto others, onto this Third World which we dress up in all our own sins and hopes.'

'Isn't that the way it's always been?' retorted Ron, who was beginning to feel bored stiff by our chatter.

I made no reply, and Xavier continued:

'Well, tell me what brings you here, Michael. And never mind about career requirements, is it really an accident that we should meet again in Acapulco? We were so fond of navel-gazing. In the end we had to leave our private selves behind, and even the fragments of the past that we thought it was possible to rebuild on . . . Look, do you remember there was one poet whom we passed over too fast in our discussions – Antonio Machado, the Andalusian? I have just been rereading him, nearly everything he wrote. Look.'

And he took a small notebook from his hip pocket and opened it at a page covered with notes scribbled in all directions.

'*The other does not exist: that is the rationalist faith, the incurable belief of human reason. Identity equals reality, as if in the final analysis everything ought to be absolutely and necessarily one and the same. But the other will not be excluded; it subsists and persists; it is that solid bone on which reason wears down its teeth.*'

As the reading went on I found myself framing a sudden but startingly sharp view of the overall picture whose details and pattern I had been allowing to disperse. Quetzalcoatl was not only a subject for a TV programme but a living reality embodied by Raven and perhaps also by the three of us here, who had come to this land of resurrection because for one reason or another, in one way or another, we wanted to drop out of sight – our own and other people's – wanted to dissolve into ghosts, devoid of flesh, blood, feeling and all human substance, in order to be totally reborn out of our own ashes. One question remained unresolved: what blood must bathe our walking skeletons before we could regain the taste for life? For Ron, who left us before the coffee arrived, the answer hardly seemed to matter. For Froggy, I wondered if it mattered and I still don't know. On the other hand for Raven and perhaps for myself the solution to the problem – or so I thought then – had its roots here, in this land of extremes.

Xavier was still talking about Machado, reminding me of what I knew about the poet from Seville. How, unable to find himself, he invented alter egos, doubles who were better situated to create an apocryphal past. Out of correction and distillation, perhaps a new configuration might emerge, a creation in the true sense.

'In 1936 the civil war broke out . . .'

And I thought about my father's unknown brother again, and the Señora, and Cartridge . . .

'Machado joined up. Poetry in the service of liberty. Speeches, pamphlets, taking public stands . . .'

And in the meantime Raven went to ground in Oaxaca.

I tried to resist. 'Froggy, surely you're not going to trot out commitment all over again? We've been through all that, haven't we? It was clear that action and literature were two different things, complementary if you like, but ultimately . . .'

I was talking off the top of my head, anything to wriggle out of the stranglehold tightening round my neck. I too was in Acapulco, I too was here for a few exotic thrills, all set to go out on the town with all expenses paid and put on a performance for stray American girls desperate for excitement. I wanted to forget about Virginia, Lippman, the Petén, and Doña Marina, my mother . . .

'By January 1939 there was only one way out, and that was exile. Machado crossed the frontier together with hundreds of thousands of other political refugees. A month later – luckily for him, you might say – he found his release by dying, at Collioure, only a few miles away from his suffering country . . .'

Exile, death . . . By way of being reborn, wasn't that just what Raven had come to Mexico to find? Why had he run away?

It all rose up again, restored to life under my eyes, and I

told my good friend Froggy my story, for the first time. He heard me out, although he was stunned and almost dismayed to have been the cause of such a confession.

'I came here to die.'

'You're off your head! Stop it, Michael, please. Come on, let's get out of here. In Acapulco the night is only just beginning!'

He was talking about fiesta, the way it was in the good old days – how old we had grown, all at once! And the word was enough to take me twenty years back, to my mother, and the Hispano, and the chapel of Los Milagros . . . I gave the Shout, the famous Mexican rallying call which was also the sound of my own true birth, in pain . . . A solitary dog barked at me out of a dingy backstreet.

'You see,' I said. 'The soul of the Chamas has been reincarnated.'

Exactly what came next is hard to say. We were sitting in a shabby *pulquería* somewhere downtown when four men just about as canned as we were took offence at the sound of two foreigners holding a conversation in English. At first they kept their distance but started to curse us and abuse us; the air was thick with insults that we perfectly understood. We were too deep in discussion to take notice, and we decided to ignore them. But one of the dockers (why on earth did I suppose that they were dockers?) came over to Xavier, and not content with a long harangue strewn with '*gringos*' and various compliments to his mother, suddenly started kicking at his chair. I rose to my feet, intending to explain to the intruder that I was as Mexican as he was, and my mother as good as his own, until he tipped his glass over my trousers and spat on the floor a few inches from my left foot. I called him *cabrón*. He caught me with an uppercut to the jaw, not a vicious one, but hard enough to cut my lower lip against my teeth. The taste of blood in your mouth . . . He wasn't very tall, not more than five foot six, but lean and wiry. His face was seamed, according to type, and I saw that he had one glass eye. I swung at that eye with my right hand, punching my full weight so that my feet came off the ground. Then the rest of them piled in, and Xavier barred the way.

I never was much of an athlete, and it used to worry Uncle Charlie. 'Brains are all right,' he would tell me when I was a boy, 'but I'm certain that your father wouldn't have wanted you to be a weakling.' Then he would carry on about their fist-fighting triumphs in the London pubs, or against the bobbies. Charlie meant well when he took me to the gymnasium when I was nine or ten years old. He taught boxing to a few neighbourhood kids whom he saw as future Carpentiers or Jack Dempseys, depending on whether they were black or white. I could take gymnastics if I had to – I could practically hear myself growing at the time – but when it came to 'putting my mitts up' against budding champions coming at me like bulldozers, I was a total flop. Poor Charlie! And it didn't improve later on, at Oxford, for instance, where I was an average kind of swimmer, and more for the fun of it than for any sporting success. Right to the end, as long as he lived, my guardian never lost hope of teaching me how to 'look after myself'. His favourite exercise was getting me to hit fences with my fists, or sometimes even a wall, 'to get those knuckles hard'. And in spite of my failure 'to take my training seriously', as Charlie complained, I have to admit that something must have stuck, because it came out in this bar-room brawl in Acapulco, the one he had been coaching me for without knowing it. How often he told me: 'Luckily for you, you have the agility of your Indian ancestors and your father's aggression.' Once, when I must have been twelve years old (it was a few months before the Señora's visit), he was delighted to hear that I had given a fair hammering to a classmate who made some racist remarks about me. When I was punished for it, Charlie sent me to another school, which is how I went to Farlow.

As for Xavier, appearances were deceptive. His elegant appearance concealed an all-round athlete, and he had been one of the best centre three-quarters in the Magdalen rugby fifteen.

All the same I would struggle to give any coherent account of our performance in that scrap in Acapulco, and I shall never know whether it was our fighting qualities that counted most, or the desperate energy produced by the state of drunkenness we had already reached before our opponents disturbed us.

Some hours later I was woken by the spatter of raindrops on my swollen face. It was daybreak, and I was lying by the side of a stony path. I felt groggy and stiff, I ached all over, and my clothes were in tatters. It took me a while to take stock of the situation, but I could see that I was alone, and I could certainly feel that I was not dead. I called out, feebly at first, then louder and louder. No answer. What had happened to Xavier? Where was I? Limping and stumbling I groped my way along the path, and although I was quite unable to tell how long it took me (whether it was twenty minutes or an hour), eventually I came to a place where the path widened and was laid with tar. A few hundred yards ahead I saw the roofs of houses.

They took care of me there, and two days later I was able to grasp what had happened. The dockers had hauled us outside the bar for a showdown, and I must have been put out of action very fast. I thought I could remember Xavier breaking loose and streaking away like the sprinter he was. If he had returned with the police – as he had shouted he would do while I collapsed, half-conscious, in the alleyway – there was nothing left to find. They had thrown me into a covered truck (I vaguely remembered the jolts along the way, and the pain in my back), then driven off and dumped me near this little village twenty miles out of town, on the road to Oaxaca . . . The funny thing was that our attackers had not taken Nicholson's money, which never left my possession (so unreliable, those Mexican hotels . . .), and I still had nearly three thousand dollars left. On the other hand, my American passport was gone – the supreme revenge!

In the time it took me to mull things over (imagine the perspectives it inevitably laid open), my mind was made up. In any case, with no papers and no luggage I felt as if I was halfway through a door which had previously been barred. A chasm yawned. The temptation was too strong.

The bus to Matamoros was due at the village the next day, and I would be the only man to board it there, a nameless traveller.

From Matamoros I wired Froggy: 'Meet me Oaxaca, if you want. *Salut, vieille noix*. Michael.'

On 15 September 1965, the day of the fiesta of the Shout, I came to my native town at last. My first impulse was to visit my mother's grave.

3

THE LAGOON WENT back to sleep. A few last drops of warm rain died on the surface of the troubled waters. But the country was a mass of steam, and from now on there was nothing to differentiate the lake shores from the humid forest, or from the invented world whose image was traced in the sky, a single cloud, immense.

Masson stood in the middle of the *caribal*, the Indian village, and met the eyes of the villagers.

It was too late to regret his hesitation to leave this inhospitable region. Three weeks before, he was supposed to have rejoined the rest of the expedition which was waiting in Campeche, whereas in fact the Engineer – that was the grandiose title the *Compañía* had bestowed upon him – had yet again deliberately allowed himself to be left behind. After all, hadn't he made a success of the mahogany campaign?

They would grumble about him in the capital, but that was as far as it would go. They couldn't do without his services. In four years the Forestera had increased its profits tenfold.

Masson owed his good results mainly to the way he had reformed the treatment of the Indians working under his control. His predecessors had displayed either fewer scruples or less intelligence by penning the natives in camps which they could not leave except to work, and using the whole range of corporal punishments if they stepped out of line. No more of that, the Engineer had ordered when he took over. The alternative was to reintegrate the peons into their natural environment and traditional way of life.

Masson often thought back to his former comrades in arms in

Europe, who would have considered his improvements as merely reformist; but in spite of the guilty conscience which regularly brought him fits of almost ungovernable depression, the fact of having to fight every inch of the way against the opponents of his theories, and especially against his own assistant, González, gave him reason and meaning enough – one clean drop in an ocean of hardship and injustice. That was the vindication and small endorsement for his improbable dreams of successful integration and a true blend of cultures, for the good of the majority.

Yet once again nature had delivered a shattering retort. Not since his arrival in this part of the world had the elements joined forces so destructively. First the rain fell for ten solid days, a vast torrent that confounded men with trees and trees with the soil from landslides off the mountains. This primal mud clung to the very pores of the skin, it stifled shouts and tears, choked the horizon and the hope of survival, ruined the supplies and wrecked the boats . . . When the party had finally struggled through to the Lacandon village – in the nick of time, because a day later and it would have been impossible to navigate a river ready to burst its banks – a miraculous calm had descended. Indians and Creoles paid homage to their respective and inseparable gods. As for Masson, he saw this as the confirmation of his own predictions. He decided to grant himself a few days' leave. Next day his companions headed north again, under a wet but milder sky. He promised González that he would be in Campeche within a week.

They had left the Domain of the Dog, the boundless place where everything, plants as well as animals, goes bent and stooped and creeps parallel to the ground, nose pointed to the centre of the earth. For up above there is no sun . . . Only humus and rot produce life. And they had returned to the World of the Horse, out in the open, where eyes could roam off again in their search for the moon. Nostrils and manes in the wind, breath galloping towards the great expanses. Over there, across the lagoon . . . So spoke Tcha K'in, Masson's guide, and the Engineer himself was not far away from thinking in like terms. In the thick logbook that never left him and for which he sometimes felt that he would have given his life, he had greeted their return to the caribal in similar words.

One day González had shouted at his boss: 'There are times when I wonder if you aren't more Indian than all those flat-noses!'

The deputy's resentment and racism had been intensified by Masson's sporadic liaison with Tcha K'in's daughter. The girl was already married, and the mother of two children, but the guide had been very insistent that the Engineer should accept the gift he offered in gratitude for his people's changed conditions. Masson was touched, but bound by scruples, and attempted to refuse, whereupon his guide took loud offence. Eventually he accepted. After all those long months in the jungle . . .

And then, Tcha K'in's daughter was still young and beautiful. So as the years passed Masson found a haven of peace, a temporary sanctuary where the man had his strength and zest for life restored, while he recorded a fresh episode in the notebooks which some day, perhaps, he would send to his surrealist friends, and have published in Paris or Berlin – just as in the good old days. Unless he stuck to his first intention: to burn his bridges and have nothing more to do, not only with the 'System' which he had evaded but with the literary pursuit itself . . . Experience first, and nothing but experience. To hell with words!

This time the Great Cyclone did not give him the opportunity to keep on and on asking the same fastidious question.

Nor did they have time to escape. They were pinned to the spot by the formidable arm which reached out of the sky and along the horizon, as fast as an arrow fired from Tcha K'in's bow could strike a target two hundred feet away.

The sky opened like a calabash slashed by a sharpened blade. Gouts of thick blood gushed out of the wound. The pool became a flood, the stream an ocean, but nothing drained away, and the frontiers of the world grew clogged with debris. The more the universal body emptied, the more it was swamped by a warm viscous plasma. The sickened earth was spewing up its entrails. Driven by the wind that whistled too fiercely to be heard, the regurgitations melted as red vapours into the air. And it started all over again, the terrible seething, the to and fro conflicting cycle.

Zigzagging to avoid the wind-blown missiles, doubled over,

now and then flattened to the ground, crawling, clutching at the smallest pebble or projecting branch, Tcha K'in and Masson fought to regain the caribal. The storm had caught them by surprise where they were fishing by the river.

Only a few hundred yards away from the hamlet, the Indian was stopped in his tracks by a heavy stone. He fell. Masson was ahead of him and he tried to turn back, but the other waved him on. The only chance was to go on, otherwise both would remain for ever . . . Masson thought about those who were in the village: Nahà and her sons, the younger only eighteen months old. He started forwards again, into the wind.

The caribal no longer existed. When the Engineer reached the first hut, which had been practically demolished, a spectacle of horror danced before him – blurred, flooded, wrecked, with no shape nor any human appearance. Then suddenly, in a photographic instant, a flash of glaring lucidity, everything resumed its place and function – men, women and children froze in their headlong flight, dogs ceased to bark, and instead of being smashed into the rocky ground, chickens went on quietly pecking at their chosen worms or insects. In the middle, smoke trickled gently upwards from the roof of Tcha K'in's hut, where Nahà waited with the evening meal.

That was the vision obliterated with a terrifying howl by the long tongue of fire which speared downward from where it had been lurking all this time behind the curtain of wind and rain, waiting for a chink to appear . . .

And the monster reserved its first blow for the house of Tcha K'in and Nahà, which was Masson's too.

The Engineer closed his eyes. With his nose in the dust and his body clamped to the ground, he listened to the crackling of wood, feathers, and flesh.

Seconds or minutes later, he stood upright under the battering of the hurricane and started towards the hut, still separated from it by a wall of wind and flame about twenty yards across.

When it was all over, Tcha K'in, who had managed to reach the caribal in spite of his broken leg, found Masson huddled in the bottom of a boat on the bank of the lagoon. Underneath him the Engineer held his logbook clutched against his stomach. The white man looked up. He was crying. Tcha K'in told him, in his language, that Nahà and her sons were dead. Their bodies had been found lying a few yards away from the incinerated hut.

Upon re-reading these pages of the manuscript, Waldo stopped at the penultimate word. He hesitated: *charred* bodies, *incinerated* hut, or the other way round. Which was the more idiomatic in German? Maybe he should stick to the original version . . . Torn between parallel feelings of anxiety and amusement, he told himself that after more than ten years in Mexico the subtleties of his mother tongue were beginning to elude him. It was high time he finished this work on *The Cyclone's Eye*.

The first signs of doubt had appeared. This time, would he still possess the necessary courage and talent? The role he was playing, and which he had chosen to play, sometimes grew heavy enough to sharpen the strains inside him and open up old wounds. How could he avoid the feeling that he was losing momentum? Hadn't it all been said and done?

Waldo Joven – that was the name by which he was known in Mexico – Waldo Joven was at a loose end. Soon he would have been living in Oaxaca for four years, a standstill which was becoming dangerous in more than one respect. Once more he had felt that urge to meet destiny halfway, and since he had not found it, not altogether at least, in the gradual subsidence which had drawn him further and further south, what alternative did he have left except a similarly spaced 'return' towards the north, and who knows, given the time and opportunity, towards his origins, across the ocean? No. The idea might tempt and excite him, but it repelled him even more. He had come to this land in pursuit of unthinkable visions. Even supposing that he had failed to catch them on the wing, that was a further reason for wanting to die here. 'Joven' meant young, in Spanish. When he had come to Mexico he had been young, alert, and reborn. Fifteen years later he already felt old, as if having banked on a free resurrection he had paid the heavy price of a faster decay. Time – oh yes, Time – had passed twice as quickly.

Although he had now decided to leave her, Waldo recollected with feeling the day when Marina Chama had made him welcome at the Hotel Universal. No questions asked. They had said everything with a single look. He knew that the mestiza with the glowing eyes and burning body had been waiting for him, and that she would be the real, the adult woman he had longed for. At once he saw Doña Marina as the living embodiment of his failing quest. And she, on her side, understood that the man from the south would make her suffer the same fate that Alfonso de Seguida, her distant ancestor, had inflicted on Sanikté, the daughter of Canek. This was no ordinary guest: he had walked carrying nothing but a heavy canvas bag, a sailor's kit bag, and a parrot sitting on his shoulder. He called it Papagayo. The stranger spoke Spanish with considerable fluency and some elegance, which derived from his habit of dwelling upon the sibilant and fricative consonants. Only an occasional guttural lapse betrayed his foreign origin.

Marina Chama was just under thirty years old at the time. Her family had long ago moved out of the swamplands to try their luck in the town of the north – not hunters now, or warriors, but shopkeepers or state employees. And that was how she had come from Tabasco to Oaxaca following a young Zapotec to whom she had found herself engaged, without really knowing what it meant, at the age of seventeen. The boy had property, and for Marina's father that was enough, for it would rescue his daughter from his own decline. Once married, the young woman found herself managing a hotel, and sooner than she imagined it was her total responsibility, for a year later her husband died of an unknown illness. The marriage had hardly been consummated when he felt the first twinges and discomforts which rapidly developed into terrible pain.

After her husband's death, Marina made up her mind that she would run the Universal to the best of her ability. She took a grip on the hotel and won respect. There had never been any other man in her life until the appearance of the foreigner whose very name sounded fatally out of place and who slipped inside her innermost defences. His presence in the hotel was a disruption; it compelled her to re-examine the persona she had created, with her instincts and feelings locked inside. Marina felt inexorably attracted to Joven, lured into weaknesses which till now she had easily resisted: the more she saw how sheer the depths stretched down, the closer she ventured to the edge.

Each step forward cost efforts that left her exhausted, tears destroying the splendid make-up which she affected as the mask for her distress, but each advance brought with it the certainty that the slightest landslip would launch her into an endless fall.

The crisis lasted for weeks, and when it came to a sudden halt, not because she willed it but because the frustrations and contradictions had resolved themselves of their own accord, the widow knew that Joven would be her lover.

As for Waldo, he spent that time hoping for some irreversible event which would cut short his flight. For two years now, ever since crossing back into Mexico, he had been propelled from town to town in constant pursuit of the anonymity he had managed to construct around himself, the fortress whose keep was the books signed Raven. Marina reminded him of Little Sun, the Indian girl he once had loved and whom circumstances – those famous devices which excuse and cancel everything – had caused him to abandon, together with their son, Red Sun. Yes, 'abandon' was the word, even if under compulsion. Waldo had called the boy Red because of the colour of his hair, which had come as a wonder to the Itzas. Red must be eight years old by now, he thought, as he straightened the manuscript of *The Cyclone's Eye*. He would never see his son again, and of all the mistakes and failures in his life, he knew that this one was the least forgivable.

Marina Chama had brought him love and devotion enough to overshadow everything else, and yet a few hours before he left her for another country, with another woman, all Waldo could think of was the son he had hardly known, except for a few months of happiness destroyed by the repercussions of the past he had done his utmost to eliminate for ever. For the rest of the world he had become Raven, the writer admired because no one knew who he really was, the man they praised for the mystery that shrouded his existence and his genius. From one book to the next, Waldo had found reasons – good or bad, it didn't matter – reasons for outliving himself.

Yet at forty years of age, the hope of perpetuity was fading. Perhaps after all he had been the victim of a farce. *Finita la commedia!* And to think that he had not even been capable of giving Marina a child. At first it had been she who rejected the possibility. Then with the years she had simply raised the question, but without insisting, the way she always did with him. No doubt that was why it had taken him so long to make up his mind about breaking off a liaison which was clearly involving him in some shameful pretences. She required so little from him, yet in the end it was he who was frightened of producing a child. 'You want to make a monster!' he snarled at Marina one day. She made no answer.

Waldo loathed all the various signs of ageing which were affecting his physical appearance: white hair, flabby skin and stomach, and then those regular pains in his bowels and liver, as if some microbe carried from the south was gnawing away at him from inside. 'What rubbish!' Sometimes he had to interrupt his labours for days on end, unable to stay seated on his work table, unable to concentrate or even think. And then he would disappear on endless benders in the bars of Oaxaca, or in Monte Alban, near the Zapotec tombs, if not on more distant travels on the pretext of having his 'business' to take care of. Here, too, Marina asked no questions, although she had suspicions.

On two or three occasions Joven had gone up to Mexico City – reluctant trips. In Oaxaca, in spite of everything, he felt relatively secure, whereas in the capital he might be exposed to some awkward or compromising encounter. Whenever possible he preferred to settle that kind of problem – business or depression – on the spot. He had his own post office box, general delivery. And after that, tequila and mescal, before regaining the safe and reassuring presence of Marina.

This time, as he boarded the train to Mexico City, Waldo felt suddenly apprehensive. Maybe he shouldn't have left when *The Cyclone's Eye* was waiting on his desk, only a few pages from the end. He had a foreboding that afterwards things would be harder, more like before. But the context and background were really becoming too stifling in Oaxaca. Hard as Marina had tried, the ghosts were bound to come knocking at the door of the Universal. There were times when Waldo felt that if it had not been for her he would already have cleared off.

Camacho's coming to power sounded the alarm. It was a signal of distress, and the feeling of persecution mingled in a frightening chorus with the memory of that dreadful crossing when he had thought he would never come out alive, and with the other more tenuous but equally haunting memory of the literary transposition in *Journey Without End*, with that wretch Harley as stoker of the doomed ship.

In the days of the presidency of Lázaro Cardenas, Waldo had believed that the old demons would never rise again. He had chosen Mexico as the land of exile because of Hidalgo, Juarez, Pancho Villa, Zapata . . . The Land of Revolution! Where the revolt of the poor did not obey the call of any ideology but that of hunger and justice. And there had been Obregón, and finally Cardenas. Back in the south Waldo had heard talk of the red and black flags (he would have paid dearly to see them, but it was still too soon for him to surface again, prisoner that he was of the initial maelstrom); they had told him that the people were sharing in the decisions and that the latifundia were at last to be divided up among the peasants. When the buried men, the living dead, emerged into the light he did indeed recognize the reminders of his own past that lived on in this country. But he hardly had time to convince himself of the effects of socialism in the Mexican vein before the demons returned. The only mistake Waldo had made when he left his jungle lair was to have posed as a refugee from the war in Spain. For a man with no papers in the port of Veracruz, anything was possible. You could call yourself Joven, be born in Barcelona on 31 October 1899, ask for asylum from a brother country, and get your naturalization fast. Before settling in Oaxaca . . . But there the rats were already at work, and from the day he first arrived they had scented the trail and made inquiries about the foreigner. One night, Marina Chama had shown them the door at the Hotel Universal. Three days later they were asking her questions in the street. Popular government or not, Oaxaca was no exception to other towns in Mexico: backed by Germany and Italy, who were looking for support from the American continent and who favoured the return to a rightist regime, fascist bands were organizing centres of resistance to the government by playing on the contradictions of the local middle classes and sowing terror among the working-class and peasant populations. So it would never be over! If these people discovered who he really was, Waldo was going to have trouble preserving the peace he had finally found, or almost found, with

Doña Marina. Whether they recognized Raven or Bremen it would come to the same thing. For them, the laureate of the American Indians and of workers in their struggles would deserve the same label as the ex-revolutionary from Munich, and that was 'Marxist scum'. Better that they should believe the tale of the Catalan anarchist, exiled, embittered, shorn of all militant ambitions and involved in some trivial literary work or other. Let him write his life story and keep out of our way!

Apparently the *cabrones* were satisfied with this version until the arrival of a new character whose presence upset the terms of the scenario. Rudolph Bach resembled a kind of monstrous albino. With his face and skin peppered with red and white blotches, head bald except for a plume of very fine, dead white hair, aquiline nose, metallic blue eyes made more intense by the absence of eyebrows, and a body so extremely thin that every joint stuck out, his appearance struck those who met him with a curious blend of disgust and fascination. It was the latter that prevailed in the end, however, because his character and intellectual brilliance redeemed his looks. He was said to be an archaeologist – at any rate that was how he introduced himself to Waldo Joven on the night of his arrival at the Universal, saying that he wanted to stay there for several months, long enough to complete his researches into the tomb cities of Mitla. With respect – at any rate – people called him the *licenciado*.

Waldo distrusted him at once. For a scholar, this Bach had some odd habits. He got up late, and spent most of his evenings reading foreign journals which he received by post. Sitting in the morning room behind his magazine or newspaper he would watch the comings and goings of the hotel guests, and of the proprietors too. Certainly no one saw much of him for the rest of the day, nor did anybody know exactly how he spent his time. Sometimes he would disappear for three or four days in a row on his supposed expeditions, but wearing city clothing – always an elegant archaeologist! 'Look at him,' Waldo whispered to Doña Marina, 'with his rimmed glasses, and cigarette-case and holder, all in gold, they're gold. And only drinks imported foreign beer! I wonder where the cash comes from . . .'

'Hush, are you jealous?'

'If you're talking about the way he keeps looking at you, he can undress you with his eyes as much as he likes, I don't give a damn! You haven't gone that far yet, have you?'

'There's no need to be so crude.'

'Oh, don't tell me you're completely indifferent to that pale white skin and that face like a Nordic god!'

'You're mad, Waldo.'

'That's quite possible. Just as it's possible that this damned Bach is here on my account.'

'. . .'

'A German. We've seen how they work in Europe, you have no idea. Panzers, Messerschmitts, incendiary bombs over Guernica, I do know them, the Germans . . . There's going to be war soon, you'll see. Not just in Spain but all over . . . Starting with a country that . . . I love, Poland . . .'

'You didn't tell me you've been there.'

'And even over here! I tell you, Marina, don't trust that man.'

What made it yet harder for Joven's companion to understand these occasional admonitions was that at other times a current of sympathy appeared to flow between the two men. They conducted some lively conversations over a glass of beer. Waldo would talk about the Indians in the south, while the other seemed fascinated by his first-hand knowledge of the subject, even though it came not from an archaeological point of view but rather from experience on the ground and an inner understanding gained from living. One day Marina surprised them talking in a language she did not understand. Later that night in their room, when she expressed her astonishment, all Waldo would tell her was: 'I studied in Berlin, a long time ago . . .'

Soon Joven was taking his new 'friend' on his nocturnal excursions, from *cantina* to *pulquería*. Both of them returned quite drunk, with plenty of commotion in the street and down the corridors of the sleeping hotel. You would think that 'the Spaniard' – as they called him in the locality – wanted to find out how far the other would go, and whether he would follow him even on his personal descent into hell. And to what ends? . . . For Marina, in any case, it was an ordeal whose ill effects it took all her moral strength to undo. She saw in the *licenciado* an element of discord and disorder which had come to play havoc with the precarious equilibrium established between herself and Joven. He was depriving her of the exclusivity of her only love. Till now, Marina had humoured many of the whims and escapades of 'the Spaniard'. He had a quick temper, and was constantly on edge if anybody got too curious about his writing work. He could do as he pleased both with her and away from her, but what she could not bear was the German playing on reflexes in Waldo which belonged to a bygone past that was not and never would be hers. But she was well aware that this protective screen was also what linked her to Waldo. For goodness' sake let him remain dark and laconic, seamless, opaque and impenetrable, rather than be the man he was now, riddled with ghosts and fancies, torn by the lightning of distant events that she did not understand. Waldo was changing. Day by day he seemed to grow more fragile and unstable, like a man wavering on his own foundations, a flame ready to wink out and die with the next puff of wind . . . No! She wanted him masculine, altogether a man. Entire, with violence, not like a blind bullock in a panic. Or else it would be better never to have met him. The more Bach's influence grew, the more she lost touch with Joven. What she had loved about him was that with the exception of the time he spent sitting at his writing desk, everything, absolutely everything, was given to her. Waldo no longer loved her as before. Shivering, she thought about the time, not long ago, when he would take her every day, sometimes even when she was unclean and would have preferred to be untouched.

Waldo was drifting away.

Marina Chama started to prepare herself for the day when he would be gone for good. She knew what remained to be done, and what it was that she intended to take from him against his will. Deep inside her lay the memory of Sanikté, the white flower.

To seal their friendship, Rudolph gave Waldo a present, a magnificent Dobermann which they baptized Kaiser. Marina rebelled. There was already Cholo, the yellow dog from the mountains. And Papagayo, who stuck, thank God, to whistling and spitting, and couldn't say a single word. Waldo explained that he too had a right to his own dog. 'Not a mongrel, a real dog. I'm sick of the stupid animals that lie about in this rotten hotel!'

'I didn't ask you to bring the parrot.'

'But that's another story. And then, Cholo and Kaiser together make a symbol, don't they?' Joven burst out laughing. 'If they weren't both males, what fine mongrels they would give us! The dark and the fair, God and the Devil, ha ha!'

Waldo became so fond of the animal that he took it on all his nocturnal wanderings. Sometimes it even made him forget about the presence of Bach. His hitherto extremely contradictory feelings about the German subsided, as if the *licenciado* was becoming part of the scenery, a familiar character in the comic opera that played daily in the streets of Oaxaca, with its cast of the good, the bad, and all the range between. It took several weeks for the ritual of the performances to be upset by an event that was worthy of the stage.

There were three of them sitting in the convertible parked crosswise in the street. Two were very young, not more than eighteen, one at the steering wheel, the other next to him. The third was in his thirties, and obese; he filled the whole of the back seat on his own, and wore a fedora and a white suit. All of them were laughing. They were also blocking the path of the Hispano, which had pulled up a few yards away from them, and when Waldo sounded his horn they only laughed louder. Under the glow of the streetlamp they were clearly visible, the three *borrachos* – for that is what Waldo thought they were at first, returning from a celebration like himself and Bach, and having some drunken fun. He was about to laugh as well, and invite them for a final drink, when the youngest of the passengers got out of the car and starting kicking at the radiator of the Hispano.

'Hey, *muchacho*, what's the matter?' shouted Joven, throwing open the door and ready to make a rush at the aggressor.

Bach held him by the arm.

'Take it easy! Don't get mixed up in this!'

'What are you expecting, Rudolph? I'm just going to cool this *niño* down. And I'm not afraid of the fat one with his belt and armband either. I know these types. They shout, they click their heels, but one little clip around the ear and they're squealing off to mother!'

And Waldo got out of the car.

Facing him was the corpulent man, his belly heaving with strangled laughter.

'Here, *gringo* . . . hee . . . that's how it is! If you . . . hee . . . can't take it, better get out! Go back where you came from!'

Waldo said nothing. He understood. The urge to punch that bag of lard was strong, but the gesture would have taken him down a road which for years he had deliberately avoided. Yet faced with this concrete presence of violence it was all he could do to contain the bursts or rage that seethed inside him. He clenched his fists, to keep them still. To succumb under the pressure of memories and this one event would mean wrecking what had been so laboriously constructed: one good right hand into a fat belly, and he'd wipe out the years of patient effort to remake a life and (almost!) to restore a virginity.

Something slammed into Waldo's back, and he was tripped as he staggered forward. He toppled over, arms outstretched, and a trash can clanged to the ground beside him with a sound of cymbals. A rat went scurrying along the gutter, and the man in the white suit roared with laughter. Up till now, Kaiser the dog had been lying, panting, in the back of the Hispano. Everything had happened very fast, but when he saw his master felled he sprang out of the seat and straight through the open door. One twisting bound and he was at the leader's throat.

Still on his hands and knees, Waldo shouted 'Kaiser!', trying to call him off, but it did no good. The Dobermann growled and tore and the fat man thrashed about like a clown in a circus. A gun fired twice, in quick succession, and the dog gave a yelp, and then fell at the feet of the screaming clown. Waldo reached out and stroked the warm fur of the dying animal, and felt its final spasms and the long tremor before the breathing stopped. He looked up wildly and his eyes met a sight that his mind rejected: Rudolph Bach, his friend, was standing by the bonnet of the Hispano with his arm jutting forward, holding a small pistol. It looked so incongruous in that bony white hand. Rudolph was no longer aiming at the dog. He was looking at Waldo, and slowly his arm traversed towards the new target.

The gun was pointing straight at Waldo's head, almost touching. He stood up. Nobody was laughing now. They were as motionless as pawns standing on a chessboard criss-crossed by reflections from the street lamp gleaming off the coachwork of the two cars. Waldo stood still, his arms dangling, his heart in his mouth, as if suspended by an invisible thread spun down from the centre of the night. He knew that the initiative was not with him. Without a word, Bach stepped over the dog's dead body and walked towards the convertible. The others followed. They all climbed into the car, which reversed, swung forward in a U-turn, gunned its motor and was quickly lost to view in the darkness. Waldo had not stirred.

Next day a young man turned up at the Universal to collect Señor Bach's belongings. As Waldo was not there, Doña Marina complied and asked no questions. Her companion had told her what had happened, and now he was hard at work in his room. There was no point in disturbing him. She said that she would see to the move in person, and felt only too happy to be rid of the intruder at last. Obviously she forgot in her secret delight the implications the incident was certain to carry for Waldo.

Bach moved into the Viejo Castillo, a ramshackle hotel about three miles out of town on the road to Parián, and a meeting place for supporters of national socialism.

Joven wondered why the *licenciado* had chosen that particular moment to remove his mask. He could easily have gone on spying with impunity and making the Universal his headquarters. The intervention of the dog did not explain a thing. It must be that Bach had collected all the information he wanted, for him to have deliberately broken contact over such an avoidable incident. Who was he protecting? A second-rate killer? But perhaps he had wanted to prevent things turning out even worse. What if it had been the fat man who had drawn and fired, not at the dog but at Joven . . . then that would imply that Bach was more attached to the Spaniard than appearances might suggest, and for reasons as obscure as they were likely to be disturbing . . . A net was tightening around Waldo, and he could see the meshes clearly. For once, he greeted the prospect of the trip to Mexico City with some relief. It would enable him to keep his distance, and draw breath. He needed to reflect.

When he returned it would be time to decide his next move. What he did not know was that the chips would already be down. He could not imagine how thoroughly the meeting with Ruth Powell would determine his choices and his future.

All the same, Joven had set off with the firm intention of sticking to his usual role as the literary agent representing the interests of Mr Raven. A few weeks earlier he had received a letter from Hollywood asking if the film rights for *The Tale of the Chimera* were still free. Waldo had written back to the producer, Powell, a familiar name, saying that they were. Then a cable had reached him from Mexico City, signed Ruth Powell. The actress, and Powell's wife, was longing to meet him and to start the ball rolling, particularly because she was hoping to play the part of Nieves, the mestiza. Arno, a young Austrian smitten with the ideals of the French Revolution, who volunteers to join the troops fighting for Miguel Hidalgo, sacrifices his and his friends' lives for her in the battle of Monte de las Cruces in October 1810.

Given the circumstances, Waldo did not resist the temptation to go and see for himself. After all, he would not want the dream factory to turn his book into a costume drama set in an exotic locale. He said that he would meet Señora Powell in a bar in the Zocalo – take it or leave it. High-handed manners for so important a lady – and good-looking, too: he remembered seeing her in *Tripwire* at the Triumfo in Oaxaca about three years before – but she was going to have to get used to his way of doing things if she wanted to make an impression on Waldo Joven. In his reply he simply insisted on the discretion which was his chief concern.

The square swarmed with people. The traffic was dense, and the circling cars, the din of horns and engines, the cries of the newspaper vendors and the hawkers of lottery tickets, the bustle of passers-by along the crowded pavements, all combined to afflict Waldo with a growing sense of strain. The ferment of the capital kindled too many memories of other crowds and other clamours. As he headed back northward, Oaxaca the Red, with its baked clay houses and the reasonable proportions of a provincial capital, had offered a viable balance between his longing for peace and quiet and his need to make contact again with white civilization. Mexico City did not suit him. He suffocated there. Caught in its tides of commotion and spinning in its eddies, he felt himself being drawn upward, and his getaway fever mounted. This was no resting place, still less a sanctuary. In Oaxaca he sometimes used to watch the sunrise from the hill where Benito Juarez holds his torch of stone above the valley, a signal of hope. The sun he loved so much in Oaxaca seemed aggressive here, the visual equivalent of the raucous squeal of thousands of knife blades being sharpened. Rather than the blazing sun of the central square he preferred the shade of the nearby side-streets. Before he left them, as he emerged from the anonymous little tourist hotel where he always stayed, Waldo had taken care to conceal himself behind a pair of heavy dark glasses.

There she was. He recognized her at once. Almost as beautiful as he had imagined, though perhaps that creamy skin was paler than in the film, and the traces of crows' feet at the corners of her eyes were artfully camouflaged by her makeup. Her flounced white dress clung to the lines of her figure as she sat composed on the edge of her chair, sipping at her granizado. The neckline displayed a hint of swelling breasts.

'Señora Powell?'

She put down her glass and looked up at him from beneath fluttering eyelashes.

'Señor Joven!'

She held out her hand, and he surprised himself by bending to kiss it as if suddenly reverting to the practice of gestures long since unlearned.

In the conversation that followed, Waldo paid scant attention to the exchange of professional remarks, but focused on observing the woman, and attempting to account for her elusive charm. He had not expected to be moved that way. Ruth – 'Do you mind if I call you Ruth?' – appeared to him like a synthesis of all the women he had known *before*, in his previous life, on the other side of the Atlantic. Carlotta in Berlin, Franziska the Muse of Munich, Vanessa in London . . . and all the others, lovers for a night, passing encounters in a port or on a pavement. Yet possessed in addition of that mysterious blend of sophistication and profound unselfconsciousness which seems to be the special secret of American women. Waldo had never met an American woman, or not like this, with the pleasure of lively conversation, and the desire to look, touch and know her. He attempted to master his feelings by telling himself that he had no business to be interested. All right, she was attractive, but the exercise of that attraction seemed to him automatic, not necessarily done for the benefit of a stranger who meant absolutely nothing to her. Waldo also told himself that what he felt was possibly nothing but an instant expression of the pressures he had been facing for the last few months. All at once he missed Marina and wished that he had never left Oaxaca. Marina, whom he still loved with a passion as consuming as all those passions which had swallowed up his life. No, the point was that it was time to move on, and to fall faster . . .

Behind the dark glasses, his eyes never left her.

'You should make the trip to Los Angeles, Señor Joven, you wouldn't regret it. There are great opportunities there for a man like you.'

'Oh no, never!'

She smiled, and laid her hand surreptitiously on his.

'Oh, really! You Mexicans are such queer people!'

Then she asked him about Raven.

'You must know who he is, surely?'

Waldo delivered his usual pitch about the world-weary writer retiring from civilization to live in an Indian village somewhere in southern Mexico. Joven had never met Raven: his 'client' had always insisted that their communications should be conducted by letter and kept to a bare minimum.

'Oh sure, I know, just like they say in the papers. But if you ask me, my friend, that is one big heap of baloney. And you know it, don't you?'

That brought Waldo down to earth again, and now he had to back-pedal. He had said too much or gone too far. Fool! Here you are, never letting anything slip out, watching every detail, and just because you take a liking to a woman you're ready to recruit another accomplice. No. Better to go back and face up to that fascist rabble at the Viejo Castillo; better to revert to the script as written by Rudolph Bach, no matter how it came out . . .

But when Ruth Powell suggested that they should go back to her hotel to sign the contract he made no objection.

'My husband had it all drawn up. I knew you'd agree in the end.'

Either way he would have signed, he reminded himself, but this formal process of clauses and subclauses took him on to safer territory. As long as it was only money they had to discuss . . .

They took a cab. Waldo forced himself to ignore his own responses when Ruth sat right up against him in the back seat. He stayed mute during the ride, except for uttering the necessary 'yes' or 'no' to punctuate the actress's long monologue as she outlined the main plans for her film. A few minutes later they were entering the foyer of the Regis. There, Waldo did not have time to wonder what attitude he should take, or what his reaction would be if Señora Powell were to invite him to her room, because they had only just set foot in the hotel when a little man with a tuft of beard on his chin hailed him and took hold of his arm.

'But I know you! It is you, Raven, the famous writer . . . I find you at last, and all by chance!'

Waldo listened in bemusement to this talking jack-in-the-box. He turned to Ruth, suspecting that she had helped to set the trap, but she seemed just as stunned as he was. The man went on chattering at full speed and unfortunately at maximum volume, so that passers-by began to stop and take an interest in the trio standing right in the middle of the lobby.

'I'm Fito Malinas, reporter for *Mañana*. I knew I was on to something, kept telling those idiots back at the office all this time. They told me I was crazy. Even old Fédé, the editor, he told me he was sick of having me waste my time chasing shadows. It's been hard going, and a long time, Señor Raven, but I found your trail. Here I was going to look in Oaxaca, and you come here and fall right into my arms. Raven! Ah!'

Waldo could not believe his ears. This was what he had always been afraid of, and worse still, it was happening in the foyer of one of the biggest hotels in Mexico City and in front of the disturbing Señora Powell, who could splash the news all over America.

'You're making a mistake. My name is Joven, Waldo Joven.'

But Fito Malinas was not to be put off, and his excited crescendo was starting to attract a crowd.

'I know the score. The post office box and everything. A clever arrangement, Señor Raven, terrific, but not good enough to fool Fito Malinas!'

'Look, let's cut the comedy. See this? It's my passport. I was born in Spain and I now have Mexican citizenship. No connection with your writer. Now let us past!!

And as much for Ruth's benefit as for their growing audience, Waldo grunted:

'Another scoop-happy reporter. These people have no respect for anything, not even honest people's private lives.'

Malinas sniggered out loud.

'Talking about papers, what do you think of this, Señor Raven?'

And he took from his inside jacket pocket a photograph that Waldo recognized at once. On the back of it, he knew, would be the words: *'National Anti-Locust Campaign, South Chiapas, April–May 1926.'* In his own handwriting.

'Who gave you that?'

'A man called Joe Cartridge, know who I mean? In his cell. I was researching a story about the old Wobbly movement for my paper, and he gave it to me so I could find you. That's what he said – "As long as you find him, that's enough!" On the left, see, with the sun helmet, that's him, and in the middle, with the field glasses slung across your shoulder, that, Señor Raven, is you. He told me, told me all about it. Twelve years ago, but you haven't changed much, eh? You didn't have the moustache, and your hair was not so grey, but it's you all right!'

'Give me that!'

He tried to snatch the photograph out of the journalist's hand, but Malinas hung on to it. They wrestled briefly, then seeing that it was a losing battle Waldo decided it was time for desperate measures. Okay, he couldn't get hold of the photo; never mind that, the point was to get away! He swung his fist hard into the other man's face, and felled him. The crowd parted with a hubbub of voices, and Waldo took advantage of their surprise to plunge into the gap, without a backward glance at the reporter who lay winded on the ground. He ran for the exit and out onto the avenue, shouldering guests and passers-by out of his way. Nothing could stop him.

He ducked into the first street on the left and raced on, never looking behind him. But the street sloped upwards slightly, and after a few dozen strides his legs grew heavy and he started to pant. He was out of condition, had been for four years, and his belly felt like lead . . . Shit! Where to now? He had to keep going, find the way out. His neck bulged, and there was a painful throbbing in his veins. A sudden stitch in his right side racked him with such a violent pain that he had to slow down. He looked round. Still no sign of pursuit, but he forced himself back into a run, halted for breath again, leaning against the fence of a construction site, and laboured on. He was stopped by the roar of a powerful engine and a screech of brakes. The police, for sure . . . He didn't dare turn round.

'Waldo! Waldo! This way . . .'

It was a woman's voice. Ruth, sitting at the wheel of a big Packard and leaning over to open the nearside door. Waldo did not hesitate. He had no choice.

The car shot off through a maze of nameless streets. Destination Hell, maybe, but now he didn't care. Waldo had scented the wild, familiar smell of adventure. It had returned again, a stronger spell than ever, and he surrendered to it.

So the two of them disappeared into the night, as both of them had longed to do, Waldo because that was his raison d'être, Ruth because it was her chance to put an end to the tedium of a marriage which had become little more than a professional convenience. For some time, Powell had been keeping his favours and his fading virility for a series of falling starlets.

For that one scorching night, the wire mattress in Waldo's room became the marriage bed for one of those meetings of sexual attraction and verbal exaltation in which private dramas and historic passions are sealed. There was no future in what they said and did, except that it kept them moving. That frightening paradox was not the least cause of their euphoria. They were forgetting; things were beginning again.

The lovers headed south in the Packard. Fito Malinas, Cartridge and Rudolph Bach might all be in collusion. Nothing would stop them now that their path was clear. The plan was for Waldo to return to Oaxaca to pick up his manuscripts, and particularly *The Cyclone's Eye*, still lying on his desk; Ruth would wait for him at the Hotel Francia while he said goodbye to

Doña Marina . . . that would be the hardest. Yet there was no bad faith in Waldo's assuming that his companion of the last four years would understand the situation. What choice did he really have? Hadn't she always known that she would carry little weight in an emergency? Emergency: it was a word Waldo was fond of. In this case an emergency meant disappearing, crossing the border and changing his life and his name, up there in Los Angeles. It meant surviving once again. How could Doña Marina miss a man whose solitary aim and theme was now reduced to sheer survival? What did she want with a man half dead? Marina embodied life – deep, dense, maternal, scarlet. Ruth was the complete opposite of the tropical jungle: even her beauty was tamed, and Waldo would never lose himself inside it as he had done in the body, the dark hair and warmth of the Indian woman . . . No, this time he wouldn't have to hack his way through to find breathing room, to avoid being choked by the imprisoning tangle of lianas. He would know where he was going in advance. It was over, and better so.

When La Chama saw him walk into the Universal, suitcase in hand, a day sooner than planned and at a time when no train could have brought him from Mexico City, she knew that the irreparable had come about. Gently she shooed away Chama, the yellow dog who lay curled at her feet and was reluctant to move. Papagayo trilled with delight on her perch.

'*Maldito!*'

The curse was aimed at the bird, not at the father of the child which had been growing inside her for three months now. If Joven had not left for Mexico City she would probably have given him the news already. She came to meet him and kissed him affectionately on the cheek, smiling as she did so. She would say nothing.

Waldo went straight up to his workroom, with Marina following.

'Do you want a beer?' she asked.

Unusually for him, Waldo refused, and that confirmed Marina's fears. He had begun to sort out the papers strewn across his desk. There was no need for him to tell her how deeply agitated he was feeling: she could read that in his face.

'You have come back to me with something on your mind, *querido*.'

'No sign of Bach and company?' he answered. 'Nobody's been asking for me, or calling on the telephone? No messages?'

'No, nothing. No one.'

'I have to leave again. An emergency.'

Marina almost spoke the words that were on the tip of her tongue – 'a woman' – but it was no good, it didn't matter. The thing that counted, the one reality, was that she was losing him. The pretext was a lesser question. The wrench was not out there in some bar or waiting in a hotel; it was here inside her that Marina was being torn. For an Itza woman, a *chingada*, jealousy had no roots, and only grief still tied her to the heart of the earth, beyond the weather and its clouds of bitter rain.

Waldo explained that he had an errand to do, helping an exile with no official papers to cross the border.

'Oh yes,' was all Marina could say.

Her calm and resignation were more than Waldo could stand, and his concern gave way to irritation. Certainly Marina might perfectly well have accepted his story: he had travelled north before on similar missions. It was part of his role as a Spaniard in exile, which he had been determined to play to the full, seeing it as an essential condition of his own security. Compared with what he had at stake, the risks were small, and in any case Waldo was not sorry to find in these minor escapades the spice that was missing from his new life. They were his fine but solid link with everything he once had been. By helping these stateless strays into the United States he could feel that he was still of some use. If they needed a man with experience in the underground life, then Waldo would not disappoint them. And some day these trips might turn out to be valuable practice for himself.

Seeing that Marina was hardly listening to his explanations, Waldo gave up the pretence.

'I've been found out, understand?'

'. . .'

'They're on my trail, right behind me. They may be in town already, I only have a few hours left.'

'Then it is you who will cross the Rio Bravo today.'

'You will join me later . . . I'll send word.'

'Unless you take the highway through Nogales . . .'

'What are you saying? . . . You will come, Marina, won't you? I'll leave you the Hispano.'

'And Papagayo too.'

'No, please don't cry. I love you.'

He took her in his arms, pulled her close and kissed her hard on the mouth. She merely stood still, with her arms by her sides.

'I do not want to die of my memories, like Sanikté the white flower . . .'

'No, Marina, my love, my life . . . Don't say that, not now. How often have I told you that you are not Sanikté, and all those lousy stories were ancient . . . no, let's not go over that again.'

'I will live. We will live.'

'Of course we'll live, *chatita mía!* And we will go on loving each other, you'll see . . . Now, give me some time to myself, please – a moment, *un momentito* . . . I have to hurry, and I must collect my manuscripts.'

'Ah, the books . . . So I have them to thank for the pleasure of one last visit.'

'Don't spoil everything, Marina. Wait downstairs. I won't be long.'

And while Waldo rounded up his papers, re-reading the final pages of *The Cyclone's Eye* as if the death of Nahà and her sons proved that he was somehow in the right, Marina Chama went down to the patio. There, in the shade of a cabled column, she could release the fire inside her. No tears remained in her dark eyes as she stared at the fresco which had been painted by an unnamed artist on one of the containing walls, and which the French architect had preserved in the construction of the building later to become the Hotel Universal. The hoarse cry that tore itself from her lungs rang out against the polychrome wall with force enough to strike the spark. The shapes came to life and the colours shimmered into a riot of mute words, painted feelings, manifold visions, symbols that spanned perspectives receding to infinity . . .

The four suns spun into each other, and out of their collision rose a serpent whose coils wound themselves around a whole race of dying men. Racked by invisible tortures, they writhed and strained. Beneath their feet long tongues of flame erupted, and as they licked upwards, wreathed in great eddies of smoke, the tortured men appeared to regain their smiles. Their faces softened, white wings sprouted from their shoulders, and they soared majestically upward to the clouds. There the Great Horse curvetted, all whinnies and flaring nostrils. In the meadow strewn with flowers it was joined by a pack of roving dogs which howled and bared their teeth, snapping at the hocks of the white charger; but each time they leaped and their jaws clashed together they came away with nothing but mouthfuls of star dust. The sky rained tears of blood and gold which met at the confluence of rivers edged with lava. Far in the distance the Volcano rumbled. But the loudest sounds came from the instruments in the frieze: flutes, *chicas* or *pequeñas*, drums, bugles, sackbuts and harps combined, a royal song. Then suddenly the fire blazed up again on the horizon, virgin, immaculate and free. And there was no more space to run to. The frontiers of the world came hurtling from all directions, to reduce themselves to straight lines converging on a single vanishing point and be lost in the darkness. A faint gleam lingered at the edge of the gloomy forest, stirring with deliquescent shadows, then slowly faded into the rolling eye of the Great White Horse. Dead . . . And there were no zopilotes to feed upon the carcass. Vultures belonged to a different universe from this place of the Apocalypse.

Marina Chama closed her eyes. Her head swam with the twilight whose golden glow flooded the patio of the Hotel Universal.

4

Of course I did not stay at the Hotel Universal. How could I, when there was nothing there to find? After the cemetery I headed for *Calle* Humboldt and discovered that it bore no resemblance to my memories. I did not recognize the houses, or even the smells and colours. The people themselves came straight out of a photographic album for the tourist trade: their faces – either too friendly or too aggressive – no longer tallied with my image of our neighbours as I thought I remembered them. I attempted to introduce myself: they answered with belches, shrugs, or that uniquely Mexican mode of elaborate speechifying, to tell me in the end, no, the Universal, *no hay*.

On the corner of the street I did see the remains of a building that must have been demolished. Was it fire, or an earthquake? The street hawker who sold me a city guide sniggered as he told me that the *casa* had been so decrepit that the municipality had to issue a demolition order. A danger to us all, *hombre!*

As I walked across that patch of waste ground littered with scorched wooden beams and rubble I thought I saw traces of paint high up on a section of the dividing wall. I hadn't dreamed that, at least: the fresco with its horses, penitents and whirling suns still danced beneath my eyes, reconstituted whole, as it looked in the old days. Unreality was those other people. Never mind them: I knew. I had seen the gravestone with the inscription 'Marina Chama, 1909–1945'.

In order to escape the vision, to stop thinking, I dived into the Bar Colón, which had kept its place all right, and was just the way I remembered. I ordered a Berreteaga, the first but not the last, because it was inside the smoky tavern that I spent nearly all of my time during my brief stay in Oaxaca. The rest of the time I lodged – for want of the Universal – at the Hotel Francia. Not because of the Señora, no – how well I remembered the day, not long before I left for England, when she told me the whole story, with a wealth of detail which I could have done without. It hurt then, and it still did. I stayed at the Francia because the guide said it was where D. H. Lawrence had written a famous letter to the critic Middleton Murry. The Oxford reflex, I suppose – after all, that is what I was, what I also was, a very British kind of intellectual. Not even the most abject skinful could wash away the signs of that education, or eradicate the behaviour and the thoughts that go with that culture.

The guide extolled the location and perfect climate of Oaxaca, and that was good news for the picture postcard buyers and the devotees of American Express. For me, Oaxaca was a nightmare. Anyway, nobody saw me as a *gringo*. I was a part of the furniture, a piece of local colour, as if I had never left the place . . .

The received wisdom has it that people drink in order to forget. The notion will seem presumptuous, but in those days I used to maintain that I drank in order to remember. With hindsight, it does appear to me that the whole thing was connected, not to any so-called father fixation but to my constant preoccupation with my own character. There is a kind of idiotic 'literary survey' in which they ask questions like 'Who is your favourite character in fiction?' If I had had to answer that question on the spur of the moment I would probably have said Don Quixote, or who knows, maybe even Moby Dick, yet my innermost conviction would have been that I myself embodied the most absorbing character in a fictional outline still to be developed. More than the sacrosanctity of fate, with its taste of stale booze out of yesterday's glass, I cared about the way fiction might be integrated into my own life.

Now, when a natural concern for critical judgement leads me to consider the question of Raven's biography – and really there was no other question – in the light of all I know, but also in the shadow of everything that has come to seem unreliable about that leaning tower of data, I tell myself that no matter how great its commitment to reality there is something apocryphal about the act of writing, from the very first word. What does it matter if the evidence alleged may be suspect, unauthentic, speculative or indeed heretical? Didn't the word originally signify 'kept secret'? That was already a lot more interesting! So the fact of being cast out from among the Churches, considered as the black sheep, examined, disputed and vindictively attacked – for ignorance of scholarly wisdom, banishment; for misjudging the way the wind blows, crucifixion! – all that hardly matters, compared to the perverse delights which are gratified in laying claim to canonical virtues. I have always preferred those books in the Bible whose authority is open to question. In my days at Farlow School it was my way of playing with fire, and of reconciling my natural atheism (and my father's too, or so I thought) and Uncle Charlie's anticlerical tirades with the necessities of a schooling shackled to State Anglicanism. I recall being particularly fond of the book of Daniel, which has in fact been judged apocryphal by one or two malicious or embittered minds, such as Renan's. Oh, the dream of Nebuchadnezzar! Read my essays, listen to my rhetoric, and you would think that I took myself for the prophet! '*If ye will not make known unto me the dream, with the interpretation thereof, ye shall be cut in pieces, and your houses shall be made a dunghill.*' But on the subject of mythology, it was Silenus who turned up at Oaxaca, even though it all got mixed up in my everyday life in a farcical uproar fit for the gods of Olympus. The lower I sank, the more those old school songs revived. It was as if Paul Arthur Smith and his series had exhausted the Mexican material which I had come to soak up, by absorbing it into the film stock, or drowning it in the whirr of the camera's motor. Adrift in my native town, I clung to landmarks out of another world. For want of finding what I sought somewhere inside, I made do with the carapace. I plodded laboriously on, carrying my house on my back. I was a tortoise, and I would have rather been a hermit crab and stolen the shell of the *borracho* with a skinful of wine, slumped against a wall in the blaze of noon with his sombrero tipped over his face. Instead I got stuck behind a table in the Bar Colón, chasing prophetic rainbows. Every time some flash of savage clarity seemed to show me that perched on the edge of my glass was the meaning of my quest, or of life, or simply of what I was doing here at the source, turned inside out like a dirty worn-out glove, I would find my head teeming with images of Midas. King Midas, with his ass's ears, impossible to hide! It was pointless to spend all night and day running through that maze of haunted streets: alcohol turns nothing into gold, speech is not silver, and asses bray, the better to live . . . Like the Phrygian king I would have liked to drink bull's blood and choke on the stuff. But the bullring of Tomalín was far away, and I wasn't brave enough to take the bus – anyway the bullfight season was nearly over.

Towards the end of his life, Raven drank because he felt diminished and degraded. At the beginning of mine – of my adult life, I mean – I was trying to do the same, not from chagrin but from innocent conviction. I believed that alcohol would give me the strength to continue – the initiatory drug that Nebuchadnezzar's mages had lacked.

In reality, the four days and almost three nights that I spent in the protective confines of the Bar Colón left me in a state of unprecedented exhaustion and depression.

The little steam train had just chugged out of the no less tiny station of San Cristóbal de Las Casas. You would think you were moving through a miniature world, for small-scale models. But suddenly the darkness was broken by the spectacular brilliance of huge curls of flame across the sky. By their light the travellers could see the metal carcasses of looming giants moving closer, a new set of tutelary gods emerging from the shadows to urge forgetful watchers to offer a respectful greeting. 'Pemex!' grunted a peasant voice, in a tone blending pride with fear. 'Pemex!' sighed a woman's more disenchanted voice. Michael Mateos cleaned a segment of dirty window with the sleeve of his jacket, as if the gesture would be enough to reduce the sight to a less staggering scale. Clouds of rain and smoke seethed together in a strange, disquieting dance. Driven by the wind, the small puffs of steam from the locomotive gave the appearance of being generated somewhere among the flares. As the *Ferrocarriles Nacionales* train picked up speed, Michael's attention was captured for a moment by the derricks and installations of the state oil company, but he quickly tired of them and huddled back into his corner by the window. He tugged the edges of his jacket together, not so much for warmth

– the carriage was stifling hot – as to disengage himself from the man on his right who kept puffing at a rank cigar. He was an Indian, as broad as he was tall, with feet hardly touching the floor, a very flat nose, bulging eyes, high, prominent cheekbones, and a dreamy, almost unreal air. In any case it was a race that Mateos did not recognize. The young man folded his arms and closed his eyes, trying to catch up on his last day's sleep. The train still had another fifty miles of jolts and grinding stops to cover before it came to Ococingo, in the hills of Chiapas. First there had been the tunnel on the first night: just after boarding the train bound for the port of Santa Cruz, Michael had fallen into a deep sleep disturbed by dreams he did not remember. Then the waiting – with an empty head and stomach – for a second, slower and more hypothetical train which would go in the direction of Tuxtla-Gutiérrez. He had arrived there without even noticing the hours and hours which had slipped by. How long had he been gone? What day had he left Oaxaca? Rattling along in the little express bound for San Cristóbal, it would have been hard for him to produce a clear answer to these questions. He was following his path, under the more and more powerful illusion that when the railroad track ran out at the edge of the jungle he would be able to recognize the trail that led to Raven. So far he had not found it, and the halt at Oaxaca had almost proved fatal. In any case it had been a mistake, and a bad one. At the end of the railway track the nightmare would end, he felt sure. He had eaten and drunk, naturally, in Tehuantepec and Santa Cruz, and at some other stations, but from now on nothing mattered except his hunger for the south and his thirst for the jungle, which increasingly tantalized and excited him the further he travelled from Oaxaca and the closer to his goal.

Yet at San Cristóbal de Las Casas a considerable surprise lay in wait for him. When he boarded the carriage, in Tuxtla-Gutiérrez, the capital of Chiapas – he was there at last! – the fiesta was already in full swing. Michael was so numb with fatigue that he could not grasp what was happening. Flounces and lace, perfumes, shouts and yelps wrapped him in a diaphanous fog of memories. He blinked his eyes and stared. Three, no, four full-breasted women were twirling and high-kicking. A grinning *muchacho* sawed furiously at a violin. And two tall characters in Stetson hats were slapping their thighs and neighing like stallions in rut. 'Damn it!' 'Up and up it goes, Flo!' Michael flinched. Americans – his countrymen! – and just the wrong moment to run into them. But already the one called Flo, whose real name was Florinda, was hauling him inside and into her dance. '*Ay que lindo!*' she whispered as she folded him in her arms. 'Excuse me,' he bleated, trying to disentangle himself but with no great conviction. The younger of the Stetsons pounced. 'Come on in, my friend, and have a drink,' he commanded in an atrocious Southern drawl, and held out a bottle of Kentucky bourbon. That was more like it. Michael gave a vacuous grin. He had nowhere to go. Behind him the girl was stroking his shoulders and neck. In front stood the hulk with the bourbon. On one side or another of the gangway sat three other girls, the cowboy's buddy, and the local fiddler. Having no choice, he might as well join in. After all it would make the time pass more cheerfully on this interminable journey. Yes, it would keep him afloat and suspended, still attached to what he was leaving behind, and not altogether immersed in what he sought. And the lull might also make time to take stock of what was really happening to him, because ever since his furtive departure from Oaxaca he had been acting like a sleepwalker, haggard and inert. Flesh, smells and muscle would inject some consistency into the situation. The movable orgy came just in time to shake him out of his zombie trance and force him to feel his three-dimensional existence, instead of taking an affected satisfaction in the role of an ethereal creature freed from the constraints of space and time, an idea, no, more than that, a symbol!

Oh, things didn't go very far. Everybody lavished caresses and compliments. They emptied two or three bottles. And when the whole bunch of them had partied to a standstill – the other travellers had not been invited, not that there were many volunteers for San Cristóbal – they sprawled across the seats and slept to the rhythm of the wheels. The train's inspector had readily turned a blind eye to the proceedings in the end carriage, assisted by the crisp ten-dollar bill that one of the Texans slipped into his hand with an explicit wink.

Florinda, Asunción, Raquel and Chinita were prostitutes travelling to their 'house' in San Cristóbal, while the two

Americans were heading for the Chiapas oilfields to market their technical knowhow. With new fields opening up, the little town was booming, and they'd had to re-open the doors of the old colonial *bordelo*. For the girls, the railway party amounted to a free performance, a kind of public relations exercise – instead of being a dead loss, the trip would guarantee at least two clients as soon as they arrived. After all, they had no idea what to expect in this hick town in the middle of nowhere. It wasn't for peanuts that they had said goodbye to city life and the bars of Veracruz. The oil workers in San Cristóbal were making big money, so people said. Three or four years among the savages, and then bye bye, with a packet of pesos. So the girls were acting out of self-interest, of course, but they also happened to be good-natured girls. You had to get some fun out of life, and there was no time like right now. Especially when what came after could be so bleak and drab . . . and they were reaching an age when the smiles would always be servile ones, supplied to order. The youngest, Chinita, was thirty-two; so she told Michael, planting a moist kiss on his cheek. 'Next week, at the Vegas, we shall give a birthday party, the girls and me. Say, you can come and drink with us. But first you have to shave. Your beard is prickly. What a pig! *Marrano!*' Mateos had neither the will nor the strength to tell her that a week from today he himself had no idea where he would be. The girls thought that he was only a *gringo* like the other two, and that he too was on his way to work for Pemex. He took care not to disappoint them.

He played his part to the hilt, accepting the invitation to drive straight to the Vegas with the girls and the two technicians. They had wheedled and wriggled so effectively that the Americans were raring for instant action before they even unpacked their bags. Michael was in a different frame of mind, which explains why the pressure of distance and solitude suddenly seemed hard to bear. Just like that, he was adrift in the virgin territory – virgin for himself and for his imagination – of the spectacular State of Chiapas . . . So he joined the procession, and before he had time to think he was sitting in the room assigned to Chinita by the madam of the house, who congratulated herself on her unexpected trade boom, and was generous with her *copitas* of welcome. '*Baja Manolo!*' That amused Mateos, and he said to himself that if there was a Christ, the aforesaid Jesus Emmanuel – 'God with us!' – must be blushing with shame. But then again, Mary Magdalene would have got him used to the idea . . . What with the little glasses of anisette and his impulse of iconoclasm, Michael found himself taking it for granted that he was going to stay here while he remained in San Cristóbal. If the señora (and the word burned his tongue) agreed to rent him a room. Where else would he go? He slipped a few bills from his wallet, taking care to keep the rest concealed – it was Nicholson's money. On a tide of enthusiasm, the Texans went upstairs, each with two girls, one with Florinda and Raquel, the other with Asunción and a resident who had joined the group. That left Chinita, for Michael.

They made love, and it felt good. Nothing like the cold mechanics of the mulatto woman in Los Angeles. A touch of fiasco . . . the kind of mishap he usually forgot very fast, with his amazing capacity for instant erasure. That day, although he was not drunk enough to give way to any adolescent illusion about Chinita's reasons for offering him her body, their loving gave Mateos an unalloyed pleasure which left him with the sense of a kind of rebirth. It was as if a stain had been washed away, or an old skin shed.

Chinita was nothing like Virginia Lippman. Yet as he entered her for the second time, Michael could not suppress the comparison. Chinita was as dark as Virginia was fair, but each of them had a beauty spot on her left breast, and the bucking of their hips had the same frenzy. Since London, he had forgotten what love-making was.

Chinita was left in no doubt about what she was giving him, and he had no means of repaying what he owed her except to reward her services at well above the going rate in that part of the world. It was ridiculous, pathetic, but what else could he do? When she saw the hundred-dollar bill she turned pale and let out a scream. '*Tanto dinero, qué locura, Dios mios!*' She would have the whole place in an uproar. 'Shh,' he hissed, 'you must promise not to tell the others or else I take it all back, okay?' She sat on the bed again and smiled at Michael. A tear welled up in one kohl-rimmed eye. Michael turned over, feeling like a fool, and pretended to go to sleep. He did not have to keep up the pretence for long, because as soon as Chinita had tiptoed from the room he fell fast asleep. He slept for a good twelve hours, and no one came to wake him.

Next day Michael Mateos took a thorough bath and a careful shave, and felt like a different man. It was when he came to get dressed that it struck him how low he had fallen: now that he was clean, he still had to put on the same dirty clothes he had worn ever since leaving Oaxaca. Enough, he told himself. It's time to find out what you're doing. This is not the way I planned things. At least I can open my eyes and look around. I've got to think. After coming all this way, let it be for something serious, not a wild-goose chase, but a tangible reality. And as he was kicking himself the meaning of the journey took shape. He finally woke up to the irreversible nature of his action. There was nothing to be done about that, and no question now of turning back. Hadn't he completed his contract, more or less? Paul Arthur Smith could handle the Virgin of Guadalupe and the remainder of the schedule . . . Michael told himself that he would go out to buy a few things, and to drop a line to his friend. Then no one would get worried about him, and it would also prevent them from hanging about waiting, or worse, coming to look for him. He scribbled a few lines which could be read as implying that his final destination was San Cristóbal and he would soon be back. Naturally he was careful not to give a hint of his intention to go further south. 'You can tell them everything's under control. Tell the boss that in a couple of weeks we can start the editing. See you soon, best wishes, Michael.' He had begun to reason again, and to calculate. After all, he was owed some time off. After coming as far as San Cristóbal you have no right to look back, when the perpetual rain forest stretches away before you, and somewhere in the heart of the sanctuary lies the secret of the Chama ancestors . . . If Raven's trail petered out there – well, he said to himself, I've come this far, and apparently for nothing, from that point of view – at least he would find Sanikté's lake, and her flowers, and Fray Sebastián's church, the weapons of Alfonso de Seguida and the image of his mother, Doña Marina, not as in the cemetery in Oaxaca, one more skeleton to hang around your neck for the festival of the Dead, but alive, embalmed in the undying scents of the Petén! After all, that might be the true objective of the adventure which had drawn him to step off the beaten track, and take the path of those generations of voluntary exiles whose offspring he was. As he emerged from the Vegas that morning, with a cheerful heart and rested body, looking up at a gentle sun and discovering the lanes and painted houses of San Cristóbal de Las Casas, Michael Mateos felt a sort of collective memory revive and cohere inside him. It was heavy; it bore massively down on him as he stood with his feet planted on ground as hard and dry as stone.

On the way to the market the open doors of a *cervecería* spread their arms. Michael stopped and looked at the barman who was arranging bottles on the counter. It was only ten o'clock in the morning and he wasn't thirsty: Chinita had brewed him a big pot of coffee. And yet the temptation was there. He resisted it.

The *zocalo* was crammed with a mass of huts and stalls, huddled together and almost piled on top of one another, so much so that one wondered whether the jostling crowd inside was not imprisoned in its gaudy tangle. A swarm of children surrounded Michael, trying to sell him combs, soap, lottery tickets and of course packets of *chicle*, the locally manufactured chewing gum. He bought some of everything. The dollar bill delighted the urchins so much that their shouting and shoving nearly degenerated into a general free-for-all. Mateos restored order by giving out a few pesos collected on his travels in the country. As soon as the gang had scattered he blamed himself for his largesse. He had caught himself in the act of neo-capitalist exploitation. Was he just like the rest, then? Because he had placed himself in the middle of his own world, because he wanted to bring his weight to bear on fate, he had come to forget that men and women were living and working around him and for him. But to tell the truth, things were not so cut and dried. Michael had trouble in formulating the categorical statements which had seemed to come naturally a short while ago. When he came up against reality he found himself clumsy and confused – a stranger.

Before going into the marketplace Mateos saw that he was standing opposite a little branch of the Banco Ejidal. He joined the line of peasants from the surrounding area, and when he reached the counter he changed the equivalent of five hundred dollars – that ought to take care of the purchases he planned to make. He kept the rest in American currency. In any case, where he was going, he wouldn't have much use for cash.

This place was not at all like Mexico City or Cuernavaca, or even Oaxaca. No woven fabrics for the tourist trade, and in fact no tourists, because once the Pemex workers were settled into their camps, further to the south, they seldom came to town. And then the intrusion of a single truck or jeep into San Cristóbal hardly counted as an organized trip. A single figure, common among the towns and villages of the central plateau, seemed to have made an appointment here with an Indian world immersed in its Indian nature: the changeless blind beggar was here too, leaning against a pillar in the arcades that surrounded the square, and muttering unintelligible words. When he came out of the Banco Ejidal Michael decided that the litany was directed at him. He went up to the old man who watched him with his empty eyes. Crouching low, he dropped a Mexican coin into the wooden bowl, and was about to stand up again when he was stopped dead by the impact of a blow against his shoulder so violent that he almost yelled with pain. The man had hit him with his walking stick, which he was holding out in front of him in a pose of authority, resting it against Michael's neck and threatening to strike again – this time fatally, perhaps.

The blind man spoke in a high clear voice that hammered out each syllable:

'I did not hear your prayer to the Virgin of those who have nothing.'

'It is for you . . . I ask nothing of the Virgin or of anyone.'

'Then take back your money, stranger.'

'You don't want it?'

'No . . . I am here to intercede. A message for a *centavo* . . .'

'Perhaps you have children?'

'Yes, but my mouth feeds upon the word of God.'

'Then that's what you keep chewing on about!'

Michael thought the man was going to hit him once again; the knotty stick was held against his shoulder in a grip of iron. But nothing happened, except that the beggar pronounced his curse. Michael Mateos, together with his father, his mother and their ancestors before them, from generation to generation, was doomed to the fiercest fires of Hell.

While the old man's grating voice growled on, the younger man was caught in a fit of helpless laughter. What a farce! But he wouldn't fall for it. He was no *gringo*, nor yet some sensitive soul to be taken in by a string of sonorous curses. He remembered. Doña Marina had taught it all to him. *Benedicite!* Amulets, fetishes – sorry, but they didn't mean much, compared with the people who submitted to them, the damned of the earth. He had already played the superstition game. He knew the rules and he had more than one trick up his own sleeve. Thanks to the assault by the mendicant miracle-worker, suddenly everything had come back to him. If only for that, he would have liked to give him the coin, and maybe even more, as he had done with Chinita – more of the money from Nicholson and Ruth which was burning his fingers. Oh, but no! Michael knew very well that the rules of the game required him to take risks.

'Here, I'm taking your money back, you bastard!'

There was no doubt in his mind about the next scene in the script. The stick would rise, and make way for him. He would stand up and walk away, while the old man muttered more of his complaints and evil spells.

It was time to start travelling again.

There were plenty of goods on sale in the market at San Cristóbal – poultry, livestock, spices, pottery, leather, agricultural equipment, even a bulldozer. The sight of the metal monster standing in one corner of the square, next to a butcher's stall, confirmed to Mateos that the world he intended to enter was no longer the place where Raven had ventured forty years ago.

He bought a big canvas bag, two complete changes of clothes – one to wear at once, plus a spare set – a poncho and various basic necessities. Lastly he found a man selling weapons from a stall surrounded by an inquisitive crowd, and duly haggled for a sheath knife, a .22 repeating rifle and clips of ammunition.

The arsenal was not essential to his plans. Michael had never been fond of martial trappings, and the sight of a weapon repelled him. Even during the celebrations after the Cuban revolution, when there was a rash of posters, particularly in his own student circle, featuring guns being brandished skywards in homage to freedom, he had been unable to quell a wince of revulsion for that gleaming polished metal and its cold lethal mechanism. A pistol, with its black mouth gaping, had no need to kill in order to be, to embody, a corpse by its mere absurd existence. Of course in the old days there had been expeditions with Uncle Charlie to the shooting galleries in the fairground at Battersea Park. Charlie had taught him how to aim and squeeze the trigger, and he had turned out to be a pretty good marksman.

While he examined the long rifle, feeling the butt snug against his shoulder and aiming along the barrel, peons and Indians gathered round with envious eyes. Suddenly Michael was not so sure that he really wanted to buy this precision carbine. It was a Remington, a good reliable weapon, Yankee-made. At first he had only meant to buy a *navaja*, a clasp-knife, to deal with the kind of ordinary tasks and problems that were bound to crop up once he entered the jungle. But here, jammed against the stall by a press of warm excited bodies, he could not prevent himself from handling the rifle and checking the sights and safety catch. Unable to put it down, or to remind himself that it was no use to him and could cause trouble, he held it, hefted it, and did not let go.

'*Cuánto?*'

Michael added a hundred pesos to the asking price to pay for the carrying case, which the dealer was selling separately. Had Raven owned a gun? It seemed not. There was no sign of a rifle in the photo unearthed by Fito Malinas, which the Mexican journalist had naturally rushed into the pages of *Mañana* a few days after the incident in the Regis – a picture later reprinted in many of the books and articles about the writer. Some sort of leather holster belted to Raven's hip had caught Michael's attention, and he had examined it under a magnifying glass and even had enlargements made, but still he could not tell for certain whether the holster contained a revolver, as he would have liked. After all, there was nothing to prove that it did not carry some sort of optical or surveying equipment – Raven had been playing the explorer for all he was worth in those days.

Before returning to the Hotel Vegas, Michael stopped at a cantina, where he sat beneath an Indian laurel eating a spit-roasted spring chicken with chillis, washed down with beer – a well-earned beer, he told himself. On the way back he passed the same *cervecería*. The weather was hot, the air humid, and his shirt clung to his back as tightly as his tongue did to his palate. He went in, swearing that one more beer would do the trick . . . Then, to remove the bitter aftertaste of the beer, he downed a couple of tequilas.

Outside the Vegas a pick-up truck in the Pemex colours was parked with its engine running. The two Texans from the train were just leaving. As soon as they saw Mateos they greeted him like an old friend, then ribbed him about the gear he was carrying slung across his shoulder, and fell about laughing at the thought that 'it looks like all three of us are going to be shooting big loads around this here country!' But first there was a job to do, and they guessed as how they'd better see it done, duty before pleasure – a Texas version of the Puritan ethic, cowboy-style. Then, 'So long, Mike,' and the truck took off in a cloud of dust while the younger of the two technicians leaned out of the window to shout a final 'See you later, alligator!' to their temporary fellow passenger.

Michael paused on the steps of the hotel-bordello, squinting into the harsh sunlight, to watch the truck recede into the distance. Adiós! he thought. I'll be surprised if we do meet again. I leave you to your steel dinosaurs, and hope to find some creatures less difficult to tame. 'The cayman never draws breath before it bites,' my mother used to say.

The Vegas was in an uproar, with people shouting and screaming from one floor to the next. Whose throat was being slit? Where was the robbery? Some fractious client refusing to fork out, or roughing up one of the girls? Chinita, perhaps? Michael was beginning to regret his spur-of-the-moment decision to put up at such an obvious trouble spot. It would have been better to go unnoticed and leave no trace of a visit whose only purpose had been to make some preparations before moving on.

The words '*gringo*' and '*americano*' kept emerging through the din. Had the Texans neglected to settle their bill? No, something was going on upstairs right now. Above the furious female chorus Michael could make out a male voice, howling, and not with pleasure. The man was clearly in pain, and begging for help. Michael recognized some English words, too crude to be mistakeable. He ran upstairs and dumped his purchases on Chinita's bed. If he stayed another night he wanted it to be with her. After this, who knew what kind of women he would find? Maybe none at all. He sighed, turned round and walked along the corridor towards the commotion. Florinda and Raquel practically flung themselves at him. 'Come quick, he is going to die on our hands. *Maldito americano!*' But what American were they talking about? '*Está enfermo!* Sick, for more than a week. Here. And he pays us to let him stay! None of us will lay a finger on him. *Está podrido!* Rotten in the belly. He smells of death. We are not nurses. Come, Miguelín, we need you. Only you can help us. Talk to him. Get that *cerdo* out of here!'

And they propelled him to the room at the end of the corridor where all the girls had gathered. They stopped their shrieking and jostling, and the running commentary subsided as the group parted to let him through. Inside, the man was whimpering. His words rang loud in the sudden hush. 'I don't wanna die! . . . Shit! . . . Gimme back my money, you bitches!' Michael stopped short in the doorway, his spine tingling. He recognized that voice, no question. Behind him, the women urged him forward: 'Go ahead, go ahead!' Another step and the smell hit him.

The man lay curled up, facing the wall, clutching his heavy stomach, a huge lunar foetus adrift on a sea of clotted amniotic fluid that overflowed the iron bedstead on to the floor – grey crumpled sheets the umbilical cord, soaked in urine, smeared with accumulated filth. Although the bare lightbulb dangling from the ceiling at the end of a long flex gave only a dim light, it was possible to discern the sweat on his back and the continual shivers rippling over livid goose-flesh.

Still he kept whimpering. He jack-knifed further, tighter, as if in an effort to contain surges of superhuman energy, then heaved a racking groan, uncurled and spread himself out again. A thick, yellowish liquid puddled beneath his naked buttocks, leaving a heavy stain on the sheets. Mateos looked away and briefly shut his eyes. Then he walked across and pulled the blanket over to cover the sick man, who felt Michael's presence and turned his head, but without shifting his body. A thick growth of beard covered his face, and the haggard, sunken eyes above it glittered with fever. A rictus twisted his lips, and a trickle of bile and saliva dripped from one corner. His skin was greenish, the pupils of his bloodshot eyes dilated, and yet, although his looks were changed beyond recognition, there was no doubt about the identity of the man who peered up at Mateos in the half light. It was George Lippman.

Seeing who the intruder was – though clearly having trouble bringing himself to believe what he saw (he was caught in the grip of the same stunned amazement that prevented Michael Mateos from speaking a single word, or making a single gesture, as if they were going to be forced to hold the pose for ever, face to face, both of them embalmed in the pervading stench) – Lippman fought to pull himself upright. Slowly he pivoted on the bed, loosened his muscles and brought his face towards the light. The shivering gave way to calmer, deeper breathing. He relaxed the pressure and made a show of mastering the illness which had overtaken him. Yet, hard as he tried, Lippman could not suppress the drainpipe gurgling that sluiced through his belly, beneath trembling hands which clenched and unclenched on the cotton blanket.

'Get them outside . . . please. Aah! Get them the fuck out of here.'

More spasms convulsed him. His body stretched out rigid and his head twisted up and back, almost to breaking point, towards the metal bars behind it. Mateos herded the women out into the corridor and closed the door. Standing six feet back from the bed where the other man was striving to contain a fresh spasm, he asked in a tone as neutral as he could make it: 'What happened?'

'Dysentery . . . their meatballs, shitballs . . . or I don't know what . . . the runs, fever, stomach ulcer, guts on fire . . . no strength left . . . no food for three days . . . hardly get these damned bitches to bring a drink . . . then their foul water, crawling with germs . . . and the whole thing starts over again in my guts . . . you saw . . . too weak to stand . . . dysentery I said, but with these women, who knows, they could slip you some virulent germ, finish you right off . . . and they've stolen every cent I had, of course!'

He snickered sardonically, but the laughter caught in his raw throat, and he gagged and spat.

'Don't talk, Lippman, you're delirious. You need a doctor.'

'If you can find one in this hole who won't just hand me over to the mortician.'

'What are you doing here anyway?'

'In this whorehouse, you mean? . . . What a kick for you, huh? . . . How you're going to enjoy telling Virginia all about this when I kick off . . . Son of a bitch!'

'Virginia? What do you mean?'

'Oh, don't worry, she's okay. She's safe and sound, all mod. con., hot and cold water, swimming pool and all . . . In Los Angeles, balling all those little pricks from UCLA! How do you like that?'

'Cut it out.'

'Well, yeah, the girls . . . I stopped off – like you did, I guess . . . then wham! . . . Hey, let me recommend Morena especially . . . Gives terrific head. I'll introduce you, Mateos . . . Now tell me, apart from being a pain in the ass, and trying to beat me to the line, what the hell are *you* doing here? Screwing around, right? More good pussy than Virginia, huh, Mateos?'

'No need to drag Virginia in . . .'

'Okay, so why don't we both cry together, that suit you?'

'You'll make the fever worse . . .'

'Oh sure, and you can just head on south, no sweat. When I'm dead . . . nothing in your way . . .' He groaned again.

'I'm getting you out of here, Lippman. Like it or not, you're getting out.'

The professor expelled a long whistling fart that broke the silence of the room like a bomb landing in a pool of mud.

'There, that's my answer.'

And he doubled up with pain and rolled over to face the wall, away from Michael's eyes. His body relapsed into a series of continual spasms and convulsions.

Mateos left the room and walked straight into a posse of girls, led by the madam, all of them waiting to see the outcome of the meeting between the two *gringos*. He had no intention of telling them anything, and when the proprietor blocked his way he ordered her: '*Un doctor! Hace falta un doctor, de prisa! . . . Tengo dinero para pagar.*'

'*Bueno*,' said the woman, and then told him in English: 'If you can pay for the *doctor*, is okay. Morena, *ve te a buscarlo, ahora mismo*.' And the rest of them cheered their sister on her way. All okay now. Let *gringos* see to *gringos*. It's their problem.

Michael's problem it was, and he did not intend to evade it. Lippman would be moved, and he would recover. The rifle still lay in its case on Chinita's bed. The crazy idea crossed his mind that he could, if he liked, get rid of Lippman – not that way, simply by not helping him – but the thought was instantly cancelled by the demands of the situation. One, the doctor and first aid. San Cristóbal was bound to have somebody who could give Lippman something to clear his stomach, and a jab for his fever. Two, wire the American consulate in Mexico City to collect the sick man and have him flown back to Los Angeles. Three, write to Virginia (he remembered her postal address) and tell her . . . what? That she needn't bother to thank him. By the time she received the letter he would be long gone, somewhere secret and out of reach, out in the perpetual rain forest. At least she would be glad to know that he was close to his goal . . . And he would end the letter: 'There's nothing to feel sorry for. Lippman loves you more than you believe. Take care. Michael M.'

Michael stuck rigorously to his plan. He did not allow himself to visit Lippman even when the doctor procured by Morena had done all he could, but confined himself to a brief talk with the man. Once he was sure that the professor was out of danger, and that he would be back on his feet after a few days in hospital in the capital, he paid the medic a generous fee. But there was no question of seeing Lippman again. He told the girls that everything was going to be okay, but they would have to look after the patient themselves from now on. 'I'm going away tomorrow. I'll leave some money for his expenses.'

If he could, Michael would have left the Hotel Vegas at once, but after going to the post office he had asked at the railway station and the first train for Ococingo did not leave until late afternoon the following day. Even then, he had no idea that the train was likely to wheeze its way out of San Cristóbal at least three hours late.

Now that he was obliged to stay at the Vegas, he said to himself that a night with Chinita, while Lippman lay stewing in his own putrid wastes at the other end of the corridor, was worth any amount of rancorous vomiting and well contrived revenge. Yet he was afraid that he might be unable to forget that sordid presence, and would think too much about the past, looking at the hooker's body, face and eyes, and seeing Virginia's. It didn't happen. Instead he could never have dreamt of an exorcism more complete, more perfectly liberating, than the wild night they spent.

Mateos had no illusions, no futile pretences; he knew that he was ready to leave. It was no longer the vortex of his own wandering fever that drew him in its wake; he felt that he belonged to another place, to an elsewhere so close that his steady hand could almost touch it.

In those days, the idea of travel had contradictory associations for me. I was the toy of volatile cross-currents whose sources and true point of intersection it was beyond me to identify. As with many other aspects of my character, this uncertainty no doubt expressed the split that divided me into two more or less equal parts.

First, my adolescent imagination had naturally succumbed to the vivid colours of Conrad and the metaphysical fables of Melville. The mythologies of the exotic sustained and intensified my longing to shatter the screen of everyday reality and halted time that still kept me separate from the romantic universe which my own father had lived and recreated. 'I am the explorer who never rests,' he wrote in *The Tale of the Chimera*. 'No hearth to hold me, no flame to warm me. What I seek is always in flight. Even if I must perish, I shall pursue it beyond the Mountain, into the Valley of Night, among the shades of death.'

But as well as that – and perhaps because Raven also had one of his characters say that 'the journey is nothing but a series of short-lived separations' – I remained relatively chary of setting any schedule of radical commitments, and even of the necessity for movement. In general, with the exception of that visit to Spain when I was sixteen, the horizon of my childhood and adolescence was a function of British insularity, ever since the day when – after the storm of the initial trauma – the *Queen Mary* landed me in Southampton. I had seen nothing, or next to nothing, of the voyage, sealed tight inside my cabin and my fears. Before departing, my memory and instinct had wiped itineraries and stopping places off the map. It was a straight line that I had to have, from one point to another, and between them, nothing! A stretch of nothingness while I waited for the second crossing, almost twenty years later, and this time through the raging sky. Then arriving, at last, in the country of my birth.

Strangely, the sense of having travelled only caught up with me when I was back at the beginning again.

It is hard to single out the exact moment later on when I was struck by the realization that the common assumption about travel 'broadening the mind' and deepening our view of people and events did not stand the test of experience. It seemed to me then that, on the contrary, the broader the field of investigation the narrower the field of thought, and the more diluted the quality of knowledge. Certainly I would be less categorical today, but have you noticed – even if it does not always express itself in an obvious way – how you are affected by your own shifts of latitude and changing rhythms of life? No matter how much preparation you have undergone, with your pocket full of guides and timetables and your hands full of maps and compasses, there is always a moment when you will be lost, or else when you will feel lost. It's no good trying to control the situation: itineraries and decisions have no effect. You will believe that you have the substance of the thing in hand, when all you have settled is the lesser details . . . The synthesis escapes you, it slips from beneath your fingers, and all that remains is the dream, the shadow of the reality you believed was in your grasp. The journey never ends, and the further it goes the more the trail fades out behind . . . Ought I to see that as the explanation, the reason emerging from the story we are following now, for the fact that I was unable to bring myself to write until after I had ceased to be in movement, after I had completed my revolution in space and time? Or to be thoroughly precise, I should speak in terms of directed displacement, a giration eventually stabilized around a given axis. And when I look harder, it is not at all the same thing, because manic travel has now given way to a venture of putting into words. Now, deliberate though the undertaking may be, and much though it is dictated by an undeniable act of will, it is bound to come up against various natural obstacles. For example I am forced to take account of my inability to write while in a train, or – more serious – in a strange room which I know I shall only be using for a day or two before moving on. In Puerto Lápiz, the hurricane and the fighting had given me enough time to get set. There's no explaining such things. After my return to Europe, during the fortnight I spent in Paris to see my son Pablo again, the most I could do was to make notes: I was incapable of focusing on the real work of style and composition. Then there was that hotel room in Warsaw, and the other one in Poznan, which I hardly ever left except for everyday necessities, in the hope of finally sorting out my affairs. In any case, I have promised myself not to leave this place, with its helpful solitude (fat flakes of snow are falling on the surrounding rooftops, a wall of grey), except in pursuit of the denouement, on the day when I set out for Schwiebus. It holds the key to the story, the solution to the Riddle. Ice and flame . . .

That reminds me of the opening words of *The Snows of Kilimanjaro*, which have always fascinated me: 'Close to the western summit there is the dried and frozen carcass of a leopard. No one has explained what the leopard was seeking at that altitude.' Although there are plenty of angles from which Hemingway does not appeal to me, and his personality and writing are the very opposite of my own tastes, there is one thing about him I have never rejected, and that is the way he constructed his own life like a novel – right to the end, with its absolute reversal, putting the shotgun barrel to his forehead! Harry, the wounded hunter, at least he had his vultures, circling above his camp. Where are my zopilotes then? Can I have forgotten them in some canyon of my memory, as if the question of whether to have them or not simply did not arise today? I would not have anyone see this matter of the journey as having merely a metaphysical connection with reality. That feeling was surely true all along the way, even in its most tortuous convolutions – the intention not to lose sight of the purely historical meaning of the journey. It is a theme bred of that same obsessive commitment to 'commitment' which people of my generation had absorbed from existentialism . . . and which it is fashionable to laugh at today. But my return from Central America leaves me with no wish either to laugh or cry.

To my surprise, I have found issues just as important in

Warsaw, when I had come to believe that I was rid of such confrontations. In Guatemala, echoes of the events in Gdansk had reached me, but very muffled by the height of the hill tops and the crackle of gunfire. When I returned to London in 1981 some of the people on the magazine tried to explain: in the five years since I had embarked on that second and vital visit to the land of my ancestors, things had shifted considerably in the world, making contours and boundaries even more hazy (I almost wrote 'crazy'). My colleagues wanted to snap me out of my 'daydreams' – that is the word they used to describe what a famous 'I-is-another' would rather have called 'the true life' – and urged me to resume control of the magazine I had created in 1968. Business was booming. Thanks to a few developments ('oh, nothing too serious') in editorial policy they had managed to build the circulation back to the great days of the 1970s. I merely reminded them that I had sold my shares and that *OFF* was nothing to do with me any more, nothing at all.

At the pub where many of our editorial conferences used to finish up in the old days, Hawkins and Rakovski got into an argument about the Polish situation. My ex-editorialist attacked Brezhnev and the Soviet Communist Party, which three days previously had had the arrogance to dictate the behaviour of the Warsaw government, but he also condemned the counter-revolutionary activities of various 'media stars' in the Solidarity movement. That set off a fierce debate with the assistant chief editor, Rakovski, whose Polish father, a Jew and a Communist, had left his country in 1937 to fight with the Brigades and Dolores Ibarruri. Rakovski denounced the restoration of television censorship, the imprisonment of the KOR dissidents, and the entire climate of repression which according to him foreshadowed direct intervention by Soviet troops. Hawkins was having none of that: according to him, the Polish people would settle their own problems in their own way. He had faith. Personally, although I did not join the argument I felt that Soviet intervention in Poland had already begun, even if no soldier had crossed the frontier and no tank had stuck its murderous snout into the fields and forests of Masuria. I did not say anything to my friends, because all that mattered now was the urgency of going there before it really was too late.

In Paris, not really to dissuade me but rather to sound me out and test me, to see whether I was still the 'windbag' she used to call me, Beatrice had talked of the poverty in Poland, the long queues outside empty shops, and the economic crisis. I didn't have the strength to recall the starving peasants of Central America – she would probably have accused me of complacency. In compensation, she sang the praises of Walesa, and painted a truly messianic portrait of the man. I had to come here before I could understand the scope and meaning of the events which are happening just as I face the key question of the second half of my life – the shorter half, but the more upright or less equivocal, I hope. And I have seen . . . I have seen positions harden into hatred. I have observed that the bloodbath machinery was ready for action once again. They talk about economic recovery, but the fact is that it is power and liberty which are at stake. A nation is rebelling in its memory, whose scope reaches far beyond the boundaries of factories and shipyards. Daily I expect something irrevocable to happen. Shall I have time to run my own derisory little errand? . . . And by the way, that reminds me once again of Comrade Ernest! After all it was Hemingway, not Raven, who went to Madrid.

Today, right next to the district where I am staying, the militia broke up a demonstration. There were numerous arrests.

I wrote a dozen pages.

Tonight, after eating a can of pork and beans heated on the gas stove which the hotel keeper has let me install in my room, I read a few pages of *Martin Eden* before I began to write again. Pablo made me a present of the book in Paris last week, in French translation, of course, hence my slow reading speed. The poor boy made his gesture without any ulterior motive, not knowing what chords the book might strike. I had taken him out, and Beatrice had been generous enough to allow me to see him back to his room in the flat on the avenue de la Motte-Picquet where she had moved after we split up. At that time she would still be at her office at Cardin's, and then she had an appointment with 'somebody' – I didn't ask who. Pablo would be glad to spend the evening with his father. The son displayed his expertise with electronic games, and in order not to look an absolute fool I felt I had to beat him at old-fashioned darts.

Pablo asked me if I had picked up the knack in America, and I told him yes, then changed the subject by suggesting that it was time to eat. 'There's cold meat, chicken and macédoine in the refrigerator,' Beatrice had whispered before leaving me on the terrace of a café in the Champs-Elysées. She had even thought to leave a bottle of Saint-Amour in sight on the kitchen table – she remembered that, too, the wine I particularly liked, which we had tasted in a little village in the Beaujolais on the first weekend we spent together, fifteen years before.

After the meal, Pablo wanted another game of darts. This time I let him win.

Then we went back to his room, where there were three or four books of comic strips lying on the bed. I asked him about his reading, and he pointed to the rows of shelves. 'Which one did you read last?' He knelt on the bed, reached for a book bound in red, and held it out to me. 'I haven't managed to finish it.' (A corner was turned down at page 82.) 'Raymond gave it to me for my birthday.' Even if he confused *The Call of the Wild* with *Martin Eden*, which is anything but a children's book, Beatrice's friend had no bad taste in literature . . .

I tried to catch Pablo's attention by telling him the story of Jack London. He listened rather absent-mindedly, occasionally fingering the buttons of his electronic Spiderman game, but not interrupting.

I set out, once again, on the journey to the Arctic, joined in the rush for the Klondike's fabulous gold and became a seal hunter in Japan, before roaming the highways of Canada and the United States as a great-hearted vagrant. What could the son of a bourgeois father – for so he was! – what could he understand about that glorying in freedom in which the humiliation of being poor became a reason to live in hope? London was clearly a man too riddled with contradictions, torn as he was between his revolutionary ideals and his appetite for immediate life, for me to be able to describe him without lapsing into ideological jargon over the head of a child of thirteen, or else into an apologia for the fallen condition and corruption of the species, which would be equally closed to an innocent mind. Or so I believed. For I noticed how Pablo stopped fidgeting for a while when I brought up the painful question of marriage and divorce, and of all the scandals that dogged the novelist's life. I was probably wrong to keep quiet about his alcoholism – 'the last chance saloon' – but I could not find the words to tell about despair and the unutterable quest for a paradise lost. Instead, I dwelt on 'the people of the abyss' and 'the iron heel', as if I set some special value on this proletarian side of the writer, or as if that was the image of Jack London I wanted to convey to my son. Yet I had to disclose the ending. How could I cheat about that? Suicide is suicide.

It made Pablo sit up.

'Like grandfather?'

'Who could have given you that idea?'

'I don't know . . . He was a great writer, wasn't he?'

'Yes, of course. But not all great writers commit suicide.'

'Really?'

'Who has spoken to you about Raven? Beatrice?'

'Well, yes . . . And Raymond too. They say they'll give me his books to read, when I'm older.'

At that moment I registered the oddity of the situation. Hadn't I come here with the intention of providing my son with the elements certain to be missing, to give him a better understanding of myself, his father? I would not tell him everything, and only the barest details of the Raven story, keeping the essentials until later, when I returned, for I was determined to return, either to Paris or London, it didn't matter, but somewhere we could see each other often. In that respect, no doubt I did not even want to admit that Pablo was Raven's grandson, and the son of the Mateos who I had been in the past, and no longer wanted to be. Yet today I am not sure that I am ready to return. No reason . . . Anyway, that night there was our curious excursion into Jack London. Both in order to stir Pablo's curiosity and to avoid having to talk about Raven, I described how some sensationalist commentators had imagined London somehow escaping death at the last minute and going to ground in Mexico, under an assumed name, to write the novels attributed to Raven.

With surprising good sense (did he know a lot more than he was admitting?), my son remarked:

'That would have really simplified things!'

In order to demonstrate that in his opinion the issue was

settled, he picked up his copy of *Martin Eden*, which lay between us on the bed, and said:

'Here, I'm giving it to you. It would be great if you took it with you.'

'To Poland?'

'Yes.'

'Don't you want to finish it?'

'It's more your sort of book than mine.'

I didn't feel strong enough to resist.

The following night I caught the train to Warsaw at the Gare du Nord. I could have gone by plane, but preferred a slower, more testing means of transport. I needed definite transitions, and time to arrange things in my mind and also to make some notes, so that I could pick up the thread of the story when I arrived.

The rhythm of the carriage wheels on the rails actually did take my mind back, and I saw myself sitting next to the Indian again, on the local line to Ococingo . . .

> The desire to write was stirring in Martin once more. Stories and poems were springing into spontaneous creation in his brain, and he made notes of them against the future time when he would give them expression.

He called himself Vittorio Pareja. Like many of the younger generation of Lacandon Indians, he had swapped his ancestral name for a patronym borrowed from the language of the conquistador. This son of Ts'ibatnah, god of the Arts, and of Ah K'ak, god of Fire and War, also spoke some Spanish, which was still quite rare among his people. That is why the inhabitants of his village had dispatched him as their delegate to San Cristóbal, to the local headquarters of Pemex, to transmit their complaints about the bulldozers and dynamiters who had destroyed one of their most productive hunting grounds, two days' march away from their caribal.

Having reached our destination some time after midnight, we met in the shed which did duty as a waiting room in that tiny railway station at the end of the line. The end of a world . . . There in the shadows where nothing could be seen was the beginning of another world, so different that the imagination made no response to it, not even fright. He sat on the hard-packed floor with his legs crossed in front of him and his back resting against the wooden wall, six feet away from me . . . Only half a dozen of us travellers had remained at the station; the rest had quickly vanished into the night, to rejoin their families living in Ococingo or the surrounding district.

Half an hour passed in almost total silence, occasionally broken by the grunt of a sleeping man or the sound of a door banging in the wind.

The Indian no longer had a cigar between his teeth: in the half-light I could see no sporadic glow from his direction. I moved slightly closer towards him, sliding along the smooth wood of the bench, and pulling the rifle case and the big kit bag along with me. He must have felt my presence, for without changing his position he murmured:

'Señor, you have a cigarette?'

The words could only be addressed to me: the others lay sprawling on the other side of the shed, and in any case he would certainly not have used 'Señor' with them.

'I don't smoke,' I replied, leaning towards him and trying to sound friendly.

'You are a missionary?' he asked, after a long moment's silence.

'Why? Why do you ask me that?'

A shallow sleep on the train had not revived me, but this man made me sit up. I still had several hours to kill in the station before sunrise, when I could resume my journey. To where? I didn't even know. So I might as well pay some attention to the Indian. Perhaps he would teach me something.

'They say . . . the white priests . . . that tobacco kills . . . a terrible sickness . . .'

In the ambient gloom it was hard to tell whether he was smiling or frowning. What should I say?'

After a further pause, he continued his sentence as if it had never stopped wheeling around his head in slow circumvolutions before rolling into a ball beneath his tongue, where the words had been macerated and chewed before being regenerated by his voice.

'. . . the knife that cuts the throat does not prevent the smoke from rising into the sky to tickle the nostrils of God . . .'

He smiled gently.

Later he told me about his brothers Pepe and Ernesto, and his aged father, Nensäk, the village chief of Milpa, though he could not tell me exactly how far from Ococingo the village was.

'It depends . . .'

'On what?'

'If the Rain god, that the northerners call Chac and we call Mensabäk, travels with you, then three days on horseback.'

'And if not?'

'That you must ask in the forest yourself, Señor.'

And he fell silent. I thought for a while about his missionary story. The word had got under my skin, although I didn't feel able to throw it back in the poor devil's face. What would he know about our ancient fears, or worse, about our contemporary agonies? Never before had the Western obsession with cancer seemed so ridiculously incongruous. And yet in my mind's eye I caught painful glimpses of Charlie O'Sullivan in his hospital bed. It was a dreadful death: to this day, nothing haunts me more. At the time, I went through it as if in a waking dream – not that I felt indifferent to it, by no means, since that death and its procession of medical litanies enacted the modern form of a fate reserved, first class, for ourselves. And it is true that when I thought of myself dying, or to this day when I try, not to imagine (is that possible?) but to envisage the final moment, then any fate seems better than such a long disintegration, including the sinister death of Raven himself.

Vittorio, who in the meantime had told me his first name, must have divined my painful state of mind, for he said to me:

'You do not belong to Pemex, you are not looking for anything but yourself, so if you like, you can come with me to Milpa.'

I thanked him warmly and accepted his offer. As the first rays of sunrise came slanting into the hut, he told me about his family. His wife was called Maria Bonita and his daughter Chata, which in Spanish means 'pretty' and 'cute'.

It wasn't easy to find a horse. Although the equine family was no longer the amazing sight that it had been to the ancestors of the local population, horses were still as rare in the region as they had been in the days of the Conquest. All the same, the peasant who had been looking after Vittorio's mule agreed, after lengthy negotiations, to part with one, a veteran with a battered saddle. He also sold us provisions for the journey. Although there was very little currency in circulation in Milpa, which was a closed economy working on the barter principle, Vittorio was absolutely determined to pay his share rather than allow me to settle the whole bill as I suggested.

I don't know why I had been so ready to attach myself to the Lacandon. Was his path really the one I was looking for? But it went southward, and that was enough for me. No doubt I also felt the need to put myself into the hands of a sort of guide.

Leaving behind us the outlying huts of the village, we set out across a succession of wooded slopes that very soon swallowed us beneath their thick mantle of vegetation. After a couple of hours of fairly easy progress the forest walls began to run with a steamy humidity. It seemed to fall in irregular layers from a high roof which I felt looming above our heads, and kept trying to discern, while I wondered about the nature of the phenomenon I was observing.

Vittorio made his way through this thick mist blanket as if there was nothing easier. I didn't dare ask too many questions, reluctant to add my ignorance to the expenses of the journey. I told myself that I had eyes to see, a skin to feel, and a body to experience the whims and alterations of a disconcerting environment. It was all the more disturbing because it so closely resembled the scene I had learned to imagine. In order to allay the unease which resulted from that dual apprehension, I talked to my companion about the underlying reasons for my coming to the region. He listened without interrupting, chewing on the cigars he had replenished in Ococingo.

> *'How little art thou acquainted, Sancho, replied Don Quixote, with the pretensions of chivalry! hold thy tongue and have patience; for the day will soon arrive, on which thy own eyes shall judge what an honourable profession it is: pray, tell us, now, what greater satisfaction can there be in this world, or what pleasure can equal that of a conqueror, who triumphs over his adversary in battle? None sure!' 'That may be, answered the squire, tho' I know nothing of the matter.'*

Vittorio Pareja and I were not seeing the same landscape. Our eyes saw the identical plants, animals and insects, but our points of view were different. He was stocky, rounded, horizontal, traversing paths and clearings with his own momentum; I was captious, vertical, cutting like a jagged blade. Here, suspension points stretching out of sight down the straight grain of our route; there the question or exclamation mark, hanging in the void of a way of thinking too organized to grasp the fluidity of the time going by. I kept watch on the Indian, so as to improve my imitation of his behaviour, his stately calm and silence, while he appeared to pay no attention to my presence, his veiled, almost drowsy gaze sliding over me with hardly more interest than if I had been a shadow. Yet we were linked by one unspoken common trait: each man respected the other's perspective. The further we advanced into the mountains, the less feasible was any confrontation. Each of us had his own landscape, and that was fine.

This impression of reality was borne out next day. I was no longer thinking about Raven, and even the most recent impressions seemed to have left my immediate memory. All that mattered were the concrete details of the journey; my mythology was gradually being replaced by the problems of the moment, which had to be settled one at a time, as they arose.

During that second day, ironically, an only too recognizable smell mingled with the various scents of the jungle, and I saw by the frown on Vittorio's face that he too did not enjoy the stink of gasoline invading the quilted atmosphere of the mahogany groves. Now and again a loud detonation thudded in the humid air. Foliage rustled, tree trunks shook, and both horse and mule reared up in fright. But Vittorio seemed unaware of the peril and went on without hesitation. I asked whether he was not afraid of us running into a dangerous situation, and he told me that before sunset we would have left the blasting zone behind us.

'Then we're coming to Milpa.'

'Not yet. Tomorrow. Tomorrow morning . . .'

IV

LA MORDIDA

1

THE LITTLE MONSTER had found the crack. The interstice. And it had crept inside the cell. As if it wasn't bad enough to be a prisoner behind walls dripping with saltpetre and filth. He could die . . . When the rebels had captured the little town, driving the government forces back towards the sierra, they might easily have marked him for execution right then. Luckily for the *gringo* they had found him asleep and snoring, at the height of the assault, on the back seat of a convertible abandoned by escaping defenders. The friend of the *federales* was also a *borrachón!* Drunkenness had saved him from the firing squad. When he sobered up it was always possible that in return for a few well timed drinks he might provide intelligence about the enemy. In addition, a man who carried a membership card of the Mexican workers' Regional Confederation could not be altogether bad, even if it made no sense to the supporters of General Obregón for a trade unionist to revel in the vice and decadence enjoyed by those loyal to the autocrat Calles. Issued in Tampico on 1 December 1925, the card gave the drunkard's name as Waldo Joven. A lot could happen in three years, and there was no telling what devils the man might have embraced in the meantime.

As he raced northward, Joven had been almost relieved to come across a detachment of the regular army. It was certainly better than falling into the hands of the fanatical Cristeros, hashishins whose drug was holy water and who, in the name of Christ and the Virgin of Gaudalupe, were murdering anyone whose appearance betrayed a Western origin – synonymous in those days with revolutionary allegiances, the *gringo* being by definition the carrier and transmitter of the most dangerous of germs: socialism. It must be said that in the name of the grand ideas of Justice and Liberty, betraying the ideals which had brought him to power, the caudillo Calles had ordered the deaths of many peasants whose only crime was to have been too blindly subservient to the authority of a Church obsessed with preserving its own privileges at the expense of social progress.

At army headquarters, Joven had at first been treated as a spy. He had had to provide proof of his good faith and pledge allegiance to the masters of the region. After that he was admitted to the officers' circle, and shared all their lesser pleasures, from drunken fiestas to bloody reprisals. After those years of jungle expeditions, and after all the hopes and illusions which had culminated in a terrible climax whose bitter taste still lingered in his mouth no matter how much tequila he swilled down it, to lapse into mere debauchery had seemed to him a very gentle punishment, a lesser evil. Champagne, complaisant mistresses and wild cavalcades in the duty wake of gleaming motor cars delayed the inroads of feeling and the pains of remorse.

All this was written – in the manuscript. The words and lines danced before his eyes, blurred by tears and sweat. Perhaps he had a fever coming on . . .

While the vultures gorged on the remains of the final corpse, the moon had sailed into a clear patch of sky. In the middle of the camp we lit a big bonfire to keep away the wild animals that might prowl in our direction, but ignoring both the flames and our own presence, the vile birds had returned for the conclusion of their feast. I rolled myself in a blanket, rested my head on my rucksack, and tried to get to sleep. In vain . . . I could not keep my mind off the dreadful sight we had witnessed, helpless, in the distance. We were halfway up the mountainside when the band of pistoleros had come surging hell for leather out of the desert. As if from a mirage . . . The villagers ran, tiny dumb silhouettes, plain commas on a sand beach soon to be blown clean, to the last speck of blood, by the scouring wind. In the plain that spread beneath our eyes, the sound of distant gunshots might have been firecrackers lit for a fiesta in honour of our coming. The women ran, doing their best to protect children who fell one after another, beads strung at regular intervals, dots of humanity which later were to signpost our progress to the ravaged village. We shouted, but our cries faded into nothing, swallowed by the universal chaos. Down there, men stood their ground, armed with pikes and machetes: one by one they fell.

I stared dumbstruck into the sky, where I wanted to see some sign of explanation – as if I did not know that the massacre of the innocents was written in the spider's web of the stars, which was being spun beneath my eyes. Never had the feeling and longing for death so overwhelmed me as it did during that seemingly tranquil dusk. In the land from which we were returning, the wise men of the past believed that a man's lifetime was the product of an equation correlating magical with solar time, and lasted no more than fifty-two years. I calculated the years I had left before the circle was completed, all the time that I would have to compound with my remorse. The expedition had undoubtedly taught me more than all the studies which had prepared me for it. Yet in that tragic instant it was once again a bookish reference which came to mind. The Dresden Codex. The Mayan treatise of astronomy and obsessive image of a serpent tipping a column of water on to the earth. Their apocalypse. Our world's end. To be washed free of all impurities at last . . . If only I could decipher the meaning of the stories that the stars began to enact before me, a ceaseless, grandiose dance of light and shadow. Human ambition exists only in relation to the weakness that underlies it. Balham, the English doctor who went with us to Chiapas, had been quite clear about this before we set out: preventive medicine had serious limitations when measured against the world's distress. He was a veteran. As for me, just out from Europe, and looking forward to my first expedition, I believed that every poison has its antidote. That was not only an error of youth but also – as I knew now – the fallacy created by a kind of reasoning which we believe to be based upon stable and permanent foundations.

Confronted by the constellations and the wanton spectacle of the turning cosmos, I longed to be a healer, and more than that, an exorcist, a magician, interpreter of our most abject dreams. I have seen the steles of ritual sacrifice, and yet I could not decode the language of the viscera. Open wounds, gaping chests, guts spilled across the ground, they did not speak one syllable of their secrets. If only I could turn to some potent liquor with the power to create the frenzied trance of the priestesses at Delphi. Wasn't it Socrates who found that 'the finest of the arts'? I would readily give all the crystal balls of our self-righteous master thinkers, and all the marked tarot packs of science and power, for one brief moment of trance and ecstasy . . . The days are past of auguries and portents; perhaps we are left with sleeplessness and hallucination. Tomorrow I shall ask K'in Ta, our guide, to give me a piece of his magic mushroom. For now, it is enough for me to record my ignorance. What do I ultimately know about the planets and their houses, spread across infinity? About Uranus and Neptune, Virgo and Scorpio? For me, Orion – is he those seven beautiful stars which twinkle at me here? – no, Orion is not a constellation, and I know nothing at all about Orion's Belt. In my state of mind, and in the present situation, what use is it to have learned one day at the university of Berlin that Orion, with his dog Sirius, was turned into stars for his rudeness in forcing his attentions on the goddess Diana! The ink of darkness spells out codes whose usage is . . .

Joven had not been able to complete the sentence. The notebook had slipped from his trembling fingers to land on the floor by the wooden sleeping platform. Before passing out, he thought how that would gladden the king rat who lived in the same cell and who was sure to come visiting again tonight.

He was delirious. The scorpion's sting was beginning its slow labour of intoxication and destruction. If no one came to his aid his blood would soon be darker than the ink in which the pages of the novel had been written. When the hot needle had lanced him out of sleep he had realized what had happened straight away. The arachnid had climbed up his leg and shot its venom into his thigh. Joven jumped up and saw the thing scuttling away along the wall. He crushed it underfoot, but the damage was done. He tore open his trouser leg and made a tourniquet. Waldo might know hardly anything about the language of the stars, but scorpions he understood. He had not had the time or opportunity to examine the one which had just stung him, and now that it was crushed it was impossible to identify its species with any certainty. As long as it isn't a *Centruroides noxius* . . . the lethal kind! If not, I'm okay. There's no use calling out: nobody will come. And these Obregonista bastards have left me here alone. I heard them yelling that their leader had been assassinated, and not by one of Calles's agents – that would have been too simple. No, a *Cristero*, a zealot, a Catholic mystic! I imagine him impaling the general on his crucifix, a Jacobean gesture. And a lot of good that does me, let me tell you!

Joven thought that if ever he got out of this, then some day he would probably write about scorpions, tarantulas and other fellow travellers. He also told himself that it would be pretty idiotic to die before the age of thirty. Ten years earlier, running through the streets and squares of Munich under a hail of bullets, he would almost have sworn that it was nothing to die before one's time. The game was worth the candle. Everything remained possible, even the feeling of an inevitable resurrection. Ever since the days when his name was Bremen, and although he did not lean towards the esoteric disciplines, a still unbridled instinct for life had prevented him from disowning the idea of metempsychosis. He often saw himself cut down by a machinegun only to rise again, a few seconds later, if not in the same flesh, then at least with the same verve, in the permanence of a breath which could not be extinguished . . . Today, the ground remained strewn with dead bodies and the wind transported nothing but a puff of choking sand.

There had been the approach, the route, the stages and forced breaks, but all that after the great transatlantic leap which had already signified much more than a cesura. Had it not been for the woman, Carlotta, whom he had found again in Hamburg, for the Ophelia who had played opposite him in *Hamlet*, would he have left London where, like it or not, he had moved into a new line of work and a different way of enduring the present and imagining the future? – thanks to Charlie though, whose part had been far more vital than that of a comrade standing by another comrade through temporary misfortunes. How far away it all seemed . . . In terms of years, the gap was narrow, yet no matter how hard he tried, Waldo Joven was unable to make contact with that immediate past: he barely connected, was almost unconcerned with the Ulrich Bremen he once had been. Maybe that was what the passage of time involved, and to subside into duration obliterated the illusion of mortality. All very commonplace . . . Yet he could not prevent himself thinking that here lay the cause of his present inability to move, to try to open the door of this wretched cell that his comic opera jailers might well have forgotten to bar! For the first time in ages, Joven no longer felt caught in a trap. The scorpion sting drew from his eyes tears that mingled with the sweat of the fever and took him back to the days of his childhood. The feeling of impunity no longer prevailed. Even the risks he had accepted until now seemed very minor compared with his first intentions.

Waldo stretched out on the straw mattress and tried to stop thinking about it all, but he could not stanch the torrent of images: beneath his closed eyelids, inside his skull, to the throbbing of the veins that swelled in his neck, time resumed its scansion of the rhythm of life. A cardiac arrest would come as a relief.

And yet, the fiercer the poison burned through his body, the stronger grew his certainty, rooted in the dark, that he was going to survive.

Without truly sensing the metamorphosis at work inside himself, Joven fell sound asleep at last. After some hours of calm unconsciousness he dreamt that men on horseback had him bound hand and foot and were taking him through the mountains. Instead of loosening their grip, his struggles only tightened his bonds and sharpened his pain. Just when this became so unbearable that it wrung a cry of defeat from his throat . . . to his great surprise he was riding utterly at liberty across a plain that stretched onward out of sight. The sun had risen on the horizon. He saw nothing but a vast glow . . .

The Capitán said:

'Your mission is concluded.'

Ramírez, Requete and the rest of the bunch burst out laughing. One soldier held out a glass and offered him a drink. It was an order not to be ignored. The *gringo* drained the glass in a single gulp, tilting his head back. When he straightened it again, his eyes running with tears and blood, a trickle of alcohol spilled out of the left-hand corner of his mouth and dribbled down his neck to disappear beneath the grubby collar of a linen shirt.

Ramírez hushed his men and spoke again:

'The Mexican people do not need parasites any longer. Fleas, lice, cockroaches, we shall not crush you under our boots: the ground would get dirty – right, *compañeros?* Idlers, you've been paid for a third-rate job too long. While types like you, Joven, were busy with the Indians, they didn't come poking their noses into our affairs with their big talk about liberty and socialism.'

Requete, the little sergeant, now came up to the former

prisoner. He clapped him on the back, while the other was racked with coughing.

'Look at these hands, Joven! Blood has washed away the dirt that clogged its pores and blackened its nails and its lines of life or luck . . . You understand, *niño?*'

And once again the Capitán commanded him to tell the story of the expedition. Yet he had told them everything – except of course exactly what had happened in Relámpagos, then back among the Lacandons, with Cartridge and Little Sun . . . The locust campaigns, the mahogany drives, they had been a success, hadn't they? And under the cloak of ethnological observations, the information about the neutrality of the southern tribes had been pretty reassuring, right? So what more did they want? It was all written down in the report, let them leave him in peace!

The Capitán said that the Governor distrusted written accounts where cunning presentation often distorted the reality.

'Señor Ramírez would like to hear it from the horse's mouth. From the beginning . . .'

Papagayo, the garrison's parrot mascot, squawked:

'Shot, all shot! *Ma-ri-cooooo-nes!*'

Joven darted a disenchanted glance at the bird, which was preening its feathers. Tomorrow he would be free. Free to resume his journey to an unknown destination – not that it mattered much to him. One thing was certain, and nothing more: it was no longer possible to go back. And that conviction gave him the strength to tell the story once again: the years of research and solitude, the fight against the jungle, the language of snakes and mosquitoes, the malaria attack, the death of the Belgian cartographer, the approach to the sacred forest, the everlasting rains, one month, two months of swarming damp, limp reptiles and *trompe-l'oeil* trees, and the monotonous series of camp sites, suspension points in the void of an existence wholly at the mercy of everyday chance . . . Then the journey downriver, the gentle chant of the rowers regularly broken by the raucous howls of invisible monkeys, a world of echoes, the womb of a female pregnant with nauseas and fevers . . . Until one day of pouring rain gave birth, not to the monsters that might have been feared, but to beings of flesh and blood, doomed to long ages of slavery. The forced exploitation of mahogany had replaced the Spaniards' wanton killing. God had allowed his own disfigurement: by the sweat of men and the salt of the earth he was baptized under a new name: Progress . . . So as to elude the snares of words and the nooses of a perverted semantics, there was another language to learn. Little less than a whole year of practising a dual heresy in which more than one traveller lost the meaning of strict efficiency. After some time, Balham – the doctor – left us, together with those who had taken more than they could stand of the insane existence that degraded us more each day. It was through them, Señor, that you received news of the expedition and were assured of its success, at least in terms of its scientific and technical objectives. Balham also explained to you the reasons that caused Cartridge and myself to stay on in that area. Think of the sketches I recorded in my notebooks. Frescoes, statuettes, temples, some of the strangest and most beautiful . . . When the civil war – (Who said anything about that, *gringo?*) – All right, when the disturbances are over, you, I mean the government, will certainly be keen to mount a new expedition to rescue all these treasures from the clutches of the surrounding vegetation. (All at once you're positively concerned about the national heritage! And why did you turn down our offer to send you back with supplies and an escort? I was even going to give you the Hispano, really! Can you imagine Cortés in a convertible?) . . . Thank you, Señor Governador . . . (And they tell me you left a woman and a bastard son behind. What the hell . . .?) . . . In payment for my work, all I want . . . I would like you to give me the parrot . . . (Papagayo?) . . . Yes, that's right. (Okay, it's yours.)

The guards had burst into the room, dragging with them a pale young man with long black hair, one holding him by the arm, the other by his hair and shoulder. His looks were knives. When they forced him to stand and face the little tribunal which had just decided the fate of Waldo Joven, he spat on the ground. That got him the butt of a soldier's gun in his stomach. It folded the boy in two, and he groaned, and spewed bile. Waldo looked away. Requete whispered in his ear, with his wine-sodden breath: 'You see, Joven, this kid, well, he tortured and then murdered a whole peasant family, women and children and all, who refused to give up the *sindicato* and join the ranks of the *Cristeros*. He had them stripped naked and whipped, to the tune of Ave Marias and Pater Nosters that he forced them to recite.'

The prisoner now stood up and screamed his hatred:

'Long live Christ the King! Long live . . .'

Requete bounded across to him, drawing his pistol. A bullet in the temple stopped the screams.

'You shouldn't have done that, Sergeant,' said Ramírez in a firm but placid tone, as the boy's body slumped to the ground in a foetal ball – the child restored to himself. 'What about the execution squad?'

'*A sus órdenes, mi Capitán!*'

Requete stood to attention, clicking his heels.

Waldo closed his eyes and sighed. He was recalling the words he had written in *Die Ziegelbrenner* after the reprisals. 'Comrades, the oppressor kills in the name of order and finance. In what name do we kill?' Basically his ideas had not changed: his beloved Bakunin's 'no freedom for the enemies of freedom' did not outrage him then as it would do later, much later on. In Los Angeles . . . even if in those days too there would still be executioners and victims. The Munich revolution had only cut off his arms; Mexico, his legs. Because the axe had spared his neck, his head was still on his shoulders, that restless brain swirling with musty eddies and creative fizz. Perhaps it was no longer any use. Worked out. And not even thirty years old. That was why that creature had been able to crawl up his leg and sting him without a reaction, momentarily, at any rate . . . Bitten. Torn. Shredded. After his fingers, his tongue, his lips – everything. Bleeding breasts. Cyanotic. Not the slightest sucking movement. The nursing breast hangs useless. The dogs bark. Between the pincers' metallic claws, skin stretches and the fragile film lets sunlight through. Standing on his little platform, the teacher writes on the blackboard: '*Mordeo, mordere.*' Riddled with misgivings, the child wonders what use all this will be to him. Bremen senior once roared, in a fit of rage, that 'latin is a language for priests, not for a mason's son'. His mother consoled the boy and promised him that he would not leave school. Yes, he had taken the bait, the hook had set deep, and when he felt himself being pulled, choking, out of the water, he had drawn great breaths of intoxicating air. The bird's beak tore at flesh grown flaccid with death. The student had remembered the poem: 'Darkness there and nothing more . . . And his eyes have all the seeming of a demon's that is dreaming.' Never – nevermore . . . The Raven.

And the lamp-light o'er him streaming throws his shadow on the floor;
And my soul from out that shadow that lies floating on the floor
Shall be lifted – nevermore!

As he set foot on the quay at Baltimore, on 26 April 1925, at five o'clock in the morning, Bremen resolved that if it came to the point of changing his identity, in memory of Edgar Allan Poe, who had died there in the gutter, he would baptize his new life in the name of Raven. But on condition that this pseudonym of last resort should never be uncovered! Meanwhile the forged papers which would see him through the doors of Mexico referred to a man named Waldo Joven.

With a kitbag over one shoulder and Papagayo on the other, the man walked up the road to Oaxaca. He knew that Raven was inside him, mingled as deeply with his blood as the scorpion's venom had been. For his remorse, and because of it, Raven would live.

In the prison of Relámpagos, in the remote Petén, old Guardi, blind with age, no longer scrawled his living memory on to sheets of scavenged paper, nor did the skylight now reveal the comforting image of Bocanegra, the faithful guardian of the temple, whose presence had partially alleviated the torment of so many years' imprisonment. A hundred miles away, by the banks of the Rio del Norte, Little Sun was dying of an unknown fever. Her son Red would learn to use words and arrows on his own. Some months before, her beloved Cartridge had left her in his turn. As for the Husband, the forest had never restored him.

All at once the ark of night enveloped the secret, and in their tomb concealed and overgrown by its dense cloak of foliage, the Gods turned their faces to the ground and allowed themselves to be forgotten, for ever.

2

RAVEN HAD WRITTEN two novellas about subjects directly inspired by the events of that period, but nothing that mentioned Calles's dictatorship and the uprising staged by the supporters of Obregón; as if he had drifted through those episodes in a state of near-paralysis, the man continually shying at the image reflected by the writer, and vice versa. One of the novellas dealt with the affair of Sacco and Vanzetti, the two Italian–American anarchists who were executed on 22 August 1927. They had been indicted and sentenced six years earlier, with no corroborating evidence, for a fatal holdup and double murder, although they had never stopped insisting on their innocence. The other novella was a fictional variation on Charles Lindbergh's transatlantic flight at the controls of *The Spirit of St Louis*. Raven turned it into a kind of positive version of his own itinerary – the other side of the fable. For example the pilot says to himself: 'When I climb into the cockpit it will be like entering a cell on Death Row. If I manage to reach Paris it will be because the governor has granted me a pardon.' A distant echo of the writer's Mexican tribulations . . .

These texts, first published in 1930 in *Vorwärts*, were reprinted in the collection published three years after the author's death by Señora Mateos, under the title of *Masters and Slaves*. Apart from their undeniable literary value, 'Infamy' and 'The Passage of Appearances' have in common the fact that they utterly contradict Professor Lippman's thesis. At the time of the events described, the man who called himself Waldo Joven had been out of the Petén for several months: the photograph published by Fito Malinas in *Mañana* was proof. I overlooked that kind of evidence for a long time. Why didn't I think of it sooner? It was obvious that Raven could not possibly have stolen both manuscripts and identity from some mysterious third party, when – even supposing that he had written the two novellas in the heat of the moment – at least four or five months had elapsed between the episode in Relámpagos and the world-famous events to which they refer. Obviously it is hard to be categorical here: when I started to cross-check the chronology – it was in the summer of 1967, during the transatlantic voyage back to Europe – I might still have been misled by the impact of the revelations emerging in the previous months. But in any case one question remained valid: Petén or not, true author or plagiarist, where did Raven get his information? How and why did a man in the back of beyond get wind of and then write variations on news which, even though it had shaken the entire world, was bound to have taken a certain amount of time to reach even the outskirts of the jungle, in the hinterland of a country torn by troubles of every description? . . . At the time when I myself was travelling through those regions, the answer to these questions remained closely related in my own mind to a whole range of more or less fully articulated conjectures about Raven's 'commitment'. On the one hand there was the epic version perpetuated by Charlie's tall stories, and on the other the contradictions inherent in the works themselves, where Raven sometimes appeared without ambiguity as the defender of the weak and oppressed, and sometimes represented a man flying from reality and pursued by a gaggle of spiteful demons who took a malicious pleasure in roasting him on the spit of his own distress. For him to make himself the spokesman for exploited Indians in *The Cyclone's Eye*, okay; for him to want to offer his own contribution to the chorus of well-meaning voices raised on behalf of Nicola Sacco, like himself an immigrant to the New World, a shoemaker by trade, who had left for Mexico in 1917 in order to avoid the draft, terrific! But then came the flaw: I did not understand – I who still dreamed of transforming the world without having made even the slightest serious gesture in that direction – and I could not stomach my father having become an *ex*-revolutionary, a stranger to the concrete struggles being fought there, before his eyes, in a country which was enacting its own original and continually changing version of the great social convulsion. I ought to have known what exile was. But Raven's bitterness was matched only by my own resentment towards him.

Breaking that deadlock has taken me some time, and it may take the writing of this book to finish the job. Not counting the developments soon to be described, a number of incidental observations contributed to this slow but consistent change of direction. For example – and for the record – the Dos Passos case. The author of *Manhattan Transfer* put in his own cent's worth with his poem 'Facing the Electric Chair' in 1927. Yet in later life the radical whose heart had bled for miners and political prisoners, the laureate of the great strikes, turned sharply to the right, supported the hawks in the Vietnam war, and backed the racist campaign of Governor Barry Goldwater! . . . And worse than Dos Passos there was Jack Kerouac, who went crawling back into the established order . . . After the road, the freedom, the women, the lure of the homosexual world, the drugs, came Mom. And that was it! Sanctuary, security, work, in other words the petit bourgeois calm of home, sweet home . . . The idol of my generation, the lone wolf and romantic, ending in the shrivelled skin of a back-porch loudmouth. Farce or tragedy? Who will tell the inside story? In 1971 or 72 – the beginning of the end, you might say! – I thought I had it taped when I wrote a piece for *OFF*, the magazine I was running in London at the time, which said: 'Kerouac was nothing but a child of the century adrift on an ocean of flimflam. That's all. The rest? Illusion, bluff. If we stick to the facts, Kerouac only made a single trip worth calling a journey through America, hitching his way along the road (and not completely, even then). That was in July 1947. The other times it was thanks to Mom: she paid for the ticket that ushered him aboard those comfy Greyhound buses with their trusty timetables. The American dream, my cushioned backside! On 21 October 1969 there was nothing but a corpse left in the little town of Lowell. The verdict was abdominal haemorrhage following a hernia. He was forty-seven . . . And Mom, alone and sick – the woman who loved him best. Such a superior high to all that lousy benzedrine. After the success of *On the Road*, all the little mugs, myself included, began to confuse “beatnik” with “freedom”, although for Kerouac the word had some tacky connection with the mysteries of beatitude. Kerouac was settling down! He was thirty-five years old, that’s all. A good boy, yes. Mom managed his royalties and countersigned his cheques. No more grass, no more smack, but booze, right on! The dharma lush . . . and paranoia too. Kerouac’s next mania was LSD – a Russki invention to sap the creative juices of the US of A. Suppose it was true! Better play safe – the twentieth-century equivalent of the Pascalian wager. Just in case, Jumping Jack Kerouac springs to attention under the sublime protection of the good old Stars and Stripes. God help us! Redemption . . . Napalm has no smell.’

You can imagine the look on the face of Rakovski, our psychedelic loyalist! . . . Although it was my magazine, and although in the ‘New Journalism’ which grew to be one of the buzz words of the decade nothing was sacred, Hawkins – the brains of the group – protested. ‘Do you realize what you’re doing, Michael? And on the front page, too. You should have told the committee. Just wait till the letters start arriving! If you cut off the branch we’re sitting on . . .’ Sitting pretty, you might have said, my dear Hawkins.

Anyway I knew even then that with Raven the case was harder, and more complicated. My scenario was realistic enough, but it applied more closely to my own case (the utopian turned cynic) than to my father’s. Unlike the writers I have just mentioned, he had no passport, no identity. What side could he join, once he had abandoned the tattered flag of rebellion for the limp banner of acceptance?

With ‘Infamy’ and ‘The Passage of Appearances’, my false conception may have led me further astray. For quite some time I tried to convince myself, on no good grounds, that Raven had remained deaf and blind to the realities of his time, and that these two conspicuous white pebbles placed on the year of 1927 just happened to have landed there by accident. As I saw it, the writer had to have preserved only a blurred, flat image of the period. Today I see how that interpretation displays a distinctive feature of my way of looking at things. I was projecting my own anguish, and imposing the grid of my own fragmented vision on a fractured mosaic whose pattern I did not know.

Isn't it through a similar effect that I have begun to write, cut off from everything, isolated behind dark walls, and shielded by a curtain of snow as visually impenetrable as a cathode tube without a picture? The circuits have been tripped, I know, and the wires cut. I'm not 'switched on' any more, as my son Pablo would say. Some people I know would object to my passivity, but I have never felt more receptive than I do now, or more tuned to the world. Outside noises (a bell, chimes at noon, the roar of traffic, the beat of footsteps, the crackle of transistor radios, the clicking of the jaws flexed by menacing metal caterpillars, the messages of solidarity, the cries of the victims . . .) reach me, muffled, filtered through the mesh of present needs. Things are happening, outside, which words will never circumvent. I am aware of that. To swap my pen for yesterday's camera would do no good. Eye-witness reporting, direct sound, hand-held, twitching screen shots, all that is finished. It is no longer a matter of technique, theory, or even experience. I can stand up, walk over to the window and look out over the unlit street climbing in steep perspective towards the white square. What does it matter whether the movement is necessary or not? I move, that's all.

3

FORTY-EIGHT HOURS after their arrival, following an interval spent either in sleep or in introductions prolonged into endless conversations, Vittorio told Michael that he was in luck. Milpa was preparing to celebrate the ritual of *balché*. No white man had been seen there for over a year, and that was pretext enough: opportunity would make the thief. As the guest of honour, the young man would have the privilege of being initiated.

'We will see if you are a man,' the Indian murmured. His wife, Maria Bonita, more commonly called Nouk in the village, gave a timid chuckle. Michael did not venture any comment or retort. He only watched and listened, fascinated. Two scruffy dogs with quizzical eyes were growling and sniffing at his legs. Vittorio shooed them away.

'Come, now I will show you the ceremonial boat and the sacred house.'

In an out-of-the-way place by the river, half hidden beneath a dense canopy of leaves and branches, lay the sacred canoe. It was an old craft, no longer river-worthy, and a number of earthenware jars stood inside it. Vittorio raised the lid of one of these, to expose a brownish liquid unevenly covered by a thick layer of froth. Mateos suppressed a grimace and told himself that the drink looked like Guinness, but the image that flashed into his mind was of the witches' cauldron in *Macbeth*.

'Tree bark mixed with pounded sugar cane and fermented. The *balché* will be ready at midday,' said Vittorio between his teeth, without removing the cigar he had lit a few moments ago on the fire where Maria Bonita was cooking sweet potatoes.

Michael was starting to get used to the fat cylinders of hand-rolled leaves that the Lacandons called *hach kuuts*; their aroma no longer caught in his throat or turned his stomach. Vittorio had offered him one the night before, and he had refused. The Indian had merely reminded him that the cigar was part of the ceremonial, and Mateos had promised to try one when the time came.

Vittorio bent down and picked up a pot of *balché*. He nodded to his friend to signal that he should take the pot from him, and as he handed over the precious load, the smile on the face of the Lacandon indicated the degree of trust and privilege he bestowed by doing so. After picking up a second vessel the Indian started back to the village. Michael followed in his footsteps, taking care not to spill the ritual liquid.

When they reached the sacred house the two men put down their cargo and sat on the ground to talk. Vittorio explained the meaning of the objects and utensils that surrounded them. Michael asked questions about every detail he could not understand. About twenty mahogany stools encircled a carpet of banana leaves. The pots of *balché* arranged at the back represented the gathering of the Lacandon gods.

Michael paid close attention, stroking the smooth surface of the mahogany. Vittorio told him: 'The roots of all living creatures form an endless chain. Each time you fell a tree, a star falls from the sky. What will happen when the men from the North have cut down all the trees?' Michael did not answer the question, but the vision of a sky without stars ran through his mind. Perhaps he had never perceived the meaning of the word 'apocalypse' as sharply as he did in that instant, and it was his own race who would be to blame. The Dutch engineer must have miscalculated. Adrian Boot – didn't he recall reading some material about him while working on the series with Paul Arthur Smith? – Boot claimed that the ten kings of ancient Mexico were the incarnation of the Beast. But far from being monsters, the Lacandons were wise and gentle. It was the Jewish astrologer Baruch Cordavoro (he had also read a paper about him) who had been correct in his forecasts. In a few weeks' time the year would be 1966. (Here Mateos realized how detached he had become from calendar time. What month was it, and what day? Only one thing seemed certain: the sun was rising to the zenith, and soon it would be time for the ceremony . . .) And what if the Evil One had amused himself by making the 9 into an upside-down 6? . . . Apocalypse now! Before leaving Oaxaca – he remembered that too, even though he had believed that he could blot out the images generated by the news – he had read in the newspapers about the start of the American bombing raids on Vietnam. How could it be missed? The Indians found in divination a way to lessen the effects of disasters. What is there left to imagine today, whether in the way of real horror or of metaphysical perversion?

Music plays, slow and harmonious, while the first puffs of copal resin drift out. Men arrive, one by one, silent presences at first, then gradually starting to laugh and chatter. Vittorio stands up to greet them, and Mateos does the same. Matter-of-factly, and with natural, open gestures, the Indian pours the *balché* into bowls which stand on the carpet of dried leaves. Then each man dips his hand into the bottom of the earthenware jars and sprinkles his neighbour's shoulder – the first offering to Kisin, the god of Darkness. Vittorio signals Michael to drink.

The first mouthful: a very sugary liquorice taste, nauseating. You have to drink it in one gulp. Ah, a bitter aftertaste, like fermented coconut milk! Strong, syrupy, but seemingly innocuous. Now all are drinking. People sit down. Pepe Trujillo, Vittorio's brother-in-law, sitting on Michael's left, offers him a *hach kuuts*. All the men, a good score of them, have come holding a fistful of cigars in each hand to fuel the ceremony, which is due to continue late into the night. No question of refusing this time. The smoke burns. The second bowl of *balché* tastes less unpalatable. Michael feels a tide of warmth running through and around him; at last he is able to unbend, loosening the pressures and tensions which had afflicted him before the ritual, when he had worried about what might happen both during and after it. He is bold enough to speak, to join in the chorus of happy voices. 'I thought the cigar would make me sick straight away.' Pepe replies: 'By itself, it certainly would. But when you mix *hach kuuts* with *balché* it doesn't matter if you sit or stand, it's the same lift you feel: perfection.' Vittorio chimes in: 'The sacred drink doesn't kick you in the head, it doesn't give you a hangover the way whisky does.' He actually uses the English word 'hangover', and Michael wonders where he picked it up. *Balché, balché!* . . . As he takes a long drag on his cigar, Mateos feels suddenly struck, as if by thunder: he has the impression of falling backwards off his stool and of being burned, alive and wriggling, on the ground . . . He sees . . . the entire nation of the monkeys of the rain forest, gathered in judgment . . . laughing at his distress. One tugs at his foot and nips his calf. Another, this one invisible, grabs him by the hair. He gives in at once, and makes his confession. Vittorio translates. Crossing the ocean . . . So vast an expanse of water, millions of rivers together, does that really exist? Yes, and gigantic creatures living in it: killer whales, dolphins, whales and sea serpents . . . Shouts of horror. Sea serpent? What inhuman world do you come from? That is not where I live, son of Kisin: our world is ringed by sovereign seas. Not possible! Yes, friends, and the white whale is the largest animal on our planet.

One Indian has staggered to his feet, already drunk. He protests. Suddenly his arm reaches up to the roof of the sacred house. He brings down a live insect between his fingers, a big praying mantis, and holds it under Mateos's nose, growling in a hoarse voice: 'If he is lying, bite him.' Nothing happens. Michael raises the *balché* to his lips again. He grows bolder: 'Do you know, friend, that this female eats her partner during the act of love, and that is how she gives birth?' The other man holds the praying mantis right up against the stranger's cheek. 'Is it true what he says? If not, bite him!' The mantis does not stir. So as not to lose face, the Lacandon says: 'She will show you the north.' He puts her down, and it seems that she turns in the right direction. It is Mateos's turn to be flabbergasted. In a victorious tone, the native concludes: 'The wind from the North will come tomorrow, and with it the rain, the immortal stream.' Michael curses to himself: will he be prevented from leaving, or does 'tomorrow' refer to an indefinite future? He hopes so, as he dips his bowl into the *balché* jar again.

Vittorio begins to chant. 'The song of the Jaguar,' Pepe whispers into Michael's ear. Michael realizes, curiously, that he has just become fully self-aware again. A mother and her son (aha, it's time to notice that not a single woman or child is present at the ceremony) are pursued by a jaguar. In order to escape from the beast, they throw themselves into the water, and are swallowed by the freezing lake. Perched on the topmost branch of a leafless tree, the jaguar sees their intertwined bodies adrift among the currents and the weeds . . . Michael whispers: 'That is what will happen when all the mahogany trees have gone and you can't make canoes any more, Vittorio.' Vittorio's song is done. He pours himself a cupful of *balché* and smiles. '*Gringo*, have you the spring and the eye of the jaguar?' Pepe, who is lighting another cigar, giggles with laughter. 'When the last tree has fallen . . . hah . . . Mensabäk will have crossed over to the other bank. Hee hee . . . There, the rain is ending. I know that all of us will soon be dead!'

Balché! Now the traveller can feel the way his mind is slowing down. He takes another drink to recover his senses, but he is out of his depth. The moist cigar leaf comes apart in his mouth. He spits, but the acrid taste lingers on his tongue and clings deep down in his throat, where words no longer come. Exclamations and protestations jostle in his head and form into a solid knot at the base of his skull, a painful tumour . . . He is choking. The men around him understand, and they give him another drink. It's the only solution: having reached the point of no return one must continue in order to emerge again on . . . the opposite bank. Michael throws up on himself, and is sprinkled with the sacred liquid.

Night has fallen in pink flame. Old Nensäk, whose body sways ceaselessly backwards and forwards, calls for the visitor to be left to sleep. His sons Ernesto and Pepe carry the unconscious young man to an empty hut. Long after that, the songs of life and death will ring out in darkness hardly broken by the fireflies of the *hach kuuts* and the wreaths of incense, to the great satisfaction of the Deity . . .

Her legs part. He spills a few drops of alcohol over her belly and down to her pubic hair. It is she who tells him to lick it up. His busy tongue and blind hands reach towards her stiffened breasts. She has dipped her own hands into the sacred liquid and massages herself. When Michael joins in the circular movement of her palm on her breast, Virginia shudders. She rears her hips towards his own quick breathing. He takes her by the hair with one hand, while with the other he holds her by the neck. All around their knotted bodies, a river of foaming *balché* ripples softly with the tempo of their caresses . . . The meanders are hard to contain in thought; they fade into the depths of an impenetrable forest. But suddenly they are racing towards the mouth of the river, with its shouting sailors and mewing gulls, the salt smell of spindrift and the call of the open sea. Sirens wail. A pirate crane joins the boarding attack, and grins sardonically as it carries off Virginia's body, ludicrously squirming between the iron hands of the machine. King Kong drums his fist on his chest in token of victory. The pain in his heart . . . Kali clasps the victim in her several arms: woman becomes goddess. Still and dead. The rutting male takes hold of his own penis and pumps it till his seed spurts over the statue's feet.

Michael wakes up with a terrible need to piss. His head is ringing, his arms and legs are numb, and it is all he can do to stand up. Vittorio appears, a silent shadow, and holds him upright. The Indian's eyes are bright but his face is impassive, as if the effects of drinking into the small hours had already worn off. 'You must piss now, Michael, piss a lot, and save your dreams from drowning.'

Mateos complies. He does not feel equal to asking his companion how he could have guessed the nature of the images which assailed him during the night. Before long Michael will tell him, diffidently, what sensual forms and moves his dreams contained. As if to excuse himself, he talks about lack of sleep, vitamin deficiency, sexual abstinence. The Lacandon listens without speaking a word. When the young man refers to Virginia, the other only remarks: 'Good for hunting, all this is a sign of plenty of game.' What about rain, is that not likely any more? Tomorrow, tomorrow . . . always tomorrow.

Vittorio says that they must get some rest, because a second *balché* ceremony is due to start in a few hours' time. That is the way it is: it is the rule. And tomorrow – he is certain – now that Michael has been initiated, he will wake with the soul of a hunter. The festival is to end with a beat after *paca*, a great delicacy among the Lacandons. 'You will even be able to use your rifle, *amigo!*'

Michael was still exhausted by the ordeal of the previous

night, and he was soon asleep again, this time covered by a thick blanket, for he had woken up shivering, although drenched in sweat. Vittorio assured him, when he asked about these symptoms, that *balché* was the finest medicine.

His second dream was more erotic than the first. A Kaiser with winged moustache and military leather harness performed an endless series of sexual permutations on a young woman who interpreted the role of Ophelia. 'O, heat dry up my brains! tears seven times salt burn out the sense and virtue of mine eye!' And the Prussian, with every heave, called: 'Helen, Helen, *ich liebe dich!* . . .' Above the lovers' heads flew a cloud of carrion birds. Soon they had pecked the sky to shreds: it was entirely restored to the dark. Black and unmoving.

When the netting around him parted to let the sun shine in, Michael basked in the warmth. He blinked, and stretched. This time there was hardly any pain in his limbs and his head was clear. Only one wish possessed him, and that was to go for a swim in the river. It was easily done: he had merely to walk for a minute or two, undress behind some bushes and dive naked into the warm, calm water. But he had not swum more than a few strokes before he found himself face to face with Maria Bonita, Vittorio's wife, who was also swimming naked. She greeted him with laughter, and when she stood up to splash water over him, Michael found her small, pear-shaped breasts right under his nose, in kissing reach. He was so taken aback by the sight that he turned away, while she went on cheerfully splashing him and called out: 'An alligator will come and bite your leg off!' But she spoke in the Mayan tongue, and Michael thought she was scolding him. When he left the water at the opposite bank he realized that he was sporting an erection. He lay face down on the sand, listened to the pounding of the blood in his veins, and waited for the last effects of the night to disappear . . .

As Vittorio had promised, the second ceremony was less difficult to undergo. Mateos might even be said to have passed his rite of passage: ecstatic with pleasure, he too sang the praises of *balché*, and with all the men assembled together there was a long discussion about the following day's hunt. From now on, he knew that he would give all the bourbon in the world, and even the tequila, for a pot of *balché*, and all the so-called soft drugs for a few Lacandon cigars – always provided that the two were combined, because separately – and Vittorio had been insistent about this – each substance could have its own surprises in store. All the same, Michael knew that he was cured. When the hunt was over he would be able to set out again with confidence, if not in the future course of his destiny, then at least in his new competence to face it . . .

The *paca*, the spotted cavy, is a rodent about the size of a full-grown hare. The Milpa area was full of them, it seemed, and particularly along the river not far downstream, a few hours' walk from the caribal, near a friendly neighbouring village. Over there, a similar ceremony had been held in preparation for the meeting of the two communities. Vittorio explained all this to Michael on the way, and later he told him that he would see a man with red hair and skin almost as white as his own. He was the half-breed son of an explorer who had passed through the region forty years ago, the same man who had left Nensäk the old single-loader rifle which Vittorio carried slung over one shoulder, with his bow and quiver over the other.

'We ran out of cartridges a long time ago,' he told Mateos, 'but ever since that time – my father first, and now me – we always bring it, so that the God of the Whites will save a few animals for us.'

'Then what about my two-two?'

'It's different for you. You have drunk *balché*, and we know that you will make good use of it.'

Mateos had had his curiosity aroused, and he questioned his guide about the red-haired man in the forest. His name was Red Sun, and some people called him 'Red' in memory of the nickname given him by his father. Michael's heart missed a beat. There was no possible doubt that this must be the Red referred to by Raven in *The Cyclone's Eye*. It would be too great a coincidence for this part of the country to contain two men with that name, whose ages fitted the known chronology. Wanting to settle the matter beyond doubt, Michael plied his friend with questions – too many of them, for Vittorio refused to say more. A sinister legend was attached to the half-breed, and though accepted by his tribe he had always been an odd man out, never completely assimilated.

In spite of all the mud and standing water, and the dense

undergrowth which obstructed the path to the hills and kept having to be hacked away with machetes, the hunting band made such good speed that the foreigner had some difficulty in keeping up. In silence, the men slid in between branches and dodged and sidestepped obstacles with disconcerting skill. It was just past dawn when they set out, and since they were heading into the depths of the wooded slopes that overlooked the river, only occasional shafts of morning light shone palely through the tops of the ceibas and sapotas. As well as the hazards of the route itself, Michael had at first to contend with a constant itching that kept him scratching at his body. In the village he had dealt with a few fleas when he woke up, or trodden unexpectedly on one of the big millipedes that the Lacandons allowed to scuttle about on their food, but this time the feeling was quite unbearable. Vittorio noticed his friend's predicament and explained that it was nothing serious, only a side-effect of *balché* for a beginner, and that the forest air would soon relieve it. Come to that, Michael felt as if what he was breathing was an acrid stink of corruption, as if all these trees and giant plants had been rotting here since the dawn of time, bathed and perhaps embalmed in this reek of death.

'That one I bled myself,' said Vittorio, pointing back to a sapota they had just passed, with a long purulent scar on its wrinkled belly. He was trying to make contact with Michael again, evade his questions and encourage him to keep walking . . . 'Down south, where you want to go, they're all over, as many as the stars in the sky. And the gum flows so thick that you can't move your feet . . . Much harder going than today, you know.'

Michael was about to reply, in tune with all the ideas which had been running through his head ever since leaving Milpa, by saying that the Lacandon people had already taught him one fundamental thing, namely that in order truly to know himself a man needs disasters, or rather his own personal disaster. To that extent, yes, exile is a moment of truth . . .

But just at that instant the dogs, whose panting had hardly been audible in the vast murmur of the forest, suddenly began to bark. They were approaching a clearing beyond which a stretch of river cut a sombre curve. In it stood a group of about a dozen men looking much the same as the young adventurer's companions. One man was conspicuous in this group, and Michael spotted him at once: taller, thinner and paler than the rest. His thick mane of hair was red and curly, his nose aquiline, his eyes almost green. And Michael also noticed that as soon as their eyes met, the mestizo turned abruptly away. Mateos understood very little about the subsequent exchange of words and objects between the men of the two villages, nor did he care, for there was only one thought in his mind. He wanted to move closer to Red, who was deep in conversation with Pepe and Ernesto, get a close look at him and study the strange family resemblance which had struck him at once. Their features were so similar that there could be no mistake: this half-brother (for that is what the man was!) appearing out of the jungle forty years later was the living image of the father whom Michael knew only on the basis of a few faded photographs of uncertain provenance. Michael, of course, looked more like his mother, Doña Marina. He was a Chama.

Try as he might, Mateos could not catch the man's attention. The hunters had split into several groups which were scattering in all directions. Michael was left to his own devices at first, but he joined up with Vittorio and three other Lacandons from Milpa. For several hours, all day until nightfall, apart from a few moments when they rested and ate a rapid meal of wild berries and bananas, nothing existed except stalking and beating for game, and that was just as plentiful as the praying mantis had promised. Mateos performed wonders with his rifle. He shot three full-grown pacas and two moorhens spotted by Vittorio. The four Indians with their bows and arrows had only killed two pacas, both of them smaller than Michael's, and they were loud in admiration. During the hunt, the young man ventured to ask a few more questions about Red Sun. Vittorio kept up a series of fairly laconic responses, with remarks such as: 'He only speaks Maya, nothing else.' Only after trying the long rifle on a *curaçao* flushed out by one of the group's two dogs did he consent to say: 'He is a witch doctor!'

That was the last straw. So much mystery was starting to irritate Mateos. Fascinating as it was, the coincidence was enough to make this part of the journey more galling than he would have wished, as if fate had gone out of its way to block his path with distractions to counter whatever he might have achieved. He was ready enough to find things obscure and evanescent, but not for their constant metamorphosis. He had not come this far only to find fresh reasons for self-pity or amazement: was Raven's genius so unfathomable that its mysteries had no end?

That night, after the sharing of the catch, when everyone had gathered in the middle of the village where Red was the witch doctor, Michael finally managed to approach this man whom he was determined to regard as a mere accident of history, the accidental by-blow of an unknown explorer and an unimportant native woman. At first the mestizo stared at him wide-eyed, obviously not understanding the meaning of the few Maya words used by Mateos to introduce himself, and not at all disturbed by his companion's physical appearance. He might have been some sort of fool, straight out of a medieval carnival. But the words he kept repeating with an almost mechanical insistence – '*tsul . . . tsoy yol . . .*' – conveyed no illusion of magical truth. Vittorio translated: 'The stranger is a good man.' And when the witch doctor hopped from one foot to another and beckoned Michael to follow, Vittorio explained: 'He wants to show you something.'

Red took him over to a hut with a thatched roof, went inside, and quickly emerged holding an object that Michael recognized at once. He was unable to curb a shudder, a ripple of excitement . . . The other held out a pair of binoculars. They were in poor condition, with one of the left-hand lenses missing and the focusing mechanism bent. But that is not what drew Michael's attention. Instead, his eyes stopped still at the initials imprinted on the leather of the strap. 'T.S.' Nothing to do with Raven, Bremen, Mateos or any other initial ever borrowed by the writer. '*Todsi-tuel.*' The mestizo alternately tapped himself on the chest and pointed at one of the stars that glimmered in the twilit sky. '*Todsi-tuel.*' Michael thought he was hearing another phrase in the Maya tongue till suddenly his mind made sense of the silly refrain. 'Todd Sitwell', that had been the name of this unlikely character's father. That was what he was so eager to tell him, as if aware of the visitor's dilemma.

Although he was relieved, and found his earlier determination restored, Michael could not help also feeling slightly disappointed. He had expected nothing out of such a meeting, and wanted nothing, yet he could not quite dismiss the idea of a possible revelation. The return to some sort of rational normality scaled down the perspective and reduced his odyssey to the level of a mere tourist expedition. Even if it gave a reason to go on looking . . . To have come all this way, and still no *real* trace of Raven! Nothing but a few tantalizing nods and winks that kept referring him back to his father's works of fiction . . .

That night, Michael experienced another sensual dream. The body that spurred and bewitched and overwhelmed him had only a short-lived echo of Virginia's: by its gestures and postures and through its waves of supple warmth, it metamorphosed into a thicker, coarser flesh, heavy breasts, a rounded belly and plump buttocks, which reminded him, just when he reared up to ejaculate, of the proportions of an Indian woman seen and observed in the village.

I don't know what made Red decide to come with me. No doubt he had some personal motive for embarking on such a reckless venture. As for Vittorio, it was as much as I could do to talk him into coming with us, and even then he made it clear that his mission would end at the place where the waters darken. I gathered from his explanation that this was at the frontier between Mexico and Guatemala. Naturally it would have been tactless to refuse his request, and I told him that he could turn back whenever he wanted, while I went on with Red.

'You are mad' – he used the word '*loco*' as if to stress that it was typical of men from the North – 'to go up the Rio Usumacinta by pirogue. Not even the best of us would risk it!'

'What about Red, then?'

'With him it's different. You know that.'

'Vittorio, remember that in Ococingo it was you who told me about those troopers long ago, the killers of Indians, who went that way.'

'*Loco!* . . . There are other ways of reaching the land of *chicle* . . .'

'We've been over that already! I'm in a hurry. Yes, I know, what I just said means nothing to you. How could I convey the meaning of urgency? If I'm not back in the Petén in a month's time . . .'

He silenced me with a remark whose scope and resonance I cannot exactly recall, but which I felt I heard echoed a year later, after my return to Europe, when I came across an extract from the *Popol-Vuh*, the sacred book of the ancient Maya: 'Why should there merely be rustling beneath the trees and bushes? Indeed – they had better have guardians.'

I know now that the words of my Lacandon friend did not bear the meaning my suggestible imagination was ready to attribute at the time. My Mexican adventure – the brawl in Acapulco, the mirages in Oaxaca, the web of roads and railways, the brothel and the market in San Cristobal, the rescue of George Lippman, the night in Ococingo's little station, the journey through the forest with Vittorio, the *balché* ceremony and finally the paca hunt and my meeting with Red – all this had reinforced my feeling of being on Raven's trail and at the same time connecting again with my maternal roots. A perfect symbiosis! As if the blind flight forward which compelled me had possessed some alchemical virtue, one of whose high points had been my initiation in the Lacandon rites . . . Until now, the sequence of events – including the Lippman episode – had been consistent with the sort of plot I might have concocted before leaving London. Nothing clashed with the frame of the standard edition, and the pieces fitted comfortably into a convenient pattern.

The first warning came from the forest. But not in the way I had expected, having keyed myself up for the confrontation with all the solemnity of a raw recruit on the eve of his first skirmish.

I thought that Vittorio was wary of the Usumacinta because of natural dangers we would have to face in peril of our lives. How was I to know that what he feared had nothing to do with the traps and hazards of an enchanted river? Death did not belong in the garden: men had imported and established it, one more commodity adrift on the troubled waters of multinational finance. I learned a brutal lesson about my mistake and Vittorio's warnings when, after hardly more than an hour on the river, we found ourselves heading straight up against a convoy of logs floating downstream with the current. We had to paddle hard to avoid colliding with the leading juggernauts, which made a thundering din as they jostled and thudded against each other. Before we came to the bend, Red had stood up in the prow to point with his finger and shout words which Vittorio did not bother to translate, instead ordering us to head for the safety of the river bank as fast as we could make it. '*Madera, madera*, mahogany!' he yelled.

Later, when we were able to set out again, I knew that our progress was going to be slower than I had allowed for: the obstacles would not be snakes and caimans but sapota and mahogany. During our enforced halt I was staggered by Vittorio's partial answers to my anxious questions. All at once I was becoming aware of a new human and geographical reality, with quite a different colour from my personal war paint. For over a century (and I should have known this, Raven, shouldn't I?) enterprises called *monterías* had been exploiting the forest timber. In 1879 alone they cut down seventy-three thousand mahogany and cedar trees, two thousand four hundred of them along the banks of the Usumacinta alone, between 17 January and 15 April of that year. Even if his people's collective memory had recorded that event, poor Vittorio would not have had such details on call, and of course these statistics are taken from research I carried out for an article published in *OFF* in 1971, under the title 'Sentence of Death', strap-line: 'Ten years from now, one of the world's largest remaining forests will no longer exist.'

So this region was neither as empty nor as innocent as I had supposed. First, as long ago as the late nineteenth century, rich landowners in the North (Tabasco) and South (Guatemala) began to harvest its timber, using the rivers to float the logs down to a port where they would be loaded and shipped, mainly to foreign destinations. And, come to think of it, I knew those cargoes: this was the mahogany which used to be the pride of English cabinet-making – Hampstead interiors, galleries in the Victoria and Albert Museum, sales at Sotheby's . . . I was only twenty-five years old, and my little European memory, which I had thought of as cram-full, was considerably too short!

Tens of millions of acres were carved up in the scramble. As in *The Cyclone's Eye*, a few dozen Massons turned a discreet blind eye while hundreds of Gonzálezes beat and whipped the hordes of migrant workers who flooded down from the North in retreat from starvation – Yaqui Indians fleeing the repression of Porfirio Diaz, convicts out of government jails, share-croppers outlawed by their bosses . . . And as Vittorio related his own fragments of the story, I remembered the passages where Raven described the condition of all these wretched drudges, for example the way they were kept as prisoners of the *montería* not by barbed wire or some sort of punitive system, but by making them use the *bodega*, the company store at the camp, to buy useless articles on credit. By treating themselves to these small luxuries, these petty mitigations of the hardships of their daily lives, they ran up debts which they could never repay. Thanks to my father, these stories were well known all over the world, and as literature I had very much admired them, yet I had to suffer that narrow escape from a real runaway log on the real Rio Usumacinta to take their proper measure. And people had died like flies, in their hundreds of thousands. Why is it only the early genocide that is remembered, the piles of bodies lying in the gold mines at Santo Domingo? What mental subterfuge, prompted by my personal quest, had put it into my head that such things belonged only to the history of the Conquest, and that the rest derived from the romantic imagination of W. H. Raven? As a rule, and especially at the age I was then, one tends to have thoughts about exporting revolutionary blueprints and rebellious ambitions, but in my case my student enthusiasm had compartmentalized its militancy, as if 'out there' were a world apart, lying somewhere far above the whole shambles of guilty good intentions. I stress this point because I don't want to give the impression that as I paddled along in my pirogue that day I was overcome by the slightest feeling of eco-political anger. Obviously there was an element of that, but it wasn't crucial. What counted was simply that I had taken a step into Raven's world, the real one . . .

The flag attached to one of the mahogany logs seemed to belong to something called the Vanguard Company. The Troncosos and Cilvetis, the Valenzuela e Hijos and Pedro Romanos had been replaced by anonymous corporations. Not only was the forest's epic history in a terminal decline, but there was no one left – neither the robber barons nor their slave labourers – to write its epitaph. Unless the Lacandons who had once been its masters were reserving their finest silences for the wake . . . They alone said and did nothing, or next to nothing. The forest's history was the world's: once it was gone, not only would a race die out, but all mankind. Their resignation was matched only by their certainty that they could number the stars.

Quite soon, before nightfall on our first day's travel, and after making room for several more rafts of logs, we reached the processing plant that belonged to the Madera Maya Company . . . a proper little port, with a flotilla of motor boats moored to a landing stage, two concrete buildings, on the river bank, three or four lumber depots . . . and above it all, a single background howl, the strident, throbbing whine of chainsaws, voices that never stopped. I wanted to have nothing to do with this spectacle, or with the men who belonged to it. The thought that I might bump into the two Texans from the train made me swear out loud. Vittorio explained, with his usual self-possession, that the stop was necessary. I had money, and he would do the bargaining for supplies. I could stay right out of it . . . We spent the night in a shed, next to the hulking, stinking bulk of an antiquated bulldozer that ran on producer gas. Nobody disturbed us. No one had been informed that some fool of a young *gringo* was canoeing upriver . . . Before I fell asleep I listened to the rain which had begun to fall not long before our arrival and which did not stop for several days. I told myself that behind the protective fence, overgrown by centuries of plant life, there might lie a Maya temple with superb frescoes unknown to modern times. With luck, the clearance crews would find and rescue them. I longed to go and see, but on the threshold of a night of solid darkness permeated by invisible rain which had drenched me to the skin as soon as I set foot in it, I was stopped short by a feeling then quite new to me, a sharp and undiluted sense of fear. Throughout the journey which had brought me into the heart of Chiapas there had been plenty of opportunities to be afraid; yet although no courage was involved (I have made it clear that I was not particularly brave), and having run a gamut of sensations ranging from surprise to abandon, with intervals of complacency and nostalgia, still I had never been subjected to that primitive reaction which tightens your throat, knots your stomach, sets your hair bristling and your limbs shaking, and makes your chest thump like a frantic drum. I stood petrified as I let myself be soaked and penetrated by the great warm raindrops which kneaded and worked me like a clay statue standing on the saturated earth, on a plinth of vast solitude. Terrorized, frozen, and surrounded by impenetrable darkness and a resounding silence, I saw a vision of the men who had worked in the forest, the whole production . . . and what made it strange was that I had drunk no *balché*, nor had I taken any other psychotropic drug. It had needed this outpost of the Madera Maya company to reincarnate Raven and Cartridge there, under my eyes.

Naked except for a short-sleeved open shirt, the American stood on the landing stage and pissed into the river. He held his cock, half stiff with a subsiding morning hard-on, and tried to hose circles on the water's surface. First thing on waking, after the last night's jag and the frustration of the last night's dreams, you take a piss! Out of the hut, and do it. Who'll think twice about it here? Well, sure, the Kraut will! He had changed a lot, lately. Who did he think he was? As the last drops of urine hit the water, Cartridge shook himself dry, then stopped, thinking it would give him ideas. And now was not the time, since Ulrich would soon be ringing the bell to put everybody to work. Say, the rain had stopped this morning. He almost hadn't noticed. It would soon be March, one of the few months in the year when this bitch of a jungle wasn't swimming in water . . .

On the opposite bank, three young Indian women watched and giggled. Unfazed, he burst out laughing before going back to his hut of boards and leaves.

Three minutes later he was joined by the Kraut. Cartridge was still lying on his bunk, propped up on one elbow and drinking his second cup of coffee.

'Joe, how many times do I have to tell you that your manners are dangerous?'

He was ready for action – clean clothes, cropped hair, close-shaved. And a pistol in his belt, of course . . . He might just as well click his heels too.

'You get on my nerves, Ulrich! I'm not here to swallow the same bullshit they serve up at home. And I thought the same went for you . . .'

'Cut it out, will you! I've had enough of ancient history, as much as you have. The stakes are different here, Joe. Utopia is on the move, don't you realize, and we are the guides.'

Cartridge collapsed onto his bed, shaking with hostile laughter.

'Tell that to the stiffs who died yesterday . . . Tell all the people who die by inches just to save themselves from starving to death where they lie. Shit, it's crazy how much you remind me of the big bosses in the States. You talk and you talk, and after that we only have to count the bodies . . .'

'Joe, we have a mission to see through.'

'In the name of the revolution, socialization and land reclamation . . . Yeah! You remember Berlin, Munich – it was that way already. And on the boat to Tampico, I had all the time in the world to tell you all about my adventures for the good of mankind. Look at us both. Don't you have the feeling we've gone off beam, or somehow got started on a wild goose chase?'

'Get dressed. The new crop has to be shipped out in a week. The rains have stopped . . .'

'Yes, I noticed. But it doesn't stop me having to take a piss.'

'If you didn't drink so much . . .'

'Since you've been living with your Indian woman, you've gone off the bottle. I don't have your distractions.'

'Shut your mouth!'

'Oh, the gentleman has his tongue back, he isn't acting the lord of the sacred grove, the Great Manitou, the Blameless One . . .'

'Joe, if it wasn't for the morality and behaviour that you complain about, we would be done for. If we don't get ourselves organized, don't stick together, don't try to bring a few rules to this wilderness, then we're finished. They are watching us, and the slightest sign of weakness and . . .'

'Okay, I see. They're trees and stumps and roots, and we uproot them, we grub them out of the ground, otherwise they plumb get in the way of progress on this dungball world!'

'Look out, Joe, I'm warning you.'

'So now it's threats! Maybe I'm going nuts, and then . . . That's what we're here for, isn't it? We all have our crises. You, with your Malinche . . .'

'Her name is Little Sun.'

'. . . with your Malinche, you already see yourself as the new Cortés, the great bringer of civilization. The Green King, Pope of the jungle, Mister Mahogany . . . the company's heavenly messenger, god of the timber cull, Master of the Garden of Eden where all sins are redeemed by hatchet and machete! And when your kingdom comes, how many men will be left to share your manna?'

'In two minutes' time I'm going to sound assembly. I want you there next to me, and something like presentable.'

Ulrich Jasper Bremen walked to the door, but he paused there to tell his fellow traveller:

'As soon as the rains return I shall be leaving for the south, prospecting for new sites. I hope I can rely on you while I'm gone.'

For over a week we paddled upriver, growing used to the clusters of logs floating down with the current. I noted the names of the lumber companies: Agua Azul, Explotadora de Terrenos, Vancouver Playwood, Wess Friker, Asserraderos Bonampak, COFOLASA . . . Some grew in number, others appeared to be dwindling. But as a whole the forest could never stop shuddering with their shrieking din. Of course there was also the natural babble of birds and monkeys, but that concert of sounds is in such harmony with its venue that it soon becomes almost unnoticeable. It equates to a kind of silence, and all that troubled this silence was the rasp of saws, the splintering of wood, the thud of axes and the loud rustling of leaves that slips into the hush which is instantly succeeded by the tree's last heavy groan as it crashes to earth.

On the fourth day, a small aircraft appeared in the sky overhead. It was flying upriver on the same course as ourselves, a Cessna like the one they used to scatter my father's ashes. That was in the same region . . . perhaps it was right where we were now. And I caught myself scanning the surrounding foliage as if all of a sudden I was about to glimpse some shred of Raven, some mysterious powder sown like a wonder fertilizer which could restore life to uprooted trees . . . The atonement! . . . An old crate – was it the one the Señora had hired twenty years ago? – buzzing along not more than five hundred feet above out heads. The backfires and misfires from its engine made a change from the infernal racket of the forest. Red, who usually seemed not to be affected by anything, beamed a broad smile at the sky. Vittorio broke his silence to say '*Avión*' in Spanish, as if on this point too he was teaching me a lesson. And he added: 'It goes to the land where the waters divide . . . where we will take leave of each other . . . There they bleed the *chicozapote*, the gum tree . . .' And in fact it was at a site belonging to the firm of Adams & Railghes, the chewing-gum manufacturers, that Vittorio said goodbye to Red and me . . .

While the Lacandon steered the pirogue, every now and then the mestizo would lean out over the prow of the boat and carefully examine the opaque surface of the river. Then, unhurriedly and silently, he would take his bow, and an arrow, and aim at an invisible target. The arrow shot into the liquid brown mass – and in the evening we feasted on a succulent yellow fish . . . Apart from his skill with bow and paddle, Red seemed utterly indifferent to the country we were passing through, which admittedly was quite monotonous, and to the ups and downs of a journey which was anything but monotonous. All through those days I watched him: each gesture seemed dictated only by the strict necessity of the moment. For him, there was no question of tomorrow, or even of just now – anyway, that was how I interpreted his behaviour. Not the faintest gleam of surprise or annoyance ever shone in his eyes. He looked, and that was all. All along, I had wanted to tell him about the mixed feelings his first appearance had brought me. He had caused me to have doubts, even if in the end I had refused to grant credence to the suspicion. I was all the more alive to the misunderstanding because communication was impossible, Vittorio having reduced his role as interpreter to a bare minimum. Red looked me straight in the face. He shook his tumbled mane and stared through half-closed green eyes. When the rain began to fall again, his powerful arm muscles swelled and glistened as if renewed in a fountain of youth. His white skin was tanned as strong and supple as leather. He was a tireless paddler, an unbelievably expert bowman, trapper, fire maker – but he did not speak my language. My way of walking was alien to him – his short quick steps never landed where my long strides led – but he understood and imitated the puma's tread.

I would have loved to talk to him about Raven, and tell him my own version to see how it stood up. And what if Todd Sitwell had belonged to the same expedition? . . . Sometimes I would imagine him answering that his father was not on that side and that his camp had backed the Indian cause. As if things could be so simply either/or, so Manichean . . .

On two or three occasions I used my rifle to shoot a monkey for the benefit of my companions. At the place where the Rio Usumacinta suddenly narrows, a few miles downstream from the Adams & Railghes station, Red had us stop the pirogue and lopped off a length of bamboo which he used to harpoon several bizarre-looking specimens of fish. They were the last meal the three of us shared together. At daybreak next morning, Vittorio woke me to say goodbye.

'Others have tried before you . . . Few have returned . . . Red, he knows the way, he has been to the Rio Muerto before. Several times. Because he is the son of a star and of the black sun . . .'

That disconcerted me, and I stammered:

'What about Todd Sitwell?'

'Red never saw him again. That is why he does not miss a chance to go looking for him. Like you, Miguelito . . .'

'What do you mean? That I too will come back again?'

'*Quién sabe!* But be careful, *hermano*. On the way back there is even greater danger . . .'

Before he left us, Vittorio gave me a handful of cigars that he had saved for me. I hugged him in my arms for a long time, sure as I was that I would never see him again, whatever happened.

At that point in my life I gave very little thought to dying. Like any good self-respecting Mexican . . . and even if that indifference actually amounted to an acceptance of death. Yet taking risks had nothing to do with any sort of defiance. It was unavoidable. And Red's determined silence made me accept the meaning of such a journey without too much reflection. Vittorio, for his own part, knew that he would be returning to Milpa. I could not go back. My momentum was too great for me to consider reversing it. The exit, if there was one, lay ahead. Without a full awareness of my reasons, I persuaded myself that retreat would bring me into great jeopardy. One thing about the unknown: at least it left my options open.

If I had felt the slightest hesitation, one strange event would probably have dispelled it. Among the cigars which Vittorio had bundled into my hand there was a small medallion carved in jade. The miniature's fine workmanship displayed two immediately identifiable profiles, one a Maya god, the other a bearded white man. The head of a conquistador! . . . Imagine my feeling when I discovered that parting token from my friend. I ran back to the river, but Vittorio was too far away to hear me call out: 'Alfonso de Seguida!' He gestured with one hand, or so I thought, although I could not tell what he meant. Even if he had shouted a reply, I would not have heard it: the rubber factory's siren had just sounded. I never found out whether the Lacandon really had divined that part of my identity, and if so, why he had said nothing about it to me. In any case, what I took for an extraordinary coincidence only increased my resolution and impatience . . .

The little tributary of the Usamacinta which told Red for certain that they were leaving the Lacandon forest and entering the land of the Itzas was difficult to navigate after the first few miles. Michael quickly realized that this was no waterway utilized by big lumber companies. A bottleneck little more than six feet wide ran between two walls of vegetation.

'Red,' he asked, 'is this the Rio Muerto?'

And the mestizo nodded his head before unsheathing his machete to slash at a liana stretched across their channel.

Day by day the tangle of branches, bamboo, twisted trees, climbing plants and water weed grew more dense and formless. Soon hardly an hour could pass without the prow of the pirogue slamming into a hidden stump, or the gunwale scraping along a slab of gummy tree bark.

In conditions like those, you soon forget about buried steles and temples. Now and then, in order to avoid the suspicion that he might be going mad, Mateos would tighten his hand around the piece of jade given him by Vittorio. He had threaded a piece of twine through the hole drilled at the top of its pyramid shape and wore it as a pendant round his neck.

The humid heat clung to his skin, and he had to touch and finger himself to make sure of his own material being. Otherwise it would be possible to believe in the presence of a single liquid continuum with oneself a mobile element within it. An oily resin dripped from the branches that arched together overhead, almost permanently shutting out the sky. In the half-light it was hard to distinguish the mud and silt of the river banks. The stench of decomposing matter hung in the air, much stronger than the smell which had made him wrinkle his nose on the outskirts of Milpa, with eddies of nauseating gases. Everything seemed to be mould and carrion. Huge mushrooms, monstrously deformed, were rotting where they stood, their stems in the water while armies of creeping and flying insects invaded their decaying caps. Michael was well aware that this was no time for jokes or literary references, but he could not prevent himself daydreaming for a while about Alice's adventures in Wonderland:

How doth the little crocodile
  Improve his shining tail,
And pour the waters of the Nile
  On every golden scale!

The rhyme kept ticking through his head, and as time drifted on he made up childish songs in which the Usumacinta and the Rio Muerto became the Tigris and Euphrates of the Mayas. And then he also recalled the couplet that Doña Marina used to whisper in his ear to make the chills run up his spine: '*Ay el caiman, que va corriendo por la barranquilla* . . .' The reptiles were rare on the major waterways, but here they thrived. A horrid seething, frantic leaps, lashing tails . . . And on top of that there was the din of the buffalo-toads, the hiss of the red and yellow snakes, the spiders with their giant webs, the hornets, flies, fleas . . . A whole world hardly seen but always present, never resting for a second, and never allowing an instant's respite or inattention. A forest of antennae and carapaces, animal arabesques merging with the roof and floor and walls of intertwining vegetation, a magma only occasionally relieved here and there by the song of the colibris or the laughter of the spider monkeys.

In the continual interplay of light and shade, shapes and contours dimmed and blurred. The universe was reduced to two specific dimensions, the curve and the horizontal. Time collapsed under its own flaccid, languishing weight. Tight throats must strain to breathe. The vice screwed down; its strangulating grasp, made irreversible by the sweat and baking heat that blighted and corroded fabrics, clothing and utensils, blended little by little with the advance of the darkness.

Michael Mateos did not realize the extent of his own physical dilapidation. His face was lost in beard and his hair was now as long as Red's. His young body responded only lethargically to the instructions of a brain now invaded by a treacherous seeping haze. Constant effort and the forcible loss of sleep had undermined his stamina and enthusiasm. He listened to the soft cooing from the miasma all around him as Ulysses swayed to the song of the sirens. Now and again some fit of fever would give him back the strength to do battle with the snake-lianas or the cyclops-insects. Time rolled, in one long, stratified tide, under his armpits, between his thighs and over his brow. The horizontal lines lay down in majesty before him and splayed their huge thighs, whores surfeited with sperm. The woman squirmed and plied him, heavy and viscous, and the man closed his eyes, sealed shut with moisture, to focus on enjoying the hole he now penetrated, and which drew him inside with a sucking, squelching sound.

He had the impression that the movement was endlessly resumed, with the metronomic regularity of a world in gestation. Contraction, explosion, expansion, contraction, and so on and on. If the reality of Genesis was other than poetic, its enactment must have resembled the lightning visions which burned into the traveller's mind. 'And the earth was without form, and void; and darkness was upon the face of the deep. And the Spirit of God moved upon the face of the waters.' But these images were overlaid by another biblical memory – the Last Judgement as painted by the artist in Oaxaca. And their collision gave rise to something like a rumble of distant thunder, a dull murmur on the threshold of awareness. The coils of the snake appeared to loosen their grip, and clouds of multicoloured birds flew upwards into a breach of clear blue sky.

For a long time – how many days, how many nights? – while the colours of reality were redrawn before his eyes, Michael believed that he was up against some new trick of his imagination. Unable to guess the duration of his imprisonment in the dimension of lies and illusion, he did not dare to look too hard at the verticality that loomed towards him now. Vertigo flattened him to the bottom of the boat, and there he lay exhausted for a few hours more. But Red was busy, parting the leaves and branches that choked their way, his energy reviving – for it seemed that he too had succumbed for one uncertain night to the general inertia. Little by little the Rio Muerto cleared and broadened. Tiny ripples began to play along the sides of the boat. At last they were through. Michael refused to believe that they had reached the other side, and kept wondering what monstrous child would be the offspring of so painful a confinement. Emergence was not possible, just another of the virgin jungle's cheats: after they had touched the darkest shore of death, how was it possible that light should still shine out? What good was it to have crossed the world of shadows in the funerary boat, if it was only to emerge into the world of the single sun?

Once again Red was standing in the bow of the pirogue, punting it along with a bamboo pole. The animal had bided its time. It sliced like an arrow through the screen of branches, aiming for the throat. Its weight and impetus unbalanced the mestizo, and he toppled into the water. In the seething and splashing it was impossible to tell one body from the other. Michael could only sit up and stare. He wanted to intervene, but an unknown force held him paralysed. The torpor which for days had permeated his limbs and seeped into his entrails prevented any movement. And yet, when Red found his footing in the shallows by the bank, literally hoisting the jaguar out of the water as it clawed at his face, the young man managed to take hold of his rifle and raise it to his shoulder. He was trembling, though. How could he shoot without the risk of hitting his friend? The screaming and growling throbbed in his aching head, and he shook it about in all directions, desperate to jerk himself awake and be restored to his full senses again. He took aim, and wavered. Down the gunsight he could see nothing but a tangle of muscles and fur. Blood gushed somewhere on Red's neck, but he had wrenched himself out of the creature's jaws and was tightening one powerful arm around its throat. It thrashed and struggled in Red's grip, and every spasm of its claws tore shreds of skin and flesh and left long lacerations on the mestizo's arms and torso. Still locked together, man and jaguar collapsed into the water again. Down on his knees, howling with pain and rage, Red was drowning the beast. Mateos fired a single shot which raised a wild cackle out of the forest. Red let go, and the body of the carnivore drifted slowly with the current to disappear beneath a half-submerged branch. Michael was leaning over the gunwale with his hand stretched out to his friend, calling: 'Red, Red, come on, this way, come on!' Only the other man's head was above the water. Instead of dragging himself across to be hauled back into the pirogue, it was as if an invisible force now took him by the legs and pulled him down. Michael shook and rocked the boat, trying to move it closer, but in vain: all he could see was a circular eddy, hardly disturbed by the few bubbles that rose and were lost on the surface. Painfully he rose to his feet and railed at the sky.

The day was breaking.

He raved on, until time – now it was quick, it hurried – gave him the uncanny feeling of landing in a form of eternity different from that of the horizontal world. A sudden, continual bout of diarrhoea stretched him in the bottom of the pirogue for a lyrical flight which felt as if it would carry him over the edge of extinction. Far in the distance he heard the clear and lively chant of waterfalls. Would he even reach them, caught in the crazy gyration which set him spinning on his own axis? He was making no headway, in spite of the now faster, ceaselessly swirling currents, trapped in a single maelstrom whose funnel kept growing around him.

It was not fear which had made him void his bowels. The sickness had taken him unawares – he should have guessed – at the most ill-timed moment. In his delirium it assumed repulsive metamorphoses: out of the hairy body of the fat black fly burst Lippman's face, a Lippman who lay down beside him, in the same sick bed, to stink and cling and shit in unison . . . Then, with his belt and pistol round his ankles and his trousers down, Raven was mounting Virginia from the rear, like a dog on a bitch, and she was squealing, this bitch, while a whole tribe of busy, hybrid insects toiled to dig a deep tunnel into her rectum, whose rings kept convulsively clenching. The great pink snake . . . the caress and the bite!

In a final effort before he sank, Michael tore the double-headed amulet from around his neck. The jade stone vanished into the roaring flood at the same time as himself.

> His wilful hands and feet began to beat and churn about, spasmodically and feebly. But he had fooled them and the will to live that made them beat and churn. He was too deep down. They could never bring him to the surface. He seemed floating languidly in a sea of dreamy vision. Colours and radiance surrounded him, and bathed him, and pervaded him. What was that? It seemed a lighthouse; but it was inside his brain – a flashing, bright white light. It flashed swifter and swifter. There was a long rumble of sound, and it seemed to him that he was falling down a vast and interminable stairway. And somewhere at the bottom he fell into darkness. That much he knew. He had fallen into darkness. And at the instant he knew, he ceased to know.

At that instant, in fact, I would practically have sworn that these lines copied from the edition of *Martin Eden* that my son had given me were not by Jack London at all, but by W. H. Raven.

V

INFIERNO

1

VIRGINIA TALKED. The analyst listened.

'Have you seen the TV pictures, Jerry? Frightening! I didn't know it could be like that! In Detroit or Alabama, maybe, but here in Los Angeles . . . There was a kid, not more than twelve or thirteen years old, his face all bruised, blood spurting from over his eye, covered in tears, screaming how he hated the pig, Whitey, who'd beat up on him, his father, his brother, his mother . . . Watts is a rotten district, and we're the ones who put the misery in there, and the rebellion. God, how far away it seems . . . What use is Black Power, if it's power over that ulcer, that heap of shit! But Jerry, you saw that photo on the front page of the *Los Angeles Times*, just like I did, the broken shop windows, the looted displays, and that cop pointing a gun at three black guys lying on the ground. Oh, I know, bad conscience, guilt! It isn't that. I told you the other day, it's all over and gone. I've never had such a strong impression as I do today, such certainty of belonging here and now. Okay, you're going to tell me that's not such a wonderful idea, with Johnson bombing North Vietnam and our guys filling up the body-bags. But I'm feeling really good, I'm telling you. You admitted it yourself . . . Jerry, you have to go see that Beatles film, *Help!* Help, SOS, that's the key word all right. It came out last week. The day after tomorrow I won't be coming. I don't need analysis any more . . . Don't talk to me about Sylvia. George was only just back on his feet again when I had to face that too. But I knew my mother was a heart case. Lately you'd have thought she couldn't wait to die – she was doing everything they'd advised her against. Last time I saw her alive we lunched at the Algonquin in New York, and she'd already finished her third whisky and her first pack of Marlboro. We gave her a Catholic funeral. It touched me, this priest who said the mass in English, the kind of minister she really liked, modern, social, the kind she might have gone to bed with, by way of doing her bit for Vatican Two. Ever since I was a little girl, and she put me on a stage to crawl, that was all I ever heard about – her soft heart, her weak heart that hurt so much if every look and all possible attention wasn't focused on her. If she could have, she would have staged a heart attack just to see, to make us see! But she went first time, without any warning, just when no one believed in her tantrums any more. And I was always scared stiff of being like her. Each time I felt my heart give a beat in my chest, I told myself I had a heart this big.' (She raised a clenched fist.) 'I've seen medics, cardiac experts – nix, they never found a thing. But for years I was convinced they were all mistaken, and I was going to die a stupid death in the bathtub, or playing tennis. Or worse, in some guy's arms. I told you that dream didn't I? But Jerry, you said it wasn't important, you said my neurosis came from somewhere else. According to you – stop me if I'm twisting your words – it was mainly a question of an ideal figure, a need to be always projecting myself. . . on to Sylvia, on Lippman, on Michael . . . And now, you tell me, on to Timothy Leary. Not a chance! Yeah, yeah, I'm sure. I know where it's at with all that stuff about beatitude and physical transparency! Have you tried LSD, Jerry? Oh, you too. Then you know what I mean. It bugs you, to hear people talk so much about the undivided ego, ludic flexibility, and what Gary Snyder calls the back-country of consciousness. You haven't read his poems? You should. Maybe you're scared of it taking your clients away! Don't laugh: I'm not being aggressive, just natural . . . According to you, I'm going to allow myself to be had again, "possessed" again. That could be, but right now I prefer possession to all the kinds of dispossession I've been through, and particularly . . . analysis. Think about it, Jerry. Be a good loser, for once . . . Oh, by the way, last night I saw *La Notte* again at the university movie club. You've seen it, naturally. George wouldn't come:

he claims the movie is "vapid" and Mastroianni a joke. I told him it was because it made him feel got at. He didn't take that kindly. I told Mildred about it when we met at the campus cafeteria, and she said there's no limit to the egoism of men. "Give him a good lesson," she said, but I told her I felt he'd had his lesson. Mildred is my best friend, remember? She knows all about what happened in London with Michael. But she isn't at all like me – that's probably why I like her. "Go ahead, keep going," she said. She doesn't have much of a notion of why I don't do like she does: with her boy friend – he's a young sax player, very hip right now – they want to be free, total freedom. They share everything, boy friends and girl friends both. I can't make that scene . . . And basically I know that Mildred is unhappy, even though she doesn't appear to be. After the movie, a couple of guys from the generative grammar course asked us over for a drink. We had a laugh, no reason to refuse. They were nice enough guys, and they were holding acid. I didn't go very far, a quiet little trip . . . Not far enough to spend the night with them. I left around one o'clock. Mildred stayed, like I knew she would. That gets on my nerves sometimes. But I like her all the same, Mildred with her Courrèges dresses, miniskirt, coloured tights, white plastic boots . . . One of the first girls on campus to dress that way. It's her personal zen . . . Talking about Mastroianni's part, we got to talking about George and Michael. Mildred claims that women are more clear-headed. Just what are these guys looking for? Well, we've already been through this. You know that I resent Lippman because of that, but – this'll seem strange to you – not Michael. And yet – oh well, that's his problem! . . .' (A long silence here.) 'I'm reading Anaïs Nin's diaries at the moment, the ones she'd always refused to publish till now. I copied out a passage to show you. Listen. "The idea of death too is connected with the feeling of guilt. Guilt is punishable by death . . . You can fall in love with your father and brother. You can rebel against your mother. You can kill your rivals. You can steal other's loves. You can betray all your loves . . . in dreams. You can be amorous and orgiastic, you can be a thousand women, in your dreams. But enact *one* of them and you are a criminal, in your own eyes, in the world's eyes, and *you are condemned to death.*" And somewhere else she explains that primitive people (I suppose that's the right word for the Indians George and Michael are so fond of), primitive peoples get a lot of their wisdom out of rituals of possession by the dead, because that knowledge is also derived from a form of dispossession. For us civilized folks, who are responsible for Watts and Hanoi, or who blow away Malcolm X, burial buries the relationship too. Sylvia's death belongs to the past, already. No blame attached . . . A natural, human, physical pain at the time, sure, but no need for exorcism. Sorry, Jerry! Some other time, maybe . . . Today I prefer that story of Anaïs Nin's, about Raven, the girl with long black hair and pale skin, who tries to adopt a real raven – she feels its wings and sharp beak and claws are her essential complement. The raven is almost extinct in the US – exterminated. A few specimens in zoos, for the last rites of veneration and superstition, homage to the night outside the enclave . . . So this woman buys a raven, and she lets it fly free in her apartment. They're a close couple, a constant marriage . . . One day, Raven is standing in front of a mirror, naked, looking at herself. The raven, in the background, suddenly seems quite small to her, reduced to the proportions that maybe it should never have outgrown. The more she stares at her own reflection, the more the raven is absorbed into the darkness all around her, even seems to merge into the girl's long hair. Until it disappears, it's utterly dead . . .'

For the first time since the beginning of the session, Jerry now intervened, but not in the way Virginia might have expected.

'When you had your abortion, did you think about suicide?'

'No!' she rasped, one note of harshness before she resumed her monologue.

That evening, George Lippman took his wife out to dinner. When they came home they made love, once, and perfunctorily. Since his return from Mexico and his stay in hospital, George was no longer the lover he once had been.

2

I'M NOT UNINFORMED about what's happening out there. I saw it all on the journey here – the queues outside the shops, sombre faces, empty eyes bloodshot with vodka, the posters – and I caught the background uproar, the general buzz proceeding from the streets and from the factories. People avoid each other's eyes and go on their way. Even had I wanted to talk, hardly anyone would have spoken a word, and to meet the activists in the free trade unions I would have had to make arrangements. That was not so very hard to do, but it must wait. While I was in Warsaw I had watched the news on the State television network, though without understanding what they were saying. I made my own interpretation of what the moving mouths were saying, pleased when I thought I recognized a familiar face in a crowd. Here in Poznan I was relieved to find that there was no TV set in my room. Yesterday, while I was rereading the chapter on Virginia, I thought I heard shots coming from the street below. I jumped to my feet in mid-sentence and quickly drew the curtains back. Not a sign . . . In the dead angle that prevented me seeing as far as the square, nothing was visible except a bus cautiously gliding through the melting snow, under the same wall of grey sky. Everything seemed to display the calm and rhythm of daily life . . . Not one militiaman in sight, nor a single passer-by, but a void that it's sometimes hard for me to get used to, even though as things are it offers me the truce, the neutral surface, that I need for writing . . . I don't want to omit anything – there are enough erasers outside! I sometimes find myself fearing for my manuscript. At night I snap awake in consternation and check to make sure that it's there, lying on the bed beside me. And I open it at random to reassure myself that the lines inside it are not part of a bad dream . . . a vast white nightmare carpet where letters fade out like footprints under falling snow.

There was a time, I admit, when I would not have trembled over a few sheets of typewriting, when I was uniquely preoccupied with the sight of my own molecules melting, like snow in the sun, with the heat of the tropics. Captured, not by the rapids of the Rio Muerto but by the stupidity of allowing my vitamin level to fall, I thought that I was finally going to be landed on the shores of Tartarus. To say that I felt disappointed when I eventually did come round would be an overstatement, but on the other hand it is true that subsequent events came as a sort of confirmation that I was no longer of this world. Rescued by what I have to call a miracle, on the river bank where I lay raving with fever in the bottom of the pirogue, by a guerrilla band retreating from a military search and destroy mission, deep into the Petén, I thought for some time – two weeks spent shivering and sweating in a hammock slung in a corner of their camp – that those hunted men were going to let me die. When I was back on my feet I then persuaded myself that they were only reluctantly accepting my presence, perhaps because of my rifle and ammunition clips, which they were not happy about giving back. Then, with no other choice available except to follow them on their travels, I began to know them better, and to be fired by their ideals. This time I was being offered an opportunity – of course it never happened – to die 'properly'. Later, when I was tried as an accomplice of guerrillas and sentenced to prison, I thought once again that nothing could rescue me from the hole I had dug myself into, and that no one in the world could possibly guess that I was there, between the four walls of a prison cell. The irony – which in those days my pride would have tried its hardest to reject – the unpredictable irony of the situation was that at the very moment when I imagined myself to be utterly alone, so far from anybody's mind that I might as well be dead (and it was this same conviction that helped me to survive the ordeal), the high technology of deliverance was already in motion. Petitions in London, demonstrations in Paris, diplomatic démarches in Washington . . . I even discovered, when we met again afterwards, that Virginia had played her own part in Los Angeles by organizing meetings at UCLA, at least one of which was chaired by Professor George Lippman. I thought that I had penetrated to the centre of the earth, I believed that I had worked my way down to the tip of the most fragile root which had sprung from its gnarled and scrubby tree to drink up the sap of my origins. And all the time my name had been front-page news all over the Western world. When I came back, I was to realize just how far away I had been from anonymous oblivion. I was given a hero's welcome, and soon was able to pick up my life again after a blaze of temporary glory. History had resumed the game without me, and I was destined for a brilliant career. What my admirers and promoters did not know was that my release had not been achieved in anything like the way they thought. Naturally I took good care not to explode their illusions about the role they might have played in the whole story.

The one and only time in my life when I fired a shot in anger at a man (not a target in a fairground shooting booth, not in a dream, but genuinely shooting to kill, faced with a figure moving through the tender light of a dawn like any other dawn), it was in circumstances which would previously have roused my fascinated interest, in line with the clichés absorbed from a certain kind of literature. Suddenly I had been plunged into a world just like the imagery made familiar to me by the novels of Asturias. Everything, from the natural luxuriance around me to the actions I felt bound to take, was so baroque here, and so Manichean, that I lost my sense of space and time and started to believe in the universality of words. Chance had introduced me to a special, startling form of existence that I would once have attributed, without turning a hair, to the pure paradigm of a certain type of Caribbean folklore. Certainly, like many young people of my generation, I had thrilled to the crackle of the guns at La Moncada, and in my longing to stand alongside Raven I had dreamed about the Sierra Maestra, and the fish swimming in the ocean of the people. But from there to brute fact . . . Nowadays, I know, this recollection will be considered commonplace, perhaps even affected and ludicrous. In the country where I am writing this account, the story that follows – and which I tell with a touch of guilty nostalgia – means nothing, has no point of reference. But at the risk of being accused of gratuitous provocation I must make room for it here, because this is the way things really happened. This reality principle was behind my joining the guerrilla group. There was no question, on my part, of the slightest wish to put myself to the test, and still less of trying to cash the kind of revolutionary prescription that other Europeans, would-be revolutionaries, were hawking in those days. It was the same old classic question, to be or not to be, but with none of the existential overtones that some contemporary critics have read into Shakespeare's lines. This was a matter of plain survival . . .

In my then state of physical exhaustion and mental collapse, the choice – if the word has any meaning in the context – was automatic. I felt that the Red's death had tied my life to an event whose decisive character brought me a little closer to Raven. We had our guilt in common. At last I was sharing something of his, and my companions told me, after I had recovered from the days of delirium in their camp, that I had endlessly repeated a single refrain: 'My father's son, a murderer's son!' When the danger was over, I went on brooding over the pangs of conscience I felt about having perhaps been responsible, indirectly, for the mestizo's death. The more my strength returned, the more I persuaded myself that the shot I fired had hit Red. In my mind I saw him choking and drowning the big cat, then emerging victorious, water streaming off his face and with a smile on his blood-flecked lips, till the bullet tore into his heaving, lacerated chest. The sinister reptile, the carnivorous monster which had dragged him off to its underwater lair, was the product of my unconscious wish to forget the absurd savagery of the scene, and seal it off behind the bulkhead of a convenient illness. That was reason enough to start up the ghost train again; it was a signal that asked me: 'How could you be such a fool as not to see that he was Raven's son?' And in that case I had just killed my own half-brother in the same way that my father had been the death of his own when he dispatched him to die in his place in the Spanish Civil War, at Teruel . . . The sense of guilt, and of fury at having lost a person essential to my fortunes, do not in themselves provide an adequate explanation of my behaviour towards the group that took me in. And yet they played a considerable part in making me accept a future and a way of life for which I was not prepared and which involved the risk of being distanced from the purpose of my journey and diverted on to a false scent made all the more enticing because it was dangerous too. Not that my personal situation signified anything to the men and women for whom my presence merely meant a dead weight to carry. On the face of it, they had no way of knowing whether I might embrace their cause, even for the time being, or whether the fact of having an extra mouth to feed would be offset by my contribution of an additional rifle and ammunition. At first they even distrusted me – I might have been one of the mercenary bounty hunters hired by the Guatemalan authorities to track down rebels. I kept quiet about my American nationality, and made full use of my one great asset, which was my fluent Spanish. As you will see, there were very few Indians in the group. I talked about my adventure with the Lacandons, which raised my stock with my new companions, and said that I wanted to reach Relámpagos. On the day I mentioned that, the man who commanded the band – everybody called him 'Jefe' – laughed out loud. 'Ah,' he roared, 'the later you get there, the better for you, unless you arrive with us and our guns!' He talked about the garrison of government troops, and also about the jail. I felt bold enough to tell him that I was an English academic, here to write a book about Raven, the writer and defender of the oppressed who had lived in the region and had even served a sentence in the prison at Relámpagos. The Jefe laughed again: 'If you knew what the cells are like, you would not go there, even for a book!' The sound of Raven's name drew the attention of a young woman whose unusual appearance had already caught my convalescent eye, and she came over to the fallen tree-trunk where the Jefe and I were sitting. She was a tall dark beauty wearing camouflage battle-dress, the perfect stereotype of a guerrilla heroine. (But I can't help that: this is the way it happened.) Her name was Lidia Valdés, and later on I learned that, along with her brother Rafael, she had given up her law course at the university of Guatemala to join the armed struggle. 'I have read the writer you speak of, compañero,' she said to me, and then turned to the Jefe and added: 'I believe he is to be trusted.'

She smiled. She had thin lips, a wide mouth, and her teeth were a brilliant white against the copper smoothness of her skin. That day she was wearing her black hair shoulder-length, although on forced marches or in action she usually kept it pinned up above her neck. To say that I stared at that mass of coiled hair, or that I could hardly take my eyes away from the stray wisps left floating at the nape of her neck, above her khaki collar, would be to minimize the intensity of the feeling: when she walked in front of me, with her machine pistol slung over her shoulder, the sway and dance of her supple body was an involuntary performance . . . At the time of our first meeting we chatted briefly about Raven. On top of a physical magnetism too powerful to ignore, that was enough to create a sexual fascination which was only intensified by its obviously one-sided nature. Whether because of my own isolation, or the imminence of danger, for the first time in my life I was in love, with all the irrational spontaneity the phrase implies . . . Till then, and even with Virginia, it will be obvious enough by now that my sexual experience had been more or less calculated and narcissistic. Now, when I watched her strip down her gun and grease it, when she enlarged on some sentence from Lenin for her comrades' benefit, or slept in her hammock in the glimmer of a dying fire, with her M2 lying across her chest, I felt raw and helpless. And her persistent refusal to consider me as anything but a travelling companion only heightened my confusion, and my sense of rapture. When for once I was not playing a seduction game, I was completely at a loss. Here too, this touch of romanticism may seem excessively appropriate to the situation, but the painful irony was that I fell into this condition at a moment when the thing appeared quite unnecessary. That may sound laughable, but to this day I would not laugh about it. Lidia told me straight away that she found *The Cyclone's Eye* 'petit-bourgeois', and that I was too. The terminology was familiar, of course: at Oxford these concepts had sustained sleepless nights of arguing about the way to change the world. But out here, finding myself in love with a woman who granted me nothing but her everyday respect, the Marxist catechism seemed to me about as displaced and irrevelant as the litany of a Catholic priest referring to the resurrection of the flesh, or a shaman's incantations to summon the rain. I suppose I ought to laugh: wasn't it a comic reality that had me lamenting like Menon over Diotima, trying to sublimate my love in the manner of Hölderlin, while Lidia saw our relationship purely as a matter of ideological education? She quoted Althusser, whom she had read two years before, on a visit to Paris, and her uncomplaining comrades heard her out. 'No tactic is feasible if it does not depend upon a strategy, and no strategy if it does not depend upon a theory.' I knew that she was right, even if the facts proved her wrong later on. And yet my sole response was to find the words of the poet hurrying through my mind:

> Each day I go about, and always seek another elsewhere,
> Pursued it long, down all the paths of the land
> . . .
> Only you, your own light, O heroine, holds you in the light
> . . .
> And not once are you alone
> . . .
> Then I too want to live!

The pointless dialogue did not end until two and a half months later, with Lidia's death. She never did yield to my advances. All I managed to do, with all my wooing, was to amuse her a little, as if my overtures and ardent talk amounted to a well-earned little sideshow, a fair reward for her services to the group. Make no mistake, though: Lidia was anything but frigid. No man could be left indifferent by the sensuality expressed in her every gesture and every step. And all of them – Cuchillo, Quevedo, El Gordito and the rest – missed no opportunity to pay a brief compliment in homage to Lidia's femininity. She took no offence, but answered with a smile or with some joke in the same vein, a boost to their manhood. But things never went any further than that, for – as I quickly learned – Lidia had their absolute respect. She was the daughter of a rich and powerful family, but she lived as they did, and shared their hurts and sacrifices. She did not only talk revolution, she spoke the language of the oppressed, and without affectation – she *was* the Revolution! . . . Unable to reach that level, I made friends with Rafael, Lidia's brother.

That was not difficult, because we genuinely took to one another. Rafael was nearly twenty-six, the same age as myself, and two years older than Lidia. Lacking the strength and energy that infused everything his sister did or said, he appeared to be far more fragile. He suffered from asthma attacks that racked his chest so violently you expected his delicate bones to shatter into a thousand pieces. 'A nuisance. I got it when I was small, and I had treatment for it, but here it's worse than anything . . . because of all the insects' – and he shuddered – 'and airborne moulds. And the humidity . . . Look, touch your shirt, it's soaking wet . . . You're not moving, you stand there waiting for them to jump you, and this bloody rain is dripping down your face, neck, back, between your legs, your balls, everywhere . . . and it creeps down into your lungs.' He cleared his throat loudly and spat out gobs of ropy sputum. The sicker he became – several times I saw him practically choking, fighting for breath – the more forceful his reasons for staying in the jungle, as if he needed that permanent mortification to atone for some secret sin . . . Rafael had joined the guerrilla war before his sister. Moving in stages, from resistance to resistance, from the plains to the mountains and finally to the Petén, he had come to the shores of Lake Tayascal about a year ago. At the time of my own arrival, Lidia had only been with them for four months. Once she told me in confidence that Rafael had gone on the run because he was afraid of his father. That struck me as odd, but although I knew the facts of Rafael's radical history I did not argue. Why did Lidia want to belittle the scope and meaning of those viciously repressed demonstrations, the sleepless nights spent drafting and cyclostyling pamphlets, the races against death, the manhunts, the infinite hopes? Like all the questions that love made me ask, but which brought no hint of an answer, this one took on a deeper resonance on the fatal day of the ambush when, with soldiers all around us, we were trying to think of ways out, loopholes to slip through and run. Rafael said: 'She isn't what you think. In Paris, and other places, there have been men. And then, against the advice of the entire Valdes family, she became engaged to a young lawyer, very committed to the movement. He was taken in a roundup by the political police, and never seen again . . .'

The day they hit us the group had been out of contact with

the National Guard for nearly five weeks. Thanks to his couriers, and help from friendly peasants, the Jefe knew that an expedition had been sent to winkle us out and exterminate us once and for all. But of course we didn't know how or where. All we knew was that they really meant business.

The Jefe – a captain who had deserted the regular army for being too 'bourgeois' – had known perfectly well that the group could not keep on harassing the regular troops in their quarters for ever. In any case, when Lidia arrived they had decided to space out their military activities for a while in favour of propaganda work aimed at the peons in the lumber camps or around the sharecropping estates in the region. Without the help of the peasants, there was no long-term future for guerrilla warfare, and in fact that was the crucial problem if they were to avoid repeating the sorry experience of the failed revolution of 1954. In that black year, troops brought in from Honduras and Nicaragua under the command of Colonel Carlos Castillo Armas overthrew the liberal reformist regime of Jacobo Arbenz, who had made the mistake of redistributing estates belonging to the big landowners or the United Fruit Company among the peasants. From then on, and no matter who was in power, it was the army that ruled the roost, under the kindly and collusive eye of the United States. General Ydigoras Fuentes, who had been in power for two years, was a carbon copy of his military predecessors. 'And if we do not succeed,' Rafael said, 'he will be replaced by another, perhaps even more cruel.' Lidia broke in. 'We have to avoid the old mistakes. Our country is unquestionably one of the most underdeveloped in the whole continent of America, and that is why the basic ground of the armed struggle must be the countryside. In the towns, the student and intellectual vanguard can only claim a secondary role, at least for the moment, until it becomes an essential link, when the time comes to take power . . .' Not all the group's members shared this point of view, and there were long arguments on the issue of whether they had gone over to the armed offensive too soon, and whether the masses were ready to receive the message. The peasants were frightened, it is true. For them, guerrillas were still thieves and murderers who drew down the wrath of the army and police on the heads of the population. It was quite easy for the authorities to draw parallels with the robber bands who for centuries had marauded the forests, hills and plains, ever since the excesses initiated by the outlaw adventurers of the Conquest era. The Jefe had been pleased when a villager agreed to pay his tribute to the Revolution in the form of a sack of cornflour and a few kilos of *frijoles*. Of course there were the natural alternatives offered by the local fauna and flora, but it was not possible to be completely reliant on the produce of hunting and fishing. As a former butcher's apprentice from Flores, and an artist with a clasp-knife, Cuchillo was the expert at cutting up game. Occasionally, food and meagre reinforcements would arrive from the guerrilla bands of the south-west. For arms supplies they were reduced to scavenging for the weapons dropped in battle by dead or wounded soldiers, or to staging lightning commando raids by ten or twelve men against the garrisons at La Libertad or Relámpagos, little towns lying in the valley a good twenty or thirty miles away from their hiding place. Obviously the distance did not make matters easier, particularly because on the way to or from the target they could not eliminate the risk of running into a patrol without being able to call in their main forces, the fifty fighting men and women left far behind them in the jungle. But the chief threat came from aircraft: if they were spotted the raiders could only dive for cover, which did not save them from murderous strafing guns . . . After an ambush, if it all went well, they would pick up two or three rifles or revolvers, with some chance of getting hold of a couple of cartridge belts, or half a dozen hand grenades, or – if their luck was really in – a submachine gun and its clips. They worked with the tools available: recruits arrived with their own equipment. The Jefe, for instance, was proud of his Matsen, which he had brought in together with a good supply of ammunition. He was an artist with a submachine gun, and the younger recruits admired him for his skill.

Once I had recovered I had to take part in a continual series of exhausting marches. The advantage of guerrilla warfare came from the band's mobility. They always showed up where they were least expected. But they did not necessarily appear in time to prevent the soldiers from burning the Indians' huts, raping their women and destroying their crops. That was how it had all begun – with fire. Aircraft had dropped incendiaries on plantations belonging to people who refused to sell out, for a pittance, to the Company. El Gordito recalled it, chewing on his wad of chicle: 'First they starved us out, then they collected us into a camp and under our eyes they tortured our women and children. They did not even bury the dead, just doused the bodies with petrol and set light to them.' El Gordito had escaped, and in his case fear had turned to hate. He volunteered for all the hopeless missions, but Lidia could not stand his harsh behaviour towards the peasants. One day I saw him cut the throat of a skinny bullock whose owner was refusing to say whether any soldiers had passed that way. I tried to intervene, but in vain. 'What do you know about it?' he snarled in my face, before he loosened his grip and shoved me out of his way.

On Christmas Eve a quarrel broke out among the men. Seven or eight christianized Indians wanted to celebrate the birth of Jesus, and in the name of the revolution, because they saw no contradiction there. The Marxists attempted to prevent them, and Lidia had to intervene before the Indians were allowed to pray and sing in peace. It was the day after this incident that I came across her standing in the river, smearing her body with *amole*, a plant used by the natives as a kind of soap. The water came up to her waist, but the rest of her body was a sight for my sore eyes. I was standing about thirty feet away, with a clump of bushes between us, and she hadn't seen me yet. Under the caress of her hands her breasts stood out, and it seemed to me that her fingertips lingered on the dark pink bud of her stiffened nipple. I took a step forward and she became aware of my presence. Slowly, she lowered herself up to her neck in the river, not to protect her nudity but simply to rinse herself off, since she immediately stood up again without displaying the slightest sign of haste or embarrassment. She went on bathing herself, and told me:

'A revolutionary should also be clean, don't you think so?'

'I admit the compañeros smell a bit!'

'Why don't you come in?'

I was already stripped to the waist, having come there to bathe with no idea that I might meet anyone else. I took off my trousers and underpants. As I entered the water, I was expecting some reaction from Lidia – she might have laughed, for instance, which would have made me feel less awkward. But not at all: she was having a dip as if this happened every day.

The water was quite cold. I scooped handfuls out of the river and gradually rubbed myself clean.

'Aren't you cold?' I asked her, trying to sound relaxed.

'You get used to it.'

'Don't you rather enjoy this?' (The innuendo was not unintentional, as she probably realized, for I sensed that she was on the defensive. You could say a lot of things about Lidia, but never that she lacked intelligence or presence of mind.)

'Does that worry you, comrade? When it comes right down to it, I wonder if you aren't really worse than the men from our country. Women and guns, they don't fit into your usual pattern, do they?'

'You're a beautiful woman, Lidia.'

'Ah! Now comes the sweet talk: how it would please you to find your precious Western romanticism of love and death out here. Look at these hands.' She held them out towards me. 'They have turned red and rough. Do you believe that sentimental exaggeration or rhetoric or mystification have anything to do with that?'

'With hands like yours, you can always love.'

'. . .'

'You say yourself that you're a woman: why do you refuse to be everything you are? I don't know what you are looking for here, or what you would like to forget, but I see you: you eat hardly anything and you drink even less. At least the men have booze to keep them warm, and when it runs out, there's always a cigar, or chewing gum. Don't you know what pleasure is?'

She did not answer. I had scored a point. Instead she left the water, walked over to her bundle of clothes and began to put them on.

'If I was Menéndez or Cuchillo,' I ventured, 'I would say, Lord, what a rear view!'

'The trouble is, Michael, that you are not Menéndez or Cuchillo. And you never will be.'

I ran across to Lidia and took her in my arms. She did not resist, but stood quite still against me. Her shirt was still open and her legs were bare. Her skin touched mine. I kissed her on the neck, and only then did she push me gently away. As she stepped back I did not attempt to hold her, despite my desire. It seemed to me that before she turned away she darted one wistful glance at my rearing cock. She was pulling her trousers on. 'Come,' I sighed. She finished buckling her belt, then turned towards me again and came up to kiss me on the cheek. As she did so, her left hand rose slowly from my balls to the top of my penis in a faint caress. Then she strode off along the footpath leading to the camp. I was rooted to the spot, mad with frustration. Some way along the path, she called back:

'For that, you are better than Menéndez or Cuchillo!'

At first I did not ask myself how I ought to interpret that remark, but although I had every reason to know there was nothing between Lidia and these men, for some time afterwards I was haunted by the image of their straining bodies – the beast with two backs! – I quickly sobered up, got dressed and ran to catch up with her. Walking back, neither of us mentioned what had happened, but she started to talk, in level tones, and with no preamble. I listened in silence.

'One has to choose . . . Last May the second, Julio took me to the movies for the last time. They were showing *Maria Candelaria*, by Emilio Fernández, a Mexican film. I had not seen it, and Julio liked it a lot; he used to say that I looked like Dolores del Rio . . . In the morning he had been in court, defending striking workers from Amatitlan. He was proud of his defence, even though he had no illusions about the verdict next day. As we left the cinema he told me that he wanted to re-read his files again: we would see each other after the trial. He left me outside my door; we kissed, but it was not a farewell kiss. In the street where he lived it was quiet – so they tell me – as quiet as usual. But a man in plain clothes was waiting with a submachine gun in the hallway of his apartment. In the sitting room, three men with revolvers started to beat him with their gun-butts as soon as he appeared. Julio fell, and they hit him in the belly, in the ribs, in the head, punching and kicking. When he passed out these men tied his hands behind his back and put a blindfold over his eyes. They threw Julio into the back of a car, and he was taken to an empty house, somewhere in the suburbs, where he was tied to a chair and interrogated. Who knows what else they made him suffer to make him talk? They wanted to have him say that he was a Cuban agent, on the basis that he went to Havana last year for a congress of intellectuals.

Julio could not deny his sympathies for Castroism. With his face in ruins and his teeth smashed, he confessed nothing but simply told them the truth. That was enough cause for him to disappear . . . Some friends in high places told me a few weeks later that he had been transferred to a prison far away, in the Petén. A prison where no one escaped and no one came back . . . You understand? . . . Rafael claims that Julio is dead. It was Cuchillo who told him. Some peasants found the body dumped in a ravine one day, and buried him, or what was left of him, because it was a mass of mutilations . . . But there's nothing to prove that the story is true . . . Until they bring me Julio's head . . .'

Instead of deterring me, the story only intensified my feelings. In the persona of the tragic widow, Lidia stood for the type of woman I was seeking, the image of my innermost nostalgia. Only let her forget Julio and she would be radiantly mine! Naturally – and even if I was not altogether aware of the fact at that moment – it was the desire itself I most prized. I did not persist because deep in my reluctant mind I must have formulated the idea that if I possessed her I would instantly lose her. Others before me have drawn attention to this masochistic element in the feeling of love. Instead of trying to bring us together, say by making myself useful to the cause, I set about building more and more barriers between Lidia and me. She was the first to be taken aback by my hostility. In order to school myself in the part I was playing, I began to see her in only her most negative aspects. From there to discovering all her faults, and dressing her up in the weeds of an untouchable lay nun, was a step I took with all the naïve determination of a flagellant happy with the pain through which he convinces himself of his own existence and identity.

That same evening, during the ideological training discussion held every day (except when there was fighting), I felt strong enough to talk against the grain.

'Do you know what's happening to Che at this moment, comrades? Well, Fidel has him in quarantine on the Isla de Pinos. An old revolutionary companion – a writer, as it happens – is keeping an eye on him. And do you know why? Simply because Guevara doesn't toe the line. He won't come to heel. Good old Ernesto disapproves of Soviet aid, and the alignment with Moscow. Moscow, the trials, does that put you in mind of anything?'

'How do you know that?' the Jefe asked.

'I read it in the *Los Angeles Times*.'

'What's it about, then?' El Gordito snorted, after noisily spitting out his mouthful of gum.

'Che isn't ready to retire. You remember his words – "One, two, three, many Vietnams . . ."'

'It's good, you talking about Vietnam!' Lidia replied ironically. I chose not to ask myself what she might be implying (did she know a lot more about me than she was saying?), and went right back on the offensive.

'A revolutionary always ends up by turning into a civil servant,' I observed in a sweeping tone.

'You are a defeatist,' Rafael answered, but with no trace of temper or annoyance: he merely stated a fact.

'Anyway, what does it matter to us?' added one of the Indians, whose name I did not know and who hardly ever broke his total silence, being utterly absorbed in his everyday work, and keeping himself ready for battle.

Seeing that it would be ill advised to persist, I kept quiet and lit the cigar the Jefe had just given me. 'That's good!' I breathed, letting out a cloud of smoke after a first deep inhalation. 'Very good!' I repeated, looking Lidia straight in the eyes. Instead of responding, she confronted me.

'This man is like Raven, the writer – the only thing he cares about, no? An idealist!' (I choked and coughed.) 'Perhaps he believes that the generals will sit still for us, or the landowners with their Yankee backers will bow out gracefully when we knock on their doors, just like that!'

And she snapped her fingers. The Jefe gazed at me and grinned. In order to disguise my embarrassment, I puffed at my cigar. Luckily Quevedo chose that moment to pick up his guitar and start to sing.

They pinned his eyes
To the lids of the night
And he made a vow
To cling to the light . . .

Next morning we raised camp, with the intention of moving our operations a little closer to Relámpagos. The Jefe made sure that the whole site was absolutely clear, with nothing left behind, no trace that we had ever been there. One day I had seen him giving a scorching tongue-lashing to old Pelayo because he had left some cigarette butts lying around. The man was about fifty years old, and paunchy, although his belly did not prevent him from running for miles without appearing to be out of breath. He may have been the one member of the group with something really shady in his past: the general opinion was that his reasons for joining had less to do with the growth of political consciousness than with having the police on his trail. The Jefe had required no further explanation: Pelayo was an expert with dynamite.

El Gordito knew the location of a narrow, impregnable canyon, and it was there that we spent New Year's Eve. This time there was unanimous agreement to celebrate the New Year. The men were tired, and the Jefe knew that a little peace and quiet, with nothing on their minds, would offer them a breathing space before they went back on the run. Personally, this halt only set me more on edge. I slept badly and my original enthusiasm was giving way to all sorts of misgivings. I was starting to wonder how it would all turn out, and whether it had been such a good idea to stay with the group. Now that I had survived the Rio Muerto it was time to think again about my life. The pressure of constant action can sometimes muffle the noises destiny makes when it comes knocking at your door. In perspective – and Lidia's challenge certainly helped to widen the gap between us – it is always the strongest drink that leaves the sharpest aftertaste. Enough is enough. I was full to suffocation, sensory overload, my own kind of asthma . . . Nature's grandiloquence and the limitless vocabulary of the jungle were making me feel sick. I couldn't keep them down! Call my condition homesickness, if you like. But it is true that I dreamed of concrete and the straight lines of motorways. I saw the wide open spaces as a diabolical trap, an instrumentality much more to be feared than the one that keeps you attached to narrow perspectives. I would have given that entire realm of snakes and insects for a cramped bed-sitter. Confinement . . . I finally understood why Raven had come back, no matter how bad his reasons. One day, you do have to return . . . to come back to yourself, into your shell. He had stopped halfway, and I forgave his weakness. Wasn't I weaker still? A few more days and I would almost be glad to find myself in prison, in the same cell as Raven, in a situation comparable to his own, and at the same age as his. At twenty-six, anything is better than death.

The only other woman in the group was Manuela the soothsayer, and during the celebration she took it into her head to tell my future. Manuela was an *ilol*, an Indian sorceress, a *bruja*. She had lost her husband and her two eldest sons in a forest fire, and had taken refuge with Agustín, her little eight-year-old, in an Itza Indian hamlet, deep in the jungle. When the guerrillas passed that way she had decided to follow them. It was no spirit of revenge that motivated her, or if it was, it never showed. She was fighting, she said, so that the gods might return . . . They had put her in charge of the cooking, and she used her pots and pans to mix the sauces intended for dressing the future. To her, Lidia and Rafael and the Jefe were *ladinos*, town folk: even if their words were sincere, they were out of key with the toucan and the humming bird.

'You have slept on the ground but you know nothing of wounds and scars.' (She carried an old deep gash on one stout cheek.) 'We are in the days of the forty-five plagues. Comes the cataclysm, and suffering will be abolished . . .'

While she mouthed her litany, Agustín was playing nearby with the top he had whittled out of the bark of a *matapalos*. Just as I was captivated by his mother's words, so I was fascinated by Agustín's skill. He would wind the lash of his little whip round the upper stem, then with a sharp flick throw the wooden top to the ground, and then pick it up again in his free hand and let it run right up his arm up to the shoulder, and when the spinning slowed he would let it back down on to the ground to whip up whatever speed he chose for more acrobatic feats. He would sit down, lie down and then leap to his feet again, pirouetting almost as rapidly as the top, and dancing round it in a spellbinding ballet whose patterns blended in my mind with the words of the Soothsayer, as if the mother's gentle chanting was spontaneously expressed in the movement of the child.

In Spanish, a top is a *peón*. The most familar meaning of the word is worker, or agricultural labourer, but a *peón* is also a pedestrian, a walker, and by extension an infantryman in the army. And to prolong the semantic whirl comes one more meaning, that of the pawn in the game of chess! Perhaps I am only invoking all these associations with hindsight; I am not sure if I broke into such a parade of aesthetic vanity in the thick of the events. All the same it does seem to me as if the combined performance of Agustín teaching tricks to his toy, Manuela nodding her head to punctuate sentences whose meaning eventually escaped me, and the Indians twirling to the sound of the flute – all this interspersed with belts of a rough hard liquor brewed up by the Soothsayer out of some wild berry, I don't know which – went so thoroughly to my head that it went ballooning away on flights of imagination I could not possibly retrace. All that was left the following day was a ferocious hangover. I had dropped like a felled tree, paralytic, and dribbling at the mouth. Manuela told me: 'We thought you were dead.' And she kissed me on both cheeks. '*Feliz año nuevo, compadre!*' Dozens of arms took turns to hold me for a waltz of friendly embraces in honour of the year 1966, which had just begun. With all that spinning, the tightening band around my head became unbearable, and I collapsed half-senseless into El Gordito's arms. He helped me to lie down. I was sick. My companions started laughing. Babble and thunder . . . the year of 1966! I rolled up in a ball, and that made me into an overturned figure 9; it plunged me back into the scalding bath where Alfonso de Seguida's body sank (I was a few decades out!); it brought me to the triple 6 of Adrian Boot's beloved Beast. It raised the curtain of the Apocalypse, and I was one of the actors . . .

They moved back to give me air, but somebody knelt down beside me, propped up my head and laid a hand on my burning forehead. It was Lidia. I saw her face through the distorting prism of the tears that sprang to my eyes. Her beauty was all the more disturbing, and drawn as I was towards the cliff's edge that my unconscious had split open below me, all I could do was to stammer:

'Tomorrow . . . I'm leaving . . . leaving you . . . for ever.'

She stroked my hair.

'Idiot!' she said. 'How you love disaster!'

I think I really did start to cry then. She allowed me to

huddle in her arms, then gently lowered me to the ground and stood up to rejoin her comrades, who were busy checking their weapons. I heard the click and snap of bolt actions and loaded magazines, and a general clash of metal that reverberated into a huge echo against the walls of the gorge which was our hiding place, harsh sounds that drummed a kind of funeral beat in counterpoint to my sobbing. Soon they drowned me out completely, which speeded my return to the surface, and a clear head . . .

Next day – so that was 2 January 1966 – I volunteered to stand guard duty at the top of the steep hill, along with Rafael and two of the Indian peasants.

The rain, which wraps you in a constant clinging mist of humidity throughout the tropical winter, had begun to fall harder. I pulled on a cape El Gordito had removed from the dead body of a national guard, and the Soothsayer handed me a beret which had belonged to her oldest son. She also held out a scrap of broken mirror: 'See how handsome you look, *chico!*' I smiled to myself: it was true, I could have been mistaken for Che Guevara! Behind my cracked reflection I saw Lidia, sitting a few yards off beneath an overhanging rock, reading a book. Without looking back I picked up my rifle and walked towards Rafael, who was waiting for me where the track turned upwards to the top of the hill. There I waved one hand over my shoulder, to say goodbye to Manuela and to Agustín, who was hunkered down next to her, Indian fashion.

When we reached the top we spread out along a stream which any would-be attacker would have to cross – possibly a tributary of the river where Lidia and I had bathed a few days before. I sat in the fork of a big ceiba, Rafael settled on a little shelf of rocks about fifty yards downstream, and the two Indians found perches in some trees further down. The vegetation was so dense in this place that it gave us a roof to shelter from the rain; filtering through a tangled layer of leaves and branches, it fell only sporadically, and then in huge drops that splashed loudly down onto the moss, or landed on the surface of the water where I saw them send out slow concentric ripples. By now it was not at all hard to adjust my vision to the forest gloom, and yet although I was used to it, each time I entered the jungle a feeling of anguish took hold of me. Secure on my branch, looking out over the ground across the stream, I began to speculate about a remark Rafael had made on the way up: 'One good thing about rain, it washes out tracks and scent . . .' I wondered whether the words were meant to reassure, or whether they signalled a need to exorcise some deadly premonition.

I must have spent about an hour up there, letting my thoughts wander, playing hide and seek with a flock of different feelings, and dithering around the only question that mattered, which was how soon I should leave. My real reason for coming on sentry duty at all was to postpone the moment of decision.

All these hazardous conjectures were conveniently stifled by a call of nature and the urge to stretch my legs. I slung my rifle over my back, slid down the tree and started walking upstream, away from Rafael's position. Two minutes elapsed, maybe less. And then I saw him. I was reaching for my fly-buttons when the silence hit me in the face, suddenly snapping me out of my distracted mood. Just like the darkness, the noise – the chatter of birds, the screech of mammals – is so intense in the tropical forest that in the end you no longer notice it. Then it is the absence of sound that makes you pay attention . . . I looked up, and he was standing no more than ten yards away, bending over the stream to fill his water-bottle. I grabbed for my gun and cocked the hammer. The clack made the soldier raise his head. He stared back in amazement and let go of the bottle, which spilled out over his feet. Then his hand darted towards the automatic rifle lying next to him. He started to unfold from his crouch, but he never had time to stand up. Two shots in quick succession, then one more. They caught him in the belly, chest and head, stitching him upwards, fired from the hip, not the shoulder. The man collapsed into the stream, turned on his face, and a shower of foam rose around him as his body sank. I stood rooted to the spot. A dark red stain floated up to the surface, close to the still bobbing head. I don't know how long I stayed there watching it grow from little spirals into thicker, slower spurts, but finally I took a grip on myself and sprinted to find Rafael. I was in such a state of panic that before I ran I forgot to collect the soldier's gun, in spite of the Jefe's reiterated instructions to the group. Tearing along, I ran smack into Rafael, who was coming to investigate. 'They're coming!' I yelled, and we dived for the shelter of the rocks. We lay there flat on our bellies with our feet in the stream, held our breath and waited for the enemy, expecting them to hit us from the west, where I had killed the scout. The silence was heavier still; you might have thought that every furred and feathered animal had deserted that garden of the dead, and that not one had ever settled in the unlikely earthly paradise. Rafael propped his submachine gun between two stones and roared: 'You see what they get!' Still in the grip of emotion, I stammered: 'What about the others . . . the camp . . . no warning . . . might not come in time.' Rafael clapped me on the shoulder: 'Don't worry about them . . . They heard . . . Up to us to hold them long enough . . . And take good aim!' A fit of coughing cut him short. I thought it would never stop, and in the ominous surrounding calm the hacking rasp of his throat and lungs filled the forest with a sinister echo. Before he had stopped coughing a grimmer din drowned every other sound. We were under fire, and it came from all directions at once, not only from the west . . . This was no single platoon, more like ten, fifteen, a company, a brigade! The whole national guard, here to exterminate us . . . They weren't here just to search, and lay ambushes: this time it was the final solution.

'Shit!' I screamed, firing ahead at random, at targets I could not see, spotting only muzzle-flash and smoke through the thickness of the undergrowth, and hearing the thud of the enemy's bullets.

'I'll stick it to the bastards,' Rafael called, kneeling and spraying the trees across the stream.

The firing lasted for a few seconds more, that felt like hours. Then it stopped, as suddenly as it had begun.

'What's happening?'

I had rolled over on to my back to reload.

'Now they'll move in,' Rafael whispered in my ear. 'They know our numbers, and what weapons we have. My friend, there are so many that we are small fry . . . What they want is the camp.'

'But they've had it, they're cornered. The only way out is up here . . . They'll be slaughtered, Rafael!'

'Us first, *hombre.*'

At that moment the sound of a voice made us sit up. 'Rafael,

Juancho . . .!' It was little Agustín. I saw him scurry through the underwood, from tree to tree.

'He'll get himself killed,' I said.

Rafael stood up, firing wildly in all directions, trying to cover the boy. Agustín was hurdling a fallen tree trunk when the bullet – a single bullet out of nowhere – hit him full in the chest. I didn't see him fall because my fists were dug into my eyes and I was howling with rage. But how could I not see Rafael, writhing beside me, riddled with bullets and covered in blood? The hullabaloo had begun again. He moaned in pain, dying but not yet dead. I saw his lips move and put my ear beside them. There was something he wanted to say. And it was then he talked about Lidia. He blamed me for my failure to love her. Rafael spat blood, and I wiped his mouth. He struggled for breath, and added with an air of quiet amusement, as if defying death:

'No, Michael, no one's trying to kill you!'

What did he mean? Was he urging me to run or to surrender? Was it a last – derisive – shaft, to remind me how incongruously out of place I seemed to him? Delirium . . . he didn't realize. The accusing words rang in my mind, and I kept repeating them. And the worst of the joke was that my stream of consciousness chose that, of all moments, to prompt my memory about the sentence, context and all. Raging and choking, I would rather have wept, but only the printed characters came to dance in my dry eyes. I was riveted by the sheer coincidence. I looked at Rafael, in the throes of death. I reached out a shaking hand and touched his arm, as if to convince myself of the reality of his martyred body. It was not possible: he hadn't read the book. And yet, almost word for word, he had repeated what Clevinger tells Yossarian in *Catch-22* about the enemy firing at him. I had read Joseph Heller's novel in Mexico, while we were shooting the series. Paul Arthur Smith had bought it for me at the airport before he caught the plane. It had only recently been published and already it was one of the books of the decade: although the action was set in the Second World War, the events in Vietnam gave it a very contemporary resonance . . . I don't know why – perhaps because I was rigid with terror and my guts were churning – but Yossarian's reply came out quite naturally. If nobody wanted to kill me – 'Then why are they shooting at me?' Rafael didn't answer, he didn't even hear my frantic appeal: he was dead. I closed his eyes and tried to scream, but no sound left my throat. The shooting had broken out again. With my chin pulled tight into my neck I threw myself flat on my face, right next to Rafael's dead body. Convulsive shudders locked the muscles of my thighs and buttocks, and a warm trickle crept between my legs, my last sensation before going under. . . I protected my head by wrapping my arms around it. From a distance it might have looked as if I was peacefully asleep, in a hypnotic trance. Only my bulging jaws still moved: I was chewing the earth . . .

Down in the canyon the dead were jerking and tossing under the hail of bullets that killed them for a second time. Sodden with rain, the bodies wallowed in spreading pools of water; soon their shapes would no longer be distinguishable from the enfolding mud. It was as if they had never existed, reclaimed by the illusion which had first engendered them, the last and dismal image of a macabre fancy.

When I went to Guatemala City ten years later, during my other visit to Central America, I made efforts to trace Lidia's and Rafael's family. It didn't take long to locate the residence of a distinguished clan whose line went back to the Conquest. No Valdés would see me. When I persisted a steward gave me to understand, with all due civility, that my presence was misplaced.

3

The sons of Heaven and Earth went tumbling down from their mountain cluster to land among the humans, in a valley of bitterness. Kronos attempted to forestall ridicule by inviting his brother Titans to a sumptuous feast. What game did he serve? A handsome young man, Dionysos. Rhea licked her lips and kneaded her belly with her clumsy hands. Boiled and spit-roasted, she thought, he would taste delicious. As yet there was no sign of Saturn . . .

'The frozen God still couchant on the earth,
And the sad Goddess weeping at his feet.'

In order for things to hold their proper place, after the poet had written these lines it was necessary for him to die of tuberculosis in Rome. Like his mother and his brother before him . . . Keats had summoned death. 'Bright star, would I were steadfast as thou art . . .' The bane was there and he felt flowers growing over him. From being too much in love with those whose trouble is the troubles of the world . . .

Rhea gave birth to Zeus. The son struck down the mother, for the Titans had devoured Dionysos. Out of the ashes sprang the first men torn between violence and beauty. Orpheus took up his lyre to sing of the divine schism which leaves no heart at rest. The Forsaken roamed for ever more over the surface of the earth. From city to city, they offered their fellows prescriptions for salvation. In vain . . . They were rejected, spurned, condemned. And as disease and starvation ravaged towns and country alike, soon there remained nothing but a single rootless people, and no prospect of atonement.

Nevertheless, the Aztecs continued to believe that after death they would return to the place of their origin, to Mictlan, the metropolis of the North, from which they had been expelled.

As soon as he laid hands on Guardi's notebooks, Michael Mateos knew that they had nothing to do with Raven. Written in a microscopic scrawl, the old man's ravings might at most have been taken for a mystical parody of some passages in *The Tale of the Chimera* or *The Cyclone's Eye*.

Now there was no doubt left in Michael's mind that Lippman had blundered. In his enthusiasm the professor had got it all mixed up: Donovan, Bieliski and Echeverria had never been in Relámpagos prison. If Cartridge had mentioned their names at the preliminary hearing it was because they belonged to the crew of the *Naxos*, on board which Joe and Bremen had first become acquainted, during the voyage from Baltimore to Tampico. Of course that still left open the question of why Cartridge had jumbled things together as he had. And furthermore, what kind of mental acrobatics had made him feel compelled or entitled to associate himself with Raven's imprisonment in the Petén? Michael could only conjecture: in the end, if anybody had projected himself on to the other, it was the American, and not the other way round . . . And on top of that, Lippman had deceived himself about the identity of a possible candidate for having initiated Raven into writing. But here, in the case of Guardi, things were anything but straightforward . . .

In addition to considering the facts that reached him in circumstances so exceptional they took him a while to digest, Mateos did not dismiss the voice of his imagination. Confinement, and the very special sense of passing time that it gives rise to, were not unconnected with this altered state of mind. He had time to condemn his father, and then to save him. He even had the leisure to forget about him now and then, almost convinced of his own guilt, as if everything – right from the start – had been his fault, whereas the other was innocent. Precisely because he didn't have much to blame himself for . . . Relámpagos with its prison terminus was the end of the dream. Illusion persisted for a while, in the patch of sky he could see through the bars. But the four walls always brought him down to the level of daily routine. No more art, only life!

'We thought you were dead, Ulrich . . . thought you'd never come back from the Petén.'

'Well, you see . . .'

Cartridge felt that Ulrich had changed. He looked thinner, his face was drawn, and he no longer possessed the haughty brisk assurance typical of those whose healthy minds inhabit a healthy body. He was losing his nerve. Seeing how much less pugnacious his friend had become – when he returned he had not even inquired into the operation's production figures, as he would have done a few months before – Joe pressed home his advantage.

'Things have changed here since you left . . . They've sent two guys down from up North. Seems your management needed improving, and they didn't trust us, the *gringos*! You wanted action, and let me tell you we've stopped counting the bodies. The graveyard had to be enlarged . . .'

Bremen sat casually sipping at his beer, as if he was not hearing what his companion had to say.

'A lot can happen in six months . . . You should have stayed.'

'You're sorry?'

'Yes.'

'Just an identification check, then bang! Into the calaboose!'

'I told you that if you crossed the frontier you were asking for trouble. You and your obsession with the stab in the back! . . . And get this straight, don't go imagining they were worried about you here. Good riddance, they thought. Everything hunky-dory . . .'

'What about Little Sun?'

'Have you seen the boy? He's walking now. And pissing by himself!'

'And her? How did she take my being gone?'

'Well, pal . . . I'd say it was lucky I was here.'

'What do you mean?'

'Nothing, nothing . . . after all, with Red needing some affection and all, there was bound . . .'

'What?'

'Hasn't she said anything?'

'. . .'

'Okay, I've been taking care of her, there!'

Bremen picked up the almost empty beer bottle and broke it on the edge of the table. Then without a word he stood up and walked out of the sombre room, leaving Cartridge to listen to the rhythmic whining of the ventilator fan driven by a generator installed by the new boss of the camp.

Ulrich returned to his log cabin and set about collecting the baggage he had unpacked only a few hours previously. It wasn't much . . . Mainly the manuscripts he had been carting around with him since Relámpagos, and which were starting to feel heavy in the bottom of his kit bag. Little Sun came over to him, with a smile on her face. He pushed her gently away, but said nothing to her, not even to voice the disgust that rose to his lips at the thought of their earlier passionate reunion. She laughed, and murmured a few words of her own tongue which he did not understand. Then she raised her voice to tell him: 'I'm going to see what Red is doing. I don't like him spending too much time by the river.' Ulrich nodded agreement, while he reloaded the revolver which had been returned to him empty upon his release from prison.

Five minutes later he was standing quite still, with tears in his eyes, in the noonday sunlight that flooded the *zocalo*, the open space surrounded on three sides by the buildings and installations of the camp. The yellow dog which had followed him so often on his hunting trips and jungle walks came rubbing up against his legs and wagging its tail. Ulrich paid it no attention.

Facing him at the other end of the square came the American, the buddy who had as good as saved his life when the *Naxos* had been caught in the storm and come close to being wrecked on the Florida reefs, off Key West. A giant wave out of the howling darkness had scoured the deck, torn Bremen from his hold and slammed him against a hatch cover. The blow to his head had left him unconscious, and if Joe hadn't left the shelter of the bridge to drag him to safety there was no doubt that the next roll of the ship would have pitched him into the sea. The *Naxos* had been forced to dock in Havana to repair the damage, in the middle of a big fiesta – rum, castanets and rumba . . . The Greek had given the crew time off. In a Baltimore bar, Bremen had made friends with Bieliski, a Russian who also seemed to be on the run from something they never talked about. Cartridge had teamed up with the Basque, Echeverria. Chance had caused the four men to sign on board the same old bucket, and among all the strong drink and soft women of Havana, they had sworn eternal friendship . . .

As Cartridge came walking towards him, Ulrich reviewed the episodes of his life on board, how they had jumped ship in Tampico docks, and how he and Joe had decided to get in touch with the labour union people while Bieliski and Echeverria re-embarked on the *Naxos* with a cargo of mahogany . . .

'Are you sick? What the hell are you doing with your kit bag?'

Bremen did not answer the American, who was looking him straight in the face. Instead he turned and walked away in the direction of the the landing stage.

'Don't mean nothin', I'm telling you. You're pulling out now? . . . And all because a poor damned woman that you'd left behind, that didn't know if you were dead or alive, wanted to go on living?'

Joe came after him and tried to take hold of his arm. Ulrich spun on his heel and swung his sailor's bag hard against the other man's chest. The blow unbalanced Cartridge, and he staggered back a few yards before sitting heavily on the ground. 'You're selfish,' he roared, 'self is all you know.' Ulrich walked three paces away, and Cartridge came charging after him like a mad bull, wrenched him round to face him and caught him with an uppercut to the chin. He was stronger than Bremen, and handier with his fists. Bremen's head rang. He dropped his kit bag and was about to throw himself at the animal he longed to flatten to the ground when he looked up and saw Little Sun running up the path towards him, crying out and holding Red in her arms.

She threw herself at his feet, and the naked boy began to cry. Bremen picked up his bag, slung it over his shoulder, and walked towards the river without a backward look. Had he turned round he would have seen Joe holding Little Sun in his arms, although he would not have been able to tell whether he was restraining her from joining him, or whether he was comforting the woman in her sorrow. He only heard the sound of Red wailing as he clung to his mother's skirts, and the American bellowing: 'Yellowbelly! You're coming off real easy here! . . . Identification check my ass! I've got your number . . . Who'd you kill down there? An Indian? No sweat, huh? Does all the damage he wants, this guy, then runs for cover with his shit-ass writing full of lies! Hey, mister genius, who you going to screw now? Never you mind, you bastard, we won't forget!'

At first I did not find what I had hoped to find at Relámpagos. But my eye was caught by an inscription scratched on one of the walls of my cell: 'Alberto Guardi, 1848–1925'. Someone had put a line through the name and date, and added the graffito '*que le den por culo*' – 'fuck him' – almost illegible on the flaky whitewashed partition wall. Its study took up practically the whole of the first day I spent in prison. The previous night they had tossed me on to the wooden slats of the bed and I had fallen instantly asleep, exhausted by the three days' forced march I'd just completed with the national guard. It had taken me some time to face up to the twin realities, first, that I was not dead, and second that I was not truly a guerrilla, protected by my American nationality, which I must have stated automatically, without realizing it, at the moment of my capture . . . I suffered no ill-treatment because, quite clearly, I was accounted neither a hero nor an enemy. Through overhearing the laconic remarks of the NCOs who commanded the detachment, I realized in the end that it even gave them a kind of kick to deliver a Yankee safe and sound to the *cárcel* in Relámpagos. One of them had announced: 'Allies, *por cierto*, but you never know!' Here, by the way, was where I became conscious of the odd and complex nature of relations between the United States and the past and present autocratic regimes of Latin America.

So on the first day my mind was absorbed in the traces left by Guardi, whose name I knew from having met it in that article by Lippman, who had found it mentioned in Cartridge's statements to the attorney general. The shock was severe, and it might have been crippling, but although I could not say why at the time, I only felt excited by the inscription, as if its implausible presence in the very cell where I had been confined actually amounted to a sign of my good faith, if not of my lucky star. For I was not conscious of the extraordinary lucky streak I had been playing: I had pushed the odds so far that it all seemed part of an inevitable chain of events.

Meanwhile at dusk, when my cell was full of shadow, picked out behind the bars by the light of the rising moon hung the silhouette of a prodigious creature which seemed at that distance to be staring back at me from insolent stone eyes. Bocanegra! The chimera! Seguida's gargoyle, and Fray Sebastián's, there she was, perched on her buttress of ruined wall, ready to take wing to whisper in my ear the words which, spoken in my mother's voice, had peopled half of all my childish fears . . . 'Doña Marina . . .' I sighed, and clasped my hands around the iron bars. The very face that Raven had described in detail in his book . . . From that moment onward, everything became possible, not by extreme coincidence, and still less under the influence of a destiny my explorations had taught me to recognize as a projection of myself on to the wide screen of life which I had been holding at arm's length, looking for a flattering reflection. Now that was gone. In the bazaar of the here and now, junk sold for a dime. As novels used to do . . . You may not believe me, but as things stand now, what do I have to gain from a lie, from disguising the truth? Certainly I have no proof of what I claim. My sole guarantee comes from the sheer authenticity of the coda to my story, particularly in the episodes following my return to Europe, if the reader will trust me so far . . .

For the moment, it is time to establish the circumstances of my meeting with Rudolph Bach, and in doing so to close the first circle, and dispose of this famous, exasperating, Raven secret which I have to be rid of at last, so that tomorrow I can go to Schwiebus and gather the fruit of my efforts in the certainty that this time there can be no more question of peeling layers of riddles and enigmas.

There was no mistaking him: this was the same Rudolph Bach, the albino that Doña Marina went out of her way to avoid, tugging me along behind her, each time we passed or spied him in the streets of Oaxaca: the man responsible for my father's exile, and therefore for my own desertion, if not for worse . . .

For me he was only a blurred image, not even a childhood memory. He had lingered in my heart as an unfocused hatred fuelled by my latent disgust for that hermetic face and spindly outline, and for eyes that stabbed me with a thousand knives whenever they came near. And yet he would pass just yards away from us, and be indifferent.

As soon as they marched me into Bach's office it all came

back, but at least a week elapsed between my arrival in Relámpagos and this confrontation, a week in which my only visitor had been a single mute warder. Well, perhaps not altogether mute, but it did not matter, because in any case he was too young to have known Guardi or my father. Out in the prison courtyard, bugles saluted the flag, orders were bawled, guns fired and horses neighed . . . And out of her scalloped niche, overgrown with leaves and creepers, the gargoyle stared down at the daily performance. A corner of her time-worn mouth was set into a sneer. When night came, the lips would open further, as if the beast was on the point of relating the day's events, or perhaps, who knows, some stranger tales, tragedies buried beneath the ruins of the church, or moonlit melodramas hidden under the beaten earth of that barrack square . . . Unable to sleep, I spent hours gazing back at her. My eyes asked questions, and that was sufficient to make her flap her wings and puff out her throat in readiness for a new story saved specially for me. As soon as I hailed her she would begin to mouth her endless litanies. So rapid a response to my calling seemed rather suspicious for the first two or three days, but the pleasure it gave me quickly came to justify such courtesan liberties. I was fascinated, possessed.

So Bach's appearance, when it came, was that much easier to accept.

He was old and sick. On the first visit, when he sat hunched behind an oak desk so vast that I wondered how it could have got there, I almost overlooked him. As I entered the room, which must have been situated at the far end of the north wing of the building (two soldiers had escorted me up a staircase and down a long dark T-shaped corridor), I was expecting to find myself facing one of the commanders in charge of the assault in the jungle, or possibly a colonel plastered with medals and decorations, or even a tribunal of nameless uniforms worthy of the Holy Office . . . For a fraction of a second I thought that the room was empty, and that what I was seeing was some sort of statue, a grim enough sight in its hieratic pose, but in keeping with the chilly bareness of the place. Some counterpart in clay of the black gargoyle, though whether it was a full-length figure or a bust I could not tell, since only the upper part was visible. It must have been placed in that strategic position by an art-loving owner whose taste ran to the sort of aesthetic extremes which would be appropriate to the military condition and exacerbated by garrison life in a backward, hostile province . . .

Yet out of this peeling stucco effigy shone a pair of eyes so extraordinarily vivid that I stood stock-still. Slowly it opened its mouth; I could hardly see its lips, but the movement appeared to be produced by the operation of powerful jaws whose sharp bones glided under the drawn skin.

'Mr Mateos? . . . I once knew a Mateos,' he pronounced in a croaking voice. He spoke English with the slighty too sharp-edged accent typical of German. The albino lifted a tremulous hand covered with repulsive-looking scales. He waved me to sit down on the chair placed facing his desk, but I pretended not to understand the gesture and stayed on my feet. I wanted him to know from the start that I was not taken in. Wearing a shirt with a mandarin collar, in a greenish grey shade that almost blended with the colour of his skin, the mercenary was obviously trying to pass himself off as a mere bureaucrat briefing himself on my case. However, I had good reasons for believing that his role could not possibly consist in an administrative function: in my memory Bach stood for some demonic presence, and before they withdrew, the soldiers had put me on my guard by barking: 'At your service, *Señor Consejero*!' I knew what kind of advice this man was liable to provide. My frozen silence was a way of conveying to him that if any discussion was to occur, it would be in the form of an interrogation and not of a civilized chat between two Europeans marooned in the tropics. I had been treated correctly since my arrival, and this was to continue throughout my period in detention. After Lidia's death, whose memory used to haunt me in the emptiness of my cell, I almost longed for an expiatory punishment, some refined torture to which I would have succumbed without ever regaining consciousness. But instead it was as if they took care not to aggravate the torment inherent in being locked up. They wanted me intact and clear-headed. And it took me several weeks and a number of talks with Bach before I grasped that these measures of clemency stemmed from a subtle tactic of misdirection. They would not break my will, which is the standard objective with political prisoners. They would spare my strength. And so as the rhythm of habit took over, I would submit to the reality principle, incapable of shouting or dreaming, heartbreak or rebellion.

At first Bach played the interrogation game, but with restraint. He spaced out our meetings and alternated between a stern and a friendly manner. He knew that time was on his side. In general he did very little talking, and would leave me sitting on my chair while he said nothing. Sometimes, when I ventured to observe him, he looked as if he was dead. Motionless in the stifling heat of his office (Relámpagos was baking hot), he resembled a desiccated mummy. He gave off a smell that made me feel queasy. It reminded me of some creature, possibly an insect, whose defensive mechanism was to secrete an obnoxious substance. When I was least expecting it his throat would be racked with spasms that made him seem on the point of choking. His eyes clouded over, the pupils were hidden beneath twitching lids, and his corneas turned bloodshot with a colour more blue than red. I would stand up, and with an icy smile on his lips he would tell me: 'We have plenty of time, Mr Mateos. Help yourself to a cigar.' I remember that the first time I accepted his offer he sent for the orderly on duty in the corridor and dispatched him to fetch us some iced tea.

He clenched his bony hand around the glass, and it was all he could do to raise it by fits and starts towards his toothless mouth. At such times I became aware that my life was at the mercy of that hand. Often, in a burst of dignity, I told myself that if it had not been for the power he seemed to enjoy among the armed forces, Bach could have been taken for a comic opera character. On the few occasions when I saw him on his feet he was leaning on a stick whose knob was carved into the head of a snake. Sometimes I would even find him swaddled in a big brown cloak with his mangy eagle's head poking out of it in a quite ridiculous way. In spite of the sweltering midsummer heat that now prevailed, no trace of sweat ever beaded the death mask of his face. All this play-acting and scene-setting was done merely to impress me. One day, after I had delivered a preposterous version of the circumstances which had caused me to take up with the guerrilla group (I belonged to an archaeological expedition, and had got lost in the jungle), he offered no comment but confined himself to putting a 78 record of Act II of *Tosca* on the ancient gramophone which sat on the left of his desk. It was Baron Scarpia giving orders for the sham execution. Then Mister Adviser stopped the recital before the death of the chief of police to tell me about his investigations on the site of Mitla, near Oaxaca. 'Isn't that where you were born, Mr Mateos?'

Without being aware of doing so, I was gradually letting go. Every effort of resistance was turned against me. Thus when I screamed out in hatred against him because of Lidia's death ('pig fascist'), he gave a nervous laugh.

'I have fewer memories than you think.'

And that was the day when he gave me Albert Guardi's notebooks.

'You will read this, my friend. Your days will pass more quickly. Fascinating, the story of this fellow who was your predecessor in your cell, a long time ago . . . All the interest that archives can possess . . . A great philosopher, this Guardi. You do not know about him? Before your time, it is true. What does a young man of your age have to do with the independence and freedom of Italy? Far away from the plotting and the intrigues, Guardi wrote it all and foresaw it all. The calibre of scholar they do not make any more, don't you think? . . . Obviously, simple minds do not see how a sympathizer with Garibaldi could secretly have devised ideas which another, a German, philosopher was developing almost simultaneously. I tell you, they never understand . . . '*For all eternity the character of the world as a whole is chaos, not because of the absence of necessity, but by reason of the absence of order, articulation, form, beauty and wisdom.*' So wrote Nietzsche, and Guardi agreed: 'The opacity of darkness and the sparkling stars of poetry are not sufficient to throw disgrace and satisfaction over the universe. There remains the eternity of silence, and the one certainty common to all, which is death. But for mercy's sake, at least let this brotherhood in death aid us to think about life.' Would you like to know what came later, Mr Mateos, or would you rather we left it till tomorrow?'

'Now.'

'As you wish . . . In 1920 the thinker went into exile. His son had been killed by blackshirts, outside the gates of a factory on strike. He had been widowed for three years, and this was his only son. In the following months he crops up in Gibraltar, and then in Kingston, Jamaica. There he sails for British

Honduras. In Belize he is treated in a clinic for an unknown illness. He escapes and breaks out across the Guatemala border, killing the guard who tries to stop him. Guardi, man of action, imagine! It is only too obvious that the old man is searching for a way to die. His life has become a burden too heavy for him to bear. Here in Relámpagos, instead of his death, he finally discovers the madness that gives meaning to his existence . . .'

'Claptrap!'

'All right. Read it and we'll see.'

As a matter of fact I could hardly wait, and by next day I had read the entire contents of the folder that Rudolph Bach allowed me to take away. Here at last was the answer to one of the key questions in the Raven mystery. Several of the notebooks were crammed with rambling meditations which cast some doubt on the mental health of the man who had composed them. Some pages were gloriously beautiful. And in the margin of one of these anthology pieces Guardi had scribbled the following lines:

> My eyes hurt. Soon I shall be blind and unable to write any more. Already I must make the best of the numbered hours when the sun slants into my cell . . . Fortunately, for the last few days I have been sharing my refuge with another man – I shall refer to him as Mateos. He is young, clear-sighted, and I like his intelligence. I have asked him if he would be willing to write to my dictation, and he has agreed.

At the foot of another page dealing with the Greek myths, I found this laconic remark:

> I do not trust him any more. Which of us two will be quicker to tire of the other to the point of killing him? M. wants me to leave him alone. He too has *his* things to write, he says! The blinkered stupidity of youth . . . Why does he refuse to help me die?

I imagined the encounter, and said to myself that the albino was seeking to re-enact the scene with me. The more I read, as hours crept by, the more I became convinced that henceforward it would no longer be possible for me to avoid the encounter. If there was any chance of getting out of this rat hole, now was the time to grasp it . . . Just between the two of us, *Señor Consejero*! He had no inkling of the effects produced by Guardi's revelations. Maybe he believed the opposite would happen, that I would be sucker enough to swallow his bait and cook myself too . . . Suddenly I felt capable of putting up a fight again. That night, even though a full moon shone, I didn't spare a glance for Bocanegra. I was engrossed in my thoughts.

Next day, Bach waited until the noonday heat was at its worst before he sent for me.

I handed back the Guardi file, and he laid it on the desk in front of him. Neither one of us spoke, each of us evidently waiting for the other to show his hand. Then in a casual tone my jailer broke the silence. 'I hope you have lunched well. Shall I send for some coffee?'

I nodded my head, without clarifying which of the two questions had elicited my agreement. The everlasting black beans had given way to some rice, and the salt pork to a piece of broiled beef.

'Sit down. Take a cigar.'

I helped myself from the box by the gramophone. He always kept it full, although he himself never smoked – 'My throat, I can't any more . . .'

As I lit the Honduras, he began to lay out in front of him the twenty-eight ivory and ebony tiles of a magnificent and precious set of dominoes which he kept in a drawer of his desk. He had enlisted me into his crazy ritual on several previous occasions, and turned a deaf ear to refusals. It was a real passion with him.

'Tangier, 1936 . . .'

'Yes, I can see what you might have been doing around there in those days.'

'Ah, my dear boy! . . .'

He taught me 'chicken' and 'matador', two variations which I didn't know, but it was the classic 'Cyprus' that he most enjoyed.

The double six made him chortle horribly. And at the moment of victory – which I usually conceded to him because the game did not concern me – he gave a triumphant squawk of 'Domino!' On the other hand, when chance compelled him to 'pass' – to lose his turn – he would wince and throw himself about in his chair as if electrodes had been clipped to his body.

That day, he lost three games in succession. After the coffee came, he insisted on having his revenge. I tried to talk about Guardi's notebooks, but he waved my approaches away. 'One more game!' he insisted, looking me straight in the eye and staring me down. He knew what he was doing. Behind his inlaid wall, the albino was building a fortress with crenellated ramparts. And in the gaps between the stones coiled the sleeping snake . . . He leaned towards me and his sickening smell made me draw back. The veins in his neck were extraordinarily pale: no blood seemed to flow there, or else it was some cold, translucent liquid . . . By its rigidity, which concealed a latent tension ready to explode at the most unexpected moment, the neck he craned towards me reminded me of a reptile's. In self-protection, the question was to know whether I was facing a rattlesnake or an anaconda, a lethal bite or powerful coils that could tighten and choke me. Mesmerized, I followed his slightest movement. With Guardi, the poison had been injected. I could feel it eating into me. But maybe that was better, I thought, than to remain a living prey, ready to be ingested all at once . . . In the corner of his pallid lips gleamed a trickle of poisonous saliva.

I cracked, and the ophidian did not let go. It came out in a rush, as if I had been drunk – Mateos, Raven, Oaxaca, I told him everything.

'Do what you like with me!'

'Calm down, please . . . Your case is not as important as you think. My government . . .'

'*Your* government?'

'Yes. That is to say . . . they find you rather an embarrassment. A few formalities to complete, and you will be free . . .'

'Another of your tricks! Like this Guardi business . . . How do I know you haven't faked the whole thing?'

'Don't you want to know the end of this business, as you call it?'

'. . .'

'Guardi did not have the strength to kill himself. He begged your father – we know now that it *was* your father – to put him to death. Mateos wavered. The ordeal went on for several days. Unable to stand it any longer, the young man reported the old man's fatal intentions to the warders. By doing so he hastened his own release. He was moved to another cell, and a few days later, at the moment of his departure, he learned of Guardi's suicide.'

'How did it happen?'

'I believe the philosopher hanged himself from the bars by tearing his shirt into strips and plaiting them into a cord.'

'You believe that, do you? And what if I told you that you are my father's killer?'

My hand shot out to sweep across the desk top and scatter his domino stronghold across the floor.

'You should not have done that,' he fretted. 'Yes, it is true . . . it could have been me. A bolshevik, a Jew, a troublemaker, a degenerate, a depraved writer, an alcoholic . . . There was no shortage of reasons . . . But listen hard, Mr Mateos Junior, there is something else that you surely will not understand, and that is that your father was my friend.'

'You? A Nazi?'

He stiffened in his chair and closed his eyes.

'Since it concerns you, I will give you proof of that friendship. First, allow me to explain that at the time of Waldo's death we had already lost the war. I was of no more use in Mexico, and there were tasks for me here.'

'But my mother pointed you out to me, I remember. I saw you.'

'You were very young. How can you be sure that I had not left Oaxaca? You would do better to make inquiries in Los Angeles, and look to the Señora.'

'That's impossible. Ruth wouldn't have been capable of anything like that.'

'Not her . . . but in her own circle . . . a sordid crime.'

'What do you know about her anyway?'

'I am sorry, you are right. I am surmising . . .'

'I'd rather hear you say that. Otherwise you'll be resurrecting that old story about the Kaiser . . .'

'Ah, now in your place I would not be making jokes, young man.'

'Go ahead, it's okay. I am the illegitimate grandson of Wilhelm the Second, which makes me the great-great-grandson of Queen Victoria! And why not the long-lost bastard line of the Borgias, while you're at it!'

'Your generation and History do not mix. Very well. That is the difference between us, Mateos, and that is why no matter what you do you will never understand anything about Raven. . . The proud descent that you dispute is without doubt the true reason for my respect for him. If it had not been for that, yes, I would have done it, I would have got rid of him.'

'So what's your proof?'

Bach levered himself painfully to his feet. Leaning on his cane, he hobbled over to a filing cabinet standing against the wall, to the left of the window. He took a key from the hip pocket of his jacket, fumbled in the lock and pulled out a drawer. He riffled through his assortment of files, then returned to his desk holding a sheaf of yellowing paper which he examined before putting it into my hands.

'There. Look at the date – 9 December 1938. Your father gave me that manuscript two days later. Waldo was drunk, and we had got into a quarrel in a *cantina*. He absolutely insisted on making me a gift of it, as a token of our reconciliation.'

'You got it by extortion. Like me, he was becoming your prisoner. You left him no choice.'

'I did not ask him for anything.'

'And how is it that this document has followed you all this way . . . nearly thirty years later?'

'Oh, there are things that one does not leave lying about in one's wake. You yourself were prepared to accuse me, weren't you? You never know what may happen . . . Also, although in our ideas we were totally opposed, I admired Raven as a writer. It was an honour for me to possess an original manuscript in his own hand. I am something of a collector, as I suppose you must have noticed.'

There was no doubt about it: this was Raven's writing, and it was his signature at the foot of the final page. Next to the title –*Bocanegra* – in smaller writing he had noted 9 December 1938.

'That's the name of the gargoyle,' I said mechanically.

'They called it that because of the hurricane of 1927 that destroyed the church,' the albino remarked.

'I thought it was supposed to be the Spanish translation of

its ancient Itza name. At least that's what Raven claimed in his book.'

'That's possible . . . but you know, if there's one thing your father never lacked, it is imagination.'

'The Kaiser too: all that could be invention.'

Rudolph Bach seemed taken aback. He hid behind his milky eyes, as I described them above. His breathing grew heavier, as if he were dropping off to sleep, and he clenched his gnarled hands.

'Why . . . why would he have lied to me about such a serious matter?'

'That's just it, you see . . . He had you cold!'

I had no grounds for sounding so assured, but the albino was flagging; this was my chance to finish him.

'History is your field, I agree. So you were screwed in advance. You fell for it. At least I don't pretend to know what a writer is. You had his hide, but that was all you had.'

'Leave me . . . I feel tired . . . Read the text and we will talk about it again.'

He never had the chance to verify his theme. Three days went by, and nobody came to escort me to Bach's office. Then one morning, very early, my attention was caught by the sound of an abnormal commotion in the barrack square. They were not cleaning weapons, or unsaddling horses, or revving engines. The shouts and orders sounded more ragged than usual. I chinned myself to the bars by the strength of my arms. Four black limousines nosed their way through the gatehouse in the outer wall, and various uniformed generals and colonels emerged with their burnished medals and spotless caps and stood about conferring on the flagstones below. Suddenly they sprang to attention and saluted. A coffin carried by six enlisted men appeared in the doorway of the chapel. There was a pause . . . A surpliced priest ran up, followed by a pair of choirboys, to bless the catafalque. A bugle sounded the last post. Movement resumed, rapid and jerky, with the comic unreality of an old-time silent newsreel. The coffin was slid inside one of the hearses, they piled back into the cars again, and the procession set off. After turning in an arc that took it directly beneath the gargoyle, it drove out through the gateway. I had no need to consult Bocanegra to learn what the warder confirmed soon afterwards, that we had just observed the last rites for the *Señor Consejero.*

Another political police official arrived in Relámpagos a week after they buried Bach, and it started all over again. The first interrogation session went very badly. I was anxious, my confidence was gone, and I didn't give much for my chances. But in fact they were playing the final act: one final deception exercise before I was handed over to the International Red Cross, which had come to inquire into my treatment. I had no idea, of course: how could I imagine that my jailers themselves had been running a shrewd publicity campaign about my 'affair', blaming the perversity of the whole concept of guerrilla insurgency, which led these poor European intellectuals so hopelessly astray? . . . It was unbelievable. Just as unbelievable as the special kind of piety I found myself practising to stiffen my own resistance: I prayed to Bocanegra to come to my rescue, and held the conversations with her that were no longer possible with Bach. I plighted her my faith, and surrendered her my memory, and I hated her.

Late one afternoon when I felt like spitting in her face, the sky went suddenly dark. It was as if a vast lid had been lowered onto the valley of Relámpagos. The heat, already stifling, grew hotter still. The walls ran with damp. Lying on my sleeping platform with my body drenched in sweat and twitching for no reason, I listened to the thudding of my heart. Night fell, and so did the thunder, and then the sky itself, in a torrent of fire, a seething incandescence, eruptions of black suns which the wind sent scudding against the prison.

All that night, and all next day and then another night the hurricane raged. I huddled in a corner of my cell. Debris fell from the ceiling. Several feet of floor split open. Two rats were cowering at the other end of the cell, and I saw their terrorized eyes imploring me to intervene, to do something. A section of masonry half-collapsed and a stone rolled towards my feet. Then came a sudden shock, and a pain in my leg which felt even sharper because I didn't know what caused it. It was like a shell-burst, shredding my brain apart. I screamed and passed out.

Afterwards, it was simply a matter, yet again, of time and due formalities. I was one of the handful of survivors. The Red

Cross did come looking for me. When they slid my stretcher into the ambulance I lifted my head for a final look at Bocanegra, and was astonished to see that she was no longer standing there on her pinnacle, with her talons digging into the wall. I turned my head and saw her lying lifeless on the ground, half buried in mud, with her beak dipped into a pool of water. Her body was intact; the lightning strike had split her off at the base.

As for the manuscript which I had tried to protect by keeping it with me, sandwiched between my shirt and my skin, I never found out what became of it. Having read and re-read it hundreds of times during those final weeks of captivity I had no difficulty in recalling and copying it, lying in the hospital bed in Guatemala City. Froggy, who was now attached to the French embassy in Mexico City, came looking for me and had me flown back to Paris. In gratitude, I gave him my version of *Bocanegra*.

At Orly they gave me the full publicity treatment, with heaving crowds and a barrage of flash cameras . . . Beatrice was there too, waiting for me.

4

BOCANEGRA *9 December 1938*

'Had I not forced them to hear, it would never have occurred to them to let me speak. For which among you sober humans could conceive without a peevish murmur that a piece of carved stone – no matter how prodigious the beauty of its forms – should presume to offer any remark upon the history which has shaped it? The man who sculpted me, not content with being dismissed by the architect, incurred the wrath of the Inquisition. The stake was raised beneath my eyes, and from the church square the flames reached up and licked around my wings. They stung my nostrils, which were pained to smell the juices and aromas of the Levantine whose hands and whole body had lavished a fatherly care and love upon my making. What aesthetic aberration could he have been found guilty of committing, to be thus subjected to the supreme punishment? The centuries since my birth have hardly been long enough to enable me to offer any certain answer to that question. Certainly I know – from having sufficiently admired them before time wore them into nothing – I know the baroque kindred who stood by my side and who presumably did not transgress the divine law. Hippogriffs like myself, they were neither more nor less monstrous: eagle's head and wings, tiger's paws, and the body of a horse . . . Evidently, beneath my eagle eyes the Levantine had carved a lion's jaws. Is it possible to see this detail as a criminal act?

'I remember that the dear man was fond of interrupting his work – he would leave me all panting and dishevelled, sweating blood and brine under the rays of the sun – to sit in the cool of the Gothic vaulting and read a book with a worn, faded binding which he always took with him. He would never be parted from it, even in bed. Sometimes, as he struck me with his chisel (I quivered with delight under the blows that gave me wings), he would recite passages from it, or murmur into my equine ears some secrets in the history of his author, Ariosto. Trembling with pleasure, and a little jealous too, I saw myself enthroned on the topmost tower of the palace of the dukes of Ferrara. (Ah, sweet Italy, the raptures I knew there. Here, in this barbarous, choking jungle where my fate has been fruitlessly expended in the quest for a meaning, it is not enough for men to gut one another to the sound of drums and trumpets, with their banners streaming in the wind, or subtle poisons simmering over the fire, but they must eat each other too. Why could they not leave that task to us, the creatures of legend, created to resolve such problems?) Now if I understood my sculptor's confidences, his own life resembled Ariosto's, at least in certain respects. Born on the shores of the Mediterranean (and not of the Adriatic, but what does that signify to me, who have never seen the sea?), the third of a family of nine children whose sire, the commander of the fortress of Peñíscola, won the greater part of his fame for his loose principles and breaches of trust . . . Not in the least like that, my Estebán (that was his name)! Or so he claimed, at any rate: no, there was no doubt concerning his identity, devil take it, I simply want to say that he did not resemble his father. In order to please this sabre-rattler, he studied law. The soldier stumbled and was accidentally killed one dark night while on his way to visit a lady. Estebán studied drawing and sculpture in Valencia, then entered the service of the local duke. The rest you know . . . Or most of it, since first he had to father a heretical bas-relief which sent him packing, rather faster than he would have wished, for the New World, where they were building such a host of monasteries and churches that even a fool could come in useful there. In the view of Estebán, *Orlando Furioso* – that was his book, and I too could thrill you with the tale of the warrior's exploits, and conjure up the treacherous Angelica, the mighty Rodomont! – was a work in which freedom of invention knew no bounds. Why be surprised if the critics took offence, as good disciples of Aristotle, against its uneven flow or provocative manner? One narrative began, and then another supervened. (Oh, how that annoyed me! I gaped in expectation of a continuation which never appeared, and from dialogue to counterpoint I was finally drawn, without realizing it, to a point whence I thought I would never return!) Bradamante moves onward, surrounded by a crowd of adventitious characters so dense that she is instantly lost to the reader's eye. The tone keeps changing quite capriciously. Yet the more it varies the more the demands of the book as a whole become clear. If you wish to know the truth, says Ariosto, turn History upside-down. What if the Trojans had defeated the Greeks and Penelope, the faithful wife, had been nothing but a slut in a world of pimps, buffoons and informers? – Digression aside, the structure – a little too scholarly, I agree – remains glaringly obvious.

'You may divine my emotion on the day when my Levantine related the episode of the hippogriff. All those fantastic stars where I cavorted in concert with my namesake! . . . By some strange effect of cosmic perpetual invention, might I be descended from an unknown race born on a distant moon? A creature even more fabulous than the legend suggests, at once ethereal and flesh and blood? More than a concept, a dream, a hurt, an atom of eternity, who knows? My non-existence might have no other tangible proof than the counter-valuation I underwent each time I tried, without success, to intercede among men. If I was to captivate and love them, I found no better means than to bewitch them. They all caressed me with their dirty, clumsy hands, and my dark mouth would utter nothing but cries of rebellion. Incoherent, untranslatable . . . The Levantine was reduced to ashes; those who had punished him perished in a hurricane that the stellar hippogriff blew at my request. (Ah, why did I not express my wish more clearly?) The men with copper faces chanted themselves hoarse to glorify my powers; the Roman lost his wits; and he who had several names cursed me, proclaiming that some day his son – but he did not say which – would call me to account for all those dead who lay upon my stony conscience.'

BOOK THREE

I

DESTINATIONS

1

THE SS *CRAVEN* had steered well clear of Ushant and its reefs, the island of shipwrecks. The stoker, an Irishman, had muttered a string of prayers, but in the clangour of the stokehold Ulrich had picked up only a single arresting sentence: 'Who sees Ushant sees his blood.' From now on, all danger was past: the ship was through the ocean's gate and facing the long crossing. No more ambushes, no enemy in hiding, only the sovereign power of the sea where death has but one, uncovered, face . . . Since Hamburg, Ulrich had had time to learn his new trade, together with the language of winds and waves. But here on the high seas he felt fragile and helpless, as if he must start all over again.

In the stokehold it was hell: as hard to breathe as to sweat. Yet there was no question of self-pity. For the first time in years he felt a kind of serenity which he could hardly explain but which was there all the same, in his body as well as in his mind. Although he did not bear suffering gladly (he was not Christian enough for that), nevertheless it seemed to him – how could he put it? – that mourning, with its cruel bite, became him. Each day as he lay in his cabin before collapsing into sleep he would read a few lines of John Bunyan, the Puritan, out of the little leather-bound volume which had been Franziska's last farewell gift: '*Now I blessed the condition of the dog and toad, and counted the estate of everything that God had made far better than this dreadful state of mine, and such as my companions' was; yea, gladly would I have been in the condition of dog or horse, for I knew they had no soul to perish under the everlasting weights of hell for sin, as mine was like to do. Nay, and though I saw this, felt this, and was broken to pieces with it, yet that which added to my sorrow was, that I could not find that with all my soul I did desire deliverance.*'

How he had once detested those Puritan scrupulosities, the curbs and corsets, nay-sayers, character-assassins, appetite-haters, castrators, slime-purveyors! . . . He would rather have thought nothing further about it, forgotten the whole thing, and drawn a line beneath it. But Franziska's condemnation kept returning, obsessively, to the beat of the engines: 'Libertine!' As if his whole destiny reduced itself to that one word . . . And he also remembered the day and the night which lately, once again, had caused his downfall . . .

The date was 10 November 1923: of that there is no doubt. Not only is it difficult to forget the kind of events which overtook Ulrich that day, but also the previous day, the 9th, had seen the fifth anniversary of Kaiser Wilhelm's abdication, and the end of the Hohenzollerns, an event he was unable to ignore . . .

Ulrich was supposed to see Charlie at six o'clock. They had arranged to meet at the Trafalgar Inn in Greenwich. O'Sullivan had no great liking for the place – too starchy for his taste – but his friend had convinced him that it was a good way to cover their tracks. In Whitechapel and all over the East End, the two companions no longer went unnoticed. After all, Ulrich had remarked, 'that was where an anarchist died in 1894, killed by the bomb he was on his way to plant.' And he added that the incident had inspired Joseph Conrad in his novel *The Secret Agent*. Charlie pulled a wry face at this remark. Certainly he recognized the writer's literary talent, and understood why Ulrich should see him as a model for the books he said he meant to write some day. But the lithographic print worker remembered some lines he had happened to come across in a book which the young German journalist had left open on his work table. Ulrich was shaving, and he had invited O'Sullivan to help himself to a cup of tea before they set off to the printer's. The book was *Under Western Eyes*, and Ulrich had ringed and underlined a paragraph that Charlie had time to read and then to re-read as he sipped his tea. '*A violent revolution falls into the hands of narrow-minded fanatics and of tyrannical hypocrites at first.*

Afterwards comes the turn of all the pretentious intellectual failures of the time. Such are the chiefs and the leaders. You will notice that I have left out the mere rogues. The scrupulous and the just, the noble, humane, and devoted natures; the unselfish and the intelligent may begin a movement – but it passes away from them. They are not the leaders of a revolution. They are its victims: the victims of disgust, of disenchantment – often of remorse. Hopes grotesquely betrayed, ideals caricatured – that is the definition of revolutionary success. There have been in every revolution hearts broken by such successes.' This had left Charlie unimpressed. Certainly his juvenile enthusiasm had become tempered by a caustic irony, and he was well aware that power corrupts and disfigures the finest causes. But that was no reason for giving up, or succumbing to a destructive scepticism whose ultimate effect was to strengthen oppressors and shore up their regimes. At the time of Charlie's visit to Berlin, the Ulrich he knew there had been so entire, so ready for self-sacrifice. How could such a man come to cherish this new illusion of replacing one brand of romanticism with another? He aired these thoughts on the way to the printer's, and Ulrich gave a snort of laughter. That annoyed Charlie, and he refused to be put off, but all his friend would yield him in reply was another quotation from Conrad, where the narrator wrote about going home: '*Say what you like, to get its joy, to breathe its peace, to face its truth, one must return with a clear consciousness*. That's Marlow, in *Lord Jim*. Do you know the story?'

Something was clearly wrong. 'You're getting my goat with your Conrad!' Yes, and ever since his friend had started going out with Vanessa Holleran, who was an active campaigner for the pacifist movement, things seemed to have been going from bad to worse.

That night the three of them were to meet at the Trafalgar Inn before going on to the dance marathon in Clapham. Ulrich and Vanessa had entered for it and Charlie was to come with them. A drink at the pub would put them in the right mood to face the ordeal to come. Vanessa was a terrific dancer. At first Ulrich, himself a fair performer, had partnered her out of friendship. Then when the relationship had grown more intimate he too had been bitten by the charleston bug. Charlie, a big, shambling man, would put up his objections – 'Off to shake a leg *again*?' – but obviously with competitions it was different. There were prizes, a chance for some extra cash to supplement the worker's meagre wages and the lineage rates earned by the journalist who occasionally translated articles from German for the *Telegraph*. As for Vanessa, she had been out of work for four months, ever since the ball bearings firm where she was employed as a secretary had closed down.

In Clapham, the first prize was as high as a hundred pounds – a fortune! True, the prize was in proportion to the target – the world record, no less. To better it they were going to have to keep on dancing for something over twenty-five hours. A dancer called Victor Hindmarsh and his partner Della Dunn had just set this time at Eshington, in Northumberland. But it couldn't stop there, the advertisements clamoured. Onward, they blared, to the limits of human endurance. Ulrich had said: 'Come on, we're going to sell our sweat and tears to these new Caesars in the capitalist circus! But never mind, it will be for the last time. We win the jackpot and it's over, Charlie, I promise!'

When he reached the pub Ulrich found his friend sitting at a table with a pint of bitter, engrossed in a newspaper.

'Hello there.'

He looked up with sad eyes.

'Is something the matter, Charlie?'

'Here, read that.' And he held out the paper with an air of despondency.

It was open at a page where, under the headline of 'The Beer Hall Uprising', Ulrich found himself reading the following lines, and forgot that Vanessa was late.

> Under cover of darkness, the ruthless General Erich von Ludendorff took over the streets of Munich, the Bavarian capital, on Thursday, together with his faithful friend Herr Adolf Hitler. Under the guise of commemorating the anniversary of the fall of the Kaiser, they planned to carry out a coup d'état.
>
> With an unerring instinct they led their men to a famous beer hall, the Bürgerbrau Keller, where the Bavarian dictator Doctor von Kahr and a number of his followers were gathered. Dr Von Kahr was delivering a tirade against Marxism when Hitler and General Ludendorff burst into the room, firing shots into the ceiling in order to create confusion.
>
> Herr Hitler then announced that the government was over-

thrown and that not only was he assuming the leadership but also proclaimed himself Chancellor of Germany. Ludendorff was to command the army. The General added: 'We are at a turning point in our country's history, in the history of the world. May God bless us!'

Some voices called for a march on Berlin. Demands were made to repeal the Treaty of Versailles and to depose President Ebert.

Everything appeared to be going 'according to plan'. The crowd applauded Ludendorff, who strutted away. Hitler's forces were in control of the town; the morning sun turned out. The 'Chancellor' and the 'Commander in Chief' were sitting in the War Ministry when loyalists stormed the building. After a brief battle, the Beer Hall Uprising was crushed.

'As long as they stick to beer halls!' Ulrich sighed.

'Now there you surprise me,' said Charlie. 'In my opinion this is a serious thing.'

'Yes, of course.'

'What worries me even more is the other article lower down the page. The mark worthless, the Berlin police desperate for dollars, people starving, riots, shops being looted . . .'

'I know. And at the Berlin Zoo the animals are so hungry that they howl all night long. No one in the district can sleep. The hyena laughs like a maniac and the wolves bay at the moon. It's a jungle!'

'Something should be done.'

'Yes.'

'A pamphlet . . .'

'Tomorrow . . . or the day after.'

'The marathon first, you mean?'

The two friends knew their eternal debate had resumed once again. Charlie was the anarchist and Ulrich the serious intellectual, and yet when it came to the point it was often the former who reacted with an appropriate sense of responsibility, as if the roles had been suddenly reversed.

Vanessa's arrival cut the argument short. Both men greeted her, and then Ulrich went over to the bar to order two gins (there was no question of drinking beer like Charlie, who would be glad to remain a spectator). When he returned to the table with the drinks he had the impression that Vanessa was looking particularly grave. Of course, the urchin haircut she had adopted nearly a month before tended to harden her features a little (he remembered her coming to see him, and the shock he had felt – for a supposedly freedom-loving, open-minded man, he had behaved like a jealous, narrow-minded idiot), and today the absence of powder and mascara, which would only be a nuisance in the marathon, further accentuated that hardness.

He would have liked to ask questions, and talk to her. Maybe on their own . . . Instead he began to talk about the rules for the Clapham contest.

They would start with demonstrations. For the wild charleston, Vanessa and Ulrich had no one to fear. Then would come the waltzes and the paso dobles. And soon, sooner than it should, would come the real question, which was the test of endurance. It wasn't enough to be good, they had to be tough as well. Right to the end . . . but the end of what? The light above the ring would be dimmed and people would shut their eyes so as not to think and to let the body's machine take over. The trick was to elude the referees' scrutiny at the right moment, and when the gong sounded, to spring to life, cover the dance floor with orderly-looking movements, allay all suspicions, slide along the tightrope, smile, keep smiling, as if there was nothing to it . . .

The three young people mounted their bicycles and went sailing down the street. They felt cheerful, almost carefree . . . The weather was fine. A soft autumn evening . . .

The ballroom entrance was choked with spectators and contestants, who were queuing for their official numbers. Behind the judges, underneath the banner, stood a cluster of half a dozen policemen. They looked as if they were waiting for instructions from a man in plain clothes who was leafing through the list of entrants. Ulrich and Charlie exchanged quick glances, but it was too late to beat a retreat. Vanessa and a flood of contestants barred the way. That left only one solution – since there was no doubt who the police must be looking for – which was to keep going, and make themselves part of the gesticulating uproar on the dance floor. There was always the possibility that the police wouldn't dare to draw too much attention to themselves, and if so, then it wouldn't be the first time the two friends had managed to slip through their fingers . . .

In the interval before the start of the competition, Ulrich and Charlie sat down on a bench next to one of the side entrances. They watched the constables stroll to the four corners of the auditorium while their leader took up a position on the other side of the open floor, opposite where they sat. Vanessa had vanished into the ladies' cloakroom to change her dress. Ulrich had not the remotest suspicion that he was never going to see her again, and for some time afterwards – in prison, on the boat to Hamburg, and then on the voyage to Baltimore – he was haunted by the notion that there had been nothing accidental about her non-appearance.

The loudspeakers blared out a march – the Entry of the Gladiators. Couples formed. Ulrich spoke softly in Charlie's ear, rose to his feet and strolled towards the changing room. The man in the brown suit did not stir. Everything was fine. What if they'd only been rattled by their own imaginations, damn it! By being outside the law . . . The corridor was surprisingly dark after the brightness of the ballroom, and Ulrich cannoned into somebody. He was about to apologize when the man took hold of his arm and his curt voice grunted: 'Sergeant Vickers, Scotland Yard. You're coming with me.' Ulrich attempted to break loose, but the men in uniform had followed him and he was already surrounded.

The following morning he was taken to the magistrates' court in Aylward Street. Having no papers, or any means of proving his identity, he was sentenced to a month in prison. As it turned out, all these proceedings were a charade, as Ulrich learned when he was taken before a new set of policemen who had their own ideas about his case. The fact that he was a journalist, and had rooms near Regent's Canal Dock, did not concern them. Their cross-examinations followed another, much more distant and secret trail. Straight away, they switched the line of questioning to Germany. Where did he come from? Why had he entered England illegally? Who was he working for? Slowly he realized that there was very little they didn't know about him. He had no secrets here – not Munich, nor his activities over there . . . They wanted to tie him into some squalid espionage inquiry. He could throw no light on that. All right, then they would deport him, hand him over to the German authorities. Not that! You can't . . . Course we can, my lad, easy as pie. I think we know a fellow at the embassy, be glad to see you again. All right, said Ulrich. Enough! You fix me up with a passport – an American passport and a safe-conduct there – and I'll tell you everything, all you want to know. Not so fast now, chum. We've got to have guarantees. One last little visit to Germany that's the ticket. You're sure you didn't leave anything behind in Hamburg? And Ulrich talked, he talked about Franziska and everything else . . . All right then, good, we'll send you back to Hamburg. You'll enjoy seeing Franziska again, won't you? You see, we're even giving you a present. But on one condition: you get the papers, your name kept out of it, the lot, provided you do a little favour for us. You can't refuse a service to democracy, can you? Otherwise we'd have to assume that you sympathized with those agitators over there, pining for the good old Imperial days . . . All right, I'll go . . . Good, we appreciate you seeing the error of your ways like this. Got to know what side you're on. That's good. And anyway it's better to work for the British Crown than kick your heels in that scruffy cell in Brixton, don't you think? When you come back – you're bound to come back, you realize? – it's a promise: the passport and the ship to Baltimore. The Americans agree. You'll see: freedom, new identity, a new trade to learn – tremendous! And once you're over there you can even leave again, go somewhere else, where you like. Well, almost . . . Anywhere but Europe. No coming back. But there's Mexico, for example . . . why not, eh? You'll have the right introductions. You ask the Yanks and they'll let you have the papers you need. Before, you had no identity, or anyway no means of proving it. Now you'll have more than enough!

On 24 December 1923, Ulrich Jasper Bremen was driven to the docks in a black limousine. A few minutes before midnight they put him on board a freighter, its name obscured in the darkness, bound for Hamburg.

2

AFTER THE RETURN journey, it took time to convince myself that the novel had to be written. After those years on the move, only the transition to my own reserve, to self-containment, might some day lead me back to the road again, if later I wished to reach a point of stillness.

A good six years went by between my return from Central America and the resurrection of my questing demon. I will come back – I assure you – to what I have just referred to as 'self-containment', but first I would like to indicate how the first symptoms of the process appeared, even if its origin can be traced back to some time before the date of 25 April 1973 when the folder from the Home Office came into my hands . . . My getting involved in the 'underground' press, as it was called in those days, certainly did not marginalize my power: there are doors which open to the mandatory degree of wealth and clout (another word that surfaced around then, curiously enough). There is nothing so unusual about rubbing shoulders with powerful men and people in government, for a fashionable journalist whose editorials mould the opinions of a key minority which happens to include a good fraction of the country's so-called intellectual elite. Two or three investigations into hot issues, a salutary scandal, and you are dining with ministers and principal private secretaries. In the course of a few years, the influence of *OFF* had grown considerably, and not only in the United Kingdom . . . We were researching a 'cultural' supplement on 'the inter-war years and the rise of fascist movements in Europe' when a 'friend' in the A-stream of the Civil Service volunteered to give me access to certain of his ministry's records. One thing led to another, and my infected curiosity made me unable to resist the temptation to find out if there was anything on file about Bremen. Considering what I knew already, I still wonder why the idea had never occurred to me before. It was obvious: those stories of Uncle Charlie's ought to have rung the bell. With a past like his, Raven was bound to have left some trace of his presence in England somewhere in the archives of the police. The arrest by Sergeant Vickers, Brixton prison, the boat to Hamburg, the confirmation of his return to England and final departure for the United States, together with a message from the FBI giving all the details of his naturalization in Mexico, it was all there, duly stored away. I haven't made anything up, not about the nature of the facts, I mean. When it came to the marathon and Vanessa (I noticed that she was never mentioned in the file), I had to rely on my old guardian's account, and he had steered clear of informing me about the deeper ins and outs of the affair. What I had learned to my cost in Mexico and Guatemala had at least convinced me of one thing: my father had undoubtedly had his visions of being a man of action, and perhaps he had even believed himself to be one, but as I saw the picture, it was only on paper, in his books, that the genuine royal roar had sounded, full-throated and unambiguous. At the end of the journey there had been the certainty of something real, the authenticity of a great writer. And only that . . . When I came back, I did not intend to imitate him, and would not presume to paraphrase. Now that I had reconstituted the outcome of the drama, and even though I didn't have the key, what did it matter if the walls of memory still stood, as sheer as ever? The anecdotal fragments were restored to a living order. Failure was no longer distinguishable from success. On the contrary, the more I grew aware of the trap I had entered as a willing victim, the more I came to see that in the fiction there was something sound. The gaps, the deficiencies, the alternation of black and white, colour and shadow, unmasked the mystification. In Oaxaca, and then in Chiapas and Relámpagos, I in turn had become a character out of a novel. How could I then have supposed that the story would have no continuation unless I was to pick up the torch – unless I too conceived the shape of this devil of a novel of which I knew nothing as yet, because the first word was still unwritten? Admire the force of the truism! And let us look at the situation with a steady eye. As far as Raven is concerned, no matter how tangled and intricate things may be, in the end they are simple: the further you pursue his invitation to go backwards in time, the deeper it lures you into an infinitude of unresolved dilemmas. It is easier to relive a life, even if only partially, than it is to 'make' one, to follow it step by step in the knowledge that choosing one path instead of another means constantly manufacturing destiny without having any means of gauging the importance or inconsequence of the move in the instant of its making. For example we know nothing, or practically nothing, about the Franziska who puts in an appearance, and yet her role is obviously a part of the Raven mystery. She touches and attracts us in advance; she even invests the young Bremen with a glamour as yet unearned. Conversely, if there has been little mention until now of the woman I married on my return from Guatemala, it is because Beatrice belongs to the 'self-containment' to which I have referred. Her story intersected mine at a point which will be fairly accurately defined when the time comes, and that should suffice . . .

I have to admit it: the visit to Bocanegra had not cured me of myths! Or not entirely . . . At that time I was living under the influence of a Papa Freud made specially pernicious because I believed in theory that I was liberated from him. My head was still cluttered with half-baked notions – for instance, that the more the father is demystified the more the son can find himself . . . The essential journey remained to be completed – a virgin path. I should have known. But who can claim to know the shortest way, I ask you! All the same, though, it is extraordinary that after having thought I was writing these notebooks for myself alone, I should now find myself angling for the attention of a collusive reader. Perhaps that requires supplying proof that the issue does not merely concern Raven and me. Perhaps it requires the reader to believe me capable of the kind of actions usually performed by characters in fiction. By then, with every schema thoroughly confused, it will be possible, who knows, to talk about unity regained . . . Reference for reference, I prefer henceforth to tell myself that my father had no account to settle with any kind of superego: his life was as speculative as, say, Daniel Defoe's. While I was at Farlow School or up at Oxford I read books like *Moll Flanders* or *Robinson Crusoe* and took them utterly at their face value. I had to reread those novels, and others by the same author, during the months that followed my marriage to Beatrice François, before I came to see their affinity with Raven's. I was struck then by the love of mystification evident in a man who could write an introduction to a novel in which he remarked that it might seem impossible for the narrator not to have personally witnessed the events described. Like my father, and like myself, Defoe had been a man of both worlds, of words and experience. He was a traveller, he spent some time in jail, he was accused of being a secret agent, and he practised several trades. His knowledge of the criminal underworld was quite as extensive as Raven's of revolution, or mine of guerrilla warfare. And like us, as a good journalist with deadlines to meet he had poked his nose into all sorts of experiences, one day shady and degrading, the next involved with the greatest causes, if not both at once. And for what? For the exclusive benefit of fictional biographies presented as authentic historical accounts! The circumstances were true, but as for the characters, it would have been a shrewd observer who could define precisely what degree of credibility they deserved.

I have no intention – that will be obvious, I hope – of introducing any notion of retrospective futility. The game – even if it does have its part in the order of existence – is what interests me least in all this. I am simply trying to articulate in clear and not too reductive terms how (and not why or wherefore) I have arrived at writing.

I would like, if I may, to cite another example. This one will be the last. For years I was possessed by the story of Bakunin's escape as told by Uncle Charlie, who thought I should know something about the man whom my father had admired sufficiently to call me after him. Michael is a fairly nondescript and unheroic name in all of its various languages, surely, and yet doesn't it wear a special aura in this (my own) story? . . . In 1861 the anarchist escaped from his Siberian prison. 'The storm is the eruption of popular life, the one force capable of sweeping away that whole world of entrenched injustices, do you see now, Michael?' And Charlie did not omit a single detail of the way Bakunin seduced his jailer's daughter, who later helped him to get away. Now history tells us that things didn't happen that way at all. The political mentor of both O'Sullivan and Raven in fact enjoyed the utmost liberty: although in exile, he had every opportunity to move from one place to another. He left Irkutsk when it suited him, took ship on the Amur river and . . . just left, that was all. Naturally it would have suited me better to stick to my guardian's version, but I was left in no doubt after reading the correspondence of Bakunin in an edition of 1896, unearthed for me by Beatrice in one of the bookstalls along the Seine, a few days before she went back to London, where we were about to settle. I was stunned by one letter from Kavelin to Herzen: 'I'm sorry for this gentleman' (he was referring to Bakunin) 'but I confess that I have little faith in him and that I do not expect anything good from him. The way he left Russia is not at all attractive.' What did he mean? Was it true that when Michael arrived in London he told Mme Ogarev in confidence that: 'In order to achieve my freedom I had to deceive some of my friends'? Call that what you like, but it was a quite surprising coincidence, wasn't it? And there was also the letter Bakunin wrote to Herzen and Ogarev from San Francisco on 3 October 1861: 'I have managed to escape from Siberia and after a long voyage down the Amur, along the coast of the Tartary Strait and through Japan I arrived in San Francisco today. But on the journey my modest savings were completely exhausted, and if I had not fallen in with a generous man who was willing to lend me two hundred and fifty dollars to take the train to New York, I would have found myself in a very awkward position. You, my friends, are too far away, and in this particular town I do not know anybody. I hope to reach New York on 6 November. If I reckon correctly this letter should reach you on the 15th, so I could hear from you by the end of the month. I hope you have already received the money which ought to have been forwarded to you from Russia on my behalf. At all events I beg you to send me five hundred dollars in New York, which if I am not mistaken comes to the hundred pounds sterling necessary for my travelling expenses . . .'

Etc. Etc. Good grief! And further on, this incredible declaration: 'My final watchword will be the destruction of

Austria . . . To serve this cause I am ready for anything: I would agree to enlist as a drummer, I would even go so far as to become the clown.' Is that all? No, there's more. 'During my voyage here I have managed to arrange a business deal which will certainly please you. Knowing how avidly the *Bell* and the *Polar Star* are read in Siberia, and how hard it is to get hold of those publications, I have made arrangements for the sale of your papers with three foreign businessmen, a German in Shanghai, an American in Japan, and another American in Nikolayevsk, which lies at the mouth of the Amur. They will take everything we send them from London on sale or return, and in this way our papers will be sold to the officers of the Russian navy and to the traders from Kyakhta who flock to the vicinity of the Amur and the Pacific Ocean every year. This way we can sell one or two hundred copies of the newspaper, a trivial quantity from the commercial point of view, but very sizeable from the political point of view.'

The course had already been set, then. I had only to follow it. And later on I only needed to get my teeth into the 'Polish question', such a passion with Bakunin, for the cycle to be completed! Oh, I hear the commotion and the snorts of scepticism. All this proves nothing, it's true, except the utter effrontery of a narrator who goes strutting about playing hero and fool simultaneously, when he puts in parallel lines that intersect, not at any infinite vanishing point but very quickly, almost immediately in fact, as always happens both in life and in fiction . . .

From the Spanish Conquest to the guerrilla resistance in Guatemala – or come to that in Vietnam – with Bocanegra, the historical chimera in the middle of the bunch – the combination of events of which I was the product, as they say, took on a certain pattern and continuity. From Alfonso de Seguida to Virginia Lippman, by way of Rudolph Bach, Raven and Lidia Valdés, separations and refusals seem to have been entirely determined by the dialectic that sustained them. It seems to me that we are living through other discontinuities today, but find ourselves unable to say exactly what it is that makes them different and unprecedented. It is as if we had entered the dimension of . . . anti-history. Not a negative, no, but a kind of white light out of another world, as in the dawn of another apocalypse . . . I remember one of the last interviews I did for my magazine, in 1975, a few weeks before I left again for Mexico. In Vienna I had been the first journalist to interview the Soviet dissident Sergei Matlev. Excuse the weakness of the word, but I am too fond of words to deprive myself of making them cough up at any price: I had not been disappointed by the *trip!* In those days we were spoiled children, only just out of our utopian infancy. Under the pavement we found nothing more than the sand from the holiday clubs, and the last wells we sank, groping in the dark, left us bone dry of everything, illusions as well as oil! Matlev predicted that in a few years' time the crunch would come in Poland. And if the pot boiled over there, then it would certainly spread to Germany, and finish God knows where . . . With 1984 around the corner! . . . The sorrowful, tragic Matlev threw Orwell in our faces with the accent of Dostoevsky! In the name of the Gulag, mysticism (hadn't I had more than my share of visionaries?), the priesthood, Evil, Original Sin, the Devil and all his works, the writer paraded the wildest of fantasies about the worst of all words. I sniggered behind my hand. I didn't take him seriously.

No more seriously than I had been ready, in different circumstances, to take that Kaiser Wilhelm story mentioned by my stepmother and brought up again by Rudolph Bach. Being the bastard offspring of such a massive historical figure never seemed to me to justify the belief that I had some sort of novelistic responsibility to bear. From where I stand, the events I have been describing carry more conviction, and my present state of mind surely cannot alter this feeling. The Edwardian Age, the 1920s, how remote they are! Provided I could find the words to describe it, I preferred the nostalgia of our present time, the undiscoverable country of the here and now. Nevertheless, more out of respect for him than through personal necessity, I owe this final tribute to Raven, his books and his legend. Even allowing for an element of self-parody, that excursion into Hohenzollern territory shows the categorical difference between my father and myself. This is his story, not mine, and that is why I now feel capable of setting it down on paper.

In *Die Ziegelbrenner*, in the midst of the revolution called the Republic of Councils, in 1919, Ulrich Jasper Bremen had printed a wild tirade in which he declared that: 'I am only the product of an era and my one ambition is to melt into the vastness of the world. Nameless, I have not the least ambition. I am no writer, no, I am nothing but the Word.' If I too have made up my mind to write, I would like to say, with neither shame nor modesty, that it was for less virtuous, rather more tainted and arrogant reasons. When he signed that article, Bremen was only replying in his then characteristically quixotic, impetuous manner, to attacks from anti-semites who inevitably believed that the magazine was a front for the secret powers of Sion. A paragraph earlier, he wrote that not a drop of Jewish blood flowed in his veins. 'I am bound to make that clear, in the name of the truth which we hold dear. However, my detractors would be mistaken if they thought that this statement contained one ounce of relief or pride. The only ancestral pride I am able to boast is not to have known them and not to have sought to know them.'

Raven, Bremen, that is my father, knew what he was saying, and I understand how he came to see things in that light. But how silly to have thought and written that he was 'only the product of an era'! Even if he had told me that himself, looking me straight in the eye while he said it, I would not have believed a word of it. His flight (don't ask me which one) and all his rambling do not prove anything: to me, they are a series of sharp denials.

Today is 9 December 1981, and I have just taken a short trip out to post a card to Pablo on his birthday. When I came back, because I ran into some difficulty in starting the chapter I had promised myself to write tonight, I started to re-read the manuscript almost from the beginning. I have smoked the last of my cigarettes. I look through the window, and there in the frozen stillness of the night I can see nothing but the glow of burning braziers and the stamping silhouettes of young militiamen trying to force a little warmth into their hands and feet.

II

HOHENZOLLERN

1

'FRANZISKA, I LOVE you.'

In the darkness of the bedroom Ulrich caressed the smooth skin of her naked back. His fingers slid slowly down her spine as if he wanted to learn all of its cambers and hollows, and the flat of his hand stopped moving when it came to the small of her back and the end of the ridge. A shiver rippled through the girl's body. 'Are you feeling cold?' He pulled the blanket up over her shoulders, then leaned down to kiss her neck, which made her curl tighter away from him. As soon as he had pulled back from her, after a strained embrace, she had turned over to face the wall, drawing her legs up into a foetal position.

Outside, the quiet of the night was broken by sporadic shooting. As time went by the crackle of gunfire slackened and grew fainter.

Around eight o'clock that morning Franziska had burst into the little furnished flat which Ulrich occupied at 84 Clemenstrasse. She was panting for breath, beside herself, and only able to gasp:

'. . . the Freikorps . . . Eric . . .'

Ulrich had no time to don his jacket. She threw herself against him, clutching at his shirt and digging her nails into his flesh.

'Gently, Franziska, please . . . I know . . . I was just on my way to join our friends at the Maria-Theresa café.'

'Don't go . . . Too late . . . They've arrested Eric and they're murdering everyone they find in the streets!'

'It was reckless to come here. You might have been . . .'

She huddled in his arms.

'Ulrich, I'm so frightened. Listen, that's a heavy gun . . . Eric, what will they do to him, what will become of him?'

'Don't be afraid. As soon as you pull yourself together I'll see what I can do.'

'No, straight away!'

Her small clenched fists drummed on his chest. He shook her, she let out a shrill cry, and he slapped her face. She collapsed in tears, and he supported her over to the divan.

Franziska Ball had arrived in Munich six months earlier, together with her aunt, to visit her cousin, the poet Eric Muhsam. The armistice had just been signed and life was resuming its course. The daughter of a wealthy Hamburg ship-builder, brought up by the strict tenets of German Protestantism, the seventeen-year-old Franziska was making the first long journey in her life, not counting visits to the spa at Ems with her parents, before the war. Even if the rather coarse Bavarian manners did shock her at first, she soon became enchanted and delighted by the free and easy, even boisterous character of the capital city of the kingdom of the South. Eric took her to the Pinakothek, the theatre, the parks and even the café, and it was there that on 6 November 1918 she first met Ulrich Bremen. He was twenty years old. During the discussion that sent the group of friends alight, he cried out: 'Comrades, the world Revolution has begun!' She did not attend the big demonstration that took place next day, on a sunlit afternoon, in Bavaria Park. Although she did not understand much about the meaning of their debates, Franziska admired the enthusiasm of these young men who forecast the coming of a new world which was going to be more free, more just, and more human. She would have liked to go with Eric (she was secretly in love with him, or thought she was), but her aunt refused permission.

'We should have been back in Hamburg by now, little one. I don't like the look of all this.'

By the time the decision was made, it would be too late, and the danger too great. Better to stay quietly in Munich, wait for the trouble to die down, and things to get back to normal. In Berlin, they feared the worst.

Eric, the tender-hearted, had told her all about the crowd at Bavaria Park, and all the joy and excitement. Kurt Eisner, in his top-hat, grey beard and prominent pince-nez, had climbed on to the platform. 'The finest words I've ever heard, Franziska. Words that no poetry could ever rival! . . . And the soldiers were captivated. They scattered through the town and fraternized with the people. Together they seized the barracks and armouries. It's the Republic, do you hear, the Republic!'

Eisner took over the government. King Ludwig III ran away. And in Berlin the workers set the example by declaring a general strike.

During all this time, Franziska had little opportunity to see much of her cousin's young friend, the journalist Ulrich Bremen, whose articles in *Die Ziegelbrenner* gave the movement an eloquent voice. Nor was she sorry to miss him, because during a meeting at Eric's house Ulrich had not stood on ceremony but had taken hold of her hand with hardly a word when she sat next to him at tea. She shot him a withering look, but he had met it with an impertinent stare that did not leave her face. It thoroughly disturbed her, and she took care not to mention it to her aunt or to Eric, whom she loved with devotion. And that was in spite of the fact that the poet had no suspicion of his cousin's feelings towards him. At best, he would address her as 'the Muse', which brought conniving smiles among the gathering . . .

In January came the elections. Eisner was beaten. Clinging to power, and supported by an active minority, he was assassinated shortly afterwards by Count Anton Arco-Valley, a young right-wing extremist. Munich now descended into total confusion, which meant among other things that there was no question of Franziska's leaving the city. The noose had tightened. Much more than Revolution, scarcity, cold and hunger were the true masters of the capital. And it was at that moment that Ulrich Bremen's behaviour suddenly changed. Until then, he had paid assiduous but quite decorous court to Franziska. When the anarchists were not meeting at the café, he would come and spend the evening at Augustenstrasse, when if he did not somehow manage to bring a little coal or a piece of meat, at least he supplied the comfort of lively conversation. After the incident of the hand – thank God it was not repeated – so much solicitude irritated Franziska. The boy was not bad-looking; if it had not been for Eric's enchanting presence she would probably have found some charm in Ulrich. What she was not sure of was his heart. Hadn't Eric once mentioned his friend's theatrical past, and a woman called Carlotta, who sounded as if she must have been much more than a fellow actor? . . . Yet the last time Ulrich had turned up at Augustenstrasse (that was in late February, and he had not been seen there since) he had scarcely opened his mouth. He just sat mute, and listened. The fact that the majority socialists had formed a government in exile in Bamberg seemed to leave him unmoved. And Franziska noticed that when Landaur was describing the intrigues of the communists Leviné and Axelrod, his eyes stared into a distant corner of the ceiling, as if his thoughts were a thousand miles away from the discussion. From that moment on, she took less stern a view of him. And in the following weeks, the girl learned to her cost that absence is often the most perverse of seduction's wiles . . .

Obviously Franziska could not imagine what had happened to Ulrich. It was not till later – much too late – that she learned the nature of the emotional shock which was disrupting his life. She resented him for the celerity with which he set about serving the cause, and even caught herself feeling jealous of Eric, who saw him nearly every day. 'What a superb example!' her cousin would tell her. 'Oh, if only all our young people displayed such a depth of self-sacrifice! . . .' And he described to her an Ulrich giving himself entirely, body and soul, to his mission. No hunger or fatigue could diminish his vitality. Working without a break, he volunteered for every task, both the wildest and the humblest. On 6 April, the day when they declared the Republic of Councils, not content with being elected on to the propaganda committee he demanded, as a privilege, to join the revolutionary tribunal.

Schwiebus, 16 January 1919

My son

Since your all too brief letter telling us that you had moved to Munich, we have heard no more news from you. You know that I have never been a very clever writer, and in the ill fortune which has hit us my clumsy pen cannot tell you what I am feeling.

Fortunately your devoted younger brother is here beside me, and it is he who is taking the trouble to write what I want to say. 'Otto,' I said to him, 'today we shall write to your brother.'

You have to know this, my dear: Carl is no longer with us to tell you how worried we have been about you. He will not scold you any more, and he will not advise you to beware of the strength of your own feelings as much as you beware of your enemies. After you left home, these three long years, he was not properly alive any more, the poor man. He loved you, Ulrich. Like a son . . . But let me put your mind at rest: he left without a warning, without knowing it. What do they call it? An embolism?

Carl was proud of you. He hoarded the newspapers you sent us, where they mentioned you. The photo of *Hamlet* at the theatre in Düsseldorf, with that girl, Carlotta Wiener. And the caption: 'A phenomenal young actor of seventeen: W. H. Raven.' We wondered just why you had chosen such a peculiar name. Your father – well, Carl – he could not bear the thought that you might be ashamed of being a Bremen. I would tell him no, you had no cause to be. Isn't that right, Ulrich?

I didn't want you to know – what good does it do? – but when he felt that he was going, Carl made me swear to tell you the truth. My God, what it costs me to revive the memory of that cursed springtime I had buried deep inside me and that Carl's love had made me forget! I have not got your talent for making words speak, Ulrich, but you have enough experience of human affairs to imagine what happened. And you know, my son, that all my life long there was never labour or punishment hard enough to pay for the sin of my young days.

Carl loved me, in secret. In the village, everybody knew it except me. You are not so old that you cannot understand the silly ideas that a poor young girl of eighteen may get into her head. When one has herded cattle all one's life, Prince Charmings do exist. And one day he came to Schwiebus . . . I cannot say his name but you will easily recognize him. A hunting party it was, all noise and colour, it turned the village topsy-turvy, and my head with it. The prince gave an open-air feast for the company – he was one of the greatest in the land. There was music, dancing, smiles, caresses, kisses . . . what a celebration! And he looked so sad and frail in spite of his proud ways and fine moustache. When hearts and heads were spinning he drew me to one side. He wanted to go for a walk with me, no one but me. Tired of his friends and important people and drum-rolls and etiquette . . . A simple girl of the kingdom, there, to the life, you see? And as we walked along the river bank – because he had sent his servants away and he waved intruders off, because he wanted to be alone – he told me about his virtuous wife who gave him so little love and so many children! You have heard about all this, I'm sure, and now you will understand who I am speaking of. And I do not blame you for the hate you must feel for your mother.

Oh, Ulrich, there are no words – well, I don't know them if there are! – for the rest of the story. Spinning and falling . . . and then the dreadful rude awakening! Two hours afterwards the handsome prince was gone, and he never set foot in our province again. He took away a shameful hunting trophy. You know how prettily those gentlemen talk! He left behind a creature wounded to death. If Carl had not been there to help me, and really to give me back the will to live for you, the son I carried in my belly, I don't think either one of us would be here today. Carl was always your father, your *true* father.

Forgive me. Not for what I did, but for shrouding myself in silence and terror, and now for the cry I send to you for love of Carl. Understand a poor mother who is condemned never to see her oldest son again, and who would at least wish to give him a reason for distrusting the speeches and humbug of those who have always led an easy life. Even here, in Schwiebus, we can feel that the earth is being shaken and that the world is in danger of falling. If I tell you all this – and think of the suffering that chokes my throat – it is because I want you to think again before you too do something stupid. Make no mistake, Ulrich, a woman like me is in no position to preach to anyone at all. Shall I be washed clean, and on the day I die shall I go to Carl with peace of mind and body? We have never blamed you for anything. When you wanted to go to the high school we bled ourselves dry to pay for your studies. How proud we were! . . . Otto, who has not been as lucky as you, will make a good worker, like his father . . . Nor did we say anything when you met that older woman, that Carlotta. And I thank the Lord that Carl never thought it was a sign of tainted blood and that your mother's bad qualities were coming out in you.

The war has spared you, my son, and I would not wish the evils that are afflicting Germany today to cause you to do anything rash. If you do not do it for me, then do it for your father.

Your loving mother,
Horminia Bremen.

Ulrich remembered. He must have been . . . four years old, that's right. One day a woman dressed in black and wearing a hat and veil had arrived at the house in a coach and four escorted by a squadron of cavalry. The burgomaster had been informed in advance that the Empress would be coming from Cronthaus castle to distribute gifts to the poor, and that, finding the Bremen family particularly deserving, she intended to make a special example of them. Orders were barked, heels clicked, crinolines rustled . . . in the silence of fear. And Carl Bremen stammered his thanks. Ulrich came in for a kiss from the great lady and an affectionate little pat on the head. 'Here, my boy, take this purse. We want a deserving son of our people to know how deeply the Emperor and I are concerned with the advancement and education of our best subjects.'

Ulrich tore up the letter after scanning it several times. He would make no reply to his mother. Never. But he picked up his pen to compose the diatribe which he would publish next day in *Die Ziegelbrenner*. 'This is hardly the time to forget the morbid fanaticism of the imperial clown. It is common knowledge, of course, that the man who used to pose as a demi-god was in reality a common seducer. This posturing warlord had no equal for slinking out of the bed of a defenceless girl (preferably an illiterate peasant, good and plump) to see some scented, periwigged young marquis for exercises unknown on the battlefield.'

At the anarchists' café, Eric Muhsam read the pamphlet then looked across at his friend, who was draining a stein of beer washed down with schnapps, and said:

'This is a bit strong, Ulrich. What's the point of it?'

'Oh, I know what you're going to say. It's all right to be a revolutionary, but you wouldn't like the old ordure of things to be soiled, isn't that it? Still attached to the grandeurs of the Empire . . . It's the upper middle class in you, bound to come out!'

'When you write something like that, it's you who don't trust the political consciousness of the masses. As if we weren't above all that!'

'Well, I'm not above it, actually. As long as we haven't torn out the canker of aristocracy, down to its deepest roots, there's still every risk of the clock being turned back again.'

'Too hard to be true . . .'

'Are you accusing me of bad faith?'

'No, no, it was just something to say . . . Ulrich, stop

drinking. Landaur and Toller are waiting at my house. Franziska may still have some tea to offer us. You like the Muse, don't you?'

Money was abolished, the birth of a radically new art proclaimed. A new law decreed that flats in Munich were no longer to contain more than three rooms. Doctor Franz Lipp, the *Räterepublik*'s commissar for foreign affairs, sent a message to Moscow complaining that his predecessor in exile had run off with the key to the ministerial lavatory. Down to the most trivial follies, hope took the lion's share, and left the scraps for realism. A radiant light shone in the April sky. Life – all of life – was going to change.

In his paper, Ulrich wrote: 'I do not, we do not belong to any party but the party of mankind. Allegiance to an order or programme and obedience to leaders lessen the freedom in whose name we are meant to be working. The sole aim of existence and of our activities is summed up in these words: to be a human being and nothing but a human being.'

On the very day of that editorial he signed fifteen death sentences. A few hours later the communists seized power. Toller gathered an army, and when it came to a confrontation with the social democrat troops Ulrich begged his friend to let him fight in the front line of the assault. Contrary to his wish, he did not meet his death there, and was recalled in triumph to Munich, where new political tasks awaited the victors. But he was worn out, and on the advice of his friend Eric he at last agreed to take a rest day. That was on the 30th of April.

'Franziska, I love you.'

He wanted to make love to her again, take her again, make himself forget the scarlet violence of the first assault. There in the warmth of the bed, as if with a caress and a heave of the hips they could obliterate the bloodshed, suffering, screams and agony.

'Let me go, Ulrich.'

'Come.'

'No . . . do you realize what we've done, what we're doing? While others are dying . . .'

'It had to be now, it had to be.'

'They'll be coming to arrest you too. Let's get away.'

'Too late. It's time for the big sweep. The Freikorps aren't arresting people, they're killing them.'

'My God, blessed be thy clemency!'

With her hair spread over her naked shoulders, Franziska sank to her knees.

'Don't let's start that again, please, Franziska. It's only love, nothing but love . . . We will be happy, you'll see.'

'Ah, you talk of happiness when Eric has probably laid down his life for us . . .'

'You can go back to your aunt's place. I'll go with you. Don't worry, I know this town well, and its backstreets too. You pack your bags and I'll take care of the rest. Now go.'

Her clothes were strewn about the bedroom. She hurried to collect them, clutching them against her to cover her nakedness. Turning her back on her lover, she began to dress again. In the racing of his senses and the fever which had driven them into each other's arms, Ulrich had had no time to be concerned with the girl's physique. It had been a sudden rush of panting, frantic movements, sighs, rips, smells, taut muscles, moans, shudders, honey and confusion. This time, the more Franziska's re-clothed body was lost to his eyes, the more aware Ulrich grew of the real object of his desire. Instead of allowing itself to be carried along on the tide of an action that made it nothing but a toy, his body was reacting to the situation. Ulrich saw the effects and outcome of the drama. He was there, lying on an unmade bed, like Sardanapalus commanding and observing the death of his wives. Would he have the courage to immolate himself? That was the whole question. Or else, like a prince for ever debauched, would he write the dissolute epitaph: 'Eat, drink, and be merry: nothing else matters'? When Franziska turned again, two tears were running down her cheeks. Ulrich lowered his head. He would not raise it again before he heard the sound of the door being closed behind the Muse.

Naturally Ulrich did not get very far. Hardly had he walked the length of Clemenstrasse when a carload of counter-revolutionaries shot out from around a corner. Three pistol-packing officers of the Freikorps and a civilian ordered him to stop. The latter – only a young man, although his hair was as white as a greybeard's – shouted out:

'I recognize him. It's that journalist, Bremen!'

They manhandled Ulrich into the car, to be driven to the war ministry. Piles of dead bodies lay in the deserted streets, and the rats were running.

What happened next remains obscure. Bremen had come unusually early to the boundary where the fickleness of the present merges into the precariousness of the future. It was only a step to turn risk into systematic doubt. The jeopardy of a severe crisis is likely to produce decisive hesitations, and the person concerned has no idea which way the pendulum will swing.

In *Tarantulas at Nightfall* – though bear in mind that there is some doubt about the book's authenticity and its author's identity – Raven introduces two characters. One of them, Robert, escapes after wounding his guard, a sort of albino with a beak of a nose. The other, Wilhelm, the first man's companion, lets himself be hauled up in front of the judges, is accused of high treason, and is finally released after having denounced his comrades and claiming to be the bastard offspring of a prince of the blood. In both cases, Robert and Wilhelm manage to be reunited with the women they love, one in Hamburg, the other in Vienna.

If we consult the historical record, its facts are no less stubborn than in fiction. Gustav Landaur was tortured and beaten to death. Leviné shot. Muhsam was jailed for five years, then released under an amnesty, and later arrested again by the Nazis, who murdered him in Oranienburg concentration camp in 1934. As for Ernst Toller, shattered by Franco's victory and the Munich pact he hanged himself in his hotel bedroom in New York, on 22 May 1939.

Raven chose the following passage from the Italian anarchist Malatesta as the epigraph for *The Cyclone's Eye*:

> The day will come, so we are firmly persuaded, when it will be possible to do good for mankind without doing harm to oneself or to others; but today it is impossible. Even the purest, most gentle of martyrs, he who would have himself brought to the scaffold for the

sake of the triumph of the good, unresisting, blessing his persecutors like the Christ of legend – even he would be doing harm. As well as the harm he would be doing to himself, but that is the way of things, he would cause bitter tears to be shed by all who have loved him.

2

Carlotta Wiener was no Ophelia. A tall woman, and quite mannishly broad at the shoulders, she had worn her dark hair shingled long before the style was legitimized by fashion and a looser morality. This enabled her to stand in for a sick or absent actor at a moment's notice, if the need arose. And in life as well, she could play to perfection on that physical ambiguity which she had made the key to her power of seduction over men. As the star of the travelling company Carlotta would never have brooked a second's rivalry for the role of Polonius's daughter. Prost, the company's producer and director, and her titular lover, was compelled to make the best of that fact. Thank goodness the repertoire offered plenty of other possibilities.

It was in Strindberg's *The Virgin Bride* that Ulrich discovered her. Carlotta Wiener was magnificent in it: the role of the unmarried mother who murders her child suited her perfectly. At the age of thirty-two, after a wayward career, she could hardly aim much higher than Prost's troupe, but in the Swedish play she regained the brilliance of her younger days.

Bremen was raw from his distant province. He knew nothing about the theatre and actresses. He had not been in Berlin for more than a couple of weeks, working as a messenger for *Der Syndicalist*, before he became a regular member of the audience that sat in a courtyard just off the Alexanderplatz. For three nights running he saw the performance of *The Virgin Bride*, and a few days later he was back watching *Die Marquise von O . . .*, which the company was giving on alternate weeks. If the young man had found Carlotta unbearably moving in the first of these plays, in the role of the girl violated while unconscious and ignorant of the identity of the man whose child she bears, the actress was simply sublime. A bit out of character, perhaps, but this detail escaped young Ulrich, who revelled night and day in a state of mental and physical exhilaration which the hard, disciplined life of the imperial high school had never allowed him even to suspect . . . The following day he stayed on after the performance and rushed to the dressing rooms to throw himself at the actress's feet, then rise to kiss her knees, thighs, stomach and at last the hands that reached down to draw him to his feet.

'Oh madame . . . I love you!' he babbled, with tears in his eyes.

She stroked his cheek: the skin was soft and beardless.

'How kind . . . But you'll tear my robe. Come, sit there. We can talk while . . .'

'May I stay, really?'

'Oh you rascal!' She kept her eyes trained on him, and looked him up and down as he perched on top of a rickety stool and almost tipped it over. She smiled, a candid smile, without any malice, and he did not blush for his clumsiness.

'I'm ravenous, you know. I shall get changed, and after that, if you like, we can talk while we eat, shall we?'

Ulrich had imagined all sorts of scenarios for this meeting. He had stood in his room rehearsing entire speeches from Kleist, intending to reproduce them again, with a melodramatic air, at the opportune moment, as declaimed in front of the fly-specked looking glass. But Carlotta caught him unawares: she proved to be even more surprising than his fizzing imagination had let him conceive. He felt at ease with her, and safe. After uttering his tribute he had intended to flit away like a ghost that rejects human existence and creeps into hiding in nethermost darkness. Instead, he stayed. He watched her, half naked, and he thought of only one thing: to become an actor himself, to incarnate a host of people and a gallery of faces, to throw off his pursuit, play out the comedy of love and woe, and dupe the enemy which had so often threatened him in the chilly dormitory of adolescence . . .

It was the first flush of Ulrich's passion. In the village, at home, and even at school, he had felt out of place, as if he floated on an unknown tide, drawn somewhere else, but where he could not tell. He had left Schwiebus and the builder's trade to go to high school, but although he made the most of the privilege, here too he felt that his future lay along a different path. Although the prospect of leaving the family fold was painful to him, and he knew that his departure would break his parents' heart, Ulrich owed it to himself to step out onto the highway of adventure, as if a sword were prodding at his back. He was attracted by the vortex whose drawback is its sheer totality. Already he felt that he wanted to be in touch with everything, and live in everything. Not knowing what roads might run to that idea, he saw in Carlotta and the theatre a means to travel there, perhaps. Unless he resolved the contradictions of his own personality, love and the ephemeral scene might exacerbate (and so, paradoxically, if not cure then at least contain) his tendency to dissipate his energies.

As for the actress, she was not unhappy to be able to make her entrance at the Schultz beer garden with such a handsome young man in tow. 'How old are you?' she had asked him with a casual air. 'Eighteen,' he told her, lying slightly. As usual, Prost had turned a blind eye, disappearing before the end of the meal, before the moment when Carlotta was obviously going to take her new conquest home with her. So much could be read in the looks she darted at him, and even more in the imperceptible tremor of her hands that the producer recognized on such occasions in the woman he loved.

The boy was no fool. His speech about the stage as a bottomless well of vicarious living for actors impressed the guests no end. It certainly pleased them more than his outburst about the war which, according to him, was imminent, so his friends on the paper had told him.

'Now Ulrich, you're not being the least bit amusing!' Carlotta protested. He was ready to charge further in his onslaught upon the dismal future that awaited them all, but the actress cut him short.

'Enough of that! Come on, let's go.'

His graduation by way of Carlotta's bed was to eradicate the last traces of romanticism from the young man's mind. The blaze and concentration of her passion overwhelmed him: soon he found himself lying in her boudoir on a ravaged bed, with nothing more to ponder than a landscape of buts and perhapses, beyond which his gaze did not reach.

Carlotta decided that he would stay.

In a week's time, the company was due to leave Berlin for the theatre at Essen, where it was to give thirty performances of *Hamlet*. No arguments: Ulrich would travel with them. They would try him out in the role of Rosencrantz. Prost never said no to his star actress, and the first rehearsals brought out her protégé's unmistakable gift for acting. Perhaps he overdid it, but Carlotta argued that with practice Ulrich would tone down his style to a quieter, more effective level. She would see to it personally. After all, he was only seventeen. Was there not every reason to have the highest hopes for the boy's future career? Prost admitted that he did have a certain temperament, you might even say class.

'He must play Hamlet!' cried Carlotta.

And the opportunity was not long in coming, because several days after the dress rehearsal old Dietrich was taken ill on stage, in the full flood of his To be or not to be. The slings and arrows of outrageous fortune interrupted his heartaches for a while (the luckless fellow claimed to have suffered several rejections by Carlotta in the past three years) and consigned him to a hospital bed and the thousand natural shocks that flesh is heir to. And Ulrich was, it is true, a superb Hamlet. You only had to see him, and hear him triumphantly declaim: 'The play's the thing, with which I'll catch the conscience of the king.'

Carlotta was all the more in love with him. To begin with, at least . . . for she quickly began to be irritated by the unstable character of a young lover who swung between domination and subservience, braggart and spoiled child. More than once she restrained herself from slapping his face.

'Filthy brat!'

'Go on, go on then! Hit me, you bitch!'

Nothing got more thoroughly on Carlotta's nerves than this way he had of striking a static pose, as pale as death, or else of ranting on to wherever the mood might carry him, with a puppet's jerking movements. In both cases she blamed him for bad acting.

'But life isn't like that!' she would shout.

'You can say that?' he would retort. 'What a nerve!'

'I think you should leave the theatre. For your own good.'

'What do you know about what's good or bad for me? . . . Too easy. You pick me up, take me on, eat me alive, and then when there's no more marrow left to suck, you throw me away. Carlotta! . . .'

'Oh please, don't whine!'

From Essen to Düsseldorf, and then to Munich, the quarrels ground on as months went by. Having gone off the rails for a moment, it looked as if both were slowly rediscovering the original goal of their respective roles. The act concluded with a sub-plot which would disappear under the pressure of the necessary development of the play. There was not even a grand separation. While Carlotta gradually resumed her relationship with Prost, Ulrich no longer had visions of the kind he had murmured in bed one day, of dying on stage in full make-up like an excommunicated Molière. Instead he had begun to frequent the city's anarchist cafés, whose life and energy lost nothing, so he said, by comparison with the antics of the theatre. The friends he made there even gave him the strength to ignore Carlotta's infidelity. 'Anyway,' he said to himself, 'how on earth can I have brought myself to fall in love with a woman almost old enough to be my mother?'

In Munich, where the company was to spend the winter, Prost decided to put on both parts of Goethe's *Faust*. Ulrich was offered, but refused, the role of the scholar rejuvenated by Mephistopheles – they would have to make do with Dietrich, who after his illness might sound rather lame when he came to give voice to: 'What heavenly image fills this magic mirror?' Prost and Carlotta made no objection when the young man spoke of leaving the company.

'You don't understand! Under the pretence of constantly remaking yourselves through the characters you play, you become incapable of wondering what you could be in the real world! I want a future to hold on to . . . Symbols, masks, pantomimes, you remind me of gods playing at theatricals. What's happened to your bodies, lungs, chests, thighs, sex? Don't you hear the beast inside us growling? What tomorrows does a shadow have?'

This was too much for Carlotta's derision to ignore.

'I suppose it was bound to come to this: a budding little Faust, just look!'

Ulrich flared up now. He called her an old bag, a plaster mask – 'only just fit to lie down and spread your legs.'

The actress flew at her short-term lover with all her claws out. Prost intervened. With calm restored, he said in the firm but affable tone he used for speaking to his actors at rehearsals:

'Man is a lie . . . Only one virtue is left to him: the possibility of living in defiance.'

There is no telling whether these words were addressed to the flesh-and-blood Carlotta and Ulrich or to their theatrical alter egos. But possibly the producer was only talking to himself . . .

III
SELF-CONTAINMENT

1

My father was no hero. No villain, either, of course. Since my return from the Petén and my encounter with his old acquaintance, Bocanegra, that much had been clear to me, even though I felt there were still more details to be added to the picture . . . not after some factual inquisition liable to generate theories whose converse would be equally unfalsifiable, but through the work of self-definition which had now been forced upon me, seeing that the sole effect of the previous sequence of events had been to regress me into limbo, into the outlandish, ambiguous state of mind that hovers between life and death. An orphan in the underworld, a Pilgrim without a saviour, and yet with a clear, quiet conscience. No matter when or where, doesn't every legacy have its limits in the end? If the boundary were natural and fluid, as people often think, in principle there would be nothing to prevent its being set further and further back, perhaps infinitely far. The ordinary urban traveller does not cross oceans and deserts; he learns every day that outside a given time and space his ticket is no longer valid! And since we are on to general-purpose precepts, cleaning and laundry thrown in, one small proverb, for want of a better one, may put my meaning straight. 'No man is a hero to his valet.' You will tell me that the saying is irrelevant, that I didn't know my father and therefore could not have been his lackey. Not physically, at any rate. All the same, my dealings with him have undoubtedly been a lot more intimate than most sons' relationships with accessible fathers. Have I overlooked some of his strengths or his weaknesses? When I came back to Europe, my exaggerated indulgence gave way to a quite different mode of thinking without my realizing it. In my mind, it wasn't just a few days or weeks since I had left Central America, but years . . . So powerful an experience should have left deep and visible traces: I treated it like a spare part of myself, stowed away somewhere and practically redundant.

I longed for triteness and monotony. Instead of seeming hopeless, everyday life took over again and offered the prospect of simple happiness. To get away from the journalists and the pull of society and politics I had to have a guide, someone who would take me in charge and point me back to reality. That person was Beatrice.

'Beatrice François,' she said. 'Xavier's cousin, remember?'

Drained by the journey, dazzled by camera flash and stunned by the uproar, at first I had not recognized her. Yet she hadn't changed very much since our brief affair at Oxford. Still the same slightly too hard, slightly too serious face, yet with that roguish gleam in her eyes which made her charm so patent once you saw it. Still the same low-key distinction in the way she dressed, which made her look older than her years, though I knew very well that it was merely a means of self-defence, a shell that covered a slender young body, fair skin, tight pear-shaped breasts, a hard triangular stomach, adolescent hips and shoulders, and inside her a soft warmth always ultimately withheld and kept intact.

We kissed one another on both cheeks. A mellow scent that used not to be there . . . Later on I was also to notice the perfection of her lacquered fingernails, whereas during her stay in England she had kept them short and natural. She no longer wore her chestnut hair cut straight across her forehead in a Beatles fringe: now it was shoulder length, and swept backwards in a fluent curve, emphasizing the ambiguity I have mentioned – the breadth of bare forehead enhanced the virile strength of the face, while the expression in her eyes was even more sensual (the eyebrows and eyelashes accented by a touch of mascara). Beatrice was a woman, chic and thoroughbred, but a woman all the same . . . and no longer a youthful memory.

She had just completed her postgraduate thesis at the Sorbonne, on the Bauhaus School, with a degree from the Ecole du Louvre. She told me about herself over the dinner her parents gave for me that night, after the formalities and the interviews. I had feared the worst when I learned that Froggy had taken charge of my reception and welfare so thoroughly that he had arranged for me to stay at the François' house, where Beatrice was still living. She had no job as yet, and she came from the sort of background where you don't have to start to put your knowledge on the market before the term is out. There was no hurry: she was hovering between a museum career and the possibility of opening a gallery of her own, with backing from Papa. I listened and found nothing much to say. No fuss was made, no questions asked, and the banker was perfectly discreet. Nobody tried to pump me about my adventures. The conversation meandered through all sorts of topics, but its relative inconsequence put me at ease. The prospect of staying in the guest room for a few days, 'while you find your bearings', began to seem like a good idea. At the airport a telegram had been waiting from Paul Arthur Smith: 'Congratulations. Champagne awaits. Editing ongoing. Phone us. Best wishes. Paul.' Next day, after twelve hours sleeping off some of my jet lag, I called London to explain that I still had quite a lot to sort out in Paris and would not be back for at least a week. Paul was very understanding: well of course, I had earned a holiday, he would explain things to the TV people, and anyway I was a star now, and they were delighted to have me on the team . . . I thanked Paul and assured him that he could rely on me to complete the film, but I did not tell him that I intended to quit television after that. It was a decision reached in my cell at Relámpagos – that if ever I got out, and even though I had no idea which way to go next, there was no question of picking up again where I had left off. Nor did I tell him anything about Beatrice. She had thought of everything, and made plans accordingly. A tourist programme for that marvellous Paris autumn of 1966, flexible enough to allow for spur-of-the-moment expeditions as well as fixed timetables, and to accommodate both my curiosity and my need to relax. There was perfection here, too, and all the better for being unobtrusive. There was no red carpet, no cotton wool either. Beatrice's attentions ended just where my own free will began, and never a word or smile or gesture further. I let myself be carried, in the belief that any movement and progress were my own achievement, dictated only by the pace of my injured leg and convalescent thinking. Paradoxically, the first symptoms of what I must describe as falling in love came to me without a sudden jolt or surge of feeling, but carried on the tide, with a momentum as smooth and uneventful as coasting along an even path . . .

The programme included lunch with a publisher from the boulevard Saint-Germain who wanted me to write a book about my 'adventures'. Beatrice told me: 'I've made the appointment, but if you don't want to go I can break it.' Actually I was interested in what the man might have to say, and in particular how much hard cash one raw and tender slice of my life might be worth. In that respect the meeting exceeded all my expectations. The publisher turned out to be likeable as well as shrewd. He promised the earth, lauded the existential criterion about there being great books rather than great writers, and waited for the pear-charlotte before offering a massive cheque in return for exclusive world rights to my story – my 'book' he called it, and kept on calling it, remorselessly, as if the writing were a mere formality, signed, sealed and delivered in advance. He outdid himself when the cognac arrived – 'a Delamain grande Champagne, one of *ze* best!' he proclaimed, and while my eardrums were still buzzing with his Gallic definite article it occurred to me how often since my return to normality I had waded through a gush of greats and grandeurs. 'My God, it's incredible!' I said to Beatrice the day after that publisher's lunch. (We were driving down route nationale 7, on our way to her parents' house in the country.) 'Is it a French obsession? You don't seem to have anything but "great" men and "great" books! Aren't you getting overloaded?' And Beatrice, to whom I had spoken about Raven, almost apologized – though not everybody was in the same position as I was, she said. I bristled a little at that, and asked her to explain herself. She side-stepped the issue very gracefully, and we ended by agreeing on our criticism of De Gaulle. Beatrice's father was a Gaullist; it was probably the only issue where she departed from the family consensus. She had no real political allegiance (or so she claimed in those days), but was simply irritated by the arrogance of the 'great man' in question.

'You see, you said it too, after all that!' Both of us laughed . . .

But to conclude this publishing episode, let us go back to what happened over that very special cognac, just as I was lighting the Montecristo number four supplied by my generous host. There was a spark of complicity in his eyes as he sent for the cigar, as if to say that smoking it would bring it all back to me.

'Actually we would like . . . hmm . . . we would be glad if you would consider following up this book – your autobiographical account would be a sort of introduction – by telling us about W. H. Raven, the great [*sic*] writer, your father.'

I made a show of calmly puffing my cigar, then blew a stream of smoke into his face and waited a moment before replying casually:

'So the papers have got hold of that?'

'The whole world knows, my dear Mr Mateos. It's fantastic! A fabulous scoop!'

'You mean the book you want to publish?'

'No, no . . . The article by that American professor, er . . .'

'George Lippman?'

'That's him . . . In *Newsweek*, and now all the rest of the media too . . . You owe him quite a debt, you know. If it hadn't been for that, you might still be in prison . . . But I'm not telling you anything you don't already know.'

'Not really. But what do you mean, "if it hadn't been for that"? For what, exactly?'

'Well, let's see, yes, chairing the international committee for your release . . . the meetings, demonstrations, pamphlets, petitions, articles, interviews . . . We know everything, or almost . . . Now it's up to you to fill in the rest – er, that is, the vital missing parts . . .'

I asked him for a few days to think it over. For the sake of appearances, and in order to stir the pot, I raised his already substantial bid by a healthy amount. He smiled and said that he too would think it over. We parted with a firm handshake.

Back at the avenue de La Bourdonnais, Beatrice took in the situation straight away. I was on the point of packing my suitcase and phoning Air France for a seat on the next plane to London when she suggested a visit to the cinema. Alain Resnais' *La guerre est finie* had just come out. Afterwards she took me to dinner in a quiet, modest little bistro in Montparnasse. We talked and argued about the film for some time, then stopped and ate in silence. I looked at her, and she looked at me. Eventually she said:

'You can't leave without getting to know the place where I was born. I shall be very glad if you can come. Mama is lending me the DS – her own, of course, not Papa's – and I will leave the little Austin for her. Tomorrow we drive down to the Beaujolais, what do you say?'

'Yes, I'd like to go.'

She hadn't asked about my meeting with the publisher. Perhaps she felt responsible for my bad mood. I told her that I would not do the book. I was expected back in London for the TV series on Mexico, and had to get down to work again. I couldn't go on living on welfare like this. She did not protest and talked about her country home . . .

We were leaving for three days. We stayed for a week. When we came back, we were engaged . . . Beatrice's parents tried every trick they knew to postpone the event, and her father's behaviour was frankly hostile, but he was pragmatic enough to realize that a hurried engagement was better than a rash liaison. His daughter was twenty-three years old. Anyway I would be returning to London to start work again and find us a place to live. There would be an interval of several months, and anything might happen in the meantime . . . We planned to marry in the spring.

Eighteen months previously, in Virginia's time, I would have been appalled by the prospect. With Lidia Valdés it would have been even more unthinkable. And during my imprisonment in Guatemala my memory had plagued me by constantly recycling an erotic parade of the women I had loved. At the time it was quite unimaginable that all this sensual ferment could centre upon any single woman, but with Beatrice our second encounter developed at a different level from sheer sexual attraction and pursuit. After such a long abstinence, certainly there was all the renewed pleasure of a woman's body, and her tranquil self-confidence as she gave it, unhurriedly, deliberately, but never holding back. But I don't want to give the impression that having lost my bearings in Central America I was now succumbing to the cautious counter-attraction of stability. Things are never that simple. In Beatrice I recognized a real woman. My mistake – though I can only discern it with hindsight – may be to have confused the wish to live with the onset of a slow consumption of being, neither seeing nor accepting the fact that the sense of being alive lies somewhere between these two extremes, at a point which may vary according to circumstance but which we alone must find and clarify.

All the same, and despite some wild fluctuations in our life together, we kept the current running between our two poles for nearly three years. Only in the fourth year was the circuit finally broken . . . Meanwhile these slow progressions from positive to negative were punctuated by two main events, the birth of Pablo and the reappearance of Virginia Lippman . . . Then, after the divorce, came another four years of neutrality and emotional disengagement after which the cold truth dawned. It hit like a sucker punch, smack on the jaw, and I went out for the count, and then out of the sheltered backwater where I had gone to ground with little more than safety first and personal gain in view. It sounds as if I am suggesting that those eight years were a long digression after the purple patch of my first visit to Central America. That isn't so, of course, but the fact remains that some periods which are hard to live through can sound quite trivial in the telling of what is intended to be an impartial story.

Thus the months I spent in London before my marriage to Beatrice passed much faster than I had anticipated. Although we had both agreed to sit out this waiting period, I couldn't help seeing it as a pointless waste of time; but my resentment was nowhere near so keen as my determination not to try to race against time on this occasion. Was it because I curbed my expectations that events pressed on to meet me? The paradox itself was no surprise. Yet two things came my way in quick succession. Their impact might have smashed me; instead I emerged more confident than ever in the strength of my grip upon the present – which was close to becoming a stranglehold.

I had only been back in London for a matter of hours when I learned that the Señora was dead – three months before, of a brain haemorrhage. No news had reached me in the Petén, of course. I wired condolences to Nicholson, and asked if there was anything I could do. In the piles of correspondence which I found waiting for me at home and at the television company (most of the bills and paperwork had been sorted out by my friends Paul and Ron, as soon as they heard that I was in jail, and not missing, presumed dead), there was a long letter from Nicholson as well as a thick envelope from a Los Angeles law office. Far from cutting me out, the Señora had made me her sole heir. Her good friend Nicholson received several hundred thousand dollars and the use of the Santa Monica property. I told him he must stay there for as long as he wanted. He rang me up a few days later to ask if I would mind flying over to Los Angeles, just a quick visit to settle the various formalities. Before I went, I phoned Beatrice.

'The Raven estate,' she said, quite placidly. 'Then you are rich . . .'

I did not ask whether the last remark was a statement or a question. In any case she did not wait for an answer but continued:

'Does this alter our plans at all?'

'What for? Now you've got a dowry after all.'

'Please, if that is a joke then keep the others to yourself.'

'It could always come in useful with your father. I'll bank the money with him!'

'What about the film, Michael?'

'We've started already. I promised Paul I'd finish the job as soon as I get back. It's a matter of a couple of weeks . . . After that, I've told them I'll be leaving.'

'Are you sure?'

'Absolutely.'

'You see yourself living on your income?'

I gave a laugh, a rather forced one.

'Don't worry, no danger of that. I have plans, you'll see . . . I shall be in Paris sooner than we planned. We can live there for a while, I'd enjoy that. I've found a house for sale here, in Onslow Gardens, right by my present flat. It's a quiet residential area. You'll like it . . . Between Paris and yourself, you'll help me work out my plans.'

Sam Nicholson was even more affable than he had been at the time of our first explosive encounter, though there was a spark of malice in his eye when he remarked on how well I had used his five thousand dollars. I must take whatever I wanted from the house – naturally it was things to do with Raven that he had in mind. Apart from a few first editions of my father's books, I didn't touch anything, and particularly not the archives collected by my stepmother.

'What's the good?' I said to Nicholson.

'I understand,' he answered. 'Do you know it all now?'

'No, but it comes to the same thing.'

In Paris came the second piece of news, another notch down the low voltage scale . . . Beatrice was pregnant. She heard that the tests were positive on the day I arrived. We arranged to bring forward our wedding day, and that made both of us happy, at least for the time being. For Beatrice had a miscarriage in January. She took it stoically: although she was badly hurt, she let nothing show. Certainly less than I did anyway, because I treated it as yet another opportunity to take my foot off the accelerator and lower the temperature, and it was Beatrice who fussed over me and had to be specially affectionate – so successfully that in three months' time she was pregnant again, with Pablo.

We lived with her parents in the meantime. The apartment in the avenue de La Bourdonnais was spacious and comfortable enough not to get too cramped. Anyway we spent the entire summer of 1967, four whole months, in Les Ferrandes, in the Beaujolais. Hubert and Sonia, my in-laws, only came down for a week in June and on two weekends, the 14th of July and the 15th of August . . . Beatrice relaxed by reading Elie Faure and Malraux – the Malraux of *The Metamorphosis of the Gods*, naturally. When I was not taking long walks through the woods by myself, I too did a great deal of reading (in particular, Daniel Defoe, after a visit to the English bookshop in the rue de Rivoli before we left Paris). As for my plans, I must confess that they were merely stagnating in my mind. Fortunately – if I can put it that way – a series of slaps in the face shook me out of my daze. Didn't I deserve them?

Beatrice was drafting the outline of a book on aesthetics that she intended to start writing after the baby was born. For me it was the subject of some poor jokes which she didn't much appreciate. Once she retorted sarcastically: 'Oh, I know I can rely on you. When it comes to outlines, you're an expert!' That day we did not say a word to each other, and I went off to brood over the lesson in the small dressing room on the second floor of the house. Brood is not quite the word: I was furious with Beatrice, but full of a morbid resentment against myself. I sat about upstairs doing nothing. Slumped in an armchair with my feet up on a pouffe (my shoes were still muddy from the morning's walk), I started to leaf through some magazines that Sonia had left in a pile on a low table. Stories about princesses and film stars, just good enough to protract my annoyance and exercise my French, which was also fairly sketchy . . . Till the moment when I came across a photo that took away my desultory apathy. Sylvia Morrison: she too had died while I was trailing around on the Rio Usumacinta. And as I stared dumbly at the actress's portrait the features blurred, and soon another face was superimposed over the clouded image, and grew sharper. Virginia's face. I must have sat peering at that picture for a long while, because by the time I emerged from my reverie the ashtray was overflowing with cigarette ends. Behind the window curtains I saw that the sun was low and red. At dinner in the vast silent kitchen I was the first to break the ice.

'What if we go back to Paris? . . . It's time for me to get back into action again.'

Against my expectation, Beatrice seemed upset by the suggestion. 'The late summer is always so beautiful at Les Ferrandes. The best moment,' she said.

Keeping quiet about the discovery I had made in the dressing room and the mixed feelings it had caused me, I set about convincing her of my good intentions.

'Nicholson and the agent I've taken on in London will be managing the Raven royalties and rights, but that's no reason . . .'

And I held forth about the pressure of world events. That same morning we had read in the local paper that General Thieu had just been elected president of South Vietnam, with support from the Americans.

'Do you see what I mean?'

'Yes . . . but frankly I can't see the connection with the "action" you mentioned . . .'

'Hubert is right. I have to invest. I can't keep on like this . . .'

'High finance! You're making me laugh!'

'Oh yes? Well, listen to this.'

And I explained how things were happening with young people all over the world, and that a turning-point in civilization was on the way ('civilization' is the word I used). From Berkeley to Peking, and from Berlin to Tokyo . . .

'I have noticed.'

'I want to start a magazine, something radically new, like nothing before . . .'

'Pop music and LSD . . . Now I see!'

'I'll make sure that you do.'

In Paris I explained my plans to Hubert. He hummed and hawed a lot, but eventually admitted that my idea had something in it.

'No need for market surveys, that's certain . . . All the same, Michael, permit me to offer you one piece of advice: Play the amateur in public, if you want, but underneath you must take things very seriously . . . If you're thinking on the right scale, I'll help you. What are you going to call this magazine?'

'*OFF*.'

'What frequency?'

'Weekly.'

'Format?'

'Tabloid.'

'Print run?'

'A hundred and fifty thousand copies. To start with.'

'What kind of presentation?'

'Nothing fancy: no glossy paper, but no lavatory paper either. Colour, lots of it. A changing layout. News about every aspect of the counter-culture, worldwide. And readers' letters to give them a voice . . .'

'Good, good, that's fine . . . You can count on me.'

The builders had been out of Onslow Gardens for several weeks, and the house was ready for occupation. I wrote to tell Paul and Ron that I was coming back. The baby was not due until early December, another three months. This was the moment to press ahead. Just as marking time had seemed like a good way to stave off uncertainty, so now my conquering enterprise seemed to me to offer my only defence against a return of the lyrical illusion. Ah! And then there was Virginia, who filled my dreams with violent passions unfulfilled. I had put up with the sexual abstinence recently imposed by Beatrice's condition, but things had been very different since that long afternoon in the dressing room at Les Ferrandes . . . I wrote in secret to Virginia, taking the gamble of sending the letter to the post office box number she'd given me two years before. The contents were fairly bland, in any case: I mentioned Sylvia Morrison, the student movement, the race riots and Virginia's own studies, and ended with a vague thank you for all that had been done for me, without indicating whether or not the doers were meant to include George Lippman. With no great hopes of a reply, I gave my London address. As a postscript I simply wrote: 'I'm married. My wife's name is Beatrice. We're expecting a child before the end of the year.'

I wanted to cut every possible corner. Once the finance had been arranged, I had to find premises and recruit the right staff. This last point was the hardest to settle: I needed my new colleagues to be both young and experienced at the same time. It was a particular state of mind I wanted, a militant attitude, so I started looking around among my old acquaintances. Rakovski, who was vegetating in an insurance company and writing science fiction in his spare time, came in at once. Hawkins joined the team after a few months; he had been public relations manager for a record company. I was in a fever of impatience, and furious at not being able to bring out a pilot issue at the end of October, in homage to Che Guevara, who had just been shot dead in a small village school room, after his capture by the Bolivian army. Till now I had been immunized against the pleasures of organization – preparing, calculating, planning, directing . . . I felt the spirit of a builder inside me.

Beatrice was still at the maternity home when Virginia's reply arrived. A postcard, with that famous picture of a hillside with the name of Hollywood in giant letters. Some small talk, and the news of a probable trip to Europe some time before spring next year . . .

The first issue of *OFF* went on sale on 1 January 1968. An exceptional vintage, bottled in Prague and Paris. It travelled well at the Mexico Olympics, where five hundred people died under the machine-guns during the demonstration in the Plaza de Tres Culturas . . . That year, at Les Ferrandes, only the Beaujolais was second-rate. Hubert didn't even bother to send us a case.

2

WASHES OF DRIZZLE slid soundlessly down the panes of the big bow-window. Even with the heavy velvet curtains drawn, you could sense the steady monotony of its exasperating presence. A comfortable darkness warmed and protected the bodies stretched side by side on the double bed. The man lay on his back, staring up at the dance of shadows on the ceiling, and jotting down words in his head. The aspirin he had taken before going to bed was having no effect. His head ached. The unfinished editorial kept nagging in his mind, and he detested the idea of leaving work undone. His partner held his rigid penis tight in her right hand, clenching it hard between her fingers, too hard, and not letting go. By raising and lowering his hips, he tried to slide this vice along the shaft of his penis, but with every plunge the nail of her little finger dug into the base of the moving shaft, where the scrotum began. Brusquely he pulled free of her grasp, rolled on to his side towards her, kissed her and nibbled at her earlobe.

'That tickles,' she said.

'Suck me,' he murmured as he kissed her neck.

'You know how I hate doing that.'

He rolled away again, on to his back, with his head pillowed on his joined hands, and closed his eyes, listening for the slightest trickle of the rain.

'What are you thinking about?'

'Nothing . . . I'm dead beat.'

'You weren't home till after one o'clock.'

'Let's not go through that any more.'

She stroked his stomach. He felt his energy begin to flow again.

'Why do you keep everything to yourself? If you talked to me about it, it might help.'

'It's odd . . .'

'What is?'

'Now and again you remind me of someone.'

'Who?'

'Someone I used to know . . . once upon a time.'

'It can't be so very long ago!'

'It doesn't matter.'

'I won't argue with you. I feel cold. Put your arms round me.'

She nestled against him, and he pulled her closer with his right arm. Their legs intertwined.

'I have an idea.'

'Don't move now.'

'Not to lose track of . . .'

'Please.'

'. . . change the character of . . .'

'Damn it!'

Her hair brushed his lips and chest.

'You smell good . . . Come here now.'

'In a hurry, hmm?'

'Not exactly.'

'You don't play by the rules.'

'Tell me what you want.'

A wail broke out in the room next door; the baby was crying in his cradle.

'Shit!'

'You go!'

The two bodies separated and the man sat on the edge of the bed as if caught in a daze, paralysed with anxiety. He was thinking about something.

'Go on!'

He groped for the bedside light switch, and at the moment he pressed it an instinctive reflex made him jerk his hand away as if he had burnt himself. His hands were damp and sticky.

He hurried next door, where the child was squalling louder still. The covers were off, his hands and feet were thrashing in the air, his face was scarlet and his eyes dry. A concentrated scream. The man picked up his howling son, who was so light that in his hurry he forgot how little he weighed; tossed him upwards and almost dropped him, but caught him just in time and pulled him against his stomach like a rugby player. The ride had stilled the child's tears, and when he was caught he sobbed once or twice, then was silent.

'You're mad!' His wife had followed him, and now she snatched the baby out of his arms. 'You might have killed him!'

She cradled her son against her bare breast, and he gurgled up at her.

The man left the room without a word.

He lit a cigarette, put on a dressing gown and shut himself up in his study to finish the uncompleted article.

When he returned to bed an hour later (but perhaps there was no telling the lapse of time) he slid beneath the covers, careful not to wake his wife, who was sleeping with her face turned towards the wall. He made no more sound than the fine rain that settled on the panes of the bow window.

As I refused to write anything about Mexico myself, I left it to Rakovski and some of our contributors to keep our readers informed about peyote, marijuana, sacred mushrooms, and the mythic unity of man and nature in the setting of a culture freed from the dualist double bind . . . I simply referred in an editorial to Artaud and the 'barbarism' of Europe! If I read it again today, I would probably be torn between laughter and nostalgia . . .

All the same, that particular issue was a big success. *OFF* was running ahead of all my expectations. The piece that William Burroughs gave us on that occasion went around the world . . . People came to see us from the *Herald Tribune* and from *Rolling Stone*, and we could tell by their excitement that their professional respect was the measure of our potential as rivals.

To say, in those days, that we would handle information as a novelist handles his characters or any other element in his fiction was a kind of provocation in itself. With the fine inconsistency which was our trademark, we might equally produce some offhand phrase – 'The novel. *The* novel? Hell, don't say that's all there is to life.' That was pretty much the way we tended to express ourselves, back then.

We took it for granted that the novel could not deal with

social reality, couldn't contain it any more. To the novelist fell myth and fable; to the journalist, action, the stuff of life, and it was for him to ride the beat and rhythms of the march of time, and focus on the moving faces of society. A style of journalism was being born, and would soon have grown up, and it was our creation. The New Journalism. Of course, while it rejected dogmas and manifestos, our revolutionary enthusiasm only added one more label to the everlasting dustbin of household brand names. Do I still need to explain my personal reasons for staying with the product? No doubt it will suffice to say that the material did not have to be 'created': it was there, in front of us. There was no need to go looking for it, or to work out how to use it, because we were immersed in its dimension, actor and observer inextricably joined. Every viewpoint deserved to be represented – the interviewee's, the spectators' (the Chorus), and the reporter's too. Our polyphony was recorded live from the street, complete with sub-dialogues, voices off, silences and streams of consciousness. The avant-garde was ourselves. The novelists had taught us nothing. We were virgins. At least, that is what I was quite determined to be convinced of . . . with the good conscience of marginality, the blessing of the general permissiveness, and the certitude that at long last I stood outside and below (underground, we used to say), actuated as we were by an equal condemnation of rampant capitalism and Stalinist bureaucracies (there we were not mistaken, but what a flimsy innocence, to believe that an intellectual process would leave feeling intact just because of some supposedly new sensibility!).

Things were going so well for my paper that we were only a few months old before we were able to afford to print a pre-publication extract from Norman Mailer's latest book, *The Armies of the Night*. Do you remember? 'One of the oldest devices of the novelist – some would call it a vice – is to bring his narrative (after many an excursion) to a pitch of excitement where the reader no matter how cultivated is reduced to a beast who can pant no faster than to ask, "And then what? Then what happens?"' And the reporter of the protest march on the Pentagon continued: 'At which point the novelist, consummate cruel lover, introduces a digression, aware that delay at this point helps to deepen the addiction of his audience.

'This, of course, was Victorian practice. Modern audiences, accustomed to superhighways, put aside their reading at the first annoyance and turn to the television set. So a modern novelist must apologize, even apologize profusely, for daring to leave his narrative, he must in fact absolve himself of the charge of employing a device, he must plead necessity.'

So, having the authority of such a famous advocate, let us plead necessity: perhaps the jury will accept a plea of mitigating circumstances . . .

There is no such thing as writing in one's head, as I had plenty of opportunities to learn throughout those years. What I conceived by night I would unmake by day, as if the action secreted its own antidote of self-mutilation and castration. From the Book of Sublimation to the Book of Nothing was a single step which a taste for both power and whisky enabled me to take with ease. If it brought me no genius, alcohol did two things for me: it gave me the feeling of scraping the bottom, and at the same time it legitimized the ambiguous roles played by my ambition and my bad conscience.

At the paper, this gave rise to all sorts of excesses – intolerance, overworking myself and others, casual affairs . . . Beatrice was not nearly so worried by these sexual escapades as by the methodical programme of disintegration I had launched against myself. She did not enjoy my womanizing, but it came to matter much less than the increasingly concrete impression that she was tied to a husband who, instead of security or protection (and contrary to his own original belief), expected nothing from his marriage but a process of inevitable destruction.

One night I returned to Onslow Gardens feeling utterly exhausted after going to press. Beatrice was asleep. I woke her, and she sat up with a start. Roaring like a stage lion, I ripped the sheets and blankets off her with a violent tug, dropped them at the foot of the bed, and pretended that I was going to eat her alive. The joke did not amuse her, and she scratched at my face with her nails. 'Idiot!' That got me excited, and I wrestled harder. 'Stop it, Michael!' She struggled underneath me, hitting out with her knees and elbows, utterly withholding herself.

'Give me your tits,' I raged, 'I love your tits,' in a voice now drained of all amusement.

'But Pablo, Pablo . . .'

'Yes, that's it, we'll wake up Pablo. A free command performance.'

I reached for the neckline of her nightdress and yanked at it sharply with both hands. The material ripped to expose her breasts. Beatrice lay still. 'Go ahead, rape me.' I gave a jeer of laughter. When I started to undo my belt I had to lift myself off her. Beatrice seized her chance to roll clear with a fluid wriggle and jump out of bed. Before I could move she was darting into the corridor. 'You wait!' I raced after her, but she had scurried downstairs and had shut herself in the kitchen. One kick at the door demolished the bolt and shattered the cathedral glass window to pieces. Beatrice stood with her back against the sink and a big kitchen knife clutched in both hands, the butt end of the handle digging into her stomach as if she had been about to commit hara-kiri . . . only in reverse, for the quivering blade was pointed towards me. Without for an instant considering the consequence for either of us, I made straight for her, at the risk of spitting myself on the tapered steel. At the very last moment Beatrice must have given an unconscious start, for she let the knife fall. Before I began to hit her about the head and face, and breasts as well, a tear had welled in the corner of her eye . . .

Beatrice slid to the ground, unstrung and defenceless. And that is where I took her, on the cold clean tiled floor of an ultra-modern fitted bourgeois kitchen. As if in a bad dream, you could say, but with this dreadfully simple and prosaic difference, that we were not dreaming.

3

I HAVE NEVER kept a diary. Today, more than ever, that would seem to me to be a pointless exercise . . . as if writing were only putting one's life on deposit, in the sense that a shopkeeper charges a deposit on the bottle you are buying from him, until you bring it back. Whether the interval between the act and its literary transcription is a matter of a second, a year or half a lifetime does not alter its nature as an absolute divide. Everything can wait, even urgency. It's a question of degree, like alcohol – that page there, how many degrees of proof? Far from being a hazard, or a subterfuge, distance makes it possible to collect whatever you have previously put in pawn to life, and put it to maximum use at a minimum cost.

There is no need for detailed accounts, day-books or documents: there are some dates which stick in your memory, and they are not necessarily what everyone agrees to recognize as the essential links in the chain of common history. One such date is 23 March 1968 . . . the day I saw Virginia Lippman again.

The news from Paris suggested an extraordinary acceleration of the social heartbeat, information confirmed by Hubert, who rang us with an apocalyptic account. According to him, bands of marauding Huns were ravaging the university of Nanterre, and he advised me not to go. To me, though, the whole thing cried out for investigation. I had heard at the paper about a man called Cohn-Bendit; I decided to go to Paris to interview him. It was good timing, because there was also to be a meeting at the Cartoucherie de Vincennes, called by the Vietnam Committee. Sartre was supposed to be speaking there. All that was well worth a brief three-day visit . . .

How could I have expected that at the end of Sartre's speech, in the middle of the standing crowd, I would suddenly catch sight of the massive outline of George Lippman, with Virginia standing next to him, both of them strenuously clapping and chanting the slogan 'Victory to the NLF'? I didn't show myself at first, but stayed hidden behind the dense crowd gathered in front of the podium, watching the Lippmans and wondering what course of action I should take. Would I go towards them? Would I speak to them? Or would I let myself drift away and behave as if they did not exist, or had walked out of my life to become two more nameless faces in the crowd? So Lippman was back on his feet again! I had left him in San Cristóbal in a pitiful state, remember, but now he looked heavier, ruddier and more jovial than he had been three years previously, in London. His face was scarlet, and he was practically laughing with delight as he listened to the speeches. It looked as if Virginia had also gained some weight, though nothing like Lippman, of course, maybe another seven or eight pounds . . . She had let her hair grow down to her shoulders: it gave her a more serious look. And she had aged, we all had! Oh, for her it was in a barely noticeable way, which doesn't count when you are twenty-five, but must surely present some terrifying prospects for Lippman . . . She turned her head in my direction; she saw me. Dragging Lippman by the sleeve, she ploughed through the throng between. I was glad to see her again, but at the same time I had been caught in a kind of panic. If the crowd behind me had not cut off my retreat, would I have stood there watching as she made her way towards me, all smiles? . . . Her husband had looked bewildered at first, as he peered around him, but then he had realized what was happening, and semaphored a stream of friendly gestures, as if to say: 'We've spotted you, stay where you are, we're on our way, don't move, we've got you now, we love you!' I thought for a moment that he was going to throw his arms around me, but then he seemed to have second thoughts.

'Mateos, what in hell are you doing here?'

'And what about you?'

'I'm here with the American delegation.'

'Oh really, so you're against it now?'

'Sh! . . . No time for explanations now, okay? After the meeting we'll have a drink . . .'

So by a stroke of perfect irony the three of us stood together with our clenched fists raised, to the tune of the Internationale, amid a forest of red and violet banners and in a dustcloud raised by the feet of thousands of demonstrators stamping in the sand of the vast derelict factory.

It was a long walk from the Cartoucherie to the buses and the Métro, so I accepted the Lippmans' offer to drive me back to the centre of Paris.

'There are four of us. Two other comrades from Los Angeles. We can squeeze up, all right?'

They had rented a car for the duration of their stay, and were making a proper tour of Europe to attend protest meetings against the war in Vietnam. Next stage, Munich and Berlin . . . They told me about it on the journey back, when naturally the presence of people who had nothing to do with our personal history stopped us exploring the state of our various scars. We dropped the two students at the door of a small hotel in the rue des Ecoles, then went to park the car, and soon we were sitting on the terrace of a bistro near the Sorbonne, I think it was called the Balzar.

'You won't learn anything there,' I said after ordering a beer.

'Where do you mean?'

'In Munich or Berlin.'

'Why do you say that? Have you been there?'

'No . . . but I know, that's all.'

Virginia chimed in:

'I thought we weren't going to say any more about that.'

'All right . . .'

But neither Lippman nor I was capable of keeping our promise. Not that we really wanted to do battle again. The last occasion had done no good to either one of us. It was more a matter of bringing things up to date, and running a test to prove to ourselves that this kind of duel had gone out of season.

'I'm making good progress with my research, did you know?'

'I'm sure you are . . . I'm not that interested any more.'

'Even if you heard that you could be a descendant of Wilhelm II himself, Kaiser Bill?'

'Oh, not you too,' I said, in a tone of pure indifference.

'Who told you?'

'The Señora.'

'Before she died?'

'Yes.'

'Well, that's it you see, my dear Michael . . . I'm not sure that you're stepmother's version was correct.'

'You're going to tell me she was lying again.'

'No, no, it isn't that . . . Just a point she couldn't possibly have known . . . Hang on to your hat, Michael: I'm on to the trail of Raven's real mother. She was playing before the royal court, while it was on vacation at Cronthaus castle. The young prince laid eyes on her . . . and the rest you know.'

'So?'

'Well, the big news is that Helen Feldman was American, and that Raven spent the first year of his life in San Francisco. Now you understand the mystery that hung around your father's so-called American origins.'

'If you say so . . .'

'After that, the boy was still less than two years old when Helen abandoned him for good. It was while she was making another visit to Germany – she must have gone back hoping to get some sort of payoff from the Emperor, even if he refused to admit paternity. So in return for a financial allowance she left him in the hands of a family of poor working people, the Bremens . . .'

'All right, Lippman, it stands up. But I have one thing I want to say to you. This is it: I really don't give a shit.'

The conversation went on like that for well over an hour. No doubt it saved us from having to look each other in the face: a sidelong angle was the best we could manage! To avoid Virginia's eyes . . . And as I focused on her lips, and the little curl of disapproval in the corner, the taste of her mouth came back to my own lips, and my sour tongue recalled the sweetness of Virginia's. Lippman was laying down his heaviest biographical artillery to prove that he knew the whole truth and nothing but the truth about my father, and all I could think about was laying his wife!

Since that afternoon in the dressing room at Les Ferrandes, my mind had been plagued by the image of my penis buried to the hilt inside her. But – as I surely must have known – history never works the same way twice, does it?

I felt that Virginia gave several indications of not being totally indifferent to my presence, close enough to touch – a knee, an elbow, a hand . . . And it was hard to convince myself that these mute appeals came only from the special illusion that memory breeds. When we parted company I left them my card, with the paper's address.

Lippman guffawed with laughter.

'So, the man is rich, and married too, huh?'

After Germany and Switzerland they planned to return to France for a while: Lippman had a programme of academic lectures to deliver.

'So the man's still on the circuit!' I chaffed him.

And they would finish their visit to Europe with a long weekend in London . . .

'Then I hope to see you there. Give me a call, Virginia.'

We saw each other, and we did what will have been imagined, though perhaps not in the terms imagined. On the basis of the material facts alone, the likeness of causes and effects might seem to confirm the idea of history repeating itself. But obviously the conditions were different! . . . Between that meeting in Paris and the reunion three months later in London, Virginia would have changed. She would have experienced the impact of the abortive revolution of May–June 1968, just time enough to lose the few certitudes which she had painfully rebuilt for herself in what I thought of as her little Californian paradise. Because I felt sure that the original student eruption would not take long to fizzle out, I didn't go to Paris myself. Rakovski would cover the events as well as I could. There was no point in being there. As a symptom of civilization in crisis, this was nothing new: *OFF* knew the score already. As for the insurrectional nature of the demonstrations, I knew too much about the machinery that links action to repression to have doubts about the outcome. Even later on, at the height of the factory occupations and the clashes at Flins and elsewhere, I would remain a sceptic. 'Not a shot fired!' Rakovski advised me to stay on the side-lines, and I had sense enough to trust his editorial judgement. Yet when I heard from Virginia's own mouth that she had been seriously involved in the Paris disturbances I could not prevent myself from asking her for an interview. At first she was very reluctant, but I spoke to George, who promised to put in a word on my behalf. 'The job comes first, Mateos. An occupational hazard!'

It was early July, the anniversary of our parting, almost three years to the day. She came to my office. I asked not to be disturbed. We recorded an interview over two hours long. I think Virginia's last words were: 'Now that it's all over, the world is going to become impossible.' She yielded quite readily to my caresses and kisses and heavy breathing, or rather she didn't reject them, but gave the impression of being somewhere else, indifferent to the crude probing of my fingers, the suction of my lips, my legs jammed in between hers . . . I bent her backwards over the desk I had hurriedly swept clear, and she let me undo her blouse, unbutton her trousers, and then pull them down below her knees, together with her briefs. I mounted her. It was over in a few quick moments, a ludicrous performance, hastened by the knowledge that it would take us nowhere. We could not turn time back to where we had been before, merely – and once again – make a perfunctory acknowledgement of having been there . . . But the fact is that only I could have supposed (before the event, need I say?) that one common natural impulse might signal a brand-new beginning.

Yet I'm not sure whether disappointment alone will account for the dismissive headline which I splashed across five columns at the head of my interview with Virginia: 'An American in Paris: "I was on the barricades at the Rue Gay-Lussac!" ' When I review that episode today I don't feel that it was actually my former mistress I was aiming at. Once again, whatever my genuine affection and no less genuine erotic attraction towards Virginia, she was paying the score I had to settle with George Lippman – not because he was her legal husband but because in spite of everything he continued to enjoy a status which I had my own good reasons to dispute: he was still the world's foremost authority on W. H. Raven.

When the article came out, Virginia and George had already left for the United States. I never saw them again. When I returned from Honduras two months ago, Hawkins and Rakovski told me that Lippman had been killed in a car accident on the San Bernardino freeway . . .

So Virginia had no chance to come and spit in my eye at the

time. On the other hand – and I didn't learn this illuminating detail until several months later, when my marriage was past retrieving – she did make a phone call to Beatrice. They met, and they told each other everything.

The fact of that encounter flabbergasted me. What crumb, what scruple of complicity was imaginable between two such dissimilar women? . . . I tried in vain to visualize my mother, Doña Marina, exchanging confidences over a pot of tea with Ruth Powell, the future Señora. No, that was too much, it was out of the question – another time and place.

The truth is that in order to understand those years it would make more sense to consult a complete edition of *OFF* than to try to digest a mass of events so fresh in our memory that they hardly seem to have happened! All that documentation is out of my hands now, and I don't miss it, but I imagine it providing the raw material for any number of still unwritten novels, each of them orchestrating the score of history in its own way, in tune with the years and fashions, with more or fewer little fictional appoggiaturas . . . I have only to riffle through some of the issues of 1969 in my mind: the disclosure of the My Lai massacre, Neil Armstrong walking on the moon, Dennis Hopper and Peter Fonda in *Easy Rider*, half a million people at Woodstock pounded by a bank of amplifiers, an echo pedal and Jimi Hendrix . . . I remember that – don't you? And in any case TV refreshes our memories every now and then with newsreel footage or contemporary history spectaculars. Well, of course, the fun didn't last very long. If I turn a few more pages, and skip a little faster, we soon come to the Middle East, the Arab oil boycott, the energy crisis, Allende's death, the CIA, destabilization, Chilean refugees and so on. 1973 . . . A few months after my divorce. With ice in my blood and a callous heart I felt immune to any wound or accident that might deflect me an inch away from my chosen itinerary. Exit Joplin, smashed by drugs and booze, and exit Hendrix: to me it meant little more than a couple of banner headlines and a rise in circulation . . . I built up *OFF*, and bought two more sinking titles (a traditionalist women's magazine which I transformed into an outpost of militant feminism, and a weekly events publication). After that, I set up an advertising agency . . . A competitor once tried to nail me in an article headed 'The Citizen Kane of the New Journalism'. I sued him. Although by now I had achieved the kind of power and prestige which only solid success can both create and maintain, for my readers I remained a marginal, if not totally anonymous figure. It was out of the question for me to become some sort of media star when our entire enterprise was based on principles of out-and-out democracy. We were not writing in our own names, but at best as spokespeople. I have to say that the timing was perfect, just when the herald was replacing the hero in my mind. The more my power appeared to be dissolving into a haze of instant improvisation, the tighter my hold on people and on things.

All this may appear to suggest that I was playing with the lash of cynicism, putting down other people the better to lacerate myself. Naturally things were not that simple. My eyes alternately melted or froze under the influence of feelings which I could not totally control. The power that gave me life would often restore my love of the lower depths. I did not feel I was lying when I wrote about the death of traditional values, or the Watergate affair, and nobody dreamed of questioning my sincerity – nobody, that is, except possible Beatrice, who said to me one night: 'I loathe it when you behave in some of your articles as if you were playing the electric guitar with simultaneous tremolo *and* vibrato!' . . . With Rakovski and Hawkins, the political debates which had once kept us arguing far into the night were turning into brief exchanges. They distrusted both me and my reactions. One day Hawkins told me: 'You're playing the conservative game: you're going to have to choose which side to be on!' I knew in my heart that he was right, but I sidestepped the issue.

'Call it the Shakespeare angle.'

'Meaning what?'

'Well, Marxist of the King Lear tendency . . .'

'Is that supposed to be funny?'

As I remember, that was in the spring of 1971. Castro had just jailed a poet slightly too crazy to be a reliable revolutionary. This bad apple had had to put his name to a long self-critical statement in which he accused himself of various infamous crimes and betrayed his best friends . . . In Rakovski's view, that was no reason for condemning Cuba and its generally positive achievements – literacy, crayfish and cigars all round . . . Right on, *compañero!*

And it was during that same spring that Beatrice was unfaithful. I won't say why or how. Or whether it mattered more or less than the rest.

In July we went to Scotland for two weeks' holiday. Pablo was three and a half. We made one last attempt to start again, and it failed, failed badly. The aftermath was even more terrible. I almost cracked up (or acted that way).

'Help me, Beatrice. I am seeing myself as I am.'

'It's over, Michael.'

'I can't bear that.'

'There's nothing I can do for you any more . . . Pablo and I will be fine.'

Lacking a centre, a point of focus, would my life go to pieces once again? Rather than a breaking point, this time I had to see things in terms of weakness, of a stubborn, narrow self-containment.

With everything under control, I had nothing of my own.

Little by little, the gall rose again, the exquisite, sickening taste of Raven . . . as if I had no appetite for anything.

Ten years had passed. Another departure wouldn't make sense, except as a bad joke. Going to some distant country to brood on one's faults was a thing of the past, and Hawkins's scathing response made no attempt to spare my feelings. Could I be feeling ashamed? How quaint! My friend Froggy told me on the telephone that Third World romanticism was over and done with: 'In theory, you should be cured by now . . . Vietnam is all over.' In theory, of course . . . To them, it was funny: they were the first to denounce the old myths, but they didn't draw the full conclusions of what followed. As they saw it, I was paying more tribute to self-hatred. They were wrong. I was dropping everything, cutting loose, not because I felt guilty, or responsible for all the world's misfortunes, but because I knew that instead I was suffering from utter indifference . . .

This time the journey was no voyage of discovery, simply the recognition of an established fact . . . I had picked up the Raven trail again, as I have explained, but I would not be leaving in order to find him, to make him over to fit the pattern of my own illusions. It was no longer a matter of taking a leap in the dark, but of the detailed, patient reconstruction and reconstitution of a route identified as such. Going back did not mean copying Raven, but *being* Raven . . .

I sold up everything, or almost everything. *OFF* would continue without me: the magazine was still riding high. The privilege of the affluent is to be able to dispossess themselves without having to provide an explanation, without remorse, or noise, or ostentation. As if a body, once undressed, did not appear in all its nudity, but remained in its Sunday best . . . an image which must represent the impression I had that I was leaving nothing. I also recall the remarks of Montaigne's that I had underlined in a fine eighteenth-century edition which Sonia, my mother-in-law, had bought in an auction near Les Ferrandes and given to me as a birthday present. Just because I had long hair and rumpled jeans, it didn't mean that I had lost my love of antique words and yellowed paper! In his essay 'On Vanity' Montaigne wrote: '*I ordinarily answer those who demand reasons for my journeys: that I know what I shun, but not what I seek. If I am told that among strangers too there may be little health, and that their manners are no better than our own, I answer, first, that it is hard* tam multae scelerum facies (*crime takes so many forms*)*! Second, that it is ever a gain to exchange a bad for an uncertain state, and that others' evils ought not to sting us like our own* . . .' And further on comes the essential corollary: '*I am content with a death in communion with itself, quiet and solitary, all my own, in keeping with my retired and private life.*'

This calm, this lull at the height of the storm, may be mistaken for some dubious form of physical and mental catalepsy. Never mind: I am ready to insist that so much assurance was not acquired by hypocrisy. Why should a sense of calm be seen as a variation on perversity? I felt good, that's all.

Not long before that second 'grand' departure for Mexico, I dreamed a reassuring dream. In it, I returned to Relámpagos, collected the remains of the gargoyle Bocanegra, took them to Puerto Lápiz and had them put on board a ship bound for Europe . . . Paul Arthur Smith would be glad that I had kept my commitments. The divine chimera, the star of the exhibition that he organized in collaboration with the former

Beatrice Mateos, would draw big crowds in the British Museum, then in the Grand Palais and all the world's major museums . . . Unfortunately a tremendous storm blew up in the Atlantic. The boat was sunk, and Bocanegra with it . . . After a long struggle with the raging elements I finally managed to reach land. Swimming a rhythmic steady crawl I proceeded up the Thames or the Seine between ranks of cheering onlookers.

If the dream did not preserve the legend, it did indicate the possibility of an acceptable conclusion.

4

'The ships you see in sea stories are Sunday ships, and their seamen are seamen out of light opera, trimming their fingernails while they chew over some silly tale of disappointed love as if they were munching flowers. Only the lowest of the lower deck have the right to talk about a seaman's life.'

These words of Raven's say enough. Talking to his terrified ministers, Philip II of Spain advised: 'Be calm!' Flimflam was okay for the journalistic interlude of the all-powerful chairman and managing director of OFF Publications Ltd. I am well aware that too much realism hinders credibility. My motivations in those days, and still more at the time of my departure, had better be left unspoken, otherwise a sudden myopia might seem to have developed, or the tempo of the story to be faltering . . . I was living my life, and that does not necessarily require elaborate documentation which would tend to conceal it. While I was distancing myself from Raven (or so I believed), it would have been shabby to claim that this very distancing conferred some unexpected romantic status *as well.* And to tell the whole story, I must confess that at the time of writing the pages in question (I'd been in Poznan for five or six days) I was paralysed by an acute attack of sciatica which forced me to keep a horizontal position not conducive to literary fluency. For several days of brute helplessness I was unable even to hobble across to my portable typewriter, and had to settle for jotting down some hasty notes on pieces of scrap paper. Actually it seems to me that the lumbar pain that put my leg out of action (the same leg that Bocanegra injured in the hurricane) came just when it was needed. Having emerged from that state of lethargy (you find it past forty!), I have been able to read the offending pages with a fresh eye. If I had to rewrite them today I would leave them as they are. There is nothing more to say. It's all there.

The same goes for the crossing, which I was determined to make on a transatlantic liner this time . . . Second class, of course! But not quite in the state of mind described by Raven in those lines from *Journey Without End* which I have quoted at the head of this chapter . . . No doubt I will have made clear my intention no longer to resort to the exotic – not that it is a register or value I mean to reject from now on, but simply out of a concern for rigour and exactitude. Far from indicating some gaping hole in my existence, the weight of the facts alone carries all possible interpretations. No question of imagining any more. Perhaps still more demanding is the opportunity to say that a destiny is also worked out in stillness. Oh, the delicious constraint of pain! Nothing was moving inside me, and yet every twang of the sciatic nerve struck unknown chords. Was it because of the snow which had not stopped falling since daybreak? In the warmth of the bed, huddled beneath a chain of aching vertebrae, on the point of sleep, a thought was self-arousing, an onanistic pleasure. It was nothing like the days in Puerto Lapiz, waiting for the fighting to break out or for the trade wind to begin to blow, with all the nerve ends titillated by a horde of invading sensations! All I could see was the wall. I revelled in the faded flowers in the dreary wall-paper, whose design was so thoroughly unexpressive that not even a wandering, feverish eye could convert it into anything but its intended form . . . I was stuck there so solidly that I was unable even to consider the idea of escaping from my own boredom and isolation. But after all, the self was not so very hateful! On the day when I managed to get out of bed, slouch to the window, and then cook myself my own idea of a meal and eat it with disproportionate enjoyment, while I grumbled about the tasteless dishes brought up by the Polish hotel manager, I said to myself that the egoism I'd often been accused of was matched only by my preoccupation with the truth. Of course, throughout the story I thought only of myself. So what? We act within our limits. I have loved as much as I was able to love. Badly, but still loving. Or perhaps too much, who knows?

Anyway, today I retire into my shell. For good. I may be criticized for that, but it won't matter, because I will have, not a clear conscience – that can wait – but the certitude of not laying a false trail. The snail's withdrawal will not prevent the careless walker's foot from crushing it: inside its blind retreat it will not even see the danger approaching. With the shadow of death hovering right above, it will never know the nature of the thing that is on the point of killing it. You can always make your mind up later on about what is, in principle, the more terrifying choice: to be forewarned or not?

Curled up in bed like this, the pain subsides until it is hardly noticeable. Wrapped in the eiderdown I close my eyes, rocked by a soft *canción de cuna*. My fingers close around a corner of the padded quilt. Its texture strokes my lips. My head snuggles further into the comforting warmth. Doña Marina is there. She smiles, leans over me, and gently scolds at me. 'Michael, stop sucking that corner, you're not a baby any more. A big boy like you . . .'

Wasn't it Flaubert who said that a cradle reminded him of a coffin? I wonder if he spoke English. Surely he must have, because one word echoes the other, with a change of consonant – womb, tomb . . .

Apart from a few incidental appearances, I have always been struck by the absence of child characters in Raven's books. The one outstanding exception comes in *Mr Steele*, though that appears to be an apprentice work, and far from my father's best. Lippman was right: *Mr Steele* is the victim of its own fine, heavy-handed feelings . . . We are in Indianapolis at the turn of the century. A family of migrant workers . . . Hermione, the mother, has high ambitions for her little son Jason Steele. She over-protects him. Carl, the father, sees and understands nothing beyond the harsh necessity of survival. For love of her son, Hermione grants the use of her body to anyone – bosses, officials, ministers – with power enough to further the boy's social emancipation. Jason is the silent witness of these proceedings. His father loses an arm in an accident at work. Hardship ensues. Hermione redoubles her extramarital exertions. Jason kills one of her lovers. He is twelve years old . . . The chapter ends. In the rest of the novel, Jason is no longer a child.

Before I sailed for Mexico, and after I had scanned the Bremen file at the Home Office, I had written to the Town Hall in Schwiebus, once a German town and now in Polish territory. From Versailles treaty to Yalta conference it had been shuttled between East and West with none of its inhabitants consulted about their position on one side or another of arbitrary frontier lines . . . All the same, the registry office records were bound to have survived all these changes, or so I told myself, automatically dismissing the idea that archives might not have been invincibly shell- and bomb-proof! In any case I had nothing to lose: if this initiative did not produce anything more than what I already knew, okay, the Lippman version would be confirmed. After all, now that I'd made up my mind to settle on Oaxaca for a few years it no longer mattered very much. Helen or Horminia? Either way, those were no ordinary grandmothers! Neither one could be ignored. But – was it because of *Mr Steele*? – my personal preference leaned heavily towards Horminia.

So I had no idea whether there was any point in my inquiry. When my letter reached the hands of the registrar, the boat would be landing me on the shores of the New World once again. This time the scion of the lines of Chama and Seguida, the descendant of those illustrious Indian and Spanish families, had remained on the quayside, on the pavement of the old Europe. His place was no longer on the other side. The Mateos who landed in Mexico did not feel exiled but at home, or very nearly – in the meantime I had naturally had to leave behind a forwarding address. I had all the time and money a man could dream of, but the Hotel Universal, mark two, would not be rebuilt in a day. For if this voyage had to be assigned an 'objective', then first of all it was to restore some life to the place where I was born, only bigger and more luxurious – four stars, one hundred and fifty rooms, packed with staff and buzzing with tourists. A real business, in good working order! Just the opposite of a chimera: a solid reality, steel girders and reinforced concrete . . . Not a rampart but a hive, with entrances, exits, corridors, ups and downs, lifts, passageways, stairs . . . like a great liner steaming ahead towards a tranquil destination, a familiar port of call.

Once the foundations had been laid, on the very site of the

old Universal, I left town for a few weeks. The journey to San Cristóbal de Las Casas was much quicker than before: I had no reason to make detours or waste time. As with the letter sent to Schwiebus, I was not hoping for any guaranteed result. A pawn had been moved on the chessboard; that didn't mean the file was open. One day at a time, and I'd see . . . Besides, there was no question any longer of discovering unknown countries or crossing hostile natural barriers. A plain return ticket would do. The risks were minimal: the birth certificate might never arrive from Poland, and furthermore the woman I was going to San Cristóbal to find could be long gone. Ten years was a lot of time, especially for a whore in the tropics. If Chinita had not left the brothel where we had made love, that could be a fatal sign. Would I find a ruin or a corpse, a syphilitic or who knows what else? But it didn't happen like that. Chinita's wish had come true: three years in San Cristóbal and she had left the place behind. They gave me an address in Mexico City, and a few days later I ran her to earth in the *cantina* off the Zocalo which she had bought with her savings . . . I bought her out at a high price, with the additional lure of appointing her the new manager of the Hotel Universal in Oaxaca. She was forty-two years old, and she accepted my proposition.

We had only to pack her bags and organize the removal, and then we were standing in front of the hotel – already two floors high. Chinita was impressed, but she thought I had bitten off more than I could chew.

When I went to the post office I found a letter from Schwiebus. Inside it was a copy of a birth certificate. Ulrich Jasper Bremen was born on 26 October 1898, the son of Carl Bremen, stonemason, and Horminia Wiener, farm girl. Because the couple were not married, the child was described as 'natural'. As well as the certificate, the Polish official had included another document which I hadn't asked for. Carl Bremen had married Horminia Wiener one month after the recorded birth of Ulrich.

'A fine love story' was Chinita's response when I told her something about it.

Had the Bremens adopted the child abandoned by Helen Feldman? That looked unlikely now. Which left the hypothesis of the Kaiser's escapade with a naïve and gullible country girl.

'Another *chingada*!' said Chinita.

'I forbid you to speak that word,' I shouted, 'especially here . . .'

'*No importa*, seeing that her man, the *real* man, loved her enough to take her together with her child.'

The incident was closed. We moved into our hotel as soon as the first ground-floor suite became habitable. For the opening there was a big reception where Oaxaca's upper crust came to stand around the swimming pool, and pretty soon, with the help of good business and competent public relations, everyone agreed that 'Señor Mateos' was a blessing for the province. A born cacique!

In those days (I am talking as if it were some prehistoric era, but actually it was only six years ago) large-scale international tourism was booming. The American, European and Asiatic charter companies sent us a stream of clients, and the Universal had no off season. One day, in the foyer, I even came across a man I'd worked with at the BBC. His name escaped me but the face was familiar. Before he remembered me I sidled away into the section closed to the public, determined not to be drawn into conversation. To tell the truth, I ought to explain that I had soon pulled out of the daily management of the hotel. Chinita was in charge of the staff, but to handle the rest I was relying on a young Zapotec accountant who had shown a sharp sense of timing as the business developed. Virgil Chamula was his name. If you ever go there, ask for Señor Chamula and mention Señor Mateos. I'm sure that you'll find a good reception. Because there is every reason for believing that Virgil, a man with a future, as they say, is still at his post there, and running the hotel, together with Chinita of course . . .

For a suburb of hell, at least you stayed in style, if your bank roll permitted . . . People came to visit the shades just as in Sicily they stroll on Etna with the firm intention of shaking Vulcan's hand and congratulating his Cyclopses. It's dandy for those winter nights where you show the holiday slides, and cultural too.

Do I sound bitter? So might you. One day Chinita informed me that she wanted a child. What do you make of that?

'Are you out of your mind?'

'Perhaps you think I am too old . . .'

'No, I'm the one who . . .'

And it was just about at that moment that I was visited by the first desire to write – a straightforward intention to begin with, but continually postponed. Then, quite unexpectedly, an idea too clear and luminous to yield anything but sizzling flashes that left me for dead. Lightning erupted in the highest spheres of my mind, yet no thunder sounded. The spark was struck, but no blaze kindled. It was as if I consumed myself in the cold, cut down on the threshold of vision.

Here too there came the first suspicions on the subject of Chinita and Virgil Chamula – an ideal solution! Since now, very slowly and laboriously, I drafted a few pages of the history of the first Hotel Universal . . . Until the day when I finally realized that far from being my enemy, time was working in my favour . . . The idea no longer thwarted the desire. I was falling into a different beat, a slower rhythm. There were no more misfires; instead, all kinds of speeds seemed feasible. For example, in a single burst I wrote the pages on my mother's death, knowing that it was not a good way to begin. But it was the way I had to go, wasn't it? Raven would come in his own good time, I felt sure.

I had to have a pretext. The need to gather material, to re-immerse myself in the atmosphere of action, was one such, and it worked. Chinita even seemed attracted by the idea of having a writer in her bed. It would be good for the prestige of the hotel. Her erotic fires rekindled for a while: the smokescreen that developed under my eyes was thick and acrid, and it delayed my departure for a few months more. I was fond of Chinita, 'my little reformed whore', with the mole on her left breast, like Virginia . . .

My plans and working notes made one great clutter in my mind. Scrub it out. I tore up the fifty or so pages I had written and . . . picked up the telephone to ask about the flight times to Mexico City and then to Guatemala City.

Against my hopes and calculations, the trip was at first uninspiring. There were too many stops and blind alleys. No Ruth Powell was waiting for me anywhere. And in Guetamala I could find only faint recollections of my Lidia Valdés. My very own star, my untouchable legend . . . I was surrounded by such a pleiad of remote and inaccessible suns that each attempt to catch them in my torn sky hunter's net left me empty-handed and exhausted, like some cosmic cosmonaut trawling seas of space explored a thousand times by bolder, more expert, or simply more previous adventurers.

On the way to Flores I grew aware with every mile I covered through jungle and sierra that my strenuous apprenticeship had not been wasted. Its lesson amounted to the self-evident fact that the beginning comes at the beginning. But I know now that it is not easy to arrive at this obvious beginning. And possibly still less easy to accept what it implies.

In Relámpagos (for I did go there!) nothing much had changed since my previous visit. For the people who lived there, I mean: for myself, it was utterly different. The ruins of the church had disappeared altogether, and in their place stood an extension of the barracks, a brick and breeze-block hangar used as a garage by the military. As for Bocanegra, the gargoyle, who will be surprised to learn that no trace of her presence remained? Unable to disclose my identity, for reasons of elementary security, I did not dare to ask about my fine and formidable chimera. Had I questioned the local population, perhaps I might have been astonished to hear them deny all knowledge of her. Rather than face that possibility I preferred to leave in a hurry. This time it was not the end of my journey. The way was open, and it led elsewhere. Further along . . . on the way to Honduras (the same route by which Guardi, the old philosopher and my father's cell mate, had secretly entered Guatemala), on the road to Puerto Lápiz, at last I found the thread and drift of all those words.

In the beginning was the hurricane.

And it arrived as I was writing the first pages of the story which has brought us here.

Epilogue

1

EACH JOURNEY BROUGHT its storm, from elementary squall to emphatic tropical cyclone. And with each new assault the explosion of life had ended in such havoc that generation after generation paid a heavier price. Whether or not he bowed to the violence of history, the individual was finally tied hand and foot by a network of convergences and intersections. One man, schooled in the language of the stars, nevertheless believed in changeless permanence. The other saw this chart of dates and places as the sole cause of his own ill fortune. And the third, thrown into prison in his turn, bringing the wheel full circle, did not dare hope even for that much: for want of descendants and a future, he invented his own strictly personal chronology . . . But in every case, each of them thought in terms of space and time: centuries torn to the four cardinal points, years shredded into ceaseless travels there and back, monstrous junctures of enchanting hours spiked with murderous instants . . . And yet a slight difference did exist, a divergence barely perceptible at first sight. In his crude astronomical glass, the cabbalist Cordavoro had taught his pupil Alfonso de Seguida that nature contains anomalies transcending human understanding. Perhaps the challenge should have been picked up, as if every folly were a path to follow. But sometimes all it takes is a little shift, the merest shade, to disturb the original design.

The winds had risen in their utmost fury, covering tracks, obliterating landmarks, annihilating latitude and longitude. So loud was the roar that in the brief spells of calm the enormous bellowing mouth hung open in the void, locked in paralysis, brooding over devastation. A single trifling breath might have changed the face of things, the face of the world; but the black hole kept silent, unable to flex its jaws. In the dense silence after the uproar there rose a torrid, sticky heat. Soon it covered the remotest traces, impregnating cracks and fissures and blocking all perspectives. It seemed both pointless and dangerous to attempt to open one's eyes. At the slightest such effort the veil of the eyelids, stuck down by seeping moisture, came near to tearing. It would have been better to be blind, to have put out one's own eyes beforehand, than to become the helpless witness of that orgy of the grotesque. Worn out, and sweating blood and water, the motionless body could do no more than listen to the muffled music of the chemical transformations gnawing and rotting from within. Must the victim expect a final deflagration at the moment of toppling into the void? Might he dream about a last true pang, an animal shriek before surrendering to the vegetable reign, and later to the mineral?

The serpent stiffened, wedged tight between the two vertical walls of a crack in the earth's crust opened up by drought. Half choked, it awaited an improbable sloughing of its scales. Its coils wore themselves out with writhing its own grave. When a light damp wind blew up once more, and the first drops of yellowish warm rain fell upon that disinherited region, the formless, supposedly annihilated mass convulsed, and seemed to heave in respiration. Gasping, the magma caught its breath again. Chewed, swallowed and digested by the living mud, only the fossil remained inert – and vitrified.

It rained so long that there was talk of a second flood. And yet the survivors who, safe in the deepest caves, had escaped the catastrophe and to whom fell the duty of perpetuating the species, were no longer willing, as their ancestors had been, to lean upon the possibility of a heaven-sent punishment which would quite rule out their own responsibility.

It rained so long that little by little the temperature fell until eventually it reached the threshold at which water is converted into ice. At first it was just a winter frost that covered town and country with a thin film of limpid crystals . . . Then, as the weeks went by, the snowflakes fell and thickened, but footprints were still visible on the layer of snow. Later, much later (the equivocal alternation of night and day preventing the survivors from noticing the steady darkening of the atmosphere), the horizon closed in upon the sight, totally blotted out by gusts of swirling whiteness, a backdrop for a play of fleeting shadows.

The frozen bodies stiffened once again. The more optimistic continued to think that this was nothing, and that the age of cataclysms had passed: after all, these present difficulties in moving about might help restore things to their proper place. No panic! Don't let's confuse repose with stagnation, they told the alarmists, those who saw visions of pillars of salt.

A curious phenomenon brought all the world together. Inexorably, the snow went on falling, but it was observed that people were no longer being ill. For young and old alike, the pattern was the same: no more preliminary shivers, no more weaknesses to conduce to bacterial invasion, no, nothing but a sudden sclerosis which, in a brutal, unexplained assault, changed life to death.

This disappearance of disease did not occur without its counterpart. Many more people began to die, and faster, so that soon no one knew where to leave the corpses that the crematoria were no longer able to absorb. And suddenly it was realized that the thick mantle of snow would make an ideal shroud, a sublime mausoleum.

One day, no doubt, a final avalanche would cover everything in one great surge, beneath a vast, immaculate winding sheet.

Even the most practised eye would detect not the slightest trace of a seam . . .

2

THE BITE OF the cold did him good. His face muscles tightened as if under the sting of a host of minute and invisible needles.

In the room which he had not left for two weeks, the temperature was hardly likely to comfort a body racked by rheumatic pains and a sitting position. Protected by several layers of wool, with a blanket over his knees, and when necessary muffled under the quilt from the bed, he had continued to write, attempting to ignore the torpor that numbed his lower limbs from the calves to the tips of his toes.

Once in the open, after a few timid, tentative steps he was reassured by his ability to move about. Breathing deeply, he filled his lungs with frosty air. It was good to feel alive. A shiver ran all the way down his back, and he pulled up the collar of his overcoat and walked towards the square.

Unusually for him, that morning he had got up early. What with a series of wakeful nights, his shifts of work had left him without a sense of hours and days, but when he inquired the hotel keeper had told him, with one finger on a timetable and a few words of broken English, that the buses for Schwiebus left very early in the morning. On top of that, he would have to allow for a half-hour walk before he reached the bus station.

They woke him at six, but only to inform him that he could not possibly leave. Serious incidents had occurred, and there was no question of leaving the hotel, still less the town. As best he could, he tried to say that it was not really a journey he had in mind, just a very quick return trip. He would leave his luggage at the hotel, and be back in forty-eight hours at the latest.

'I won't waste any time,' he said to himself as he packed one case. 'Just call in at the Town Hall to run an eye over whatever information they have stored in the archives, then a visit to this Joseph and Gertrud Bremen who are supposed to remember little Ulrich as a boy . . . My family . . .'

The manuscript lay in a large envelope at the bottom of a travelling bag, under a pile of dirty washing.

'After Schwiebus, I'll stop off here to collect all this stuff . . . then back to London straight away. As soon as I've settled a few details with my agent I'll fly on to Los Angeles. Nicholson will find me a room in the Señora's house – my house, idiot – and I can polish the writing at leisure . . . And maybe, if she still wants anything to do with me, find Virginia again. Genuinely . . . With no ulterior motive . . .'

He ran his tongue over his chapped lips. The icy wind flicked his eyes, and they brimmed with tears. Walking down the street, he grew aware of the silence that surrounded him. About three hundred yards away, in the square, through the film of moisture that he wiped away with the back of his sleeve, he could make out the distant figures of men standing like ragged punctuation in the snow. Some appeared static, as if petrified by the cold, while others were in perpetual motion, liquid and elastic.

Before leaving the hotel he had switched on the small transistor radio which he had bought in Paris during his walk with Pablo, but which had not left the suitcase throughout his stay in Poznan. Of course he could only pick up Polish broadcasts – continuous classical music. Then, suddenly, a solemn voice, reading out an official statement. Then more music. And again that solemn, impersonal voice.

'I hereby announce that on this day we have constituted a military council of public safety and that, in accordance with the constitution, at midnight the Council of State proclaimed a state of war throughout the country.'

Not understanding a word of the speech, he stowed the radio in the travelling bag, next to the manuscript.

He picked up the telephone and tried to call Warsaw to book a seat on the plane. No sound. The lines were cut. After another failed attempt, on the spur of the moment he dialled Beatrice's number in Paris, then Rakovski's in London. No connection.

Downstairs, the desk clerk tried to stop him. 'Curfew . . .' The word was unmistakable. The message was clear. One more reason to go and see. There was sure to be a bus to Schwiebus: the country, a blank space where there was probably nothing going on.

'Prison,' said the man, and abandoned the struggle with a sigh.

At the crossroads he came up to a sizeable roadblock: *zomos*, belonging to the anti-riot squads of the militia, stood to attention with loaded weapons beside three armoured vehicles. They checked his identity. The American passport travelled from hand to hand until an officer came over and ordered him back to his hotel. So he turned back, but then ducked into an alley that led to the parallel street. Still heading for the square, he now mingled with a group of demonstrators who occupied the middle of the roadway – about fifty men, and some women too . . . A murmur went up as he passed, but they let him walk on. Hugging the walls along the pavement he ran into a few other scattered knots of young people. One of them handed him a leaflet and he took it mechanically: on the printed page with its mostly indecipherable characters he nevertheless recognized a slogan printed in capital letters. Although he had kept clear of what was happening in the country he could not fail to have noticed the words on walls all over Warsaw, ever since his arrival. *'Solidarity is not dead as long as we are alive.'*

All at once, just as he reached the end of the avenue which opened onto the broad prospect of the square he would now have to cross, a mass of striking workers swarmed around him, running in all directions. The dry coughing of teargas grenade launchers broke out from all four corners of the square, a characteristic sound, and one he knew well. He plunged into the heart of the crowd. If he ran fast, and his still mending hip and leg held out, he should have no problem reaching the buildings on the opposite side. A hundred yards, maybe less . . . Then he would stay under cover, as long as he had to. And he wouldn't be all that far from the bus station.

He forged on through the moving crowd, shouldering people out of his way. The main action seemed to be further to his left, although the cloud of gas appeared to be rising higher and higher and threatening the middle of the square. A sudden surge backwards stopped him in his tracks, and although he fought to go forward, a forest of arms pushed him back and barred his path. But soon the human saplings began to fall, as if mown down by a giant chain saw, swaying and falling, one after another . . . one on top of another. The swish of truncheons was drowned by the more shrill, incessant hissing of the water cannons.

Angling to his right, he broke away from the surrounding scrum. Visibility was down to twenty yards. Coughing and crying, but now no longer running, he kept on.

Under his feet the snow had melted, black puddles alternating with grey slush.

He no longer felt cold. His body was sweating, and from his panting mouth came dense puffs of steam that drifted away to merge with the strange vaporous compound blending morning mist with riot gases.

'I'm not in danger,' he grunted, to reassure himself, because he was starting to regret his foolhardiness. Things were more serious than he had imagined, and he was angry with himself for his failure to sum up the situation. Really inexcusable! He of all people ought to have known, and even anticipated this!

There in front of him, barely five yards away, a *zomo* stood stock-still, legs planted solidly apart, shield and truncheon raised. He seemed to be waiting for Michael. Only two choices: confrontation, face to face, 'him or me', or else retreat and flight. But behind him was one vast uproar, a wall of voices that seemed to be collapsing under the impact of an invisible war machine whose clicks and clanks and heavy mechanical growl were coming closer by the second.

The blow landed on his shoulder. He raised an arm to protect himself and dropped to one knee. Another blow caught him on the temple. He toppled sideways into a puddle of water. The contact with the icy liquid prevented him from passing out. He shook himself. The man in the boots and helmet had vanished. 'Kaiser's bastard, Raven's son, stand up!' a voice cried out. The voice of the blind prophet of San Cristóbal, perhaps . . . The syllables dinned painfully into the wounded man's skull. His clenched hand pressed against his bleeding ear.

He staggered to his feet.

A dull rumbling came from somewhere behind him. Like the

breaking of surf in a spring tide . . . No longer moving, still, he listened.

With difficulty, he turned his head to stare back at the thunder. The words that formed inside him hung suspended on his lips, unspoken . . .

'But . . . but I'm no . . . hero.'

The monster was so close that he did not see her dark mouth open and spit fire. Caught off his balance, the traveller fell beneath the creature's caterpillar paws. At the moment when she passed over his body, no doubt vexed to have her progress marred by that unexpected little jolt, the beast spread her fabulous wings, and so proclaimed her displeasure and her triumph.